BURT FRANKLIN: RESEARCH & SOURCE WORKS SERIES 516
American Classics in History & Social Science 138

A JOURNEY

IN THE

BACK COUNTRY

A JOURNEY

IN THE

BACK COUNTRY

BY

FREDERICK LAW OLMSTED

AUTHOR OF "A JOURNEY IN THE SEABOARD SLAVE STATES," "A JOURNEY IN TEXAS,"
"WALKS AND TALKS OF AN AMERICAN FARMER IN ENGLAND," ETC.

BURT FRANKLIN
NEW YORK

Published by BURT FRANKLIN
235 East 44th St., New York, N.Y. 10017
Originally Published: 1860
Reprinted: 1970
Printed in the U.S.A.

S.B.N. 26218
Library of Congress Card Catalog No.: 73-97842
Burt Franklin: Research and Source Works Series 516
American Classics in History and Social Science 138

PREFACE.

THIS is the third volume of a work, the first of which was a narrative of a journey in the sea-board districts of the older slave States; the second, of a rapid tour west of the Alleghanies, and of a winter spent in Texas. This volume concludes and somewhat focalizes the observations of those, its narrative being, in part, of the hill-country people, and mainly of those who are engaged in, or are most directly affected by, the great business of the South—the production of cotton. The record of facts, except as regards the domestic life of the people, is less elaborate than in the other volumes, because, reference being made to previous observations, less detail is needed to give a full statement of that which was seen by the writer. Facts of general observation and conclusions of judgment form a larger part of this volume than of the others, because they are appropriately deduced from all preceding details. It was prepared for the press nearly in its present form, and announced for publication three years ago. A chapter was then intended to be added upon the natural history of southern politics, before preparing which, I was interrupted by unanticipated duties. Upon recent examination it was found that the facts recorded had not lost significance, and that the volume might be published without revision or addition. As the topic of slave insurrection is considerably discussed, I will here observe that all its narrative portion had been printed, and that all the matter of the last chapter bearing upon that subject had been written, some time before the John Brown plot is supposed to have been formed.

The controlling considerations which now induce the publication of the volume are, first, that after publishing the former volumes, to leave untold what is reported in this, would be to leave my story untrue through incompleteness; secondly, that the agitation growing out of the condition of the South is now graver, and the truth more impor-

tant to be known, than ever before. Before preparing this volume, I
had given more than two years' careful study simply to the matter of
fact of the condition of the people, especially the white people, living
under a great variety of circumstances where slavery is not pro-
hibited. There has been no publication of observations made with
similar advantages, and extended over so large a field. I may add
that few men could have been so little inclined to establish previously formed opinions as I was when I began my journey in
the South. I left a farm in New York to examine farms in Virginia.
The Fillmore compromises had just been accomplished; a reaction from
a state of suspicion and unwholesome excitement was obvious in the
public mind. Looking upon slavery as an unfortunate circumstance,
for which the people of the South were in no wise to blame, and the
abolition of which was no more immediately practicable than the abrogation of hospitals, penitentiaries, and boarding-schools, it was with
the distinct hope of aiding in this reaction, and of aiding those disposed
to consider the subject of slavery in a rational, philosophical, and con-
ciliatory spirit, that I undertook, at the suggestion of the editor of the
New York Times, to make a personal study of the ordinary condition
and habits of the people of the South. I believed that much mischief
had resulted from statements and descriptions of occurrences which
were exceptional, as if they were ordinary phenomena attending
slavery. I had the most unquestioning faith, that while the fact of
slavery imposed much unenviable duty upon the people of the South,
and occasioned much inconvenience, the clear knowledge of which
would lead to a disposition of forbearance, and encourage a respectful
purpose of assistance (such as soon after this found an expression in
the organization of the Southern Aid Society), there was at the same
time a moral condition of the human race, in connection with slavery—that there was an expression of peculiar virtues in the South,
too little known or considered, the setting forth of which would do
good.

I will not here conceal for a moment that I was disappointed in the
actual condition of the people of the South, citizen and slave; that the
more thoroughly and the longer I was acquainted with that which is
ordinary and general, the greater was my disappointment. In the
present aspect of affairs, it would be an affectation of moderation if I
refrained from expressing my conviction that the larger part of the
people of the South are in a condition which can not be too much de-

plored, the extension and aggravation of the causes of which can not be too firmly and persistently guarded against.

The subjection of the negroes of the South to the mastership of the whites, I still consider justifiable and necessary, and I fully share the general ill-will of the people of the North toward any suggestion of their interfering politically to accomplish an immediate abolition of slavery. This is not from idolatry of a parchment, or from a romantic attachment to the word Union; it certainly is not from a low estimation of the misfortune of slavery, or of the flagrant wrong of the laws and customs of the slave States. It is from a fair consideration of the excellence of our confederate constitution when compared with other instruments of human association, and from a calculation of the chances of getting a better, after any sort of revolution at this time, together with the chances of thereby accomplishing a radical and satisfactory remedy for the evils which must result from slavery. I do not see that a mere setting free of the blacks, if it could be accomplished, would surely remedy these evils. An extraction of the bullet does not at once remedy the injury of a gun-shot wound; it sometimes aggravates it.

It does not follow, however, that the evils of slavery must continue to be as great as at present. Nor does it follow that consideration of these evils at the North must be either futile or impertinent, for they are by no means limited in their action to the people of the Slave States, and there are matters in the discussion of which the people of the North have a constitutional right to be heard, the decision of which may greatly help to perpetuate or to limit them.

The emancipation of the negroes is evidently not a matter to be accomplished by this generation, but again it does not follow that even emancipation can not be anticipated, or the way of accomplishing it in some degree prepared. The determination that it shall not be, is much more impracticable, fanatical, and dangerous, than argument for immediate abolition. The present agitation of the country results less from the labors of abolitionists than from the conceit, avarice, and folly of wealthy owners of slaves. These constantly, and by organized action, endeavor to reverse the only line of policy by which safety and peace can, in the nature of things, be secured to the people of the South; for there are moral forces, as well as material, in nature, and there is the same folly in expecting to overcome the one as the other.

It would be presumptuous in any man to predict when, or in what manner, slavery is to end, but, if the owners of slaves were so disposed, it appears to me that there would be no difficulty whatever, politically, financially, or socially, in diminishing the evil of slavery, and in preparing the way for an end to it. It is to be hoped that elements will, by-and-by, come into play, the nature of which we can not now imagine, which will make a peaceful end more practicable than it now appears. Whitney's invention has, to all appearance, strengthened the hold of slavery a thousand times more than all labors directly intended for that purpose. A botanical discovery, a new motive power, the decease of some popular fallacy, a physical, or mental, or moral epidemic, a theological reformation, a religious revival, a war, or a great man fortunately placed, may, in a single year, do more to remove difficulties than has thus far been done in this century.

Popular prejudice, if not popular instinct, points to a separation of black from white as a condition of the abolition of slavery. It may be hoped that something will occur which will force, or encourage and facilitate, a voluntary and spontaneous separation. If this is to be considered as a contingency of emancipation, it is equally to be anticipated that an important emigration of whites to the slave districts will precede it.* I do not now say that it is, or is not, right or desirable, that this should be so, but, taking men as they are, I think a happy and peaceful association of a large negro, with a large white population, can not at present be calculated on as a permanent thing. I think that the emancipation from slavery of such part of the existing actual negro population as shall remain in the country until the white population is sufficiently christianized, and civilized, and properly educated to understand that its interests are identical with its duty, will take place gradually, and only after an intermediate period of systematic pupilage, restraint, and encouragement, of such a nature as is suggested in this volume.

To be more explicit: it seems to me to be possible that a method of finally emancipating the slaves and of immediately remedying many of the evils of slavery, without an annihilation of that which the State

---

* If gold fields as attractive as those of California should, for instance, be discovered and opened to adventurers in Mississippi, slavery would be practically abolished in that State within two years. Cotton culture would be more profitable work than gold digging, but not until something else had once drawn free laborers to a cotton district in large numbers.

has made property, or conceded to be held as property, may be eventually based on these accepted facts: That a negro's capacities, like a horse's, or a dog's, or a white man's, for all industrial purposes, including cotton-growing and cotton-picking, must be enlarged by a voluntary, self-restrained, self-urged, and self-directed exercise of those capacities. That a safely-conducted cultivation and education of the capacities of the slaves will, of necessity, increase the value of the slaves, and that the slaves may thus be made to pay, year by year, for their own gradual emancipation.

I do not suppose that in one generation or two the effects of centuries of barbarism and slavery are to be extinguished. I do not think negroes are ever to become Teutons or Celts, but I do suppose that negroes may become thoroughly civilized, thoroughly independent individuals, and thus of tenfold more value in the commonwealth than they are. I know, for a certainty, that the most dogged have a capacity for some improvement, even within their own lives; that the most valuable cotton-pickers are capable of being made yet more valuable; and I do not believe that even ten years of careful, judicious, and economical cultivation of this capacity, with all the negroes of a large plantation, would fail to earn some pecuniary as well as moral reward.

But a vain delusion possesses the South that slavery carries with it certain defined advantages for the master class. (I do believe, after a careful study, that there are no such advantages.) Owing to this delusion, moral forces in nature, as irresistible as the laws of climate, are blindly disregarded, or held in contempt, and the hope lives that a power, found paramount within the South itself, must yet control the continent. This hope makes light of all present evils growing out of slavery, or attributes them to causes which it gives the purpose to remove. Not till it is decisively and finally dispelled, can any general policy for remedying the evils of slavery be initiated, or even an individual slaveholder be permitted to govern his property in a manner consistent with what would otherwise be the requirements of Christianity, civilization, and a sound and far-seeing economy.

In the preparation of this book, my conscious first purpose has been to obtain and report facts of ordinary life at the South, not to supply arguments. Lest it should be thought I had some concealed purpose to advocate by my selection of facts, I have here frankly set forth the inner plans and theories for which it might have been agreeable to me to have gained the approval of its readers. The facts of my personal observation fill the greater part of the book, though I have not neglected others obtained at second hand in the South. There are various theories and purposes for which these facts may be turned to account. Their influence need not be, and should not be, the same with all that it has been with me, but I believe that there are few who will chance to read to whom they will not afford some entertainment and instruction.

CONTENTS.

CHAPTER I.

THE VALLEY OF THE LOWER MISSISSIPPI.

CHAPTER II.

THE PROPERTY ASPECT OF SLAVERY.

CHAPTER III.

A TRIP INTO A PART OF NORTHERN MISSISSIPPI.

CHAPTER IV.

THE INTERIOR COTTON DISTRICTS.

CHAPTER V.

THE PIEDMONT COTTON DISTRICTS.

CHAPTER VI.

THE HIGHLANDERS.

CHAPTER VII.

PATRIARCHAL LIFE IN VIRGINIA, AND IN GENERAL.

CHAPTER VIII.

SLAVERY EXTENSION; SOUTHERN COMMERCE AND COTTON SUPPLY; PRESENT CONDITION AND CHARACTER OF THE CITIZENS OF THE SOUTH; THE CAUSES AND THE REMEDY.

CHAPTER IX.

CHARACTER AND MANNERS.

CHAPTER X.

THE DANGER OF THE SOUTH.

CHAPTER I.

THE VALLEY OF THE LOWER MISSISSIPPI.

A COTTON MAN.

A DEEP notch of sadness marks in my memory the morning of the May day on which I rode out of the chattering little town of Bayou Sara, and I recollect little of its suburbs but the sympathetic cloud-shadows slowly going before me over the hill of St. Francis. At the top is an old French hamlet, and a very American tavern.

One from among the gloomy, staring loungers at the door, as I pass, throws himself upon a horse, and overtaking me, checks his pace to keep by my side. I turn toward him, and full of aversion for the companionship of a stranger, nod, in such a manner as to say, "Your equality is acknowledged; go on." Not a nod; not the slightest deflection of a single line in the austere countenance; not a ripple of radiance in the sullen eyes, which wander slowly over, and, at distinct intervals, examine my horse, my saddle-bags, my spurs, lariat, gloves, finally my face, with such stern deliberation that at last I should not be sorry if he would speak. But he does not; does not make the smallest response to a further turning of my head, which acknowledges the reflex interest excited in my own mind; his eyes remain fixed upon me, as if they were dead. I can no longer endure it in silence, so I ask, in a voice attuned to his apparent humor,

" How far to Woodville ?"

The only reply is a slight grunt, with an elevation of the chin.

" You do n't know ?"

" No."

" Never been there ?"

" No."

" I can ride there before night, I suppose ?"

No reply.

" Good walker, your horse?"

Not a nod.

" I the ght mine pretty good."

Not a sneer, or a gleam of vanity, and Belshazzar and I warmed up together. Scott's man of leather occurred to my mind, and I felt sure that I could guess my man's chord. I touched it, and in a moment he became animated, civil ; hospitable even. I was immediately informed that this was a famous cotton region ; " when it was first settled up by 'Mericans, used to be reckoned the gardying of the world, the almightiest rich sile God Almighty ever shuck down ; gettin' thinned down powerful fast now, though ; nothin' to what it was. All ou't owned by big-bugs." Finally he confided to me that he was an overseer for one of them, " one of the biggest sort." This greatest of the local hemipteras was not now on his plantation, but had " gone North to Paris or Saratogy, or some of them places."

Wearing no waistcoat, the overseer carried a pistol, without a thought of concealment, in the fob of his trowsers. The distance to Woodville, which, after he had exhausted his subject of cotton, I again tried to ascertain, he did not know, and would not attempt to guess. The ignorance of the more brutalized slaves is often described by saying of them that they can not

count above twenty. I find many of the whites but little more
intelligent. At all events, it is rarely that you meet, in the plantation districts, a man, whether white or black, who can give
you any clear information about the roads, or the distances between places in his own vicinity. While in or near Bayou Sara
and St. Francisville, I asked, at different times, ten men, black and
white, the distance to Woodville (the next town to the northward
on the map). None answered with any appearance of certainty,
and those who ventured to give an opinion, differed in their estimates as much as ten miles. I found the actual distance to be,
I think, about twenty-four miles. After riding by my side for a
mile or two, the overseer suddenly parted from me at a fork in
the road, with hardly more ceremony than he had used in joining me.

THE LANDSCAPE.—ROSE HEDGES.

For some miles about St. Francisville the landscape has an
open, suburban character, with residences indicative of rapidly
accumulating wealth, and advancement in luxury among the proprietors. For twenty miles to the north of the town, there is on
both sides a succession of large sugar and cotton plantations.
Much land still remains uncultivated, however. The roadside
fences are generally hedges of roses—Cherokee and sweet brier.
These are planted first by the side of a common rail fence, which,
while they are young, supports them in the manner of a trellis ;
as they grow older they fall each way, and mat together, finally
forming a confused, sprawling, slovenly thicket, often ten feet in
breadth and four to six feet high. Trumpet creepers, grape-
vines, green-briers, and in very rich soil, cane, grow up through
the mat of roses, and add to its strength.   It is not as pretty as

a trimmer hedge, yet very agreeable, and the road being sometimes narrow, deep and lane like, delightful memories of England
were often brought to mind.

There were frequent groves of magnolia grandiflora, large
trees, and every one in the glory of full blossom. The magnolia
does not, however, show well in masses, and those groves, not
unfrequently met, were much finer, where the beech, elm, and
liquid amber formed the body, and the magnolias stood singly
out, magnificent chandeliers of fragrance. The large-leafed magnolia, extremely beautiful at this season of the year, was more
rarely seen.

THE PLANTATIONS.

The soil seems generally rich, though much washed off the
higher ground. The cultivation is directed with some care to
prevent this. Young pine trees, however, and other indications
of impoverishing agriculture, are seen on many plantations.

The soil is a sandy loam, so friable that the negroes, always
working in large gangs, superintended by a driver with a whip,
continued their hoeing in the midst of quite smart showers,
and when the road had become a poaching mud.

Only once did I see a gang which had been allowed to dis-
continue its work on account of the rain. This was after a
very heavy thunder-shower, and the appearance of the negroes
whom I met crossing the road in returning to the field, from
the gin-house to which they had retreated, was remarkable.

First came, led by an old driver carrying a whip, forty of
the largest and strongest women I ever saw together; they
were all in a simple uniform dress of a bluish check stuff, the
skirts reaching little below the knee; their legs and feet were

bare; they carried themselves loftily, each having a hoe over the shoulder, and walking with a free, powerful swing, like *chasseurs* on the march. Behind them came the cavalry, thirty strong, mostly men, but a few of them women, two of whom rode astride on the plow mules. A lean and vigilant white overseer, on a brisk pony, brought up the rear. The men wore small blue Scotch bonnets; many of the women, handkerchiefs, turban fashion, and a few nothing at all on their heads.

The slaves generally of this district appear uncommonly well—doubtless, chiefly, because the wealth of their owners has enabled them to select the best from the yearly exportations of Virginia and Kentucky, but also because they are systematically well fed.

The plantation residences were of a cottage class, sometimes with extensive and tasteful grounds about them.

An old gentleman, sensible, polite, and communicative, and a favorable sample of the wealthy planters, who rode a short distance with me, said that many of the proprietors were absentees—some of the plantations had dwellings only for the negroes and the overseer. He called my attention to a field of cotton which, he said, had been ruined by his overseer's laziness. The negroes had been permitted at a critical time to be too careless in their hoeing, and it was now impossible to recover the ground thus lost. Grass grew so rampantly in this black soil, that if it once got a good start ahead, you could never overtake it. That was the devil of a rainy season. Cotton could stand drouth better than it could grass.*

* " FINE PROSPECT FOR HAY.—While riding by a field the other day, which looked as rich and green as a New England meadow, we observed to

The inclosures are not often of less area than a hundred acres. Fewer than fifty negroes are seldom found on a plantation ; many muster by the hundred. In general the fields are remarkably free from weeds and well tilled.

I arrived shortly after dusk at Woodville, a well-built and pleasant court-town, with a small but pretentious hotel. Court was in session, I fancy, for the house was filled with guests of somewhat remarkable character. The landlord was inattentive, and, when followed up, inclined to be uncivil. At the ordinary —supper and breakfast alike—there were twelve men beside myself, all of them wearing black cloth coats, black cravats, and satin or embroidered silk waistcoats ; all, too, sleek as if just from a barber's hands, and redolent of perfumes, which really had the best of it with the exhalations of the kitchen. Per-

a man sitting on the fence, ' You have a fine prospect for hay, neighbor.' ' Hay! that 's *cotton, sir*,' said he, with an emotion that betrayed an excitement which we cared to provoke no further; for we had as soon sport with a rattlesnake in the blind days of August as a farmer at this season of the year, badly in the grass. * * *

"All jesting aside, we have never known so poor a prospect for cotton in this region. In some instances the fields are clean and well worked, but the cotton is diminutive in size and sickly in appearance. We have seen some fields so foul that it was almost impossible to tell what had been planted.

" All this backwardness is attributable to the cold, wet weather that we have had almost constantly since the planting season commenced. When there was a warm spell, it was raining so that plows could not run to any advantage; so, between the cold and the rain, the cotton crop is very unpromising. * * *

"The low, flat lands this year have suffered particularly. Thoroughly saturated all the time, and often overflowed, the crops on them are small and sickly, while the weeds and grass are luxurious and rank.

" A week or two of dry hot weather will make a wonderful change in our agricultural prospects, but we have no idea that any sort of seasons could bring the cotton to more than an average crop."—*Hernando (Miss.) Advance*, June 22, 1854.

haps it was because I was not in the regulation dress that I
found no one ready to converse with me, and could obtain
not the slightest information about my road, even from the
landlord.

I might have left Woodville with more respect for this de-
corum if I had not, when shown by a servant to my room,
found two beds in it, each of which proved to be furnished
with soiled sheets and greasy pillows, nor was it without re-
iterated demands and bribery of the servant, that I succeeded
in getting them changed on the one I selected. A gentleman
of embroidered waistcoat took the other bed as it was, with
no apparent reluctance, soon after I had effected my arrangements. One wash-bowl, and a towel which had already been
used, was expected to answer for both of us, and would have
done so but that I carried a private towel in my saddle-bags.
Another requirement of a civilized household was wanting, and
its only substitute unavailable with decency.

The bill was excessive, and the hostler, who had left the
mud of yesterday hanging all along the inside of Belshazzar's
legs, and who had put the saddle on so awkwardly that I
resaddled him myself after he had brought him to the door,
grumbled, in presence of the landlord, at the smallness of the
gratuity which I saw fit to give him.

The country, for some distance north of Woodville, is the
most uneven, for a non-mountainous region, I ever saw. The
road seems well engineered, yet you are nearly all the time
mounting or descending the sides of protuberances or basins,
ribs or dikes. In one place it follows along the top of a
crooked ridge, as steep-sided and regular for nearly a quarter

of a mile, as a high railroad embankment. A man might jump off anywhere and land thirty feet below. The ground being too rough here for cultivation, the dense native forest remains intact.

"IMPORTANT TO BUSINESS MEN."

This ridge, a man told me, had been a famous place for robberies. It is not far from the Mississippi bottoms.

"Thar could n't be," said he, "a better location for a feller that wanted to foller that business. There was one chap there a spell ago, who built himself a cabin t' other side the river. He used to come over in a dug-out. He could paddle his dug-out up the swamp, you see, to within two mile of the ridge; then, when he stopped a man, he 'd run through the woods to his dug-out, and before the man could get help, he 'd be t' other side the Mississippi, a sittin' in his housen as honest as you be."

The same man had another story of the ridge:

"Mr. Allen up here caught a runaway once, and started to take him down to Woodville to the jail. He put him in irons and carried him along in his waggin. The nigger was peaceable and submissive till they got along onto that yer ridge place. When they got thar, all of a sudden he gin a whop like, and over he went twenty foot plum down the side of the ridge. 'Fore Allen could stop his hoss he 'd tumbled and rolled himself 'way out of sight. He started right away arter him, but he never cotched a sight on him again."

HILL-SIDE COTTON CULTURE.

Not far north of the ridge, plantations are found again, though

the character of the surface changes but little. The hill-sides
are so plowed that each furrow forms a narrow terrace. After
the first plowing, thus scientifically directed, the lines are followed in subsequent cultivation, year in and year out, so long
as enough soil remains to grow cotton with profit.   On the
hills recently brought into cultivation, broad, serpentine ditches,
having a fall of from two to four inches in a rod, have been
frequently constructed : these are intended to prevent the formation of more direct gullies, during heavy rains.   Of course,
these precautions are not perfectly successful, the cultivated
hills in spite of them losing soil every year in a melancholy
manner.

ABANDONED PLANTATIONS.

I passed during the day four or five large plantations, the
hill-sides gullied like icebergs, stables and negro quarters all
abandoned, and given up to decay.

The virgin soil is in its natural state as rich as possible. At
first it is expected to bear a bale and a half of cotton to the
acre, making eight or ten bales for each able field-hand. But
from the cause described its productiveness rapidly decreases.

Originally, much of this country was covered by a natural
growth of cane, and by various nutritious grasses. A good
northern farmer would deem it a crying shame and sin to attempt to grow any crops upon such steep slopes, except grasses
or shrubs which do not require tillage. The waste of soil
which attends the practice is much greater than it would be
at the North, and, notwithstanding the unappeasable demand
of the world for cotton, its bad economy, considering the subject nationally, can not be doubted.

If these slopes were thrown into permanent terraces, with turfed or stone-faced escarpments, the fertility of the soil might be preserved, even with constant tillage. In this way the hills would continue for ages to produce annual crops of greater value than those which are at present obtained from them at such destructive expense—from ten to twenty crops of cotton rendering them absolute deserts. But with negroes at $1000 a head and fresh land in Texas at $1 an acre, nothing of this sort can be thought of. The time will probably come when the soil now washing into the adjoining swamps will be brought back by our descendants, perhaps on their heads, in pots and baskets, in the manner Huc describes in China, which may be seen also in the Rhenish vineyards, to be relaid on the sunny slopes, to grow the luxurious cotton in.

The plantations are all large, but, except in their size and rather unusually good tillage, display few signs of wealthy proprietorship. The greater number have but small and mean residences upon them. No poor white people live upon the road, nor in all this country of rich soils are they seen, except *en voyage*. In a distance of seventy-five miles I saw no houses without negro-cabins attached, and I calculated that there were fifty slaves, on an average, to every white family resident in the country under my view. There is a small sandy region about Woodville, which I passed through after nightfall, and which of course my note does not include.

I called in the afternoon, at a house, almost the only one I had seen during the day which did not appear to be the residence of a planter or overseer, to obtain lodging. No one was at home but a negro woman and children. The woman said that her master never took in strangers ; there was a man a few miles

further on who did ; it was the only place she knew of where I
was likely to be entertained.

I found the place : probably the proprietor was the poorest
white man whose house I had passed during the day, but he had
several slaves ; one of them, at least, a first-class man, worth
$2,000.

Just before me, another traveler, a Mr. S., from beyond
Natchez, had arrived. Learning that I was from Texas, he immediately addressed me with volubility :

"Ah ! then you can tell us something about it, and I would be
obliged to you if you would. Have you been out west about
Antonio ? Ranchering's a good business, eh, out west there,
is n't it ? Can a man make thirty per cent. by it, eh ? I hear
so ; should think that would be a good business. But how much
capital ought a man to have to go into ranchering, good, eh ? so
as to make it a good business ?"

He was a middle-aged, well-dressed man, devouring tobacco
prodigiously ; nervous and wavering in his manner ; asking questions, a dozen at a breath, and paying no heed to the answers.
He owned a plantation in the bottoms, and another on the upland ; the latter was getting worn out, it was too unhealthy for
him to live in the bottoms, and so, as he said, he had had " a
good notion to go into ranchering, just for ease and pleasure."

" Fact is, though, I've got a family, and this is no country for
children to be raised in. All the children get such foolish notions. I do n't want my children to be brought up here—ruins
everybody ; does sir, sure—spoils 'em ; too bad ; 'tis so, too bad ;
can't make any thing of children here, sir—can't sir ; fact."

He had been nearly persuaded to purchase a large tract of
land at a point upon a certain creek where, he had been told, was

a large court-house, an excellent school, etc. The waters of the
creek he named are brackish, the neighboring country is a desert
and the only inhabitants, savages. Some knavish speculator had
nearly got a customer, but could not quite prevail on him to purchase until he examined the country personally. He gave me
no time to tell him how false was the account he had had, but
went on, after describing its beauties and advantages :

"But negro property is n't very secure there, I'm told. How
is't? Know?"

"Not at all secure, sir; if it is disposed to go, it will go—the
only way you could keep it would be to make it always contented to remain. The road would always be open to Mexico; it
would go when it liked."

"So I hear. Only way is, to have young ones there and keep
their mothers here, eh? negroes have such attachments, you
know; do n't you think that would fix 'em, eh? No? No, I
suppose not; if they got mad at any thing, they'd forget their
mothers, eh? Yes, I suppose they would; can't depend on niggers; but I reckon they'd come back; only be worse off in Mexico—eh?"

"Nothing but—"

"Being free, eh? get tired of that, I should think—nobody to
take care of them. No, I suppose not; learn to take care of
themselves."

Then he turned to our host and began to ask him about the
neighbors, many of whom he had known when he was a boy, and
been at school with. A sorry account he got of nearly all.
Generally they had run through their property; their lands had
passed into new hands; their negroes had been disposed of; two
were now, he thought, "strikers" for gamblers in Natchez.

" What is a striker ?" I asked the landlord at the first opportunity.

" Oh ! to rope in fat fellows for the gamblers ; they do n't do that themselves, but get somebody else. I do n't know as it is so ; all I know is, they do n't have no business, not till late at night ; they never stir out till late at night, and nobody knows how they live, and that's what I expect they do. Fellows that come into town flush, you know—sold out their cotton and are flush—they always think they must see every thing, and try their hands at every thing—these fellows bring 'em in to the gamblers, and get 'em tight for 'em you know."

" How's —— got along since his father died ?" asked Mr. S.

" Well, ——'s been unfortunate. Got mad with his overseer ; thought he was lazy and packed him off ; then he undertook to oversee for himself, and he was unfortunate. Had two bad crops. Finally the sheriff took about half his niggers. He tried to work the plantation with the rest, but they was old, used-up hands, and he got mad that they would not work more, and tired o' seein' 'em, and 'fore the end of the year he sold 'em all."

A MISSISSIPPI FAST MAN.

Another young man, of whom he spoke, had had his property managed for him by a relative till he came of age, and had been sent North to college. Two years previously he returned and got it into his own hands, and the first year he ran it in debt $16,000. He had now put it back into the hands of his relative to manage, but continued to live upon it. " I see," continued our host, " every time any of their teams are coming back from town they fetch a barrel or a demijohn. There is a parcel of fellows, who, when they can't liquor anywhere else, always go to him."

" But how did he manage to spend so much the first year,—in gambling ?"

" Well, he gambled some and he run horses.   He do n't know any thing about a horse, and of course he thinks he knows every thing.   Those fellows up at Natchez would sell him any kind of a tacky for four or five hundred dollars, and then after he'd had him a month, they'd ride out another and make a bet of five or six hundred dollars they'd beat him.   Then he'd run with 'em, and of course he'd lose it."

" But sixteen thousand dollars is a large sum of money to be worked off even in that way in a year," I observed.

" Oh, he had plenty of other ways.   He'd go into a bar-room, and get tight and commence to break things.   They'd let him go on, and the next morning hand him a bill for a hundred dollars.   He thinks that's a smart thing, and just laughs and pays it, and then treats all around again."

By one and the other, many stories were then told of similar follies of young men.   Among the rest, this :

A certain man had, as was said to be the custom when running for office, given an order at a grocery for all to be " treated" who applied in his name.   The grocer, after the election, which resulted in the defeat of the treater, presented what was thought an exorbitant bill.   He refused to pay it, and a lawsuit ensued. A gentleman in the witness box being asked if he thought it possible for the whole number of people taking part in the election to have consumed the quantity of liquor alleged, answered :

" Moy Goad! Judge" (reproachfully).   " Yes, sir!   Why, I've been charged for a hundred and fifty drinks *'fore breakfast,* when I've stood treat, and I never thought o' disputin' it."

EDUCATION.

At supper, Mr. S., looking at the daughter of our host, said: "What a pretty girl that is. My dear, do you find any schools to go to out here—eh? I reckon not. This is n't the country for schools. There'll not be a school in Mississippi 'fore long, I reckon ; nothing but Institutes, eh? Ha! ha! ha! Institutes, humph! Do n't believe there's a school between this and Natchez, is there?"

" No, sir."

" Of course there is n't."*

" What sort of a country is it, then, between here and Natchez ?" I asked. " I should suppose it would be well settled."

" SWELL-HEADS."

" Big plantations, sir, nothing else—aristocrats ; swell-heads I call them, sir—nothing but swell-heads, and you can't get a night's lodging, sir. Beyond the ferry, I'll be bound, a man

---

* " Sectional excitement" has given a great impetus to educational projects in the South, and the Mississippi newspapers about this time contained numerous advertisements of a similar character to the following:

CALHOUN INSTITUTE—FOR YOUNG LADIES; MACON, NOXUBEE COUNTY, MISSISSIPPI.—W. R. POINDEXTER, A. M., Principal and Proprietor.—The above School, formerly known as the " Macon Female Institute," will be reopened on the first of October, 1855, with an entirely new corps of teachers from Principal down. Having purchased the property at public sale, and thus become *sole proprietor,* the Principal has determined to use all means he can now command, as well as he may realize for several years yet to come, in building, refitting and procuring such appurtenances as shall enable him to contribute his full quota, as a professional man, to the progress of the great cause of " SOUTHERN EDUCATION."

might die on the road 'fore he'd get a lodging with one of them, eh, Mr. N. ? so, is n't it ? 'Take a stranger in, and I'll clear you out !' That's the rule. That's what they tell their overseers, eh ? Yes sir; just so inhospitable as that—swell-heads ! swell-heads, sir, every plantation—can't get a meal of victuals or a night's lodging from one of them, I do n't suppose, not if your life depended on it. Can you, Mr. N. ?"

"Well, I believe Mr. ——, his place is right on the road, and it's half way to the ferry, and I believe he tells his overseer if a man comes and wants something to eat, he must give it to him, but he must not take any pay for it, because strangers must have something to eat. They start out of Natchez, thinking it's as 't is in other countries; that there's houses along, where they can get a meal, and so they do n't provide for themselves, and when they get along about there, they are sometimes desperate hungry. Had to be something done."

" Do the planters not live themselves on their plantations ?"

" Why, a good many of them has two or three plantations, but they do n't often live on any of them."

"Must have ice for their wine, you see," said Mr. S., "or they'd die; and so they have to live in Natchez or New Orleans; a good many of them live in New Orleans."

"And in summer they go up into Kentucky, do they not ? I've seen country houses there which were said to belong to cotton-planters from Mississippi."

" No, sir; they go North, to New York, and Newport, and Saratoga, and Cape May, and Seneca Lake—somewhere that they can display themselves worse than they do here; Kentucky is no place for that. That's the sort of people, sir, all the way from here to Natchez, and all round Natchez, too,

and in all this section of country where there's good land.
Good God! I would n't have my children educated, sir, among
them, not to have them as rich as Dr. ——, every one of them.
You can know their children as far off as you can see them—
young swell-heads! You 'll take note of 'em in Natchez. Why,
you can tell them by their walk; I noticed it yesterday at the
Mansion House. They sort o' throw out their legs as if they
had n't got strength enough to lift 'em and put them down in
any particular place. They do want so bad to look as if they
were n't made of the same clay as the rest of God's creation."

Some allowance is of course to be made for the splenetic temperament of this gentleman, but facts evidently afford a justification of his sarcasms. And this is easily accounted for. The
farce of the vulgar-rich has its foundation in Mississippi, as in
New York and in Manchester, in the rapidity with which certain values have advanced, especially that of cotton, and, simul-
taneously, that of cotton lands and negroes.* Of course, there
are men of refinement and cultivation among the rich planters
of Mississippi, and many highly estimable and intelligent persons outside of the wealthy class, but the number of such is
smaller in proportion to that of the immoral, vulgar, and ignorant newly-rich, than in any other part of the United States.
And herein is a radical difference between the social condition

---

* As "a Southern lawyer," writing for *Harper's Weekly* (February, 1859)
observes: "The sudden acquisition of wealth in the cotton-growing region
of the United States, in many instances by planters commencing with very
limited means, is almost miraculous. Patient, industrious, frugal, and self-
denying, nearly the entire amount of their cotton-crops is devoted to the increase of their capital. The result is, in a few years large estates, as if by
magic, are accumulated. The fortunate proprietors then build fine houses,
and surround themselves with comforts and luxuries to which they were
strangers in their earlier years of care and toil."

of this region and that of the sea-board slave States, where there are fewer wealthy families, but where, among the people of wealth, refinement and education are much more general.

I asked how rich the sort of men were of whom he spoke.

" Why, sir, from a hundred thousand to ten million."

" Do you mean that between here and Natchez there are none worth less than a hundred thousand dollars ?"

" No, sir, not beyond the ferry. Why, any sort of a plantation is worth a hundred thousand dollars; the niggers would sell for that."

" How many negroes are there on these plantations ?"

" From fifty to a hundred."

" Never over one hundred ?"

" No; when they 've increased to a hundred they always divide them; stock another plantation. There are sometimes three or four plantations adjoining one another, with an overseer for each, belonging to the same man; but that is n't general—in general, they have to strike off for new land."

" How many acres will a hand tend here ?"

" About fifteen—ten of cotton, and five of corn; some pretend to make them tend twenty."

" And what is the usual crop ?"

" A bale and a half to the acre on fresh land and in the bottom. From four to eight bales to a hand they generally get; sometimes ten and better, when they are lucky."

" A bale and a half on fresh land ?   How much on old ?"

" Well, you can't tell—depends on how much it 's worn and what the season is, so much. Old land, after a while, is n't worth bothering with."

" Do most of these large planters who live so freely, anticipate their crops as the sugar planters are said to—spend the money, I mean, before the crop is sold ?"

" Yes, sir, and three and four crops ahead generally."

" Are most of them the sons of rich men ? are they old estates ?"

" No, sir ; many of them were overseers themselves once."

" Well, have you noticed whether it is a fact that these large properties seldom continue long in the same family ? Do the grandsons of wealthy planters often become poor men ?"

" Generally the sons do ; almost always their sons are fools, and soon go through with it."

" If they do n't kill themselves before their fathers die," said the other.

" Yes ; they drink hard and gamble, and of course that brings them into fights."

This was while they were smoking on the gallery after supper. I walked to the stable to see how my horse was provided for ; when I returned they were talking of negroes who had died of yellow fever while confined in the jail at Natchez. Two of them were spoken of as having been thus " happily released," being under sentence of death, and unjustly so, in their opinion.

THE LOWER LAW.

A man living in this vicinity having taken a runaway while the fever was raging in the jail, a physician advised him not to send him there. He did not, and the negro escaped ; was some-time afterward recaptured, and the owner learned from him that he had been once taken and not detained according to law. Being a patriotic man, he made a journey to inquire into the matter, and was very angry. He said, " Whenever you catch a nigger again, you send him to jail, no matter what's to be feared. If he dies in the jail, you are not responsible. You've done your duty, and you can leave the rest to Providence."

"That was right, too," said Mr. P. "Yes, he ought to a' minded the law; then if he'd died in jail, he'd know 'twas n't his fault."

Next morning, near the ferry house, I noticed a set of stocks, having holes for the head as well as the ankles; they stood unsheltered and unshaded in the open road.

I asked an old negro what it was.

"Dat ting, massa?" grinning; "well, sah, we calls dat a ting to put black people, niggers in, when dey misbehaves bad, and to put runaways in, sah. Heaps o' runaways, dis country, sah. Yes, sah, heaps on 'em round here."

Mr. S. and I slept in the same room. I went to bed some time before him; he sat up late, to smoke, he said. He woke me when he came in, by his efforts to barricade the door with our rather limited furniture. The room being small, and without a window, I expostulated. He acknowledged it would probably make us rather too warm, but he should n't feel safe if the door were left open. "You do n't know," said he; "there may be runaways around."

He then drew two small revolvers, hitherto concealed under his clothing, and began to examine the caps. He was certainly a nervous man, perhaps a madman. I suppose he saw some expression of this in my face, for he said, placing them so they could be easily taken up as he lay in bed, "Sometimes a man has a use for them when he least expects it. There was a gentleman on this road a few days ago; he was going to Natchez. He overtook a runaway, and he says to him, 'bad company's better'n none, boy, and I reckon I'll keep you along with me into Natchez.' The nigger appeared to be pleased to have company, and went along, talking with him, very well, till they came to a thicket place about six miles from Natchez, and then he told him he reckoned he would not go any further with him. ' What! you black rascal,' says he ; ' you mean you won't go in with me; you step out and go straight ahead, and if you turn your face till you get into Natchez, I'll shoot you.' ' Aha ! massa,' says the nigger, mighty good-natured, ' I reckon you haint got no shootin' irons,' and he bolted off into the thicket, and got away from him."

The carpentry of the house, as usual, was so bad that we did not suffer at all perceptibly, for ventilation.

At breakfast, Mr. S. came rather late. He bowed his head as he took his seat, and closed his eyes for a second or two ; then, withdrawing his quid of tobacco and throwing it in the fire-place, he looked round with a smile, and said :

" I always think it a good plan to thank the Lord for His mercies. I 'm afraid some people 'll think I 'm a member of the church. I aint, and never was. Wish I was. I am a Son, though [of Temperance?] Give me some water, girl; coffee first—never too soon for coffee. And never too late, I say. Wait for any thing but coffee. These swell-heads drink their coffee after they 've eaten all their dinner. I want it with dinner, eh ? Do n't nothing taste good without coffee, I reckon."

Before he left, he invited me to visit his plantations, giving me careful directions to find them, and saying that if he should not have returned before I reached them, his wife and his overseer would give me every attention if I would tell them he told me to visit them. He said again, and in this connection, that he believed this was the most inhospitable country in the world, and asked, "as I had been a good deal of a traveler, did n't I think so myself?" I answered that my experience was much too small to permit me to form an opinion so contrary to that generally held.

If they had a reputation for hospitality, he said, it could only be among their own sort. They made great swell-head parties; and when they were on their plantation places, they made it a point to have a great deal of company ; they would not have any thing to do if they did n't. But they were all swell-heads, I might be sure; they 'd never ask anybody but a regular swell-head to see them.

His own family, however, seemed not to be excluded from the swell-head society.

Among numerous anecdotes illustrative of the folly of his neighbors, or his own prejudices and jealousy, I remember none which it would be proper to publish but the following:

REFUSING A NOBLE TITLE.

"Do you remember a place you passed [describing the locality] ?"

"Yes," said I ; "a nice house, with a large garden, and a lawn with some statues or vases in it."

"I think it likely ; got a foreign gardener, I expect; that 's all the fashion with them ; a nigger is n't good enough for them. Well, that belongs to Mr. A. J. Clayborn. [?] He's got to be a very rich man; I suppose he 's got as many as five hundred people on all his places. He went out to Europe a few years ago, and some-time after he came back, he came up to Natchez. I was there with my wife at the same time, and as she and Mrs. Clayborn came from the same section of country, and used to know each other when they were girls, she thought she must go and see her. Mrs. Clayborn could not talk about any thing but the great people they had seen in Europe. She was telling of some great nobleman's castle they went to, and the splendid park there was to it, and how grandly they lived. For her part, she admired it so much, and they made so many friends among the people of quality, she said, she did n't care if they always staid there; in fact, she really wanted Mr. Clayborn to buy one of the castles, and be a nobleman himself; 'but he would n't,' says she; 'he's such a strong Democrat, you know.' Ha! ha! ha! I wonder what old Tom Jeff. would have said to these swell-head Democrats."

WHERE ARE ALL THE POOR PEOPLE?

I asked him if there were no poor people in this country. I could see no houses which seemed to belong to poor people.

" Of course not, sir—every inch of the land bought up by the swell-heads on purpose to keep them away. But you go back on to the pine ridge. Good Lord! I 've heard a heap about the poor folks at the North; but if you ever saw any poorer people than them, I should like to know what they live on. Must be a miracle if they live at all. I do n't see how these people live, and I 've wondered how they do a great many times. Do n't raise corn enough, great many of them, to keep a shoat alive through the winter. There 's no way they can live, 'less they steal."

EXPERIENCE OF A FOREIGN TOURIST.

At the ferry of the Homochitto I fell in with a German, originally from Dusseldorf, whence he came seventeen years ago, first to New York; afterward he had resided successively in Baltimore, Cincinnati, New Orleans, Pensacola, Mobile, and Natchez. By the time he reached the last place he had lost all his money. Going to work as a laborer in the town, he soon earned enough again to set him up as a trinket peddler; and a few months afterward he was able to buy "a leetle coach-dray." Then, he said, he made money fast; for he would go back into the country, among the poor people, and sell them trinkets, and calico, and handkerchiefs, and patent medicines. They never had any money. "All poor folks," he said; "dam poor; got no money; oh no; but I say, dat too bad, I do n't like to balk you, my friend; may be so, you got some egg, some fedder, some cheeken, some rag, some sass, or some skin vot you kill. I takes dem dings vot they have, and ven I gets my load I cums to Natchez back and sells dem, alvays dwo or dree times so much as dey coss me; and den I buys some more goods. Not bad beesnes—no. Oh, dese poor people dey deenk me is von fool ven I buy some dime deir rag vat dey bin vear; dey calls me de ole Dutch cuss. But dey do n't know nottin' vot it is vorth. I deenk dey neever see no money; may be so dey geev all de cheeken vot dey been got for a leetle breastpin vot cost me not so much as von beet. Sometime dey be dam crazy fool; dey know not how do make de count at all. Yees, I makes some money, a heap."

NATCHEZ.

From the Homochitto to the suburbs of Natchez, a good half day's ride, I found the country beautiful; fewer hills than before, the soil very rich, and the land almost all inclosed in plantations, the roadside boundaries of which are old rose-hedges. The road is well constructed; often, in passing through the hills, with high banks on each side, coped with thick and dark, but free and sportive hedges, out of which avenues of trees growing carelessly and bending angel-like over the traveler, the sentiment of the most charming Herefordshire lanes is reproduced. There are also frequent woods, of a park-like character in their openness; the trees chiefly oak, and of great hight. Sometimes these have been inclosed with neat palings, and slightly and tastily thinned out, so as to form noble grounds around the residences of the planters, which are always cottages or very simple and unostentatious mansions. Near two of these are unusually good ranges of negro-houses. On many of the plantations, perhaps most, no residence is visible from the road, and the negro-quarters, when seen, are the usual comfortless cabins.

Within three miles of the town the country is entirely occupied by houses and grounds of a villa character; the grounds usually exhibiting a paltry taste, with miniature terraces, and trees and shrubs planted and trimmed with no regard to architectural and landscape considerations. There is, however, an abundance of good trees, much beautiful shrubbery, and the best hedges and screens of evergreen shrubs that I have seen in America. The houses are not remarkable.

I was amused to recognize specimens of the " swell-head" fraternity, as described by my nervous friend, as soon as I got into the villa district. First came two boys in a skeleton wagon, pitching along with a racking pony, which ran over Jude; she yelped, I wheeled round, and they pulled up and looked apologetic. She was only slightly hurt, but thereafter gave a quicker and broader sheer to approaching vehicles than her Texas experience had taught her to do.

Then came four indistinct beards and two old, roué-looking men, all trotting horses; the young fellows screaming, breaking up, and swearing. After them cantered a mulatto groom, white-gloved and neatly dressed, who, I noticed, bowed politely, lifting his hat and smiling to a ragged old negro with a wheelbarrow and shovel, on the footpath.

Next came—and it was a swelteringly hot afternoon—an open carriage with two ladies taking an airing. Mr. S. had said the swell-heads had " got to think that their old mammy niggers were not good enough for their young ones ;" and here, on the front seat of the carriage, was a white and veritable French bonne, holding a richly-belaced baby. The ladies sat back, good-looking women enough, and prettily dressed, but marble-like in propriety, looking stealthily from the corners of their eyes without turning their heads. But the dignity of the turn-out chiefly reposed in the coachman, an obese old black man, who should have been a manufacturer of iced root-beer in a cool cellar, but who had by some means been set high up in the sun's face on the bed-like cushion of the box, to display a great livery top-coat, with the wonted capes and velvet, buttoned brightly and tightly to the chin, of course, and crowned by the proper narrow-brimmed hat, with broad band and buckle ; his elbows squared, the reins and whip in his hands, the sweat in globules all over his ruefully-decorous face, and his eyes fast closed in sleep.

The houses and shops within the town itself are generally small, and always inelegant. A majority of the names on the signs are German ; the hotel is unusually clean, and the servants attentive ; and the stable at which I left Belshazzar is excellent, and contains several fine horses. Indeed, I never saw such a

large number of fine horses as there is here, in any other town of
the size.   In the stable and the hotel there is a remarkable number of young men, extraordinarily dressed, like New York clerks
on their Sunday excursions, all lounging or sauntering, and often
calling at the bar; all smoking, all twisting lithe walking-sticks,
all "talking horse."

THE BLUFF.

But the grand feature of Natchez is the bluff, terminating in
an abrupt precipice over the river, with the public garden upon
it.   Of this I never had heard, and when, after seeing my horse
dried off and eating his oats with great satisfaction—the first
time he has ever tasted oats, I suppose—I strolled off to see the
town, I came upon it by surprise.   I entered a gate and walked
up a slope, supposing that I was approaching the ridge or summit of a hill, and expecting to see beyond it a corresponding
slope and the town again, continuing in terraced streets to the
river.   I found myself, almost at the moment I discovered that
it was not so, on the very edge of a stupendous cliff, and before
me an indescribably vast expanse of forest, extending on every
hand to a hazy horizon, in which, directly in front of me, swung
the round, red, setting sun.

Through the otherwise unbroken forest, the Mississippi had
opened a passage for itself, forming a perfect arc, the hither
shore of the middle of the curve being hidden under the crest of
the cliff, and the two ends lost in the vast obscurity of the Great
West.   Overlooked from such an eminence, the size of the Mississippi can be realized—a thing difficult under ordinary circumstances; but though the fret of a swelling torrent is not wanting,
it is perceptible only as the most delicate chasing upon the

broad, gleaming expanse of polished steel, which at once shamed all my previous conceptions of the appearance of the greatest of rivers. Coming closer to the edge and looking downward, you see the lower town, its roofs with water flowing all around them, and its pigmy people wading, and laboring to carry upward their goods and furniture, in danger from a rising movement of the great water. Poor people, emigrants and niggers only.

I laid down, and would have reposed my mind in the infinite vision westward, but was presently disturbed by a hog which came grunting near me, rooting in the poor turf of this wonderful garden. I rose and walked its length. Little more has been done than to inclose a space along the edge, which would have been dangerous to build upon, to cut out some curving alleys now recaptured by the grass and weeds, and to plant a few succulent trees. A road to the lower town, cutting through it, is crossed by slight wooden foot-bridges, and there are some rough plank benches, adorned with stenciled "medical" advertisements. Some shrubs are planted on the crumbling face of the cliff, so near the top that the swine can obtain access to them. A man, bearded and smoking, and a woman with him, sitting at the extreme end, were the only visitors except myself and the swine.

As I am writing there is a bustle in the street. A young man is being lifted up and carried into the bar-room. He is insensible. A beautiful mare, from which he has evidently been thrown, is led back from around the corner quivering with excitement.

I could find no reading-room; no recent newspapers except *The Natchez Free Trader*, which has nothing but cotton and river news, and steamboat puffs; no magazines but aged Harpers; and no recent publications of any sort are for sale or to be seen at the booksellers'; so, after supper, I went to the cliff again, and most exquisite and solemn was the scene: the young moon shining through rents in the clouds, the great gleaming crescent of water below, the dim, ungapped horizon—the earth sensibly a mere swinging globe.

Of all the town, only five Germans, sitting together, but smoking in silence, had gathered here for evening worship.

As I returned up the main street, I stopped opposite a house from which there came the sound of excellent music—a violin and piano. I had heard no music since I was in Western Texas, and I leaned upon a lamp-post for an hour, listening. Many stopped near me for a few minutes, and went on. At length, a man who had remained some time addressed me, speaking in a foreign tongue. " Can't you speak English?" said I.

" You are not an American?"

" Yes."

" I should tzink it not."

" I am; I am a New Yorker."

" So?—O yes, perhaps, but not zis country."

" What are you?"

" Italian."

" Do you live here?"

" Yes."

" Are there many Italians in Natchez?"

" Yes—some many—seven. All big dam rascaal. **Yes.** Ha! ha! ha! True. Dam rascaal all of us."

" What do you do for a living here?"

" For me it is a cigar-store; fruit; confectionery."

" And the rest ?"

" Oh, everytzing. I do n't expect dem be here so much long now."

" Why—what will they do ?"

" Dey all go to Cuba. Be vawr zair soon now. All go. All dam rascaal go, can go, ven ze vawr is. Good ting dat for Natchez, eh ? Yes, I tzink."

He told me the names of the players ; the violinist, an Italian, he asserted to be the best in America. He resided in Natchez, I understood, as a teacher; and, I presume, the town has metropolitan advantages for instruction in all fashionable accomplishments. Yet, with a population of 18,601, the number of children registered for the public schools and academies, or " Institutes," of the county seat, is but 1,015 ; and among these must be included many sent from other parts of the State, and from Arkansas and Louisiana ; the public libraries contain but 2,000 volumes, and the churches seat but 7,700.*

Franklin, the next county in the rear of the county in which Natchez is situated (Adams), has a population of 6,000, and but 132 children attending school.

Mr. Russell (*North America : its Agriculture and Climate*, page 258) states that he had been led to believe that " as refined society was to be found at Natchez as in any other part of the United States," but his personal observation was, that " the chief frequenters of the best hotel were low, drunken fellows."

---

* This may be compared with the town of Springfield, county of Sangammon, Illinois, in which, with a population of 19,228 (nearer to that of Natchez than any other town I observe in the free States), the number of registered school children is 3,300, the public libraries contain 20,000 volumes, and the churches can accommodate 28,000 sitters.

LABOR AND WAGES.—TOWN AND COUNTRY.

The first night after leaving Natchez I found lodging with a German, who, when I inquired if he could accommodate me, at once said, " Yes, sir, I make it *a business* to lodge travelers."

He had a little farm, and owned four strong negro men and a woman and children. All his men, however, he hired out as porters or servants in Natchez, employing a white man, a native of the country, to work with him on his farm.

To explain the economy of this arrangement, he said that one of his men earned in Natchez $30 a month clear of all expenses, and the others much more than he could ever make their labor worth to him. A negro of moderate intelligence would hire, as a house-servant, for $200 a year and his board, which was worth $8 a month; whereas he hired this white fellow, who was strong and able, for $10 a month; and he believed he got as much work out of him as he could out of a negro. If labor were worth so much as he got for that of his negroes, why did the white man not demand more? Well—he kept him in whiskey and tobacco beside his wages, and he was content. Most folks here do not like white laborers. They had only been used to have niggers do their work, and they did not know how to manage with white laborers; but he had no difficulty.

FOOD OF THE SLAVES.

I asked if $8 would cover the cost of a man's board? He supposed it might cost him rather more than that to keep the white man; $8 was what it was generally reckoned in town to cost to keep a negro; niggers living in town or near it were expected to have " extras;" out on the plantations, where they did not get any thing but bacon and meal, of course it did not cost so much. Did he know what it cost to keep a negro generally upon the plantations? It was generally reckoned, he said, that a nigger ought to have a peck of meal and three pounds of bacon a week; some did n't give so much meat, but he thought it would be better to give them more.

"You are getting rich," I said. "Are the Germans generally, hereabouts, doing well? I see there are a good many in Natchez."

"Oh yes; anybody who is not too proud to work can get rich here."

The next day, having ridden thirty tedious miles, about six o'clock I called at the first house standing upon or near the road which I had seen for some time, and solicited a lodging. It was refused, by a woman. How far was it to the next house? I asked her. Two miles and a half. So I found it to be, but it was a deserted house, falling to decay, on an abandoned plantation. I rode several miles further, and it was growing dark and threatening rain before I came in sight of another. It was a short distance off the road, and approached by a private lane, from which it was separated by a grass plat. A well-dressed man stood between the gate and the house. I stopped and bowed to him, but he turned his back upon me and walked to the house. I opened a gate and rode in. Two men were upon the gallery, but as they paid no attention to my presence when I stopped near them, I doubted if either were the master of the house. I asked, "Could I obtain a lodging here to-night, gentlemen?" One of them answered, surlily and decidedly, "No." I paused a moment that they might observe me—evidently a stranger benighted, with a fatigued horse, and then asked, "Can you tell me, sir, how far it is to a public house?" "I do n't know," answered the same man. I again remained silent a moment. "No public houses in this section of the country, I reckon, sir," said the other. "Do you know how far it is to the next house on the road, north of this?" "No," answered one. "You'll find one about two miles or two miles and a half from here," said the other. "Is it a house in which I shall be likely to get a lodging, do you know?" "I do n't know, I'm sure."

"Good night, gentlemen; you'll excuse me for troubling you. I am entirely a stranger in this region."

A grunt, or inarticulate monosyllable, from one of them, was the only reply, and I rode away, glad that I had not been fated to spend an evening in such company.

Soon afterward I came to a house and stables close upon the road. There was a man on the gallery playing the fiddle. I asked, "Could you accommodate me here to-night, sir?" He stopped fiddling, and turned his head toward an open door, asking, "Wants to know if you can accommodate him?" "Accommodate him with what?" demanded a harsh-toned woman's voice. "With a bed, of course—what do you s'pose—ho! ho! ho!" and he went on fiddling again. I had, during this conversation, observed ranges of negro huts behind the stables, and perceived that it must be the overseer's house of the plantation at which I had previously called. "Like master, like man," I thought, and rode on, my inquiry not having been even answered.

I met a negro boy on the road, who told me it was about two miles to the next house, but he did not reckon that I would get in there. "How far to the next house beyond that?" "About four miles, sir, and I reckon you can get in there, master; I've heerd they did take in travelers to that place."

Soon after this it began to rain and grow dark; so dark that

I could not keep the road, for soon finding Belshazzar in difficulty, I got off and discovered that we were following up the dry
bed of a small stream. In trying to get back I probably crossed
the road, as I did not find it again, and wandered cautiously
among trees for nearly an hour, at length coming to open country and a fence. Keeping this in sight, I rode on until I found
a gate, entering at which, I followed a nearly straight and tolerably good road full an hour, at last coming to a large negro-
" settlement."

AN OVERSEER AT HOME.

I passed through it to the end of the rows, where was a cabin
larger than the rest, facing on the space between the two lines of
huts. A shout here brought out the overseer. I begged for a
night's lodging; he was silent; I said that I had traveled far,
was much fatigued and hungry; my horse was nearly knocked
up; and I was a stranger in the country; I had lost my road,
and only by good fortune had found my way here. At length,
as I continued urging my need, he said :

"Well, I suppose you must stop. Ho, Byron ! Here, Byron,
take this man's horse, and put him in *my* stable. 'Light, sir,
and come in."

Within I found his wife, a young woman, showily dressed—a
caricature of the fashions of the day. Apparently, they had
both been making a visit to neighbors, and but just come home.
I was not received very kindly, but at the request of her husband
she brought out and set before me some cold corn-bread and fat
bacon.

Before I had finished eating my supper, however, they both
quite changed their manner, and the woman apologized for not

having made coffee. The cook had gone to bed and the fire
was out, she said. She presently ordered Byron, as he brought
my saddle in, to get some "light-wood" and make a fire ; said
she was afraid I had made a poor supper, and set a chair by the
fire-place for me as I drew away from the table.

I plied the man with inquiries about his business, got him interested in points of difference between Northern and Southern
agriculture, and soon had him in a very sociable and communicative humor. He gave me much overseer's lore about cotton
culture, nigger and cattle maladies, the proper mode of keeping
sweet potatoes, etc. ; and when I proposed to ride over the plantation with him in the morning, he said he " would be very
thankful of my company."

I think they gave up their own bed to me, for it was double,
and had been slept in since the sheets were last changed; the
room was garnished with pistols and other arms and ammunition,
rolls of negro-cloth, shoes and hats, handcuffs, a large medicine
chest and several books on medical and surgical subjects and far-
riery ; while articles of both men's and women's wearing apparel
hung against the walls, which were also decorated with some
large patent-medicine posters. One of them is characteristic of
the place and the times.*

---

* THE WASHINGTON REMEDIES—TO PLANTERS AND OTHERS.—These
Remedies, now offered to the public under the title of the Washington Remedies, are composed of ingredients, many of which are not even known to
Botany. No apothecary has them for sale ; they are supplied to the sub-
scriber by the native red-men of Louisiana. The recipes by which they are
compounded have descended to the present possessor, M. A. MICKLEJOHN,
from ancestors who obtained them from the friendly Indian tribes, prior to
and during the Revolution, and they are now offered to the public with that
confidence which has been gained from a knowledge of the fact that during
so long a series of years there has never been known an instance in which

REVIEW OF A FIRST-RATE COTTON PLANTATION.

We had a good breakfast in the morning, and immediately afterward mounted and rode to a very large cotton-field, where the whole field-force of the plantation was engaged.

It was a first-rate plantation. On the highest ground stood a large and handsome mansion, but it had not been occupied for several years, and it was more than two years since the overseer had seen the owner. He lived several hundred miles away, and the overseer would not believe that I did not know him, for he was a rich man and an honorable, and had several times been where I came from—New York.

The whole plantation, including the swamp land around it, and owned with it, covered several square miles. It was four miles from the settlement to the nearest neighbor's house. There were between thirteen and fourteen hundred acres under cultivation with cotton, corn, and other   crops, and two hundred hogs running at large in the swamp. It was the intention that corn and pork enough should be raised to keep the slaves and cattle. This year, however, it has been found necessary to purchase largely, and such was probably usually the case,* though

they have failed to perform a speedy and permanent cure. The subscribers do not profess these remedies will cure *every* disarrangement of the human system, but in such as are enumerated below they feel they can not fail· The directions for use have only to be strictly followed, and however despairing the patient may have been, he will find cause for blissful *hope* and renewed *life.*

These preparations are no Northern patent humbug, but are manufactured in New Orleans by a Creole, who has long used them in private practice, rescuing many unfortunate victims of disease from the grave, after they have been given up by their physicians as incurable, or have been tortured beyond endurance by laceration and painful operations.

* "The bacon is almost entirely imported from the Northern States, as well

the overseer intimated the owner had been displeased, and he
" did not mean to be caught so bad again."

There were 135 slaves, big and little, of which 67 went to field
regularly—equal, the overseer thought, to 60 able-bodied hands.
Beside the field-hands, there were 3 mechanics (blacksmith, carpenter and wheelwright), 2 seamstresses, 1 cook, 1 stable servant,
1 cattle-tender, 1 hog-tender, 1 teamster, 1 house servant (overseer's cook), and one midwife and nurse. These were all first-
class hands; most of them would be worth more, if they were
for sale, the overseer said, than the best field-hands. There was
also a driver of the hoe-gang who did not labor personally, and
a foreman of the plow-gang. These two acted as petty officers
in the field, and alternately in the quarters.

There was a nursery for sucklings at the quarters, and twenty
women at this time who left their work four times each day, for
half an hour, to nurse their young ones, and whom the overseer
counted as half-hands—that is, expected to do half an ordinary
day's work.

DESERTERS AND DETECTIVES.

He had no runaways out at this time, but had just sold a bad
one to go to Texas. He was whipping the fellow, when he
turned and tried to stab him—then broke from him and ran
away. He had him caught almost immediately by the dogs.

as a considerable quantity of Indian corn. This is reckoned bad management by intelligent planters. * * * On this plantation as much Indian
corn was raised as was needed, but little bacon, which was mostly imported
from Ohio. The sum annually paid for this article was upward of eight
hundred pounds. Large plantations are not suited to the rearing of hogs; for
it is found almost impossible to prevent the negroes from stealing and roasting the young pigs." Mr. Russell, visiting the plantation of a friend near
Natchez.—*North America : its Agriculture*, etc., p. 265.

After catching him, he kept him in irons till he had a chance to sell him. His niggers did not very often run away, he said, because they were almost sure to be caught. As soon as he saw that one was gone he put the dogs on, and if rain had not just fallen, they would soon find him. Sometimes, though, they would outwit the dogs, but if they did they almost always kept in the neighborhood, because they did not like to go where they could not sometimes get back and see their families, and he would soon get wind of where they had been ; they would come round their quarters to see their families and to get food, and as soon as he knew it, he would find their tracks and put the dogs on again. Two months was the longest time any of them ever kept out. They had dogs trained on purpose to run after niggers, and never let out for any thing else.

DRIVING.

We found in the field thirty plows, moving together, turning the earth from the cotton plants, and from thirty to forty hoers, the latter mainly women, with a black driver walking about among them with a whip, which he often cracked at them, sometimes allowing the lash to fall lightly upon their shoulders. He was constantly urging them also with his voice. All worked very steadily, and though the presence of a stranger on the plantation must have been rare, I saw none raise or turn their heads to look at me. Each gang was attended by a " water-toter," that of the hoe-gang being a straight, sprightly, plump little black girl, whose picture, as she stood balancing the bucket upon her head, shading her bright eyes with one hand, and holding out a calabash with the other to maintain her poise, would have been a worthy study for Murillo.

DAYS AND HOURS OF LABOR.

I asked at what time they began to work in the morning. "Well," said the overseer, "I do better by my niggers than most. I keep 'em right smart at their work while they do work, but I generally knock 'em off at 8 o'clock in the morning Saturdays, and give 'em all the rest of the day to themselves, and I always gives 'em Sundays, the whole day. Pickin' time, and when the crap's bad in grass, I sometimes keep 'em to it till about sunset, Saturdays, but I never work 'em Sundays."

"How early do you start them out in the morning, usually ?"

"Well, I do n't never start my niggers 'fore daylight except 'tis in pickin' time, then maybe I get 'em out a quarter of an hour before. But I keep 'em right smart to work through the day." He showed an evident pride in the vigilance of his driver, and called my attention to the large area of ground already hoed over that morning; well hoed, too, as he said.

"At what time do they eat?" I asked. They ate "their snacks" in their cabins, he said, before they came out in the morning (that is before daylight—the sun rising at this time at a little before five, and the day dawning, probably, an hour earlier); then at 12 o'clock their dinner was brought to them in a cart— one cart for the plow-gang and one for the hoe-gang. The hoe-gang ate its dinner in the field, and only stopped work long enough to eat it. The plow-gang drove its teams to the "weather houses"—open sheds erected for the purpose in different parts of the plantation, under which were cisterns filled with rain water, from which the water-toters carried drink to those at work. The mules were fed as much oats (in straw), corn and fodder as they would eat in two hours; this forage having been brought to the weather houses by another cart. The plowmen had nothing to do but eat their dinner in all this time. All worked as late as they could see to work well, and had no more food nor rest until they returned to their cabins.* At half past nine o'clock the drivers, each on an alternate night, blew a horn, and at ten visited every cabin to see that its occupants were at rest, and not lurking about and spending their strength in fooleries, and that the fires were safe—a very unusual precaution; the negroes are generally at liberty after their day's work is done till they are called in the morning. When washing and patching were done, wood hauled and cut for the fires, corn ground, etc., I did not learn : probably all chores not of daily necessity, were reserved for Saturday. Custom varies in this respect. In general, with regard to fuel for the cabins, the negroes are left to look out for themselves, and they often have to go to "the swamp" for it, or at least, if it has been hauled, to cut it to a convenient size, after their day's work is done. The allowance of food was a peck of corn and four pounds of pork per week, each. When they could not get "greens" (any vegetables) he generally gave them five pounds of pork. They had gardens, and raised a good deal for themselves; they also had fowls, and usually plenty of eggs. He added, "the man who owns this plantation does more for his niggers than any other man I know. Every

---

* This would give at this season hardly less than sixteen hours of plodding labor, relieved by but one short interval of rest, during the daylight, for the hoe-gang. It is not improbable. I was accustomed to rise early and ride late, resting during the heat of the day, while in the cotton district, but I always found the negroes in the field when I first looked out, and generally had to wait for the negroes to come from the field to have my horse fed when I stopped for the night. (See Journey in Texas, p. 82.) I am told, however, and I believe, that it is usual in the hottest weather, to give a rest of an hour or two to all hands at noon. I never happened to see it done. The legal limit of a slave's days work in S. Carolina is 15 hours.

Christmas he sends me up a thousand or fifteen hundred dollars' [equal to eight or ten dollars each] worth of molasses and coffee, and tobacco, and calico, and Sunday tricks for 'em. Every family on this plantation gets a barrel of molasses at Christmas." (Not an uncommon practice in Mississippi, though the quantity is very rarely so generous. It is usually made somewhat proportionate to the value of the last crop sold.)*

Beside which, the overseer added, they are able, if they choose, to buy certain comforts for themselves—tobacco for instance—with money earned by Saturday and Sunday work. Some of them went into the swamps on Sunday and made boards—"puncheons" made with the ax. One man sold last year as much as fifty dollars' worth.

Finding myself nearer the outer gate than the "quarters," when at length my curiosity was satisfied, I did not return to the house. After getting a clear direction how to find my way back to the road I had been upon the previous day, I said to the overseer, with some hesitation lest it should offend him, "You will allow me to pay you for the trouble I have given you?" He looked a little disconcerted by my putting the question in this way, but answered in a matter-of-course tone, "It will be a dollar and a quarter, sir."

This was the only large plantation that I had an opportunity of seeing at all closely, over which I was not chiefly conducted by an educated gentleman and slave owner, by whose habitual impressions and sentiments my own were probably somewhat influenced. From what I saw in passing, and from what I heard

* I was told by a gentleman in North Carolina, that the custom of supplying molasses to negroes in Mississippi, was usually mentioned to those sold away from his part of the country, to reconcile them to going thither

by chance of others, I suppose it to have been in no respect an unfavorable specimen of those plantations on which the owners do not reside.   A merchant of the vicinity recently in New York tells me that he supposes it to be a fair enough sample of plantations of its class.   There is nothing remarkable in its management that he had heard.   When I asked about molasses and Christmas presents, he said he reckoned the overseer rather stretched that story, but the owner was a very good man.   A magistrate of the district, who had often been on the plantation, said in answer to an inquiry from me, that the negroes were very well treated upon it, though not extraordinarily so.   His comparison was with plantations in general.*   He also spoke well of the overseer.   He had been a long time on this plantation—I think he said, ever since it had begun to be cultivated.   This is very rare; it was the only case I met with in which an overseer had kept the same place ten years, and it was a strong evidence of his comparative excellence, that his employer had been so long satisfied with him.   Perhaps it was a stronger evidence that the

* In Debow's Resources of the South, vol. i., p. 150, a table is furnished by a cotton planter to show that the expenses of raising cotton are "generally greatly underrated."   It is to be inferred that they certainly are not underrated in the table.   On "a well improved and properly organized plantation," the expense of feeding one hundred negroes, "as deduced from fifteen years' experience" of the writer, is asserted in this table to be $750 per annum, or seven dollars and a half each; in this sum is included, however, the expenses of the "hospital and the overseer's table."   This is much less than the expense for the same purposes, if the overseer's account was true, of the plantation above described.   Clothing, shoes, bedding, *sacks for gathering cotton, and so forth,* are estimated by the same authority to cost an equal sum—$7.50 for each slave.   I have just paid on account of a day laborer on a farm in New York, his board bill, he being a bachelor living at the house of another Irish laborer with a family.   The charge is twenty-one times as large as that set down for the slave.

owner of the negroes was a man of good temper, systematic and thorough in the management of his property.*

The condition of the fences, of the mules and tools, and tillage, which would have been considered admirable in the best farming district of New York—the dress of the negroes and the neatness and spaciousness of their "quarters," which were superior to those of most of the better class of plantations on which the owners reside, all bore strong testimony to a very unusually prudent and provident policy.

I made no special inquiries about the advantages for education or means of religious instruction provided for the slaves. As there seems to be much public desire for definite information upon that point, I regret that I did not. I did not need to put questions to the overseer to satisfy my own mind, however. It was obvious that all natural incitements to self-advancement had been studiously removed or obstructed, in subordination to the general purpose of making the plantation profitable. The machinery of labor was ungeared during a day and a half a week, for cleaning and repairs; experience having proved here, as it has in Manchester and New York, that operatives do very much better work if thus privileged. During this interval, a limited play to individual qualities and impulses was permitted in the culture of such luxuries as potatoes and pumpkins, the repair of garments, and in other sordid recreations involving the least possible

---

* "I was informed that some successful planters, who held several estates in this neighborhood [Natchez] made it a rule to *change their overseers every year*, on the principle that the *two* years' service system is sure to spoil them." —*Russell's North America : its Agriculture*, etc., p. 258.

"Overseers are changed every year; a few remain four or five years, but the average time they remain on the same plantation does not exceed two years."—*Southern Agriculturist*, vol. iv., p. 351.

intellectual friction. Regarding only the balance sheet of the
owner's ledger, it was admirable management. I am sorry to
think that it is rare, where this is the uppermost object of the
cotton-planter, that an equally frugal economy is maintained ; and
as the general character of the district along the Mississippi,
which is especially noticeable for the number of large and very
productive plantations which it contains, has perhaps been sufficiently drawn in my narrative, I will now present, in a collective form, before entering a different region, certain observations
which I wish to make upon the peculiar aspect of slavery in that
and similar parts of the southern States.

CHAPTER II.

THE PROPERTY ASPECT OF SLAVERY.

In a hilly part of Alabama, fifty miles north of the principal
cotton-growing districts of that State, I happened to have a
tradesman of the vicinity for a traveling companion, when we
passed a rather large plantation. Calling my attention to the
unusually large cluster of negro cabins, he observed that a rugged range of hills behind them was a favorite lurking-ground for
runaway negroes. It afforded them numerous coverts for concealment during the day, and at night the slaves of this plantation would help them to find the necessaries of existence. He
had seen folks who had come here to look after niggers from
plantations two hundred miles to the southward. "I suppose,"
said he, "'t would seem kind o' barbarous to you to see a pack
of hounds after a human being?"

"Yes, it would."

"Some fellows take just as much delight in it as in runnin' a
fox. Always seemed to me a kind o' barbarous sport." [A
pause.] "It's necessary, though."

"I suppose it is. Slavery is a custom of society which has
come to us from a barbarous people, and naturally, barbarous
practices have to be employed to maintain it."

"Yes, I s'pose that's so. But niggers is generally pretty well
treated, considering. Some people work their niggers too hard,
that's a fact. I know a man at ——; he's a merchant there, and

I have had dealings with him ; he's got three plantations, and he puts the hardest overseers he can get on them. He is all the time a' buying niggers, and they say around there he works 'em to death. On these small plantations, niggers ain't very often whipped bad; but on them big plantations, they've got to use 'em hard to keep any sort o' control over 'em. The overseers have to always go about armed; their life would n't be safe, if they did n't. As 't is, they very often get cut pretty bad." (Cutting is knifing—it may be stabbing, in south-western parlance).

"In such cases, what is done with the negro?"

'Oh, he gets hung for that—if he cuts a white man : that's the law; 'intent to kill,' they call it; and the State pays the owner what he's worth, to hang him."

He went on to describe what he had seen on some large plantations which he had visited for business purposes—indications, as he thought, in the appearance of "the people," that they were being "worked to death." "These rich men," he said, "were always bidding for the overseer who would make the most cotton; and a great many of the overseers did not care for any thing but to be able to say they had made so many bales in a year. If they made plenty of cotton, the owners never asked how many niggers they killed."

I suggested that this did not seem quite credible; a negro was a valuable piece of property. It would be foolish to use him in such a way.

"Seems they don't think so," he answered. "They are always bragging—you must have heard them—how many bales their overseer has made, or how many their plantation has made to a hand. They never think of any thing else. You see, if a man did like to have his niggers taken care of, he could n't bear to be always hearing that all the plantations round had beat his. He'd think the fault was in his overseer. The fellow who can make the most cotton always gets paid the best."*

Overseers' wages were ordinarily from $200 to $600, but a real driving overseer would very often get $1,000. Sometimes they'd get $1,200 or $1,500. He heard of $2,000 being paid one fellow.† A determined and perfectly relentless man—I can't recall his words, which were very expressive—a real devil of an overseer, would get almost any wages he'd ask; because, when it was told round that such a man had made so many bales to the hand, everybody would be trying to get him.

The man who talked in this way was a native Alabamian, ignorant, but apparently of more than ordinarily reflective habits, and so situated as to have unusually good opportunities for observation. In character, if not in detail, I must say that his in-

---

* Another person in this vicinity observed to me, that it was one of the effects of the increasing demand for cotton, that planters who would formerly have discharged an overseer for cruel usage of his slave, now thought it right to let him have his own way. " If he makes cotton enough, they do n't think they ought to interfere with him."

† "Editors of *Delta :* Under the head of ' Home Reforms,' in your paper of the 19th ultimo, I find views and opinions in regard to the institution of slavery identical with those long entertained by myself, and embodied, some years ago, in a communication to your predecessors.

" I hold, sirs, that no gentleman will intentionally injure or oppress a poor slave or others under his authority or protection; and I insist upon the justice and propriety of a rigid enforcement of our humane laws, no matter by whom violated, or how high the offender. * * *

" The defective education and consequent habits of the overseers of the South, with a few exceptions, disqualify them for the high and sacred trust confided to them; and yet the extravagant salaries which they receive (from one to three thousand dollars) [*i. e.,* on sugar plantations] should command the services of men of exemplary character and distinguished abilities."— *New Orleans Delta, Dec.,* 1856.

formation was entirely in accordance with the opinions I should
have been led to form from the conversations I heard by chance,
from time to time, in the richest cotton districts.   That his statements as to the bad management of large plantations, in respect
to the waste of negro property, were not much exaggerated,
I find frequent evidence in southern agricultural journals.   The
following is an extract from one of a series of essays published in
The Cotton Planter, the object of which is to present the economical advantages of a more mixed system of agriculture than
is usually followed in the cotton region.   The writer, Mr. M. W.
Phillips, is a well-known, intelligent and benevolent planter, who
resides constantly on his estate, near Jackson, Mississippi :

"I have known many in the rich planting portion of Mississippi especially, and others elsewhere, who, acting on the policy of the boy in
the fable, who 'killed the goose for the golden egg,' accumulated
property, yet among those who have relied solely on their product in
land and negroes, I doubt if this be the true policy of plantation economy.   With the former every thing has to bend, give way to large
crops of cotton, land has to be cultivated wet or dry, negroes to work,
cold or hot.   Large crops planted, and they must be cultivated, or
done so after a manner.   When disease comes about, as, for instance,
cholera, pneumonia, flux, and other violent diseases, these are more
subject, it seemeth to me, than others, or even if not, there is less vital-
ity to work on, and, therefore, in like situations and similar in severity,
they must sink with more certainty; or even should the animal economy rally under all these trials, the neglect consequent upon this ' cut
and cover' policy must result in greater mortality.   Another objection,
not one fourth of the children born are raised, and perhaps not over
two thirds are born on the place, which, under a different policy, might
be expected.   And this is not all: hands, and teams, and land must
wear out sooner ; admitting this to be only one year sooner in twenty
years, or that lands and negroes are less productive at forty than at
forty-two, we see a heavy loss.   Is this not so ?   I am told of negroes
not over thirty-five to forty-five, who look older than others at forty-
five to fifty-five.   I know a man now, not short of sixty, who might
readily be taken for forty-five ; another on the same place full fifty (for
I have known both for twenty-eight years, and the last one for thirty-
two years), who could be sold for thirty-five, and these negroes are
very leniently dealt with.   Others, many others, I know and have
known twenty-five to thirty years, of whom I can speak of as above.

As to rearing children, I can point to equally as strong cases; aye, men who are, 'as it were,' of one family, differing as much as four and eight bales in cropping, and equally as much in raising young negroes. The one scarcely paying expenses by his crop, yet in the past twenty-five years raising over seventy-five to a hundred negroes, the other buying more than raised, and yet not as many as the first.

"I regard the 'just medium' to be the correct point. Labor is conducive to health; a healthy woman will rear most children. I favor good and fair work, yet not overworked so as to tax the animal economy, that the woman can not rear healthy children, nor should the father be over-wrought, that his vital powers be at all infringed upon.

"If the policy be adopted, to make an improvement in land visible, to raise the greatest number of healthy children, to make an abundance of provision, to rear a portion at least of work horses, rely on it we will soon find by our tax list that our country is improving: * * * Brethren of the South, we must change our policy. *Overseers are not interested in raising children, or meat, in improving land, or improving productive qualities of seed, or animals. Many of them do not care whether property has depreciated or improved, so they have made a crop to boast of.*

" As to myself, I care not who has the credit of making crops at Log Hall, and I would prefer that an overseer, who has been one of my family for a year or two, or more, should be benefited; but this thing is to be known and well understood. I plant such fields in such crops as I see fit; I plant acres in corn, cotton, oats, potatoes, etc., as I select, and the general policy of rest, cultivation, etc., must be preserved which I lay down. A self-willed overseer may fraudulently change somewhat in the latter, by not carrying out orders—that I can not help. What I have written, I have written, and think I can substantiate."

From the *Southern Agriculturist*, vol. iv., page 317 :

" OVERSEERS.

* * * "When they seek a place, they rest their claims entirely on the number of bags they have heretofore made to the hand, and generally the employer unfortunately recognizes the justice of such claims.

" No wonder, then, that the overseer desires to have entire control of the plantation. No wonder he opposes all experiments, or, if they are persisted in, neglects them; *presses every thing at the end of the lash ; pays no attention to the sick, except to keep them in the field as long as possible ; and drives them out again at the first moment, and forces sucklers and breeders to the utmost.* He has no other interest than to make a big cotton crop. And if this does not please you, and induce you to increase his wages, he knows men it will please, and secure him a situation with."

From the Columbia *South Carolinian :*

* * *   " Planters may be divided into two great classes, viz., those who attend to their business, and those who do not. And this creates corresponding classes of overseers. The planter who does not manage his own business must, of course, surrender every thing into the hands of his overseer. Such a planter usually rates the merits of the overseer exactly in proportion to the number of bags of cotton he makes, and of course the overseer cares for nothing but to make a large crop. To him it is of no consequence that the old hands are worked down, or the young ones overstrained ; that the breeding women miscarry, and the sucklers lose their children ; that the mules are broken down, the plantation tools destroyed, the stock neglected, and the lands ruined : *so that he has the requisite number of cotton bags, all is overlooked ;* he is reëmployed at an advanced salary, and his reputation increased. Everybody knows that by such a course, a crop may be increased by the most inferior overseer, in any given year, unless his predecessors have so entirely exhausted the resources of the plantation, that there is no part of the capital left which can be wrought up into current income. * * *   Having once had the sole management of a plantation, and imbibed the idea that the only test of good planting is to make a large crop of cotton, an overseer becomes worthless. He will no longer obey orders ; he will not stoop to details ; he scorns all improvements, and *will not* adopt any other plan of planting than simply to work lands, negroes, and mules to the top of their bent, which necessarily proves fatal to every employer who will allow it.

" It seems scarcely credible, that any man owning a plantation will so abandon it and his people on it entirely to a hireling, no matter what his confidence in him is. Yet there are numbers who do it habitually ; and I have even known overseers to stipulate that their employers should not give any order, nor interfere in any way with their management of the plantation. There are also some proprietors of considerable property and pretension to being planters, who give their overseer a proportion of the crop for his wages ; thus bribing him by the strongest inducements of self-interest, to overstrain and work down every thing committed to his charge.

" No planter, who attends to his own business, can dispense with agents and sub-agents. It is impossible, on a plantation of any size, for the proprietor to attend to all the details, many of which are irksome and laborious, and he requires more intelligence to assist him than slaves usually possess. To him, therefore, a good overseer is a blessing. But an overseer who would answer the views of such a planter is most difficult to find. The men engaged in that occupation who combine the most intelligence, industry, and character, are allured into the service of those who place all power in their hands, and are utimately spoiled."

An English traveler writes to the London *Daily News* from Mississippi (1857) :

"On crossing the Big Block river, I left the sand hills and began to find myself in the rich loam of the valley of the Mississippi. The plantations became larger, the clearings more numerous and extensive, and the roads less hilly, but worse. Along the Yazoo river one meets with some of the richest soil in the world, and some of the largest crops of cotton in the Union. My first night in that region was passed at the house of a planter who worked but few hands, was a fast friend of slavery, and yet drew for my benefit one of the most mournful pictures of a slave's life I have ever met with. He said, and I believe truly, that the negroes of small planters are, on the whole, well treated, or at least as well as the owners can afford to treat them. Their master not unfrequently works side by side with them in the fields. * * * But on the large plantations, where the business is carried on by an overseer, and every thing is conducted with military strictness and discipline, he described matters as being widely different. *The future of the overseer depends altogether on the quantity of cotton he is able to make up for the market.* Whether the owner be resident or non-resident, if the plantation be large, and a great number of hands be employed upon it, the overseer gets credit for a large crop, and blame for a small one. His professional reputation depends in a great measure upon the number of bales or hogsheads he is able to produce, and neither his education nor his habits are such as to render it likely that he would allow any consideration for the negroes to stand in the way of his advancing it. His interest is to get as much work out of them as they can possibly perform. His skill consists in knowing exactly how hard they may be driven without incapacitating them for future exertion. The larger the plantation the less chance there is, of course, of the owner's softening the rigor of the overseer, or the sternness of discipline by personal interference. So, as Mr. H—— said, a vast mass of the slaves pass their lives, from the moment they are able to go afield in the picking season till they drop worn out into the grave, in incessant labor, in all sorts of weather, at all seasons of the year, without any other change or relaxation than is furnished by sickness, without the smallest hope of any improvement either in their condition, in their food, or in their clothing, which are of the plainest and coarsest kind, and indebted solely to the forbearance or good temper of the overseer for exemption from terrible physical suffering. They are rung to bed at nine o'clock, almost immediately after bolting the food which they often have to cook after coming home from their day's labor, and are rung out of bed at four or five in the morning. The interval is one long round of toil. Life has no sunny spots for them. Their only refuge or consolation in this world is in their own stupidity and grossness. The nearer they are to the beast, the happier they are likely to be. Any mental or moral rise is nearly sure to bring unhappiness with it."

The same gentleman writes from Columbus:

" One gets better glimpses of the real condition of the negroes from conversations one happens to overhear than from what is told to one's-self—above all, when one is known to be a stranger, and particularly an Englishman. The cool way in which you hear the hanging of niggers, the shooting of niggers, and the necessity for severe discipline among niggers talked of in bar-rooms, speaks volumes as to the exact state of the case. A negro was shot when running away, near Greensboro', a small town on my road, the day before I passed through, by a man who had received instructions from the owner to take him alive, and shoot him if he resisted. I heard the subject discussed by some 'loafers' in the bar, while getting my horse fed, and I found, to my no small—I do not know whether to say horror or amusement—that the point in dispute was not the degree of moral guilt incurred by the murderer, but the degree of loss and damage for which he had rendered himself liable to the owner of the slave in departing from the letter of his commission. One of the group summed up the arguments on both sides, by exclaiming, ' Well, this shootin' of niggers should be put a stop to, that's a fact.' The obvious inference to be deduced from this observation was, that ' nigger shootin' ' was a slight contravention of police regulations—a little of which might be winked at, but which, in this locality, had been carried to such an extent as to call for the interference of the law."

At Jackson, Mississippi, the door of my room at the hotel, opened upon a gallery where, late at night, a number of servants had been conversing together in an animated manner. After some time, a white man joined them, and they immediately became quiet, reserved, and respectful. He was evidently a coarse, vulgar man, in a gossiping humor. Talking of a recent sale of negroes in town, led him to boast to these slaves of his own attractive qualities as a slaveowner. He had got, he said, a parcel of likely gals which he could sell any day for a great deal more'n they were worth to him. He had been on the pint of doing it several times, but he could n't, because they was of his own raisin', and every time they heard he was talking of it, they 'd come and cry so they 'd make him change his mind. He expected he was a kind of a soft-hearted man, and he could not part with them gals more'n he could with his own children. He always carried shootin'-irons with him, but he never yet shot a nigger— never shot a nigger. Some folks was mighty quick to shoot a nigger, but nary one of his niggers ever got shot, and he did n't expect they ever would—long as they behaved themselves.

This was said and repeated in a tone which would indicate that he thought such moderation quite laudable, and that it would highly recommend him to the niggers whom he was then addressing. They answered him in a manner which showed their sense of his condescension in thus talking to them, if not of his forbearance in the use of shootin'-irons.

I do not think that I have ever seen the sudden death of a negro noticed in a southern newspaper, or heard it referred to in conversation, that the loss of property, rather than the extinction of life, was not the evident occasion of interest. The following paragraphs are examples coming first in a search therefor:

" We are informed that a negro man, the property of Mr. William Mays of this city, was killed last Thursday by a youth, the son of Mr. William Payne, of Campbell county. The following are the circumstances, as we have received them. Two sons of Mr. Payne were shooting pigeons on the plantation of Mr. Mays, about twenty miles from this place, and went to the tobacco-house, where the overseer and hands were housing tobacco; one of the boys had a string of pigeons and the other had none. On reaching the house, the negro who was killed asked the boy who had no pigeons, ' where his were.' He replied that he killed none, but could kill him (the negro), and raised his gun and fired. The load took effect in the head, and caused death in a few hours. The negro was a valuable one. Mr. Mays had refused $1,200 for him."—Lynchburg Virginian.

" A valuable negro boy, the property of W. A. Phipps, living in the upper end of this county, was accidentally drowned in the Holston river a few days ago."—Rogersville Times.

" Mr. Tilghman Cobb's barn at Bedford, Va., was set fire to by lightning on Friday, the 11th, and consumed. Two negroes and three horses perished in the flames."—New Orleans Daily Crescent.

I have repeated these accounts, not to convey to the reader's mind the impression that slaves are frequently shot by their masters, which would be, no doubt, a mistaken inference, but to show in what manner I was made to feel, as I was very strongly in my journey, that what we call the sacredness of human life, together with a great range of kindred instincts, scarcely attaches at all, with most white men, to the slaves, and also in order to justify the following observation;—that I found the lives, and the comfort of negroes, in the great cotton-planting districts especially, habitually regarded, by all classes, much more from a purely pecuniary point of view, than I had ever before supposed they could be; and yet, that, as property, negro life and negro vigor were generally much less carefully economized than I had always before imagined them to be.

As I became familiar with the circumstances, I saw reasons for this, which, in looking from a distance, or through the eyes of travelers, I had not been able adequately to appreciate. I will endeavor to explain:

It is difficult to handle simply as property, a creature possessing human passions and human feelings, however debased and torpid the condition of that creature may be; while, on the other hand, the absolute necessity of dealing with property, as a thing, greatly embarrasses a man in any attempt to treat it as a person. And it is the natural result of this complicated state of things, that the system, of slave-management, is irregular, ambiguous, and contradictory—that it is never either consistently humane or consistently economical.

LARGE SLAVE ESTATES.

As a general rule, the larger the body of negroes on a plantation or estate, the more completely are they treated as mere property, and in accordance with a policy calculated to insure the largest pecuniary returns. Hence, in part, the greater proportionate profit of such plantations, and the tendency which everywhere prevails in the planting districts to the absorption of small, and the augmentation of large estates. It may be true, that among the wealthier slaveowners, there is oftener a humane disposition, a better judgment, and a greater ability to deal with their dependents indulgently and bountifully, but the effects of this disposition are chiefly felt, even on those plantations where the proprietor resides permanently, among the slaves employed about the house and stables, and perhaps a few old favorites in the quarters. It is more than balanced by the difficulty of acquiring a personal interest in the units of a large body of slaves, and an acquaintance with the individual characteristics of each. The treatment of the mass must be reduced to a system, the ruling idea of which will be, to enable one man to force into the same channel of labor the muscles of a large number of men, or various, and often conflicting wills.

The chief difficulty is to overcome their great aversion to labor. They have no objection to eating, drinking, and resting, when necessary, and no general disinclination to receive instruction. If a man own many slaves, therefore, the faculty which he values highest, and pays most for, in an overseer, is that of making them work. Any fool could see that they were properly supplied with food, clothing, rest, and religious instruction.

SLAVERY AS A MISSIONARY SYSTEM.

In the county of Liberty, in Georgia, a Presbyterian minister has been for many years employed exclusively in laboring for the moral enlightenment of the slaves, being engaged and paid for this especial duty by their owners. From this circumstance, almost unparalleled as it is, it may be inferred that the planters of that county are, as a body, remarkably intelligent, liberal, and thoughtful for the moral welfare of the childlike wards Providence has placed under their care and tutorship. According to my private information, there is no body of slaveowners more, if as much so, in the United States. I heard them spoken of even as far away as Virginia and Kentucky. I believe, that in no other district has there been displayed as general and long-continued an interest in the spiritual well-being of the negroes. It must be supposed that nowhere else are their circumstances more happy and favorable to Christian nurture.*

After laboring thirteen years with a zeal and judgment which had made him famous, this apostle to the slaves of Liberty was called to the professorship of theology in the University of South Carolina. On retiring from his field of labor as a missionary, he addressed a valedictory sermon to his patrons, which has been

---

* In White's Statistics of Georgia (page 377), the citizens of Liberty county are characterized as " unsurpassed for the great attention paid to the duties of religion."—Dr. Stevens, in his History of Georgia, describes them as " worthy of their sires," who were " the moral and intellectual nobility of the province," "whose accession was an honor to Georgia, and has ever proved one of its richest blessings."—In the biography of General Scrivens, the county of Liberty is designated "proud spot of Georgia's soil!"—Dr. J. M. B. Harden, in a medical report of the county, says, " the use of intoxicating drinks has been almost entirely given up" by its people.—White says (Statistics, 373), "the people of Liberty, from their earliest settlement, have paid much attention to the subject of education. Excellent schools are found in different portions of the county, and it is believed a greater number of young men from Liberty graduate at our colleges than from any [other] section of Georgia. Indeed, it has been proverbial for furnishing able ministers and instructors."

published. While there is no unbecoming despondency or absence of proper gratitude for such results as have rewarded his protracted labor, visible in this document, the summing up is not such as would draw unusual cheers if given in the report of an African missionary at the Tabernacle or Exeter Hall. Without a word on which the most vigilant suspicion could rest a doubt of his entire loyalty to the uttermost rights of property which might be claimed by those whom he addressed, he could not avoid indicating, in the following passages, what he had been obliged to see to be the insurmountable difficulty in the way of any vital elevation of character among those to whom he had been especially charged to preach the gospel wherewith Christ blessed mankind :

"They are [his pastoral charge], in the language of Scripture, '*your money.*' They are the source, the means of your wealth; by their labor do you obtain the necessaries, the conveniences, and comforts of life. The increase of them is the general standard of your worldly prosperity : without them, you would be comparatively poor. *They are consequently sought after and desired as property, and when possessed, must be so taken care of and managed as to be made profitable.*

"Now, it is exceedingly difficult to use them as money; to treat them as property, and at the same time render to them that which is just and equal as immortal and accountable beings, and as heirs of the grace of life, equally with ourselves. They are associated in our business, and thoughts, and feelings, with labor, and interest, and gain. and wealth. Under the influence of the powerful feeling of self-interest, there is a tendency to view and to treat them as instruments of labor, as a means of wealth, and to forget, or pass over lightly, the fact that they are what they are, under the eye and government of God. There is a tendency to rest satisfied with very small and miserable efforts for their moral improvement, and to give one's self but little trouble to correct immoralities and reform wicked practices and habits, should they do their work quietly and profitably, and enjoy health, and go on to multiply and increase upon the earth."

This is addressed to a body of " professing evangelical Christians," in a district in which more is done for the elevation of the slaves than in any other of the South. What they are called to witness from their own experience, as the tendency of a system which recognizes slaves as absolute property, mere instruments of labor and means of wealth, " exceedingly difficult" for them to resist, is the *entirely irresistible effect* upon the mass of slaveholders. Fearing that moral and intellectual culture may injure their value - as property, they oftener interfere to prevent than they endeavor to assist their slaves from usir꜇ the poor opportunities that chance may throw in their way.

Moreover, the missionary adds :

" The current of the conversation and of business in society, in respect to negroes, runs in the channel of interest, and thus increases the blindness and insensibility of owners.   * * *   And this custom of society acts also on the negroes, who, seeing, and more than seeing, *feeling and knowing, that their owners regard and treat them as their money—as property only*—are inclined to lose sight of their better character and higher interests, and, in their ignorance and depravity, to estimate themselves, and religion, and virtue, no higher than their owners do."

Again, from tne paramount interest of owners in the property quality of these beings, they provide them only such accommodations for spending the time in which they are not actively employed, as shall be favorable to their bodily health, and enable them to comply with the commandment, to " increase and multiply upon the earth," without regard to their moral health, without caring much for their obedience to the more pure and spiritual commands of the Scriptures.

" The consequent mingling up of husbands and wives, children and youths, banishes the privacy and modesty essential to domestic peace and purity, and opens wide the door to dishonesty, oppression, violence, and profligacy. The owner may see, or hear, or know little of it. His servants may appear cheerful, and go on in their usual way, and enjoy health and do his will, yet their actual moral state may be miserable. * * * *If family relations are not preserved and protected, we can not look for any considerable degree of moral and religious improvement.*"

It must be acknowledged of slavery, as a system, not only in Liberty county, but as that system finds the expression of the theory on which it is based in the laws of every southern State, that family relations are not preserved and protected under it. As we should therefore expect, the missionary finds that

" One of the chief causes of the immorality of negroes arises from the indifference both of themselves and of their owners to their family relations."

Large planters generally do not allow their negroes to marry off the plantation to which they belong, conceiving " that their own convenience and interest, and," says the missionary, " the comfort and *real* happiness of their people" are thereby promoted. Upon this point, however, it is but just to quote the views of the editor of the *Southern Agriculturist*, who, in urging planters to adopt and strictly maintain such a regulation, says : " If a master has a servant, and no suitable one of the other sex for a companion, he had better give an extra price for such an one as his would be willing to marry, than to have one man owning the husband, and the other the wife."

But this mode of arranging the difficulty seems not to have occurred to the Liberty county missionary ; and while arguing against the course usually pursued, he puts the following, as a pertinent suggestion :

" Admitting that they are people having their preferences as well as others, *and there be a supply*, can that love which is the foundation and essence of the marriage state, be forced ?"

Touching honesty and thrift among the negroes, he says :

" While some discipline their people for every act of theft committed against their interests, they have no care whatever what amount of pilfering and stealing the people carry on *among themselves.* Hence, in some places, thieves thrive and honest men suffer, until it becomes a practice 'to keep if you can what is your own, and get all you can besides that is your neighbor's.' Things come to such a pass, that the saying of the negroes is literally true, 'The people live upon one another.'"

Referring to the evil of intemperance, it is observed :

"Whatever toleration masters use toward ardent spirits in others, they are generally inclined to use none in respect to their servants; and in effecting this reformation, masters and mistresses should set the example; for without example, precepts and persuasions are powerless. Nor can force effect this reformation as surely and perfectly as persuasion—appealing to the character and happiness of the servant himself, the appeal recognizes him in such a manner as to produce self-respect, and it tends to give elevation of conduct and character. I will not dwell upon this point."

He will not dwell on this point; yet, is it not evident that until this point can be dwelt upon, all effort for the genuine Christianization of the negro race in the South must be puerile?

SLAVERY AS AN EDUCATIVE SYSTEM.

"The mental faculties will be most developed where they are most exercised, and what gives them more exercise than the having a multitude of interests, none of which can be neglected, and which can be provided for only by varied efforts of the will and intelligence ? * * *

"It is precisely these cares and anxieties which tend to make the independent proprietor a superior being to an English day-laborer. * * *

"If there is a first principle in intellectual education, it is this, that the discipline which does good to the mind is that in which the mind is active, not that in which it is passive."—*Principles of Political Economy, by J. Stuart Mill.*

The benefit to the African which is supposed to be incidental to American slavery, is confessedly proportionate to the degree in which he is forced into intercourse with a superior race and made subject to its example. Before I visited the South, I had believed that the advantages accruing from slavery, in this way, far outweighed the occasional cruelties, and other evils incidental to the system. I found, however, the mental and moral condition of the negroes, even in Virginia, and in those towns and districts containing the largest proportion of whites, much lower than I had anticipated, and as soon as I had an opportunity to examine one of the extensive plantations of the interior, although one inherited by its owner, and the home of a large and virtuous white family, I was satisfied that the advantages arising to the blacks from association with their white masters were very trifling, scarcely appreciable indeed, for the great majority of the field-hands. Even the overseer had barely acquaintance enough with the slaves individually, to call them by name; the owner could not determine with confidence if he were addressing one of his own chattels, by its features. Much less did the slaves have an opportunity to cultivate their minds by intercourse with other white people. Whatever of civilization, and of the forms, customs and shibboleths of Christianity they were acquiring by example, and through police restraints might, it occurred to me, after all, but poorly compensate the effect of the systematic withdrawal from them of all the usual influences which tend to nourish the moral nature and develop the intellectual faculties, in savages as well as in civilized free men.

This doubt, as my northern friends well know, for I had habitually assumed the opposite, in all previous discussions of the slavery question, was unexpected and painful to me. I resisted it long, and it was not till I had been more than twelve months in the South with my attention constantly fixed upon the point that I ceased to suspect that the circumstances which brought me to it were exceptional and deceptive. It grew constantly stronger with every opportunity I had of observing the condition, habits and character of slaves whom I could believe to present fair examples of the working of the system with the majority of those subject to it upon the large plantations.

The laborers we see in towns, at work on railroads and steamboats, about stations and landings; the menials of our houses and hotels, are less respectable, moral and intelligent than the great majority of the whole laboring class of the North. The traveler at the South has to learn that there the reverse is the case to a degree which can hardly be sufficiently estimated. I have been obliged to think that many amiable travelers who have received impressions with regard to the condition of the slaves very different from mine, have failed to make a sufficient allowance for this. The rank-and-file plantation negroes are not to be readily made acquaintance with by chance or through letters of introduction.

SLAVE MANAGEMENT ON THE LARGEST SCALE.

The estate I am now about to describe, was situated upon a tributary of the Mississippi, and accessible only by occasional steamboats; even this mode of communication being frequently interrupted at low stages of the rivers. The slaves upon it formed about one twentieth of the whole population of the county, in which the blacks considerably out-number the whites. At the time of my visit, the owner was sojourning upon it, with his family and several invited guests, but his usual residence was upon a small plantation, of little productive value, situated in a neighborhood somewhat noted for the luxury and hospitality of its citizens, and having a daily mail, and direct railroad and telegraphic communication with New York. This was, if I am not mistaken, his second visit in five years.

The property consisted of four adjoining plantations, each with its own negro-cabins, stables and overseer, and each worked to a great extent independently of the others, but all contributing their crop to one gin-house and warehouse, and all under the general superintendence of a bailiff or manager, who constantly resided upon the estate, and in the absence of the owner, had vice-regal power over the overseers, controlling, so far as he thought fit, the economy of all the plantations.

The manager was himself a gentleman of good education, generous and poetic in temperament, and possessing a capacity for the enjoyment of nature and a happiness in the bucolic life, unfortunately rare with Americans. I found him a delightful companion, and I have known no man with whose natural tastes and feelings I have felt, on so short acquaintance, a more hearty sympathy. The gang of toiling negroes to him, however, was as essential an element of the poetry of nature as flocks of peaceful sheep and herds of lowing kine, and he would no more appreciate the aspect in which an Abolitionist would see them than would VIRGIL have honored the feelings of a vegetarian, who could only sigh at the sight of flocks and herds destined to feed the depraved appetite of the carnivorous savage of modern civilization. The overseers were superior to most of their class, and, with one exception, frank, honest, temperate and industrious, but their feelings toward negroes were such as naturally result from their occupation. They were all married, and lived with their families, each in a cabin or cottage, in the hamlet of the slaves of which he had especial charge. Their wages varied from $500 to $1,000 a year each.

These five men, each living more than a mile distant from either of the others, were the only white men on the estate, and the only others within several miles of them were a few skulking vagabonds. Of course, to secure their own personal safety and to efficiently direct the labor of such a large number of ignorant indolent, and vicious negroes, rules, or rather habits and customs, of discipline, were necessary, which would in particular cases be liable to operate unjustly and cruelly. It is apparent, also, that, as the testimony of negroes against them would not be received as evidence in court, that there was very little probability that any excessive severity would be restrained by fear of the law. A provision of the law intended to secure a certain privilege to slaves, was indeed disregarded under my own observation, and such infraction of the law was confessedly customary with one of the overseers, and was permitted by the manager, for the reason that it seemed to him to be, in a certain degree, justifiable and expedient under the circumstances, and because he did not like to interfere unnecessarily in such matters.

In the main, the negroes appeared to be well taken care of and abundantly supplied with the necessaries of vigorous physical existence. A large part of them lived in commodious and well-built cottages, with broad galleries in front, so that each family of five had two rooms on the lower floor, and a loft. The remainder lived in log-huts, small and mean in appearance, but those of their overseers were little better, and preparations were being made to replace all of these by neat boarded cottages. Each family had a fowl-house and hog-sty (constructed by the negroes themselves), and kept fowls and swine, feeding the latter during the summer on weeds and fattening them in the autumn on corn *stolen* (this was mentioned to me by the overseers as if it were a matter of course) from their master's corn-fields. I several times saw gangs of them eating the dinner which they had brought, each for himself, to the field, and observed that they generally had plenty, often more than they could eat, of bacon, corn-bread, and molasses. The allowance of food is weighed

and measured under the eye of the manager by the drivers, and
distributed to the head of each family weekly : consisting of—
for each person, 3 pounds of pork, 1 peck of meal ; and from January to July, 1 quart of molasses. Monthly, in addition, 1 pound
tobacco, and 4 pints salt. No drink is ever served but water,
except after unusual exposure, or to ditchers working in water,
who get a glass of whisky at night. All hands cook for themselves after work at night, or whenever they please between
night-fall and daybreak, each family in its own cabin. Each
family had a garden, the products of which, together with eggs,
fowls and bacon, they frequently sold, or used in addition to their
regular allowance of food. Most of the families bought a barrel
of flour every year. The manager endeavored to encourage this
practice, and that they might spend their money for flour instead
of liquor, he furnished it to them at rather less than what it cost
him at wholesale. There were many poor whites within a few
miles who would always sell liquor to the negroes, and encourage
them to steal, to obtain the means to buy it of them. These
poor whites were always spoken of with anger by the overseers,
and they each had a standing offer of much more than the in-
trinsic value of their land, from the manager, to induce them to
move away.

The negroes also obtain a good deal of game. They set
traps for raccoons, rabbits and turkeys, and I once heard the
stock-tender complaining that he had detected one of the vagabond whites stealing a turkey which had been caught in his pen.
I several times partook of game while on the plantation, that
had been purchased of the negroes. The stock-tender, an old
negro, whose business it was to ride about in the woods and keep
an eye on the stock cattle that were pastured in them, and who

was thus likely to know where the deer ran, had an ingenious way of supplying himself with venison. He lashed a scythe blade or butcher's knife to the end of a pole so that it formed a lance ; this he set near a fence or fallen tree which obstructed a path in which the deer habitually ran, and the deer in leaping over the obstacle would leap directly on the knife. In this manner he had killed two deer the week before my visit.

The manager sent to him for some of this venison for his own use, and justified himself to me for not paying for it on the ground that the stock-tender had undoubtedly taken time which really belonged to his owner to set his spear. Game taken by the field-hands was not looked upon in the same light, because it must have been got at night when they were excused from labor for their owner.

The first morning I was on the estate, while at breakfast with the manager, an old negro woman came into the room and said to him, "Dat gal's bin bleedin' agin dis mornin'."

"How much did she bleed ?"

"About a pint, sir."

"Very well; I'll call and see her after breakfast."

"I come up for some sugar of lead, master ; I gin her some powdered alum 'fore I come away."

"Very well; you can have some."

After breakfast the manager invited me to ride with him on his usual daily round of inspection through the plantations.

PLANTATION WORK-HOUSE.

On reaching the nearest "quarters," we stopped at a house, a little larger than the ordinary cabins, which was called the loom-house, in which a dozen negroes were at work making shoes, and manufacturing coarse cotton stuff for negro clothing. One of the hands so employed was insane, and most of the others were cripples, invalids with chronic complaints, or unfitted by age, or some infirmity, for field-work.

MEDICAL SURVEY.

From this we went to one of the cabins, where we found the sick woman who had been bleeding at the lungs, with the old nurse in attendance upon her. The manager examined and prescribed for her in a kind manner. When we came out he asked the nurse if any one else was sick.

"Oney dat woman Carline."

"What do you think is the matter with her?"

"Well, I do n't tink dere's anyting de matter wid her, masser; I mus' answer you for true, I do n't tink anyting de matter wid her, oney she's a little sore from dat whippin' she got."

We went to another cabin and entered a room where a woman lay on a bed, groaning. It was a very dingy, comfortless room, but a musquito bar, much patched and very dirty, covered the bed. The manager asked the woman several times what was the matter, but could get no distinct reply. She appeared to be suffering great pain. The manager felt her pulse and looked at her tongue, and after making a few more inquiries, to which no intelligible reply was given, told her he did not believe she was ill at all. At this the woman's groans redoubled. "I have heard of your tricks," continued the manager; "you had a chill when I came to see you yesterday morning; you had a chill when the mistress came here, and you had a chill when the master came. I never knew a chill to last the whole day. So you 'll just get up now and go to the field, and if you do n't work smart, you 'll get a dressing; do you hear ?"

We then left. The manager said that he rarely—almost never —had occasion to employ a physician for the people. Never for accouchements; the women, from their labor in the field, were not subject to the difficulty, danger, and pain which attended women of the better classes in giving birth to their offspring.

Near the first quarters we visited there was a large blacksmith's and wheelwright's shop, in which a number of mechanics were at work. Most of them, as we rode up, were eating their breakfast, which they warmed at their fires. Within and around the shop there were some fifty plows which they were putting in order. The manager inspected the work, found some of it faulty, sharply reprimanded the workmen for not getting on faster, and threatened one of them with a whipping for not paying closer attention to the directions which had been given him. He told me that he once employed a white man from the North, who professed to be a first-class workman, but he soon found he could not do nearly as good work as the negro mechanics on the estate, and the latter despised him so much, and got such high opinions of themselves in consequence of his inferiority, that he had been obliged to discharge him in the midst of his engagement.

The overseer of this plantation rode up while we were at the shop, and reported to the manager how all his hands were employed. There were so many at this and so many at that, and they had done so much since yesterday. "There's that girl, Caroline," said the manager; "she's not sick, and I told her she must go to work; put her to the hoeing; there's nothing the matter with her, except she's sore with the whipping she got. You must go and get her out." A woman was passing at the

time, and the manager told her to go and tell Caroline she must
get up and go to work, or the overseer would come and start
her. She returned in a few minutes, and reported that Caroline
said she could not get up. The overseer and manager rode toward the cabin, but before they reached it, the girl, who had
probably been watching us from the window, came out and went
to the field with her hoe. They then returned to me and continued their conversation. Just before we left the overseer, he
said, "I think that girl who ran away last week was in her cabin
last night." The manager told me, as we rode on, that the people often ran away after they have been whipped, or something
else had happened to make them angry. They hide in the
swamp, and come in to the cabins at night to get food. They
seldom remain away more than a fortnight, and when they come
in they are whipped. The woman, Caroline, he said, had been
delivered of a dead child about six weeks before, and had been
complaining and getting rid of work ever since. She was the
laziest woman on the estate. This shamming illness gave him
the most disagreeable duty he had to perform. Negroes were
famous for it. "If it was not for her bad character," he continued, "I should fear to make her go to work to-day; but her
pulse is steady, and her tongue perfectly smooth. *We have to
be sharp with them ; if we were not, every negro on the estate
would be abed.*"

CLOTHES AND CLEANLINESS.

We rode on to where the different gangs of laborers were at
work, and inspected them one after another. I observed, as we
were looking at one of the gangs, that they were very dirty.
"Negroes are the filthiest people in the world," said the man-

ager ; "there are some of them who would not keep clean twenty-four hours at a time if you gave them thirty suits a year." I asked him if there were any rules to maintain cleanliness. There were not, but sometimes the negroes were told at night that any one who came into the field the next morning without being clean would be whipped. This gave no trouble to those who were habitually clean, while it was in itself a punishment to those who were not, as they were obliged to spend the night in washing.

They were furnished with two suits of summer, and one of winter clothing each year. Besides which, most of them got presents of some holiday finery (calico dresses, handkerchiefs, etc.), and purchased more for themselves, at Christmas. One of the drivers now in the field had on a splendid uniform coat of an officer of the flying artillery. After the Mexican war, a great deal of military clothing was sold at auction in New Orleans, and much of it was bought by planters at a low price, and given to their negroes, who were greatly pleased with it.

HOURS OF LABOR.

Each overseer regulated the hours of work on his own plantation. I saw the negroes at work before sunrise and after sunset. At about eight o'clock they were allowed to stop for breakfast, and again about noon, to dine. The length of these rests was at the discretion of the overseer or drivers, usually, I should say, from half an hour to an hour. There was no rule.

OVERSEERS.

The number of hands directed by each overseer was considerably over one hundred. The manager thought it would be better economy to have a white man over every fifty hands, but the difficulty of obtaining trustworthy overseers prevented it. Three of those he then had were the best he had ever known. He described the great majority as being passionate, careless, inefficient men, generally intemperate, and totally unfitted for the duties of the position. The best overseers, ordinarily, are young men, the sons of small planters, who take up the business temporarily, as a means of acquiring a little capital with which to purchase negroes for themselves.

PLOW-GIRLS.

The plowing, both with single and double mule teams, was generally performed by women, and very well performed, too. I watched with some interest for any indication that their sex unfitted them for the occupation. Twenty of them were plowing together, with double teams and heavy plows. They were superintended by a male negro driver, who carried a whip, which he frequently cracked at them, permitting no dawdling or delay at the turning; and they twitched their plows around on the head-land, jerking their reins, and yelling to their mules, with apparent ease, energy, and rapidity. Throughout the Southwest the negroes, as a rule, appear to be worked much harder than in the eastern and northern slave States. I do not think they accomplish as much daily, as agricultural laborers at the North usually do, but they certainly labor much harder, and more unremittingly. They are constantly and steadily driven up to their work, and the stupid, plodding, machine-like manner in which they labor, is painful to witness. This was especially the case with the hoe-gangs. One of them numbered nearly two hundred hands (for the force of two plantations was working together), moving across the field in parallel lines, with a considerable degree of precision. I repeatedly rode through the lines at a canter, with other horsemen, often coming upon them suddenly, without producing the smallest change or interruption in the dogged action of the laborers, or causing one of them to lift an eye from the ground. A very tall and powerful negro walked to and fro in the rear of the line, frequently cracking his whip, and calling out, in the surliest manner, to one and another, "Shove your hoe, there! shove your hoe!" But I never saw him strike any one with the whip.

DISCIPLINE.

The whip was evidently in constant use, however. There were no rules on the subject, that I learned; the overseers and drivers punished the negroes whenever they deemed it necessary, and in such manner, and with such severity, as they thought fit. "If you do n't work faster," or "If you do n't work better," or "If you do n't recollect what I tell you, I will have you flogged," are threats which I have often heard. I said to one of the overseers, "It must be very disagreeable to have to punish them as much as you do?" "Yes, it would be to those who are not used to it—but it's my business, and I think nothing of it. Why, sir, I would n't mind killing a nigger more than I would a dog." I asked if he had ever killed a negro? "Not quite," he said, but overseers were often obliged to. Some negroes are determined never to let a white man whip them, and will resist you, when you attempt it; of course you must kill them in that case. Once a negro, whom he was about to whip in the field, struck at his head with a hoe. He parried the blow with his whip, and drawing a pistol tried to shoot him, but the pistol missing fire he rushed in and knocked him down with the butt of it. At another time a negro whom he was punishing, insulted and threatened him. He went to the house for his gun, and as he was returning, the negro, thinking he would be afraid of spoiling so valuable a piece of property by firing, broke for the woods. He fired at once, and put six buck-shot into his hips. He always carried a bowie-knife, but not a pistol, unless he anticipated some unusual act of insubordination.* He always kept a pair of pistols ready loaded over the mantel-piece, however, in case they should be needed. It was only when he first came upon a plantation that he ever had much trouble. A great many overseers were unfit for their business, and too easy and slack with the negroes. When he succeeded such a man, he had hard work for a time to break the negroes in, but it did not take long to teach them their place. His conversation on this subject was exactly like what I have heard said, again and again, by northern shipmasters and officers, with regard to seamen.

PUNISHMENT.

The severest corporeal punishment of a negro that I witnessed at the South, occurred while I was visiting this estate. I suppose however, that punishment equally severe is common—in fact, it must be necessary to the maintenance of adequate disci-

---

* " On Monday last, as James Allen (overseer on Prothro's plantation at St. Maurice), was punishing a negro boy named Jack, for stealing hogs, the boy ran off before the overseer had chastised him sufficiently for the offense. He was immediately pursued by the overseer, who succeeded in catching him, when the negro drew a knife and inflicted a terrible gash in his abdomen. The wounds of the overseer were dressed by Dr. Stephens, who pronounces it a very critical case, but still entertains hope of his recovery."— *Nachitoches Chronicle.*

pline on every large plantation. It is much more necessary than on shipboard, because the opportunities of hiding away and shirking labor, and of wasting and injuring the owner's property without danger to themselves, are far greater in the case of the slaves than in that of the sailors, but above all, because there is no real moral obligation on the part of the negro to do what is demanded of him. The sailor performs his duty in obedience to a voluntary contract; the slave is in an involuntary servitude. The manner of the overseer who inflicted the punishment, and his subsequent conversation with me about it, indicated that it was by no means an unusual occurrence with him. I had accidentally encountered him, and he was showing me his plantation. In going from one side of it to the other, we had twice crossed a deep gully, at the bottom of which was a thick covert of brushwood. We were crossing it a third time, and had nearly passed through the brush, when the overseer suddenly stopped his horse exclaiming, " What's that ? Hallo ! who are you there ?"

It was a girl lying at full length on the ground at the bottom of the gully, evidently intending to hide herself from us in the bushes.

" Who are you there ?"

" Sam's Sall, sir."

" What are you skulking there for ?"

The girl half rose, but gave no answer.

" Have you been here all day ?"

" No sir."

" How did you get here ?"

The girl made no reply.

" Where have you been all day ?"

The answer was unintelligible.

After some further questioning, she said her father accidentally locked her in, when he went out in the morning.

"How did you manage to get out ?"

"Pushed a plank off, sir, and crawled out."

The overseer was silent for a moment, looking at the girl, and
then said, "That won't do—come out here." The girl arose at
once, and walked towards him ; she was about eighteen years of
age. A bunch of keys hung at her waist, which the overseer
espied, and he said, "Ah, your father locked you in ; but you
have got the keys." After a little hesitation, the girl replied
that these were the keys of some other locks; her father had the
door-key.

Whether her story were true or false, could have been ascertained in two minutes by riding on to the gang with which her
father was at work, but the overseer had made up his mind as to
the facts of the case.

"That won't do," said he, "get down on your knees." The
girl knelt on the ground ; he got off his horse, and holding him
with his left hand, struck her thirty or forty blows across the
shoulders with his tough, flexible, "raw-hide" whip. They were
well laid on, as a boatswain would thrash a skulking sailor, or as
some people flog a baulking horse, but with no appearance of
angry excitement on the part of the overseer. At every stroke
the girl winced, and exclaimed, "Yes, sir !" or "Ah, sir !" or
"Please, sir !" not groaning or screaming. At length he stopped
and said, "Now tell me the truth." The girl repeated the same
story. "You have not got enough yet," said he, "pull up your
clothes—lie down." The girl without any hesitation, without a
word or look of remonstrance or entreaty, drew closely all her
garments under her shoulders, and lay down upon the ground

with her face toward the overseer, who continued to flog her with the rawhide, across her naked loins and thigh, with as much strength as before. She now shrunk away from him, not rising, but writhing, groveling, and screaming, "Oh, do n't, sir! oh, please stop, master! please, sir! please, sir! oh, that's enough, master! oh, Lord! oh, master, master! oh, God, master, do stop! oh, God, master! oh, God, master!"

A young gentleman of fifteen was with us; he had ridden in front, and now, turning on his horse looked back with an expression only of impatience at the delay. It was the first time I had ever seen a woman flogged. I had seen a man cudgeled and beaten, in the heat of *passion, before, but never flogged with a hundredth part of the severity used in this case. I glanced again at the perfectly passionless but rather grim business-like face of the overseer, and again at the young gentleman, who had turned away; if not indifferent he had evidently not the faintest sympathy with my emotion. Only my horse chafed with excitement. I gave him rein and spur and we plunged into the bushes and scrambled fiercely up the steep acclivity. The screaming yells and the whip strokes had ceased when I reached the top of the bank. Choking, sobbing, spasmodic groans only were heard. I rode on to where the road coming diagonally up the ravine ran out upon the cotton-field. My young companion met me there, and immediately afterward the overseer. He laughed as he joined us, and said,

"She meant to cheat me out of a day's work—and she has done it, too."

"Did you succeed in getting another story from her?"

"No; she stuck to it."

"Was it not perhaps true?"

"Oh no, sir, she slipped out of the gang when they were going to work, and she's been dodging about all day, going from one place to another as she saw me coming. She saw us crossing there a little while ago, and thought we had gone to the quarters, but we turned back so quick, we came into the gully before she knew it, and she could do nothing but lie down in the bushes."

"I suppose they often slip off so."

"No, sir; I never had one do so before—not like this; they often run away to the woods and are gone some time, but I never had a dodge-off like this before."

"Was it necessary to punish her so severely?"

"Oh yes, sir," (laughing again.) "If I had n't punished her so hard she would have done the same thing again to-morrow, and half the people on the plantation would have followed her example. Oh, you've no idea how lazy these niggers are; you northern people do n't know any thing about it. They'd never do any work at all if they were not afraid of being whipped."

We soon afterward met an old man, who, on being closely questioned, said that he had seen the girl leave the gang as they went to work after dinner. It appeared that she had been at work during the forenoon, but at dinner-time the gang was moved and as it passed through the gully she slipped out. The driver had not missed her. The overseer said that when he first took charge of this plantation, the negroes ran away a great deal—they disliked him so much. They used to say 't was hell to be on his place; but after a few months they got used to his ways, and liked him better than any of the rest. He had not had any run away now in some time. When they ran away they would generally return within a fortnight. If many of them went off,

or if they staid out long, he would make the rest of the force
work Sundays, or deprive them of some of their usual privileges
until they returned.   The negroes on the plantation could always
bring them in if they chose to.   They depended on them for
their food, and they had only to stop the supplies to oblige them
to surrender.

NAMES.

Afterward, as I was sitting near a gang with an overseer and
the manager, the former would occasionally call out to one and
another by name, in directing or urging their labor.   I asked if
he knew them all by name.   He did, but the manager did not
know one fifth of them.   The overseer said he generally could
call most of the negroes on a plantation by their names in two
weeks after he came to it, but it was rather difficult to learn
them on account of there being so many of the same name, distinguished from each other by a prefix.   " There's a Big Jim
here, and a Little Jim, and Eliza's Jim, and there's Jim Bob,
and Jim Clarisy."

" What's Jim Clarisy ?—how does he get that name ?"

" He's Clarisy's child, and Bob is Jim Bob's father.   That fel-
low ahead there, with the blue rag on his head, his name is
Swamp; he always goes by that name, but his real name is
Abraham, I believe ; is it not, Mr. [Manager] ?"

" His name is Swamp on the plantation register—that 's all I
know of him."

" I believe his name is Abraham," said the overseer ; " he told
me so.   He was bought of Judge ——, he says, and he told me
his master called him Swamp because he ran away so much.
He is the worst runaway on the place."

MORAL EDUCATION OF THE NEGROES.

I inquired about the increase of the negroes on the estate, and the manager having told me the number of deaths and births the previous year, which gave a net increase of four per cent.— on Virginia estates it is often twenty per cent—I asked if the negroes began to have children at a very early age. "Sometimes at sixteen," said the manager. "Yes, and at fourteen," said the overseer; "that girl's had a child"—pointing to a girl that did not appear older than fourteen. "Is she married?" "No." "You see," said the manager, "negro girls are not remarkable for chastity; their habits indeed rather hinder them from having children. They'd have them younger than they do, if they would marry or live with but one man, sooner than they do.* They often do not have children till they are twenty-five years old." "Are those who are married true to each other?" I asked. The overseer laughed heartily at the idea, and described a disgustingly "Free Love" state of things. "Do you not try to discourage this?" "No, not unless they quarrel." "They get jealous and quarrel among themselves sometimes about it," the manager explained, " or come to the overseer and complain, and he has them punished." "Give all hands a damned good hiding," said the overseer. "You punish for adultery, then, but not for fornication?" "Yes," answered the manager, but "No," replied the overseer, "we punish them for quarreling; if they don't quarrel I don't mind any thing about it, but if it makes a muss, I give all four of 'em a warming."

* Mr. Russell makes an observation to the same effect with regard to the Cuba plantations, p. 230.

BLACK, WHITE, AND YELLOW.

Riding through a large gang of hoers, with two of the over-seers, I observed that a large proportion of them appeared to be thorough-bred Africans. Both of them thought that the "real black niggers" were about three fourths of the whole number, and that this would hold as an average on Mississippi and Louisiana plantations. One of them pointed out a girl—"That one is pure white; you see her hair?" (It was straight and sandy.) "She is the only one we have got." It was not uncommon, he said, to see slaves so white that they could not be easily distinguished from pure-blooded whites. He had never been on a plantation before, that had not more than one on it.* "Now," said I, " if that girl should dress herself well, and run away, would she be suspected of being a slave ?"

"Oh, yes; you might not know her if she got to the North, but any of us would know her."

" How ?"

" By her language and manners."

" But if she had been brought up as house-servant ?"

" Perhaps not in that case."

---

* " A woman, calling herself Violet Ludlow, was arrested a few days ago, and committed to jail, on the supposition that she was a runaway slave belonging to A. M. Mobley, of Upshur county, Texas, who had offered through our columns a reward of fifty dollars for her apprehension. On being brought before a justice of the peace, she stated that she was a white woman, and claimed her liberty. She states that she is a daughter of Jeremiah Ludlow, of Pike county, Alabama, and was brought from that country in 1853, by George Cope, who emigrated to Texas. After arriving in Texas, she was sold by George Cope to a Docter Terry, in Upshur county, Texas, and was soon after sold by him to a Mrs. Hagen, or Hagens, of the same county. Violet says that she protested against each sale made of her, declaring herself a free woman. She names George Gilmer, Thomas Rogers,

The other thought there would be no difficulty ; a slave girl would always quail when you looked in her eyes.

I asked if they thought the mulattoes or white slaves were weaker or less valuable than the pure negroes.

" Oh, no ; I'd rather have them a great deal," said one. " Well, I had not," said the other; " the blacker the better for me." " The white ones," added the first, " are more active, and know more, and I think do a good deal the most work." " Are they more subject to illness, or do they appear to be of weaker constitutions ?" One said they were not, the other that they did not seem to bear the heat as well. The first thought that this might be so, but that, nevertheless, they would do more work. I afterwards asked the manager's opinion. He thought they did not stand excessive heat as well as the pure negroes, but that, from their greater activity and willingness, they would do more work. He believed they were equally strong, and no more liable to illness ; had never had reason to think them of weaker consti-

John Garret, and others, residents of Pike county, Alabama, as persons who have known her from infancy as the daughter of one Jeremiah Ludlow and Rene Martin, a widow at the time of her birth, and as being a free white woman, and her father a free white man. Violet is about instituting legal proceedings for her freedom."—*Shreveport Southwestern.*

" Some days since, a woman named Pelasgie was arrested as a fugitive slave, who has lived for more than twelve years in this city as a free woman. She was so nearly white that few could detect any traces of her African descent. She was arrested at the instance of a man named Raby, who claimed her as belonging to an estate of which he is heir-at-law. She was conveyed to the First District guard-house for safe keeping, and while there she stated to Acting Recorder Filleul that she was free, had never belonged to Raby, and had been in the full and unquestioned enjoyment of her freedom in this city for the above mentioned period. She also stated that she had a house, well furnished, which she was in the habit of letting out in rooms."— *New Orleans Picayune.*

tution. They often had large families, and he had not noticed
that their children were weaker or more subject to disease than
others. He thought that perhaps they did not have so many
children as the pure negroes, but he had supposed the reason to
be that they did not begin bearing so young as the others, and
this was because they were more attractive to the men, and perhaps more amorous themselves. He knew a great many mulattoes living together, and they generally had large and healthy
families.

Afterwards, at one of the plantation nurseries, where there were
some twenty or thirty infants and young children, a number of
whom were evidently the offspring of white fathers, I asked the
nurse to point out the healthiest children to me, and of those
she indicated, more were of the pure, than of the mixed breed. I
then asked her to show me which were the sickliest, and she did
not point to any of the latter. I then asked if she noticed any
difference in this respect between the black and the yellow children. " Well, dey do say, master, dat de yellow ones is de sickliest, but I can't tell for true dat I ever see as dey was."

RELIGION.

Being with the proprietor and the manager together, I asked
about the religious condition of the slaves. There were " preachers" on the plantations, and they had some religious observances
on a Sunday ; but the preachers were the worst characters among
them, and, they thought, only made their religion a cloak for
habits of especial depravity.* They were, at all events, the most

* The bad character of slave preachers in general, I have often heard assumed in conversation, as if it were notorious, and it seems always to have
been so. On the records of the Superior Court of Augusta, Georgia, in

deceitful and dishonest slaves on the plantation, and oftenest required punishment. The negroes of all denominations, and even those who ordinarily made no religious pretensions, would join together in exciting religious observances. These gentlemen considered the religious exercises of the negroes to be similar, in their intellectual and moral character, to the Indian feasts and war-dances, and did not encourage them. Neither did they like to have white men preach on the estate; and in future they did not intend to permit them to do so. It excited the negroes so much as to greatly interfere with the subordination and order which were necessary to obtain the profitable use of their labor. They would be singing and dancing every night in their cabins, till dawn of day, and utterly unfit themselves for work.

I remarked that I had been told that a religious negro was considered to be worth a third more, because of his greater honesty and steadiness.

"Quite the contrary," they both assured me, for a religious negro generally made trouble, and they were glad to get rid of him.

I have no doubt these opinions were sincere. Probably these gentlemen held different views of the intellectual and moral capabilities of the African race from those entertained by the Liberty planters. I did not infer, however, that they shared the most advanced views of southern philosophers on this subject. Perhaps I should briefly indicate to what point these have reached, before pursuing the subject further.

Cotemporaneously with the anatomico-metaphysical studies of Dr. Wilkinson and of Dr. Doherty, in London, Doctors Nott and Gliddon of Mobile, and Professor Cartwright of the University

1790 "the number of negroes calling themselves parsons, going about the country," is presented as a nuisance.—*White's Statistics of Georgia.*

of Louisiana, have been laboring in a similar field with different purposes and to much more practical ends.

The general character of the results with which they are rewarded will be sufficiently shown by a few extracts from a profound discourse delivered by the latter gentleman, before a convocation of the University of Mississippi :

" Is he a son of Adam ? Does his peculiar physical conformation stand in opposition to the BIBLE, *or does it prove its truth ?* * * * Anatomy and physiology have been interrogated, and the response is that the Ethiopian or Canaanite is unfitted, from his organization and the physiological laws predicated in that organization, for the responsible duties of a free man. * * * When the original Hebrew of the Bible is interrogated, we find in the significant meaning of the original name of the negro, the identical fact set forth, which the knife of the anatomist at the dissecting table, has made appear : as if the revelations of anatomy, physiology, and history were a mere re-writing of what Moses wrote. * * * A knowledge of THE GREAT PRIMARY TRUTH that the negro is a slave by nature, and can never be happy, industrious, moral or religious, in any other condition than the one he was intended to fill, is of great importance to the theologian and the statesman, and to all those who are at heart seeking to promote his temporal and future welfare. * * * It is this defective hematosis, or atmosperization of the blood conjoined with a deficiency of cerebral matter in the cranium and an excess of nervous matter distributed to the organs of sensation and assimilation, that is the true cause of that debasement of mind which has rendered the people of Africa unable to take care of themselves."

Dr. Cartwright dwells with such pardonable enthusiasm upon the inestimable value of these researches in the positive proof they afford of what was so long suspected by the students of the middle ages—the truth of the Bible—that he omits any consideration of them in another aspect, in which they will appear still more interesting to the earnest Christian souls to whom he addresses himself. Let us, for instance, passing from the sacred record and the pages of ancient history, interrogate the explorers of Africa, and see to what practical conclusions we are at once irresistibly led. Did Mungo Park, or Lardner, or Anderson, or

Robertson, or Livingstone, or Bayard Taylor, or Captain Canot, in all their various wanderings, ever find existing in a single tribe of the true Negro, Ethiopian or Canaanitish race, a true Christian church, of indigenous origin and growth? If not, what are we to infer? Certainly not that we are to oppose the evident will of divine Providence, by preaching the religion of white men to this race. No, the proper and only divinely designated duty of a Canaanite's soul has been, for countless ages, fetish-worship, devotion, that is, to some person, animal, thing, or things—cotton, corn bread, hog, pumpkins and Sunday-tricks for instance.

Let no whining fanatic say that the whole race is not thus condemned to fetishism, that many tribes have been found to recognize a supreme Spirit, to look forward to a happy existence after death, etc. So there are known to be legislative assemblies among some tribes, and elective kings who hold office only during good behavior—there is, in fact, every thing among the Africans which Professor Cartwright says there is not, but the question yet remains, are these true Canaanites?—a question the superficial observer is not likely to answer. For after all, mere blackness of the skin no more authorizes a being otherwise in the likeness of a man, to be detained as a slave, or to be forbidden the Bible, than mere whiteness of the skin shows an entire fitness for the responsible duties of a freeman, or proves a clean heart to be within.

Real, God-ordained, unchangeable Canaanites and fetish-worshipers, Professor Cartwright has proved, can only be surely known by a careful analysis of the "mental functions," and a close scrutiny of "the membranes, muscles, and tendons, of all the fluids and secretions, and of the brain, the nerves, the chyle, and all the humors." ، You must examine the bones of the alleged Canaanite; if he be a genuine specimen, they contain ╅ phosphate of lime, and — gelatine : and as for his eyes, they will be furnished with "something like the membrana nictitans formed by a preternatural enlargement of the plica lunaris in the inner canthus." *

It is fortunate that this, the surest test of the true Canaanite, is the most readily applied, and involves no use of the dissecting knife. Let a man's color be what it may, if an examination of the eye discloses the preternatural enlargement of the plica lunaris in the inner canthus there can be no danger in treating him as a slave, a Canaanite ; a fore-ordained goat.†

Thus are these great discoveries immediately applied to further the ends of human justice. The North boasts of the greater speed of its railroads, and the celerity of its printing-presses, pin-making and hog-chopping machines, but true to its higher instincts, the South brings its discoveries to bear upon the administration of criminal jurisprudence, and thus fur-

---

* Was my friend the overseer a disciple of science and of Cartwright, and did he therefore look in the white woman's eyes, to see if she were a slave? There are "secrets of the craft" among overseers, I have been told. Was this among them—"to detect a white-skinned slave, pretending to be free, see if there be not a preternatural enlargement of the plica lunaris, in the inner canthus, having the semblance of a membrana nictitans ?"

† "However zealously," says that true conservative journal, the Richmond Whig, "however zealously a negro seeks to affect innocence, the eye always betrays guilt and a great evil capacity. Bill, the slave of Mrs. Elizabeth Johnson, who stole the coat and five dollars from Richard, a slave of T. Cauthorn, who works on board the canal boat Glazebrook, was ordered thirty by the Mayor on yesterday, in disregard of the most solemn protestations of innocence on the part of Bill. There was an amount of villainy reflected in his eyes that could well contradict all the protestations he could utter for a month."

nishes the crowning glory of the genius of the nineteenth century.

Unfortunately a knowledge of these grand and harmonious
truths is as yet but imperfectly disseminated in the South itself,
and all kinds of explanations and defenses of slavery are made
by simple men who are uninstructed in the beautiful and satisfactory theories based upon them.

If I had asked my friends on the estate last described, for instance, by what right they held their people in subjection, and
on what principle they governed them, they would probably have
answered somewhat thus :

" We have been brought up in slavery ; it has always existed
around us unquestioned and unquestionable. Perhaps it is wrong
in a comprehensive view, but if so, habit prevents us from real-
izing it. It seems to us as much the natural relation of the
white and the black, and of those who come of the black, as
marriage is of the man and the woman. To see a negro free
from the special government of some one of our superior race
seems to us a phenomenon as exceptional and as much in need
of investigation and reform as it does to you to see him held to
involuntary servitude. We are not disposed to argue the matter
—the negroes are a chief part of our property, inherited of our
fathers and improved by us. If you undertake to destroy that
property we will stand on its defense with arms.

" As for religion, we respect it, but we do not respect cant nor
fanatical superstition under the name of religion. Perhaps the
negro might be trained and educated, if we began with him
young, to a capacity for better things : certainly our household
servants seem in general much superior in character to the field-
hands. But to give him such an education would not be safe,

nor could it at present be afforded. We need his whole force to supply the demand for cotton, we can not therefore try dangerous experiments with him. As to the effect of this on ourselves you must remember that the negro is in our eyes, not a man, as he is in yours, but simply a negro ; therefore our sympathies for those of our own race are not blunted, as it seems to you they must be, by the severities we have to employ with our unruly and disobedient slaves."

Possibly, after all, in the present state of science, such an explanation would have quite as favorable an influence on the mind of the majority of honest anti-slavery men, would do quite as much to lessen the disgust with which some persons view the whole business, as the medico-theological treatises to which so much importance is attached by the more advanced minds of the South.

And here I must observe, that after taking no little pains to obtain the views of the enlightened admirers and defenders of the institution of slavery, I have failed to find a single writer among the hosts with whom the religious bearings of the system form a favorite topic, who even makes an attempt to assault the real position occupied with regard to it by the advocates of emancipation. This position, as I understand it, does not involve a denial that the descendants of a certain number of savages, dispersed and incorporated socially in a previously civilized and educated community of Christians, will acquire habits of life more in accordance with the moral standard of that community than they would possess had they never emerged from the primitive barbarism of their ancestors, but only maintains that after having been so incorporated during several generations, their spiritual development is at length likely to be more rapid if they are allowed to regulate the

disposition of their own time and labor, and to freely enjoy the
returns of that labor, than if they continued to be held in a state
of complete vassalage in these and other respects ; and that this
is still more true, if for the purpose of keeping them in such vassalage, the ordinary facilities for intellectual improvement, so essential to civilization and religion, are carefully withheld from
them.

Nor can I refrain from remarking here on the folly of that
disdainful temper, so habitual with southern controversialists,
(and which so few of them attempt even rhetorically to disguise,)
toward those whom they deem their enemies in the matter of
slavery. They fire so wide of their opponents' position, that
their books and speeches often serve only as arguments against
themselves, in the minds of honest inquirers. This Asiatic policy of supreme contempt may still answer in the South, but except with the recent immigrants, it is no longer successful in hin-
dering the growth of anti-slavery principles at the North, yet the
only other weapon generally employed, even by the ablest of its
advocates, is a shallow pretense of· resorting for testimony to the
results of scientific investigations, and to statistical inductions.

" It is fortunate for slavery that the controversy with abolition is reduced to an issue of fact and argument.   The plausible fallacies of the
abolitionists will disappear before the revelations of the census.   Casuists may dispute over the nice distinctions of ethical science until all
just perceptions of right and wrong are confounded, but statistics will
speedily and conclusively determine the effect of slavery as an economic
and social institution.   Already has it been shown by irresistible argument, that the proportion of wealth to the individual in a slaveholding community, greatly exceeds that in the free States.   Even in the
North, candid men concede that their liberty is rapidly degenerating
into license and anarchy.   The following statistics, exhibiting a comparative view of northern and southern society in respect to two most
important elements, are pregnant with instruction and encouragement
to the slaveholding community :

FROM THE CENSUS OF 1850.

States.	Population.	No. of Churches.	No. of Criminals.
Maine	583,169	945	62
Massachusetts	994,514	1,475	301
New Hampshire	317,976	626	77
Vermont	314,120	599	39
Connecticut	370,792	734	145
Rhode Island	147,545	228	24
New York	3,097,394	4,134	1,080
New Jersey	489,555	813	135
Pennsylvania	2,311,786	3,566	302
Delaware	91,532	180	6
Total	8,718,383	13,300	2,171
Maryland	583,034	909	200
Virginia	1,421,661	2,383	188
North Carolina	869,039	1,795	14
South Carolina	668,507	1,182	19
Georgia	906,185	1.862	85
Alabama	771,623	1,373	23
Mississippi	606,526	1,016	81
Louisiana	517,762	306	160
Tennessee	1,002,717	2,014	187
Kentucky	982,405	1,845	141
Total	8,329,459	14,685	1,098

With a less population by half a million, the ten southern States have above a thousand more churches than the ten northern States which boast loudest of their morality and enlightenment. With an excess of only half a million in population, the ten free States have double the number of criminals which are found in ten corresponding slave States. Such revelations will complete the revolution of public opinion in respect to slavery."

This imposing array of figures was originally marshaled, with the comments attached, by the Richmond Enquirer, but has since been repeatedly used to point a similar moral by the journals and orators of the North who are allied with that respectable "Democratic" organ. The folly of such a display is precisely like that of the Chinese generals who draw up their warriors in a position from which they are expected to throw terror into the ranks of their advancing adversaries, by frightful grimaces and menacing gestures, but in which they are quite unnecessarily exposed to the fire of their deadliest artillery. The Commissioner of the Census himself, a most careful, though sincerely loyal partisan of slavery, is at once seized and made to serve the guns of the anti-slavery partisan whenever his attention is called to this bugga-boo of figures. In a work entitled "*A Statistical View of the United States*," published and extensively given away in the free as well as the slave States, by Congress, Mr. DeBow observes, commenting upon the census returns of churches (p. 133) that they do not undertake to show the number of members of the churches or the number of attendants on their worship; that in the rural districts there are "thousands of buildings—rude sheds or log houses"—which are enumerated as church edifices, and which are used both as school houses and places of worship. The northern man knows that there can be but an extremely small proportion of the northern churches which have no bet-ter accommodation for their meetings than a rude shed or log school house. On turning over a few pages he finds the informa-tion set out by Mr. DeBow again that while the average value of the church edifices in New England and the Middle States is over $4000 each, in the Southern Seaboard and Central it is less than $1000; that in the Northwestern it is $1200 and in the Southwestern $900, (p. 139); that in the ten States above men-tioned (of which it is to be noted that one of the so-called northern is a slave State,) the amount of church accommodation for each square mile of territory is, in the northern, equal to one hundred and three; in the southern, to thirty-seven; while in the north-ern States there are on an average four hundred and thirty-seven church edifices to every thousand square miles, and in the slave States but one hundred and thirty-six. By a very simple calcu-lation he ascertains from the figures furnished by Mr. DeBow, that in the ten northern States mentioned, the people have paid for their churches more than three times as much as those of the ten southern, and the former unitedly will accommodate seven hundred and fifty thousand more worshipers than the latter. A little inquiry of travelers, or an examination of the reports of the Southern Aid Society, will satisfy him that while there are few northern churches in which religious instruction is not regularly given at least once a week, and in the great majority of cases much more frequently, and that by an educated man, engaged and paid for this purpose, this is by no means the case with those edifices in the slave States returned as churches. This indeed might be inferred from the marked absence of comfort in a large proportion of the houses of worship at the South, as also from their remoteness and inaccessibility to a great part of the inhabitants of the district to which they belong.

Then as to the "number of criminals," he finds in the census only returns of such as are confined in the prisons, jails, etc., of the different States. Under these heads he will look in vain for figures corresponding to those arranged by the Virginia Commissioner Lin. At page 166, however, Mr. DeBow furnishes the following statement respecting the inmates of the prisons of the United States :

	Native Whites.	Foreign Whites.	Colored, including slaves.
Slaveholding States, . . .	988	370	323
Free States, ...	2271	1129	565

	In every 10,000 native whites.	In every 10,000 foreign whites.	In every 10,000 colored.
Slaveholding States, . . .	$1\frac{673}{1000}$	$11\frac{684}{1000}$	$0\frac{938}{1000}$
Free States, ...	$1\frac{991}{1000}$	$5\frac{368}{1000}$	$28\frac{440}{1000}$

The defense of Lynch law which is so commonly made at the South has made it notorious that the administration of criminal justice in that portion of our country is very imperfect, and that comparatively a small fraction of those offending against the laws can be brought to a regular trial; and it is also well known to many that in several of the slave States but a small proportion of the criminals convicted in courts of justice are sentenced to confinement in jails or penitentiaries, but that they are punished by whipping, exposure in the pillory, and branding with a hot iron, modes of correction long ago abandoned in all the free States. And as to the number of colored persons in the jails of the North, as compared with the South, we turn again to Mr. DeBow (Industrial Resources of the South,) and under the head of Negroes (vol. ii., page 249) we find this explanation of the remarkable disproportion between the amount of valuable labor- —capital under lock and key in the former and in the latter part of the country.

"On our estates we dispense with the whole machinery of public police, and public courts of justice. Thus we try, decide, and execute the sentences in *thousands of cases*, which, in other countries, would go into courts."

To what effect, then, have those tables been arranged, except to awaken suspicions, in the mind of the careful student, of the solidity of all the foundations of the recent, hastily constructed "Southern Democratic" philosophy? Suspicions which will be abundantly confirmed, as my experience would indicate, if he will observe and investigate honestly, its alleged premises, whether psychological or ethnological, in a sufficient number of instances to warrant any safe and confident deductions.

What southern writer has investigated with impartiality the subject of emancipation in the British West Indies? We have in our Democratic journals on the one side, and in the Abolition journals on the other, abundant *ex parte* statements of the re-

sults of that act, but I have yet to see an attempt made by an
American to form an honest judicial conclusion upon the subject,
resulting from any respectable study of evidence, except by persons whom southern writers assume to be unworthy of their attention. Southern writers and their northern allies utterly ignore the position, statements and arguments of their opponents
on this subject, and content themselves with repeated displays of
evidence which they appear to regard as incontrovertible, when
in reality it entirely overshoots the position of those who defend
the Emancipation Act. I am not at all willing to be classed with
these defenders myself, yet it is my impression that wherever
they get the ear of the public in this country, they are having it
all their own way, because their opponents disdain to cope with
them. But there is also another class, to which I profess to belong myself, and which numbers in its ranks, I suspect, most of
the thinking men at the North, which holds the opinion that however untimely, and perhaps injudicious and rash in method the
act of negro emancipation in the British West Indies may have
been, the original design was both right in itself, and reasonable in
its anticipations, both philanthropic and economical, and is thus
justified in the results. I certainly have seen no evidence drawn
from West India emancipation, cited by any of those writers who
so delight in parliamentary returns of exports and imports, value
of estates, etc., which are not satisfactorily replied to by temperately written books (such as Mr. Bigelow's little volume of personal
observations in Jamaica,) which are in every tolerable library at
the North. On the other hand, I know of no attempt to refute
much respectable evidence derived from the English islands, that
is favorable to this view, and before the public. Is such evidence
unknown and unconsidered at the South ? If so, the alleged

success on the part of the latter in an issue of fact and argument, will prove fallacious, for the abolitionists will not fail to put it within reach of every candid, thoughtful mind in the free States.

RELIGIOUS CHARACTERISTICS OF THE SLAVES.

The frequency with which the slaves use religious phrases of all kinds, the readiness with which they engage in what are deemed religious exercises, and fall into religious ecstacies, with the crazy, jocular manner in which they often talk of them, are striking and general characteristics. It is not at all uncommon to hear them refer to conversations which they allege, and apparently believe themselves to have had with Christ, the apostles, or the prophets of old, or to account for some of their actions by attributing them to the direct influence of the Holy Spirit, or of the devil. It seems to me that this state of mind is fraught with more danger to their masters than any to which they could possibly have been brought by general and systematic education, and by the unrestricted study of the Bible, even though this involved what is so much dreaded, but which is, I suspect, an inevitable accompaniment of moral elevation, the birth of an ambition to take care of themselves. Grossly ignorant and degraded in mind, with a crude, undefined, and incomplete system of theology and ethics, credulous and excitable, intensely superstitious and fanatical, what better field could a cunning monomaniac or a sagacious zealot desire in which to set on foot an appalling crusade?

The negro races, compared with the white, at least with the Teutonic, have greater vanity or love of approbation, a stronger dramatic and demonstrative character, more excitability, less exact or analytic minds, and a nature more sensuous, though, (perhaps from want of cultivation,) less refined. They take a real pleasure, for instance, such as it is a rare thing for a white man to be able to feel, in bright and strongly contrasting colors, and in music, in which nearly all are proficient to some extent. They are far less adapted for steady, uninterrupted labor than we are, but excel us in feats demanding agility and tempestuous energy. A Mississippi steamboat manned by negro deck-hands will wood up a third quicker than one manned by the same number of whites, but white laborers of equal intelligence and under equal stimulus will cut twice as much wood, split twice as many rails, and hoe a third more corn in a day than negroes. On many plantations, religious exercises are almost the only habitual recreation not purely sensual, from steady dull labor, in which the negroes are permitted to indulge, and generally all other forms of mental enjoyment are discouraged. Religious exercises are rarely forbidden, and a greater freedom to individual impulses and talent is allowed while engaged in them than is ever tolerated in conducting mere amusements or educational exercises.

Naturally and necessarily all that part of the negro's nature which is otherwise suppressed, bursts out with an intensity and vehemence almost terrible to witness, in forms of religious worship and communion, and a "profession" of piety which it is necessary to make before one can take a very noticeable part in the customary social exercises, is almost universal, except on plantations where the ordinary tumultuous religious meetings are discouraged, or in towns where other recreations are open to the slaves.*

---

* The following newspaper paragraph indicates the wholesale way in which slaves may be nominally Christianized:

" REVIVAL AMONG THE SLAVES.—Rev. J. M. C. Breaker, of Beaufort, S. C.,

RELIGIOUS INSTRUCTION OF SLAVES.

With regard to the religious instruction of slaves, widely different practices of course prevail. There are some slaveholders, like Bishop Polk of Louisiana, who oblige, and many others who encourage, their slaves to engage in religious exercises, furnishing them certain conveniences for the purpose, as described at page 449 of the "Seaboard Slave States." Among the wealthier slave owners, however, and in all those parts of the country where the enslaved portion of the population outnumbers the whites, there is generally a visible, and often an avowed distrust of the effect of religious exercises upon slaves, and even the preaching of white clergymen to them is permitted by many with reluctance.* The prevailing impression among us, with re-

---

writes to the *Southern Baptist* that within the last three months he has baptized by immersion three hundred and fifty persons, *all of them, with a few exceptions, negroes.* These conversions were the result of a revival which has been in progress during the last six months. On the 12th inst., he baptized two hundred and twenty-three converts—all blacks but three—and the ceremony, although performed with due deliberation, occupied only one hour and five minutes. This is nearly four a minute, and Mr. Breaker considers it a demonstration that the three thousand converted on the day of Pentecost could easily have been baptized by the twelve apostles—each taking two hundred and fifty—in an hour and thirteen minutes."

* "Bishop Polk, of Louisiana, was one of the guests. He assured me that he had been all over the country on Red River, the scene of the fictitious sufferings of 'Uncle Tom,' and that he had found the temporal and spiritual welfare of the negroes well cared for. He had confirmed thirty black persons near the situation assigned to Legree's estate. He is himself the owner of four hundred slaves, whom he endeavors to bring up in a religious manner. He tolerates no religion on his estate but that of the Church, he baptizes all the children, and teaches them the catechism. All, without exception, attend the Church service, and the chanting is creditably performed by them, in the opinion of their owner. Ninety of them are communicants, marriages are celebrated according to the Church ritual, and the state of morals is satisfactory. Twenty infants had been baptized by the

gard to the important influence of slavery in promoting the spread of religion among the blacks, is an erroneous one in my opinion. I have heard northern clergymen speak as if they supposed a regular daily instruction of slaves in the truths of Christianity to be general. So far is this from being the case, that although family prayers were held in several of the fifty planters' houses in Mississippi and Alabama, in which I passed a night, I never in a single instance saw a field-hand attend or join in the devotion of the family.

In South Carolina, a formal remonstrance, signed by over three hundred and fifty of the leading planters and citizens, was presented to a Methodist clergyman who had been chosen by the Conference of that State, as being a cautious and discreet person, to preach especially to slaves. It was his purpose, expressly declared beforehand, to confine himself to verbal instruction in religious truth. "Verbal instruction," replied the remonstrants, " will increase the desire of the black population to learn. * * * Open the missionary sluice, and the current will swell in its gradual onward advance. We thus expect *a progressive system of improvement* will be introduced, or will follow from the nature and force of circumstances, which, if not checked, (though it may be shrouded in sophistry and disguise,) *will ultimately revolutionize our civil institutions."*

bishop just before his departure from home. and he had left his whole estate, his keys, etc., in the sole charge of one of his slaves, without the slightest apprehension of loss or damage. In judging of the position of this Christian prelate as a slave owner, the English reader must bear in mind that, by the laws of Louisiana, emancipation has been rendered all but impracticable, and that, if practicable, it would not necessarily be, in all cases, an act of mercy or of justice."—*The Western World Revisited.* By the Rev. Henry Caswall, M. A., author of "America and the American Church," etc. Oxford, John Henry Parker, 1854.

The missionary, the Rev. T. Tupper, accordingly retired from the field. The local newspaper, the Greenville Mountaineer, in announcing his withdrawal, stated that the great body of the people were manifestly opposed to the religious instruction of their slaves, even if it were only given orally.

Though I do not suppose this view is often avowed, or consciously held by intelligent citizens, such a formal, distinct, and effective manifestation of sentiment made by so important an integral portion of the slaveholding body, can not be supposed to represent a merely local or occasional state of mind, and I have not been able to resist the impression, that even where the economy, safety and duty of some sort of religious education of the slaves is conceded, so much caution, reservation and restriction is felt to be necessary in their instruction, that the result in the majority of cases has been merely to furnish a delusive clothing of Christian forms and phrases, to the original vague superstition of the African savage.

THE CHURCH RECUMBENT.

Upon the value of the statistics of "colored church membership," which are often used as evidence that the evils of slavery are fully compensated by its influence in Christianizing the slaves, some light is thrown by the following letter from the white pastor of a town church in that part of the South in which the whites are most numerous, and in which the negroes enjoy the most privileges.

" *To the Editor of the Richmond (Va.) Religious Herald.*

* * * "The truth is, the teachings of the pulpit (at least among Baptists) have nothing to do with the matter. Let me furnish a case in proof. Of two churches which the writer serves, his immediate predecessor was pastor for about twenty-five years. It would be only necessary to give his name, to furnish the strongest and most satisfactory assurance that nothing which ever fell from his lips could be construed into the support of ignorance, superstition, or fanaticism. During the five or six years I have served these churches, whatever may have been my errors and failings, (and I am ready to admit that they have been numerous and grievous enough, in all conscience,) I know I have never uttered a sentiment which could be tortured into the support of the superstitions prevailing among the colored people. And yet, in both these churches, the colored members are as superstitious and fanatical as they are elsewhere. Indeed, this was to be expected, for I certainly claim no superiority over my brethren in the ministry, and I am satisfied that many of them are far better qualified than I am to expose error and to root out superstition. This state of things, then, is not due to the teachings of the pulpit. Nor is it the result of private instructions by masters. Indeed, these last have been afforded so sparingly, till within a few years since, that they could produce but little effect of any sort. And, besides, those who own servants, and are willing to teach them, are far too intelligent to countenance superstition in any way. I repeat the inquiry, then, why is it that so many of our colored members are ignorant, superstitious and fanatical? It is the effect of instructions received from leading men among themselves, and the churches are responsible for this effect, in so far as they receive into fellowship those who have listened to these instructions, ground their hopes upon them, and guide their lives by them. Whatever we may say against superstition, so long as we receive into our churches those who are its slaves, they will believe that we think them Christians; and, naturally relying on our judgment as expressed by their reception, they will live deluded, and die but to be lost.

"But some one will say, 'we never receive colored persons when they manifest these superstitions—when they talk of visions, dreams, sounds,' etc. This is right, as far as it goes. In every such case they should be rejected. But superstition of a fatal character often exists where nothing is said about dreams and visions. It is just as fatally superstitious to trust in prayers and feelings, as in dreams and visions. And this is the sort of superstition which now prevails among the colored people. They have found that sights and sounds will not answer before the whites, and now, (reserving these, perhaps, for some chosen auditory of their own color,) they substitute prayers and feelings. In illustration permit me to record, in no spirit of levity, the stereotyped experience which generally passes current, and, in ninety-nine cases out of a hundred, introduces the colored candidate into the church. The pastor is informed, by one of the 'colored deacons,' that a man wishes to offer to the church with a view to baptism. The fact is announced, a meeting of the church called, and the candidate comes forward.

"*Pastor.* 'Well, John, tell me in a few words, in your own way, your religious experience. What have been your feelings, and what are your present hopes and purposes?'

" *John.* ' I see other people trying, and so I thought I would try too, as I had a soul to save. So I went to pray, and the more I pray the wus I felt; so I kept on praying, and the more I pray, the wus I felt. I felt heavy—I felt a weight—and I kept on praying till at last I felt light—I felt easy—I felt like I loved all Christian people—I felt like I loved everybody.'

" Now, this is positively the whole of the experience which is generally related by colored candidates for baptism. There may be a slight variation of expression now and then, but the sense is almost invariably the same. On this experience, hundreds have been received into the churches—I have received many upon it myself. I am somewhat curious to know how many of the seventy, baptized by my good brother Bagby, told this tale. I 'll warrant not less than fifty. Have any of us been right in receiving persons on such a relation as this ? In the whole of it, there is not one word of gospel, not one word about sorrow for sin, not one word about faith, not one word about Christ. I know that all these things are subsequently brought out by questions; and were this not the case, I have no idea that the candidate would be in any instance received. *But that these questions may be understood, they are made necessarily ' leading questions,'* such as suggest their answers ; and consequently, these answers are of comparatively little value. * * * I am aware that, as brother Bagby suggests, private instructions by masters have been too much neglected. *But these can accomplish but little good, so long as they are counteracted by the teachings of leading colored members, in whose views, after all our efforts, the colored people will have most confidence.*"

Not the smallest suggestion, I observe, in all the long article from which the above is derived, is ventured, that the negroes are capable of education, or that their religious condition would improve if their general enlightenment of mind were not studiously prevented.

" I have often heard the remark made," says the Rev. C. C. Jones, in a treatise on the " Religious Instruction of Slaves," printed at Savannah, Georgia, 1842, " by men whose standing and office in the churches afforded them abundant opportunity for observation, that the more they have had to do with colored members, the less confidence they have been compelled to place in their Christian professions."

A portion of a letter written for publication by the wife of the pastor of a church in the capital of Alabama, given below, naively reveals the degree of enlightenment prevailing among the Christianized Africans at a point where their means of instruction are a thousand times better than they are on an average throughout the country.

"Having talked to him seriously, and in the strongest light held up to him the enormity of the crime in forsaking his lawful wife and taking another, Colly replied, most earnestly, and not taking in at all the idea of guilt, but deeply distressed at having offended his master:

"'Lor, Massa Harry, what was I to do, sir? She tuk all I could git, and more too, sir, to put on her back; and tellin' de truf, sir, dress herself as no poor man's wife hav' any right to. I 'monstrated wid her, Massa, but to no purpose; and den, sir, w'y I jis did all a decent man could do—lef' her, sir, for some oder nigger better off 'an I is.'

"'Twas no use. Colly could not be aroused to conscientiousness on the subject.

"Not one in a thousand, I suppose, of these poor creatures, have any conception whatever of the sanctity of marriage; nor can they be made to have; yet, strange to say, they are perfect models of conjugal fidelity and devotion, while the temporary bondage lasts. I have known them to walk miles after a hard day's work, not only occasionally, but every night, to see the old woman, and cut her wood for her, etc. But to see the coolness with which they throw off the yoke is diverting in the extreme.

"I was accosted one morning in my husband's study by a respectable-looking negro woman, who meekly inquired if Mr. B. was at home.

"'No, he is not. Is it any thing particular you want?—perhaps I can help you.'

"'Yes, ma'am; it's partickler business wid hisself.'

"Having good reason to believe it was the old story of 'a mountain in labor and brought forth a mouse,' I pressed the question, partly to save my better half some of the petty annoyances to which he was almost daily subjected by his sable flock, and partly, I own, to gratify a becoming and laudable curiosity, after all this show of mystery. Behold the answer in plain English, or rather nigger English.

"'I came to ask, please ma'am, if I might have another husband.'

"Just at this crisis, the Oracle entered, who, having authority, by a few spoken words, to join together those whom no man may put asunder, these poor people simply imagine him gifted with equal power to annul the contract with a breath of his mouth.

"I was heartily amused to find that this woman was really no widow, as I had supposed, but merely from caprice, or some reason satisfactory to herself, no doubt, took it into her head to drop her present spouse and look out for another. The matter was referred to the 'Quarterly

Conference,' where an amusing scene occurred, which resulted in the discomfiture of the disconsolate petitioner, who returned to her home rather crest-fallen.

"These quarterly conference debates, for flights of oratory, and superlativeness of diction, beggar all description. Be it understood, that negroes, as a class, have more 'business' to attend to than any other people—that is, provided they can thereby get a chance to 'speak 'fore white folks.' To make a speech is glory enough for Sambo, if he happen to have 'the gift of gab;' and to speak before the preacher is an honor unparalleled. And, by the way, if the preacher have will and wit enough to manage and control the discordant elements of a negro Quarterly Conference, he will be abundantly rewarded with such respect and gratitude as man seldom may lay claim to. They account him but a very little 'lower than the angels;' and their lives, their fortunes, and their sacred honor, are equally his at command. But wo be to the unfortunate pastor who treats them with undue indulgence; they will besiege him daily and hourly with their petty affairs, and their business meetings will be such a monopoly of his time and patience, that but for the farcical character of the same, making them more like dramatic entertainments than sober realities, he would be in despair. Far into the short hours of morning will they speechify and magnify, until nothing but the voice of stern authority, in a tone of command not to be mistaken, can stop the torrent."

An Alabama gentleman whom I questioned with regard to the chastity of the so-called pious slaves, confessed, that four negro women had borne children in his own house, all of them at the time of delivery members in good standing of the Baptist church, and none of them calling any man husband. The only negro man in the house was also a church member, and he believed that he was the father of the four children. He said that he did not know of more than one negro woman whom he could suppose to be chaste, yet he knew hosts who were members of churches.*

* "A small farmer," who "has had control of negroes for thirty years and has been pursuing his present system with them for twenty years," and who "owning but few slaves is able," as he observes, "to do better by them" than large planters, writing to Mr. DeBow, says, "I have tried faithfully to break up immorality. I have not known an oath to be sworn for a long time. I know of no quarreling, no calling harsh names, and but little

A northern clergyman who had been some years in another town in Alabama, where also the means of instruction offered the slaves were unusually good, answered my inquiry, What proportion of the colored members of the churches in the town had any clear comprehension of the meaning of the articles of faith which they professed? "certainly not more than one in seven."

The acknowledgment that "the colored people will, in spite of all our efforts, have more confidence in the views of leading colored members," made by the writer of the letter taken from the "Religious Herald," has been generally made by all clergymen at the South with whom I have conversed. A clergyman of the Episcopal church, of very frank and engaging manners, said in my presence that he had been striving for seven years to gain the confidence of the small number of Africans belonging to his congregation, and with extreme humility he had been lately forced to acknowledge that all his apparent success hitherto had been most delusive. When asked how he accounted for it, he at once ascribed it to the negro's habitual distrust of the white race, and in discussing the causes of this distrust he asked how, if he pretended to believe that the Bible was the Word of God, addressed equally to all the human race, he could explain to a negro's satisfaction why he should fear to put it directly into his hands and instruct him to read it and judge for himself of his duty? A planter present, a member of his church, immediately observed that these were dangerous views, and advised him to be cautious in the expression of them. The laws of the country forbade the

stealing. *Habits of amalgamation, I can not stop.* I can only check it in name. I am willing to be taught, for I have tried every thing I know." He has his field-negroes attend his own family prayers on Sunday, prayer meetings at four o'clock Sunday mornings, etc.—*DeBow's Resources*, vol. ii., p. 337.

education of negroes, and the church was, and he trusted always would remain, the bulwark of the laws. The clergyman replied that he had no design to break the laws, but he must say that he considered that the law which withheld the Bible from the negro was unnecessary and papistical in character.*

The " Methodist Protestant," a religious newspaper edited by a clergyman, in Maryland, where the slave population is to the free only in the ratio of one to twenty-five, lately printed an account of a slave auction in Java (translated from a Dutch paper), at which the father of a slave family was permitted to purchase his wife and children at a nominal price, owing to the humanity of the spectators. The account concluded as follows :

" It would be difficult to describe the joy experienced by these slaves on hearing the fall of the hammer which thus gave them their liberty ; and this joy was further augmented by the presents given them by numbers of the spectators, in order that they might be able to obtain a subsistence till such time as they could procure employment.

" These are the acts of a noble generosity that deserve to be remembered, and which, at the same time, testify that the inhabitants of Java begin to abhor the crying injustice of slavery, and are willing to entertain measures for its abolition."

To give currency to such ideas, even in Maryland, would be fatal to what clergymen call their " influence," and which they

---

* The " Southern Presbyterian," in reviewing some observations made before a South Carolina Bible Society, in which it had been urged that if slaves were permitted to read the Bible, they would learn from it to be more submissive to the authority which the State gives the master over them, says that the speaker " seems to be uninformed of the fact that the Scriptures are read in our churches every Sabbath day, and those very passages which inculcate the relative duties of masters and servants in consequence of their textual, i. e. legally prescribed connections, are *more frequently read* than any other portions of the Bible."

everywhere value at a rather dangerous estimate; accordingly, in the editorial columns prominence is given to the following salvo to the outraged sensibilities of the subscribers :

"SLAVE AUCTION IN JAVA.

"A brief article, with this head, appears on the fourth page of our paper this week. It is of a class of articles we *never select*, because they are very often manufactured by paragraphists for a purpose, and are not reliable. It was put in by our printer in place of something we had *marked out*. We did not see this objectionable substitute until the outside form was worked off, and are therefore not responsible for it."*

THE EDUCATION OF THE WHITE RACE, UNDER THE NECESSITIES OF THE PRESENT SYSTEM.

The habitual caution imposed on clergymen and public teachers must, and obviously does have an important secondary effect, similar to that usually attributed by Protestants to papacy, upon the minds of all the people, discountenancing and retarding the free and fearless exercise of the mind upon subjects of a religious or ethical nature, and the necessity of accepting and apologizing for the exceedingly low morality of the nominally religious slaves, together with the familiarity with this immorality which all classes acquire, renders the existence of a very elevated standard of morals among the whites almost an impossibility.†

---

* Organized action for the abolition of slavery in the island of Java, has since been authentically reported.

† Twice it happened to come to my knowledge that sons of a planter, by whom I was lodged while on this journey—lads of fourteen or sixteen—who were supposed to have slept in the same room with me, really spent the night, till after daybreak, in the negro cabins. A southern merchant, visiting New York, to whom I expressed the view I had been led to form of the evil of slavery in this way, replied that he thought I over-estimated the evil to boys on the plantations, but that it was impossible to over-estimate it in

In spite of the constant denunciations by the southern newspapers, of those who continued to patronize northern educational
institutions, I never conversed with a cultivated Southerner on
the effects of slavery, that he did not express a wish or intention
to have his own children educated where they should be free
from demoralizing association with slaves.   That this association
is almost inevitably corrupting and dangerous, is very generally
(I may say, excepting by the extremest fanatics of South Carolina, universally) admitted.   Now, although the children of a few
wealthy men may, for a limited period, be preserved from this
danger, the children of the million can not be.   Indeed, it requires a man of some culture, and knowledge of the rest of the
world, to appreciate the danger sufficiently to guard at all diligently against it.   If habitual intercourse with a hopelessly low
and immoral class is at all bad in its effects on young minds, the
people of the South are, as a people, educated subject to this bad
influence, and must bear the consequences.   In other words, if
the slaves must not be elevated, it would seem to be a necessity
that the citizens should steadily degenerate.

Change and grow more marked in their peculiarities with
every generation, they certainly do, very obviously.   "The

towns. "I have personal knowledge," he continued, "that there are but
two lads, sixteen years old, in our town, [a small market town of Alabama,]
who have not already had occasion to resort to remedies for the penalty of
licentiousness." "When on my brother's plantation, just before I came
North," said another southern merchant, on his annual visit to New York,
" I was informed that each of his family-servants were suffering from ——, and
I ascertained that each of my brother's children, girls and boys, had been informed of it and knew how and from whom it had been acquired.   The negroes being their familiar companions, I tried to get my brother to send them
North with me to school.   I told him he might as well have them educated
in a brothel at once, as in the way they were growing up."

South" has a traditional reputation for qualities and habits in which I think the southern people, as a whole, are to-day more deficient than any other nation in the world. The southern gentleman, as we ordinarily conceive him to be, is as rare a phenomenon in the South at the present day as is the old squire of Geoffrey Crayon in modern England. But it is unnecessary to argue how great must be the influence; upon people of a higher origin, of habitual association with a race systematically kept at the lowest ebb of intellect and morals. It has been elaborately and convincingly described by Mr. Jefferson, from his personal experience and observation of his neighbors. What he testified to be the effect upon the Virginians, in his day, of owning and associating with slaves, is now to be witnessed to a far greater and more deplorable extent throughout the whole South, but most deplorably in districts where the slave population predominates, and where, consequently, the action of slavery has been most unimpeded.*

---

* Jefferson fails to enumerate, among the evils of slavery, one of its influences which I am inclined to think as distinct and as baneful to us nationally as any other. How can men retain the most essential quality of true manhood who daily, without remonstrance or interference, see men beaten, whose position renders effective resistance totally impracticable—and not only men, but women, too! Is it not partially the result of this, that self-respect seldom seems to suggest to an angry man at the South that he should use any thing like magnanimity? that he should be careful to secure fair play for his opponent in a quarrel? A gentleman of veracity, now living in the South, told me that among his friends he had once numbered two young men, who were themselves intimate friends, till one of them, taking offense at some foolish words uttered by the other, challenged him. A large crowd assembled to see the duel, which took place on a piece of prairie ground. The combatants came armed with rifles, and at the first interchange of shots the challenged man fell disabled by a ball in the thigh. The other, throwing down his rifle, walked toward him, and kneeling by his side, drew a bowie knife, and deliberately butchered him. The crowd of bystanders not only

ABSENTEEISM.

What proportion of the larger cotton plantations are resided upon by their owners, I am unable to estimate with confidence. Of those having cabin accommodations for fifty slaves each, which came under my observation from the road, while I was traveling through the cotton districts bordering the Mississippi river, I think more than half were unprovided with a habitation which I could suppose to be the ordinary residence of a man of moderate wealth. In the more fertile and less healthy districts, I should judge that the majority of slaves are left by their owners to the nearly unlimited government of hireling overseers the greater part of the time. Some of these plantations are owned by capitalists, who reside permanently and constantly in the North or in Europe. Many are owned by wealthy Virginians and Carolinians, who reside on what are called the "show plantations" of those States; plantations having all the character, though never the name, of mere country-seats, the exhausted soil of which will scarcely produce sufficient to feed and clothe the resident slaves, whose increase is constantly removed to colonize these richer fields of the West.

Still a large number are merely occasional sojourning places of their owners, who naturally enough prefer to live, as soon as they can afford to do so, where the conveniences and luxuries belonging to a highly civilized state of society are more easily obtained than they can ever be in a country of large plantations.

---

permitted this, but the execrable assassin still lives in the community, has since married, and, as far as my informant could judge, his social position has been rather advanced than otherwise, from thus dealing with his enemy. In what other English—in what other civilized or half-civilized community would such cowardly atrocity have been endured?

It is rare that a plantation would have a dozen intelligent families residing within a day's ride of it.   Any society that a planter
enjoys on his estate must, therefore, consist in a great degree of
permanent guests.   Hence the name for hospitality of wealthy
planters.   A large plantation is necessarily a retreat from general
society, and is used by its owner, I am inclined to think, in the
majority of cases, in winter, as Berkshire villas and farms are in
summer by rich people of New York and Boston.   I feel assured
that this is the case with the plantations upon the Mississippi,
and the bayous of Louisiana, upon the Arkansas, the Yazoo, and
the Red rivers, and in the lowlands of Carolina and Georgia.   I
have never been on a plantation numbering fifty field-hands, the
owner of which was accustomed to reside steadily through the
year upon it.   Still I am aware that there are many such, and
possibly it is a minority of them who are regularly absent with
their families from their plantations during any considerable part
of the year.

The summer visitors from the South to our northern water-
ing places are, I judge, chiefly of the migratory, wealthy class.
Such persons, it is evident, are much less influenced in their
character and habits, by association with slaves, than any other
at the South.   Their household arrangements, and the customs of
their house-servants must, of course, assimilate to those of cultivated families in other parts of the world.   The Irish gentleman
and the Irish peasant are not more unlike, in their habits and
manners, than some of these large planters and the great multitude of slave owners.

The number of the very wealthy is, of course, small, yet as the
chief part of the wealth of these consists in slaves, no inconsiderable proportion of all the slaves belong to men who deputize

their government in a great measure to overseers. It may be computed, (not however with confidence), from the census of 1850, that about one half the slaves of Louisiana and one third those of Mississippi and Arkansas, belong to estates of not less than fifty slaves each, and of these, I believe, nine tenths live on plantations which their owners reside upon, if at all, but transiently.

The number of plantations of this class, and the proportion of those employed upon them to the whole body of negroes in the country, is, as I have said, rapidly increasing. At the present prices of cotton the large grower has such advantages over the small, that the owner of a plantation of fifty slaves, favorably situated, unless he lives very recklessly, will increase in wealth so rapidly and possess such a credit that he may soon establish or purchase other plantations, so that at his death his children may be provided for without reducing the effective force of negroes on any division of his landed estate. The excessive credit given to such planters by negro dealers and tradesmen renders this the more practicable. The higher the price of cotton the higher is that of negroes, and the higher the price of negroes the less is it in the power of men of small capital to buy them. Large plantations of course pay a much larger per centage on the capital invested in them than smaller ones ; indeed the only plausible economical defense of slavery is simply an explanation of the advantages of associated labor, advantages which are possessed equally by large manufacturing establishments in which free laborers are brought together and employed in the most effective manner, and which I can see no sufficient reason for supposing could not be made available for agriculture did not the good results flowing from small holdings, on the whole, counterbalance them. If the present high price of cotton and the present scarcity of labor at the South continues, the cultivation of cotton on small plantations will by and by become unusual, for the same reason that hand-loom weaving has become unusual in the farm houses of Massachusetts.

But whatever advantages large plantations have, they accrue only to their owners and to the buyers of cotton; the mass of the white inhabitants are dispersed over a greater surface, discouraged and driven toward barbarism by them, and the blacks upon them, while rapidly degenerating from all that is redeeming in savage-life, are gaining nothing valuable of civilization.

In the Report of the Grand Jury of Richland District, South Carolina, in *eighteen hundred and fifty-four*, calling for a reestablishment of the African slave trade,* it is observed, "as to the morality of this question, it is scarcely necessary for us to allude to it; when the fact is remarked that the plantations of Alabama, Mississippi, Louisiana and Texas have been and are daily settled by the removal of slaves from the more northern of the slave States, and that in consequence of their having been raised in a more healthy climate, and in most cases trained to pursuits totally different, the mortality even on the best-ordered farms is so great that in many instances the entire income is expended in the purchase of more slaves from the same source in order to replenish and keep up those plantations, while in *every case* the condition of the slave, if his life is spared, is made worse both physically and morally. * * * And if you look at the subject in a religious point of view, the contrast is equally striking, for when you remove a slave from the more northern to

* Richland District contains seven thousand white, and thirteen thousand slave population. The Report is published in the Charleston Standard, October 12th, 1854.

the more southern parts of the slaveholding States, you thereby diminish his religious opportunities."

I believe that this statement gives an exaggerated and calumnious report of the general condition of the slaves upon the plantations of the States referred to, containing, as they did in 1849, one third the whole slave population of the South—but I have not been able to resist the conviction that in the districts where cotton is now grown most profitably to the planters, the oppression and deterioration of the negro race is much more lamentable than is generally supposed by those who like myself have been constrained, by other considerations, to accept it as a duty to oppose temperately but determinately the modern policy of the South, of which this is an immediate result. Its effect on the white race, I still consider to be infinitely more deplorable.

In the important work of Dr. Davy on the West Indies, I find the following description of the poor whites of Barbadoes, who, by a comparison with Sir Charles Lyell's observations, and my own descriptions at pages 414, and 506, of the "Seaboard Slave States," it may be seen correspond not only morally and intellectually, but remarkably also, in their physical appearance, with those of the old cotton plantation districts of the South.

"Relative to the whites, they may be divided into two classes—the poor laboring portion of them constituting the majority, and the smaller portion of them consisting of those in easy or in affluent circumstances.

"The former are in many respects remarkable, and not less so in appearance than in character. Their hue and complexion are not such as might be expected; their color resembles more that of the Albino than of an Englishman. When exposed a good deal to the sun in a tropical climate, it is commonly of a sickly white, or light red, not often of a healthy brown; and they have generally light eyes and light-colored, sparse hair. In make they bear marks of feebleness, rather tall, loosely jointed, with little muscular development. In brief, their general appearance denotes degeneracy of corporeal frame, and reminds one of exotic plants vegetating in an uncongenial soil and climate.

"In character, morally and intellectually, they show marks also of degeneracy, not less than physically. They are generally indolent and idle, ignorant and improvident, and often intemperate. Is it surprising, then, that they are poor, and objects of contempt? * * * What they are they have been made undoubtedly by circumstances, and this in the course of a few generations."*

Similar phenomena are found in the free race, I believe, wherever large slave-plantations are common. Whether a gradual elevation of the slaves, would prove the entire destruction of the poor whites, as is held at the South, is certainly very doubtful. The effect of emancipation in Barbadoes, upon the whites, after some half dozen years only, is thus described by Dr. Davy:

"Previous to emancipation, the planters, for every sixty acres of land, had to provide a man for the militia (the chief purpose of which was to guard against the insurrection of their slaves). * * * He was supplied by his principal with a gun and ammunition, and had a house and two acres of land free of rent, on which he raised some vegetables and kept a cow, or two or three goats. Very idle himself, his wife worked with the needle, and got money for making clothes for the negroes" (p. 66). "Now that they are obliged to support themselves as they can, they are variously employed. Those who possess a little land, or who rent a few acres, cultivate chiefly those crops which require least labor, and the smallest means, such as ground provisions, arrow-root, aloes, and perhaps a little cotton. I have seen one of them at work in a manner not a little characteristic: a hoe in one hand and umbrella in the other, which he held over his head, and a face-cloth over his face (a relief from reflected heat). Some who have been taught to read and write are employed as book-keepers by the proprietors of the larger estates, with a pay of about six dollars a month and board and lodging. Some are chiefly occupied in fishing. * * * Some gain a livelihood as carters and grooms, and some as field-laborers, a kind of labor which, when slaves were employed as laborers, they would have resisted *as insupportable degradation.* * * * All of them have the aristocratic feeling in its worst sense, the class pride acquired in time of slavery when they were an important portion of the privileged order; and it is marked in their manners and bearing. * * * They are not to be considered as altogether irreclaimable" (p. 71).

* "The West Indies, * * * founded on notes and observations collected during a three years' residence." By John Davy, M. D., F. R. S., etc., Inspector General of Army Hospitals.

CHAPTER III.

A TRIP INTO A PART OF NORTHERN MISSISSIPPI.

Vicksburg, March 18.—I arrived at this place last night, about sunset, and was told that there was no hotel in the town except on the wharf-boat, the only house used for that purpose having been closed a few days ago on account of a difference of opinion between its owner and his tenant.

There are no wharves on the Mississippi, or any of the southern rivers. The wharf-boat is an old steamboat, with her paddle boxes and machinery removed and otherwise dismantled, on which steamboats discharge passengers and freight. The main deck is used as a warehouse, and, in place of the furnace, has in this case a dram shop, a chandler's shop, a forwarding agency, and a telegraph office. Overhead, the saloon and state-rooms remain, and with the bar-room and clerk's office, kitchen and barber's shop, constitute a stationary though floating hostelry.

Though there were fifty or more rooms, and not a dozen guests, I was obliged, about twelve o'clock, to admit a stranger who had been gambling all the evening in the saloon, to occupy the spare shelf of my closet. If a disposition to enjoy occasional privacy, or to exercise a choice in one's room-mates were a sure sympton of a monomania for incendiarism, it could not be more carefully thwarted than it is at all public houses in this part of the world.

Memphis, March 20.—I reached here this morning in forty-eight hours by steamboat from Vicksburg; distance four hundred miles; many stoppages and against the current; fare $10.

Here, at the "Commercial Hotel," I am favored with an unusually good-natured room-mate. He is smoking on the bed—our bed—now, and wants to know what my business is here, and whether I carry a pistol about me; also whether I believe that it is n't lucky to play cards on Sundays; which I do most strenuously, especially as this is a rainy Sunday, and his second cigar is nearly smoked out.

This is a first-class hotel and has, of course, printed bills of fare, which, in a dearth of other literature, are not to be dropped at the first glance. A copy of to-day's, is presented on the opposite page.

Being in a distant quarter of the establishment when a crash of the gong announced dinner, I did not get to the table as early as some others. The meal was served in a large, dreary room exactly like a hospital ward; and it is a striking illustration of the celerity with which every thing is accomplished in our young country, that beginning with the soup, and going on by the fish to the roasts, the first five dishes I inquired for, when at last I succeeded in arresting one of the negro boys, were "all gone," and as the waiter had to go to the head of the dining-room, or to the kitchen, to ascertain this fact upon each demand, the majority of the company had left the table before I was served at all. At length I said I would take any thing that was still to be had, and thereupon was provided immediately with some grimy bacon, and greasy cabbage. This I commenced eating, but I no sooner paused for a moment, than it was suddenly and surreptitiously removed, and its place supplied, without the expression of any desire on my part, with some other Memphitic chef d'œuvre,

COMMERCIAL HOTEL.

BY D. COCKRELL.

BILL OF FARE.

MARCH 20.

SOUP.

Oyster.

FISH.

Red.

BOILED.

Jole and green.
Ham.
Corned beef.
Bacon and turnips.
Codfish egg sauce.
Beef heart egg sauce.
Leg of mutton caper sauce.
Barbecued rabits.
Boiled tongue.

ROAST.

Veal.
Roast pig.
Muscovie Ducks.
Kentucky beef.
Mutton.
Barbecued shoat.
Roast bear meat.
Roast pork.

ENTREES.

Fricasee pork.
Calf-feet mushroom sauce.
Bear sausages.
Harricane tripe.
Stewed mutton.
Browned Rice.
Calf feet madeira sauce.
Stewed turkey wine sauce.
Giblets volivon.
Mutton omelett.
Beef's heart fricasced.
Cheese macaroni.
Chicken chops robert sauce.
Breast chicken madeira sauce.
Beef kidney pickle sauce.
Cod fish baked.
Calf head wine sauce.

FRUIT.

Almonds.
Rasins.
Pecans.

VEGETABLES.

Boiled Cabbage.
Turnips.
Cold Slaugh.
Hot slaugh.
Pickled beets.
Creole hominy.
Crout cabbage,
Oyster plant fried.
Parsneps gravied.
Stewed parsneps.
Fried cabbage.
Sweet potatoes spiced.
Carrot.
Sweat potatoes baked.
Cabbage stuffed.
Onions, boiled.
Irish potatoes creamed and mashed.
Irish potatoes browned.
Boiled Shellots.
Scolloped carrots.
Boiled turnips drawn butter.
White beans.

PASTRY.

Currant pies.
Lemon custard.
Rice pudding.
Cocoanut pie.
Cranberry pies.
Sliced potato pie.
Chess cake.
Irish pudding.
Orange custard.
Cranberry shapes.
Green peach tarts.
Green peach puff paste.
Grape tarts.
Huckle berry pies,
Pound Cake,
Rheubarb tarts.
Plum tarts.
Calves feet jelly.
Blamonge.
Oranga jelly.

a close investigation of which left me in doubt whether it was
that denominated " sliced potato pie," or " Irish pudding."

I congratulate myself that I have lived to see the day in which
an agitation for reform in our GREAT HOTEL SYSTEM has been commenced, and I trust that a Society for the Revival of Village Inns
will ere long form one of the features of the May anniversaries.

A stage coach conveyed the railroad passengers from the hotel
to the station, which was a mile or two out of town. As we
were entering the coach the driver observed with a Mephisto-
phelean smile that we " need n't calculate we were gwine to ride
very fur " and accordingly, as soon as we had got into the country
he stopped and asked all the men passengers to get out and walk,
for, he added, " it was as much as his hoses could do to draw the
ladies and the baggage." It was quite true; the road was so
bad that the horses were obliged to stop frequently with the
diminished load, and as there was a contract between myself
and the proprietors by which, for a stipulated sum of money by
me to them in hand duly paid, they promised to convey me, as
well as my little baggage, I thought it would have been no more
than honest if they had looked out beforehand to have either a
stronger team, or a better road, provided. As is the custom
of our country, however, we allowed ourselves to be thus robbed
and forced to tiresome labor with great good nature, and waded
along through mud ankle-deep, joking with the driver and ready
to put our shoulders to the wheels if it should be necessary.
Two pieces of our baggage were jerked off in heavy lurches of
the coach ; the owners picked them up and carried them on their
shoulders till the horses stopped to breathe again. The train of
course had waited for us, and it continued to wait until another
coach arrived, when it started twenty minutes behind time.

After some forty miles of rail, nine of us were stowed away in another stage coach. The road was bad, the weather foul. We proceeded slowly, were often in imminent danger of being upset, and once were all obliged to get out and help the horses draw the coach out of a slough; but with smoking, and the occasional circulation of a small black bottle, and a general disposition to be as comfortable as circumstances would allow, four hours of stage coaching proved less fatiguing than one of the smoky rail-cars.

Among the passengers was a " Judge," resident in the vicinity, portly, dignified and well informed ; and a young man, who was a personal friend of the member of Congress from the district, and who, as he informed me, had, through the influence of this friend, a promise from the President of honorable and lucrative employment under government. He was known to all the other passengers, and hailed by every one on the road-side, by the title of Colonel. The Judge was ready to converse about the country through which we were passing, and while perfectly aware, as no one else seemed to be, that it bore any thing but an appearance of prosperity or attractiveness to a stranger, he assured me that it was really improving in all respects quite rapidly. There were few large plantations, but many small planters or rather farmers, for cotton, though the principal source of cash income, was much less exclusively an object of attention than in the more southern parts of the State. A larger space was occupied by the maize and grain crops. There were not a few small fields of wheat. In the afternoon, when only the Colonel and myself were with him, the Judge talked about slavery in a candid and liberal spirit. At present prices, he said, nobody could afford to own slaves, unless he could engage them almost exclusively in cotton-growing. It was undoubtedly a great injury to a region like this, which was not altogether well adapted to cotton, to be in the midst of a slaveholding country, for it prevented efficient free labor. A good deal of cotton was nevertheless grown hereabouts by white labor—by poor men who planted an acre or two, and worked it themselves, getting the planters to gin and press it for them. It was not at all uncommon for men to begin in this way and soon purchase negroes on credit, and eventually become rich men. Most of the plantations in this vicinity, indeed, belonged to men who had come into the country with nothing within twenty years. Once a man got a good start with negroes, unless the luck was much against him, nothing but his own folly could prevent his becoming rich. The increase of his negro property by births, if he took good care of it, must, in a few years, make him independent. The worst thing, and the most difficult to remedy, was the deplorable ignorance which prevailed. Latterly, however, people were taking more pride in the education of their children. Some excellent schools had been established, the teachers generally from the North, and a great many children were sent to board in the villages—county-seats—to attend them. This was especially true of girls, who liked to live in the villages rather than on the plantations. There was more difficulty in making boys attend school, until, at least, they were too old to get much good from it.

The "Colonel" was a rough, merry, good-hearted, simple-minded man, and kept all the would-be sober-sides of our coach body, in irrepressible laughter with queer observations on passing occurrences, anecdotes and comic songs. It must be confessed that there is no charge which the enemies of the theater bring against the stage, that was not duly illustrated, and that with a broadness which the taste of a metropolitan audience would scarcely permit. Had Doctor —— and Doctor —— been with me they would thereafter for ever have denied themselves, and discountenanced in others, the use of such a means of travel. The Colonel, notwithstanding, was of a most obliging disposition, and having ascertained in what direction I was going, enumerated at least a dozen families on the road, within some hundred miles, whom he invited me to visit, assuring me that I should find pretty girls in all of them, and a warm welcome, if I mentioned his name.

He told the Judge that his bar-bill on the boat, coming up from New Orleans, was forty dollars—seventeen dollars the first night. But he had made money—had won forty dollars of one gentleman. He confessed, however, that he had lost fifteen by another, " but he saw how he did it. He did not want to accuse him publicly, but he saw it and he purposed to write to him and tell him of it. He did not mean to insult the gentleman, only he did not want to have him think that he was so green as not to know how he did it."

While stopping for dinner at a village inn, a young man came in to the room where we all were, and asked the coachman what was to be paid for a trunk which had been brought for him The coachman said the charge would be a dollar, which the young man thought excessive. The coachman denied that it was so, said that it was what he had often been paid; he should not take less. The young man finally agreed to wait for the decision of the proprietor of the line. There was a woman in the room; I noticed no loud words or angry tones, and had not supposed that there was the slightest excitement. I observed, however, that there was a profound silence for a minute afterwards, which was interrupted by a jocose remark of the coachman about the delay of our dinner. Soon after we reëntered the coach, the Colonel referred to the trunk owner, in a contemptuous manner. The Judge replied in a similar tone. " If I had been in the driver's place, I should have killed him, sure," said the Colonel. With great surprise, I ventured to ask for what reason. " Did not you see the fellow put his hand to his breast when the driver denied that he had ever taken less than a dollar for bringing a trunk from Memphis ?"

" No, I did not ; but what of it ?"

" Why, he meant to frighten the driver, of course."

" You think he had a knife in his breast ?"

" Of course he had, sir."

" But you would n't kill him for that, I suppose ?"

" When a man threatens to kill me, you would n't have me wait for him to do it, would you, sir ?"

The roads continued very heavy ; some one remarked, " There's been a heap of rain lately," and rain still kept falling. We passed a number of cotton wagons which had stopped in the road ; the cattle had been turned out and had strayed off into the woods, and the drivers lay under the tilts asleep on straw.

The Colonel said this sight reminded him of his old camp-meeting days. He used to be very fond of going to camp meetings. " I used to go first for fun, and oh ! Lord, haint I had some fun at camp meetings ? But after a while I got a conviction—need n't laugh, gentlemen. I tell you it was sober business for me. I'll never make fun of that. The truth just is, I am a melancholy case ; I thought I was a pious man once, I did—I'm damned if I did n't. Do n't laugh at what I say, now ; I do n't want fun made of that ; I give you my word I experienced religion, and I used to go to the meetings with as much sincerity and soberness as anybody could. That was the time I learned to sing—learned to pray too, I did; could pray right smart. I did think I was a converted man, but of course, I aint, and I 'spose 'twarnt the right sort, and I do n't reckon I shall have another chance. A gentleman has a right to make the most of this life, when he can't calculate on any thing better than roasting in the next. Aint that so Judge? I reckon so. You must n't think hard of me, if I do talk wicked some. Can't help it."

So common is this sort of effervescing mixture of impiety and theology at the South, I doubt if the Colonel was not perfectly sincere, though probably not wholly unconscious of drollery, in these remarks. At a Sunday dinner-table, at a village inn, two or three men took seats, who had, as they said, "been to the preachin'." A child had been baptized, and the preaching had been a defense of infant baptism.

"I'm damned," said one, " ef he teched on the primary significance of baptism, at all—buryin' with Jesus."

" They wus the weakest arguments for sprinklin' that ever I heerd," said another—a hot, red-faced, corpulent man—" and his sermon was two hours long, for when he stopped I looked at my watch. I thought it should be a lesson to me, for I could n't help going to sleep. Says I to Uncle John, says I—he sot next to me, and I whispered to him—says I, ' When he gits to Bunker Hill, you wake me up,' for I see he was bound to go clean back to the beginnin' of things."

"Uncle John is an Episcopalian, aint he?"

" Yes."

" Well, there aint no religion in that, no how."

" No there aint."

"Well now, you would n't think it, but I've studied into religion a heap in my life."

"Do n't seem to have done you much good."

"No it haint, not yet, but I've studied into it, and I know what it is."

"There aint but one way, Benny."

"I know it."

"Repent of your sins, and believe in Christ, and be immersed, that's all."

"I know it."

"Well, I hope the Lord 'll bring you to it, 'fore you die."

"Reckon he will—hope so, sure."

"You would n't hardly think that fat man was a preacher himself, would you?" said the landlady to me, after they left.

"Certainly not."

"He is, though, but I do n't think much of that sort," and the landlady immediately began to describe to me the religious history of the neighborhood. It was some different here, she said, she reckoned, in reply to a remark of mine, from what it was at the North. Most respectable people became pious here before they got to be very old, especially ladies. Young ladies were always gay and went to balls till they were near twenty years old, but from eighteen to twenty-five they generally got religion, and then they stopped right short and never danced or carried on any after that. Sometimes it was n't till after they were married, but there were n't many ladies who had children that warn't pious. She herself was an exception, for she had three children and had not got religion yet; sometimes she was frightened to think how old she was—her children growing up about her; but she did so like dancing—she hoped her turn would come—she knew it would—she had a pious and praying mother, and she reckoned her prayers must be heard, and so on.

I was forced by the stage arrangements to travel night and day. The Colonel told me that I should be able to get a good supper at a house where the coach was to stop about midnight—" good honest fried bacon, and hot Christian corn-bread—nothing like it to fill a man up and make him feel righteous. You get a heap better living up in this country than you can at the St. Charles, for all the fuss they make about it. It's lucky you'll have something better to travel on to-night than them French friterzéed Dutch flabbergasted hell-fixins : for you'll have the———" (another most extraordinary series of imprecations on the road over which I was to travel).

Before dark all my companions left me, and in their place I had but one, a young gentleman with whom I soon became very intimately acquainted. He was seventeen years old, so he said ; he looked older; and the son of a planter in the "Yazoo bottoms." The last year he had " follered overseein'" on his father's plantation, but he was bound for Tennessee, now, to go to an academy, where he could learn geography. There was a school near home at which he had studied reading and writing and ciphering, but he thought a gentleman ought to have some knowledge of geography. At ten o'clock the next morning the stage coach having progressed at the rate of exactly two miles and a half an hour, for the previous sixteen hours, during which time we had been fasting, the supper-house, which we should have reached before midnight, was still ten miles ahead, the driver sulky and refusing to stop until we reached it. We had been pounded till we ached in every muscle. I had had no sleep since I left Memphis. We were passing over a hill country which sometimes appeared to be quite thickly inhabited, yet mainly still covered with a pine forest, through which the wind moaned lugubriously.

I had been induced to make this trip, in no slight degree by reading the following description in a statistical article of DeBow's Review :

" The settling of this region is one among the many remarkable events in the history of the rise of the western States. Fifteen years ago it was an Indian wilderness, and now it has reached and passed in its population other portions of the State of ten times its age, and this population, too, one of the finest in all the West. Great attention has been given to schools and education, and here, [at Memphis,] has been located the University of Mississippi ; so amply endowed by the State, and now just going into operation under the auspices of some of the ablest professors from the eastern colleges. There is no overgrown wealth among them, and yet no squalid poverty ; the people being generally comfortable, substantial, and independent farmers. Considering its climate, soil, wealth, and general character of its inhabitants, I should think no more desirable or delightful residence could be found than among the hills and sunny valleys of the Chickasaw Cession."*

And here among the hills of this Paradise of the South-West, we were, Yazoo and I—he, savagely hungry, as may be guessed from his observations upon " the finest people of the West," among whose cabins in the pine-wood, toiled our stage-coach.

The whole art of driving was directed to the discovery of a passage for the coach among the trees and through the fields, where there were fields, adjoining the road—the road itself being impassable.   Occasionally, when the coachman, during the night, found it necessary, owing to the thickness of the forest on each side, to take to the road, he would first leave the coach and make a survey with his lantern, sounding the ruts of the cotton-wagons, and finally marking out a channel by guiding-stakes which he cut from the

* See " Resources ;" article, " Mississippi," etc.

underwood with a hatchet, usually carried in the holster. If after diligent sounding, he found no passage sufficiently shallow, he would sometimes spend half an hour in preparing one, bringing rails from the nearest fence, or cutting brushwood for the purpose. We were but once or twice during the night called upon to leave the coach, or to assist in road-making, and my companion frequently expressed his gratitude for this—gratitude not to the driver, but to Providence, who had made a country, as he thought, so unusually well adapted for stage coaching. The night before, he had been on a much worse road, and was half the time, with numerous other passengers, engaged in bringing rails, and prying the coach out of sloughs. They had been obliged to keep on the track, because the water was up over the adjoining country. Where the wooden causeway had floated off, they had passed through water so deep that it entered the coach body. With our road of to-day, then, he could only express satisfaction; not so with the residents upon it. "Look at 'em", he would say, "Just look at 'em! What's the use of such people's living? 'pears to me I'd die if I could n't live better 'n that. When I get to be representative, I'm going to have a law made that all such kind of men shall be took up by the State and sent to the penitentiary, to make 'em work and earn something to support their families. I pity the women; I haint nuthin agin them; they work hard enough, I know; but the men—I know how 'tis. They just hang around groceries and spend all the money they can get—just go round and live on other people, and play keerds, and only go home to nights; and the poor women, they hev to live how they ken."

"Do you think it's so? It is strange we see no men—only women and children."

"Tell you they 're off, gettin' a dinner out o' somebody. Tell you, I know it 's so. It 's the way all these people do. Why, there's one poor man I know, that lives in a neighborhood of poor men, down our way, and he's right industrious, but he can't get rich and he never ken, cause all these other poor men live on him."

"What do you mean? Do they all drop in about dinner time?"

"No, not all on 'em, but some on 'em every day. And they keep borrowin' things of him. He haint spunk enough to insult 'em. If he 'd just move into a rich neighborhood and jest be a little sassy and not keer so much about what folks said of him, he'd get rich; never knew a man that was industrious and sassy in this country that did n't get rich, quick, and get niggers to do his work for him. Anybody ken that 's smart. Thar 's whar they tried to raise some corn. Warn't no corn grew thar; that 's sartin. Wonder what they live on? See the stalks. They never made no corn. Plowed right down the hill! Did you ever see any thing like it? As if this sile warn't poor enough already. There now. Just the same. Only look at 'em! 'Pears like they never see a stage afore. This ain't the right road, the way they look at us. No, sartin, they never see a stage. Lord God! see the babies. They never see a stage afore. No, the stage never went by here afore, I know. This damned driver 's just taken us round this way to show off what he can do and pass away the time before breakfast. Could n't get no breakfast here if he would stop—less we ate a baby. That 's right! step out where you ken see her good; prehaps you 'll never see a stage again; better look now, right sharp. Yes, oh yes, sartin; fetch out all the babies. Haint you go no more? Well, I

should hope not. Now, what is the use of so many babies?
That's the worst on 't. I'd get married to-morrow if I was n't
sure I'd hev babies. I hate babies, can't bear 'em round me and
won't hev 'em. I would like to be married. I know several
gals I'd marry if 'twarn't for that. Well, it's a fact. Just so. I
hate the squalling things. I know I was born a baby, but I
could n't help it, could I? I wish I had n't been. I hate the
squallin' things. If I had to hev a baby round me I should kill it."

"If you had a baby of your own, you'd feel differently about
it."

"That's what they tell me. I s'pose I should, but I do n't
want to feel differently. I hate 'em. I hate 'em."

The coach stopped at length. We got out and found ourselves on the bank of an overflowed brook. A part of the
bridge was broken up, the driver declared it impossible to ford
the stream, and said he should return to the shanty, four miles
back, at which we had last changed horses. We persuaded him
to take one of his horses from the team and let us see if we could
not get across. I succeeded in doing this without difficulty,
and turning the horse loose he returned. The driver, however,
was still afraid to try to ford the stream with the coach and mails,
and after trying our best to persuade him, I told him if he returned he should do it without me, hoping he would be shamed
out of his pusillanimity. Yazoo joined me, but the driver having
again recovered the horse upon which he had forded the stream,
turned about and drove back. We pushed on, and after walking
a few miles, came to a neat, new house, with a cluster of old
cabins about it. It was much the most comfortable establishment we had seen during the day. Truly a "sunny valley"
home of northern Mississippi. We entered quietly, and were re-

ceived by two women who were spinning in a room with three outside doors all open, though a fine fire was burning, merely to warm the room, in a large fire-place, within. Upon our asking if we could have breakfast prepared for us, one of the women went to the door and gave orders to a negro, and in a moment after, we saw six or seven black boys and girls chasing and clubbing a hen round the yard for our benefit. I regret to add that they did not succeed in making her tender. At twelve o'clock we breakfasted, and were then accommodated with a bed, upon which we slept together for several hours. When I awoke I walked out to look at the premises.

The house was half a dozen rods from the high road, with a square yard all about it, in one corner of which was a small enclosure for stock, and a log stable and corn-crib. There were also three negro cabins; one before the house, and two behind it. The house was a neat building of logs, boarded over and painted on the outside. On the inside, the logs were neatly hewn to a plane face, and exposed. One of the lower rooms contained a bed, and but little other furniture; the other was the common family apartment, but also was furnished with a bed. A door opened into another smaller log house in the rear, in which were two rooms—one of them the family dining-room; the other the kitchen. Behind this was still another log erection, fifteen feet square, which was the smoke-house, and in which a great store of bacon was kept. The negro cabins were small, dilapidated and dingy; the walls were not chinked, and there were no windows—which, indeed, would have been a superfluous luxury, for there were spaces of several inches between the logs, through which there was unobstructed vision. The furniture in the cabins was of the simplest and rudest imaginable kind, two or three beds with dirty clothing upon them, a chest, a wooden stool or two, made with an ax, and some earthenware and cooking apparatus. Every thing within the cabins was colored black by smoke. The chimneys of both the house and the cabins were built of splinters and clay, and on the outer side of the walls. At the door of each cabin were literally "heaps" of babies and puppies, and behind or beside it a pig-stye and poultry coop, a ley-tub and quantities of home-carded cotton placed upon boards to bleach. Within each of them was a woman or two, spinning with the old-fashioned great wheel, and in the kitchen another woman was weaving coarse cotton shirtings with the ancient rude hand-loom. The mistress herself was spinning in the living-room, and asked, when we had grown acquainted, what women at the North could find to do, and how they could ever pass the time, when they gave up spinning and weaving. She made the common every-day clothing for all her family and her servants. They only bought a few "store-goods" for their "dress-up" clothes. She kept the negro girls spinning all through the winter, and at all times when they were not needed in the field. She supposed they would begin to plant corn now in a few days, and then the girls would go to work out of doors. I noticed that all the bed-clothing, the towels, curtains, etc., in the house, were of homespun.

The proprietor, who had been absent on a fishing excursion, during the day, returned at dusk. He was a man of the fat, slow-and-easy style, and proved to be good-natured, talkative and communicative. He had bought the tract of land he now occupied, and moved upon it about ten years before. He had made a large clearing, and could now sell it for a good deal more than he gave for it. He intended to sell whenever he could get a

good offer, and move on West. It was the best land in this part
of the country, and he had got it well fenced, and put up a nice
house: there were a great many people that like to have these
things done for them in advance—and he thought he should not
have to wait long for a purchaser. He liked himself to be clearing land, and it was getting too close settled about here to suit
him. He did not have much to do but to hunt and fish, and the
game was getting so scarce it was too much trouble to go after
it. He did not think there were so many cat in the creek as
there used to be either, but there were more gar-fish. When he
first bought this land he was not worth much—had to run in
debt—had n't but three negroes. Now, he was pretty much out
of debt and owned twenty negroes, seven of them prime field-
hands, and he reckoned I had not seen a better lot anywhere.

During the evening, all the cabins were illuminated by great
fires, and, looking into one of them, I saw a very picturesque
family group; a man sat on the ground making a basket, a woman lounged on a chest in the chimney corner smoking a pipe,
and a boy and two girls sat in a bed which had been drawn up
opposite to her, completing the fireside circle. They were talking and laughing cheerfully.

The next morning when I turned out I found Yazoo looking
with the eye of a connoisseur at the seven prime field-hands,
who at half past seven were just starting off with hoes and axes
for their day's work. As I approached him, he exclaimed with
enthusiasm :

" Are n't them a right keen lookin' lot of niggers ?"

And our host soon after coming out, he immediately walked
up to him, saying :

" Why, friend, them yer niggers o' yourn would be good for

seventy bales of cotton, if you 'd move down into our country."

Their owner was perfectly aware of their value, and said every thing good of them.

" There 's something ruther singlar, too, about my niggers; I do n't know as I ever see any thing like it anywhere else."

" How so, sir ?"

" Well, I reckon it 's my way o' treatin' 'em, much as any thing. I never hev no difficulty with 'em. Hen't licked a nigger in five year, 'cept maybe sprouting some of the young ones sometimes. Fact, my niggers never want no lookin' arter; they jus tek ker o' themselves. Fact, they do tek a greater interest in the crops than I do myself. There 's another thing—I 'spose 't will surprise you—there ent one of my niggers but what can read; read good, too—better 'n I can, at any rate."

" How did they learn ?"

" Taught themselves. I b'lieve there was one on 'em that I bought, that could read, and he taught all the rest. But niggers is mighty apt at larnin', a heap more 'n white folks is."

I said that this was contrary to the generally received opinion.

" Well, now, let me tell you," he continued ; " I had a boy to work, when I was buildin', and my boys jus teachin' him night times and such, he warn't here more 'n three months, and he larned to read as well as any man I ever heerd, and I know he did n't know his letters when he come here. It did n't seem to me any white man could have done that; does it to you, now ?"

" How old was he ?"

" Warn't more 'n seventeen, I reckon."

" How do they get books—do you get them for them ?"

"Oh, no ; get 'em for themselves."

" How ?"

" Buy 'em."

" How do they get the money ?"

" Earn it."

" How ?"

" By their own work.   I tell you my niggers have got more money 'n I hev."

" What kind of books do they get ?"

"Réligious kind a books ginerally—these stories ; and some of them will buy novels, I believe.   They wou't let on to that, but I expect they do it."

They bought them of peddlers.   I inquired about the law to prevent negroes reading, and asked if it allowed books to be sold to negroes.   He had never heard of any such law—did n't be- lieve there was any.   The Yazoo man said there was such a law in his country.   Negroes never had any thing to read there.   I asked our host if his negroes were religious, as their choice of works would have indicated.

"Yes ; all on 'em, I reckon.   Do n't s'pose you 'll believe it, but I tell you it 's a fact ; I haint heerd a swear on this place for a twelvemonth.   They keep the Lord's day, too, right tight, in gineral."

" Our niggers is mighty wicked down in Yallerbush county," said my companion ; " they dance ."

" Dance on Sunday ?" I asked.

" Oh, no, we do n't allow that."

" What do they do then—go to meeting ?"

" Why, Sundays they sleep mostly ; they 've been at work hard all the week, you know, and Sundays they stay in their cabins and sleep and talk to each other. There's so many of 'em together they do n't want to go visiting off the place."

" Are your negroes Baptists or Methodists ?" I inquired of our host.

" All Baptists ; niggers allers want to be ducked, you know. They ain't content to be just titch'd with water ; they must be ducked in all over. There was two niggers jined the Methodists up here last summer, and they made the minister put 'em into the branch ; they would n't jine 'less he 'd duck 'em."

" The Bible says baptize, too," observed Yazoo.

" Well, they think they must be ducked all under, or 't ain't no good."

" Do they go to meeting ?"

" Yes, they hev a meeting among themselves."

" And a preacher ?"

" Yes ; a nigger preacher."

" Our niggers is mighty wicked ; they dance !" repeated Yazoo.

" Do you consider dancing so very wicked, then ." I asked.

" Well, I do n't account so myself, as I know on, but they do you know—the pious people, all kinds, except the 'Piscopers ; some o' them, they do dance themselves, I believe. Do you dance in your country ?"

" Yes."

" What sort of dances—cotillions and reels ?"

" Yes ; what do you ?"

" Well, we dance cotillions and reels too, and we dance on a plank ; that 's the kind of dancin' I like best."

" How is it done ?"

" Why, do n't you know that ? You stand face to face with

your partner on a plank and keep a dancin'. Put the plank up
on two barrel heads, so it 'll kind o' spring. At some of our
parties—that 's among common kind o' people, you know—it 's
great fun. They dance as fast as they can, and the folks all
stand round and holler, ' *Keep it up, John !*' ' *Go it, Nance !*'
' *Do n't give it up so !*' ' *Old Virginny never tire !*' ' *Heel and
toe, ketch a fire !*' and such kind of observations, and clap and
stamp 'em."

"Do your negroes dance much ?"

"Yes, they are mighty fond on 't. Saturday night they dance
all night, and Sunday nights too. Daytime they sleep and rest
themselves, and Sunday nights we let 'em dance and sing if they
want. It does 'em good, you know, to enjoy theirselves."

"They dance to the banjo, I suppose ?"

"Banjos and violins; some of 'em has got violins."

"I like to hear negroes sing," said I.

"Niggers is allers good singers nat'rally," said our host. "I
reckon they got better lungs than white folks, they hev such
powerful voices."

We were sitting at this time on the rail fence at the corner of
a hog-pen and a large, half-cleared field. In that part of this
field nearest the house, among the old stumps, twenty or thirty
small fruit trees had been planted. I asked what sorts they were.

"I do n't know—good kinds tho', I expect ; I bought 'em for
that at any rate."

"Where did you buy them ?"

"I bought 'em of a feller that came a peddlin' round here last
fall ; he said I'd find 'em good."

"What did you pay for them ?"

"A bit apiece."

"That's very cheap, if they 're good for any thing; you are sure they 're grafted, arn't you?"

"Only by what he said—he said they was grafted kinds. I've got a paper in the housen he gin me, tells about 'em; leastways, he said it did. They 's the curosest kinds of trees printed into it you ever heerd on. But I did.not buy none, only the fruit kinds."

Getting off the fence I began to pick about the roots of one of them with my pocket-knife. After exposing the trunk for five or six inches below the surface, I said, "You've planted these too deep, if they 're all like this. You should have the ground dished about it or it won't grow." I tried another, and after picking some minutes without finding any signs of the "collar," I asked if they had all been planted so deeply.

"I do n't know—I told the boys to put 'em in about two feet, and I expect they did, for 'they fancied to have apple-trees growin'."

The catalogue of the tree-peddler, which afterwards came into my possession, quite justified the opinion my host expressed of the kinds of trees described in it. The reader shall judge for himself, and I assure him that the following is a literal transcript of it, omitting the sections headed "Ancebus new," "Camelias," "Rhododendrums," "Bubbs Pæony," "Rosiers," "Wind's flowers of the greatest scarcity," "Bulbous Roots, and of various kinds of graines."

SPECIAL CATALOGUE

OF THE PLANTS, FLOWERS, SHRUBS IMPORTED BY
ROUSSET
MEMBER OF SEVERAL SOCIETIES.

At PARIS (France), boulevard of Hopital, and at CHAMBERY, faubourg de Mache.

Mr Rousset beg to inform they are arrived in this town , with a large assortment of the most rare vegetable plants, either flowerd or fruit bearer, onion bulbous, seeds, &c., &c. Price very moderate.

Their store is situated

CHOIX D'ARBRES A FRUIT.

CHOICE OF FRUIT TREES.
PEAR TREES.

1 Good Louisa from Avranche.
2 Winter's Perfume.
3 Saint-John-in-Iron.
4 Leon-the-Clerc.
5 Bergamot from England.
6 Duchess of Angoulème.
7 Goulu-Morceau.
8 Tarquin Pear.
9 Summer's Good (large) Christian.
10 Good Turkisk Christian.
11 Grey (large) Beurré.
12 Royal Beurré from England.

1 Bon-Chrétien d'été.
2   —   d'hiver.
3   —   de Pâque.
4 Doyenné blanc.
5 Duchesse d'Angora-New.
6 Belle Angevine. fondante.
7 Crassane d hiver.
8 Louise d'Orleans. sucré.
9 Double fleur hâtif.
10 Angélique de Tour.

1 Borgamotte de Milan, gros.
2   —   d'Aiençon, très-gros.
3 Beurré gris d'hiver.
4   —   Amanlis.
5   —   d'Hardenpont, précoce.
6 Fortuné, fondant.
7 Josephine, chair fine.
8 Martin-sec, sucré.
9 Messire, gris.
10 Muscat d'eté.
11 Doyenné d'automne.
12   —   d'hiver, sucré.
13 Virgouleuse fondonte.
14 Bezy-Lamotte.
15 Gros-Blanquet.

APPLES

1 Renetto of Spain.
2   —   Green.

3 Apple Coin.
4   —   Friette.
5 Calville, white, winter's fruit.
6   —   red, autumn's fruit.
7   —   red, winter's fruit.
8 Violet or of the Four-Taste.
9 Renette from England, or Gold Apple.
10 Golded Renette, yellow, backwards plant.
11 White — of a great perfume.
12 Renette, red, winter's fruit.

1 Renette, yellow, hearly fruit.
2   —   grey, very delicate.
3   —   Princess noble.
4 Apple d'Api.
5   —   d'Eve.
6 Winter's Postophe.
7 Plein gney fenouillet. ·
8 Renette franc.
9   —   of St. Laurent.
10 Sammers Numbourg.
11 Belle du Havre.
12 Belle Hollandaise.

1 Violet Apple or of the 4 taste ; the fruit.
    may by preserved 2 years.
2 Princess Renette, of a gold yellow,
    spotted with red of a delicious taste.
3 White Renette from Canada, of which
    the skin is lite scales strange by its
    size.
4 The Cythère Apple.
5 The Caynoite Apple.
6 Apple Trees with double flowers.
    Blooms twice a year, Camélia's
    flowers like.
106 others kinds of Apples of the newest
    choice.

APRICOTS.

1 The Ladie's Apricots.
2 The Peack Apricots.
3 The Royal Apricots.
4 The Gros Muscg Apricots.
5 The Pourret Apricots.
6 Portugal Apricots.

7 Apricats monstruous from America, of a gold yellow, of an enormous size, and of the pine's apple taste

PEACH TREES.

1 Peach Grosse Mignonne.
2 — Bello Beauty.
3 — Godess.
4 — Beauty of Paris.
5 — from Naples! said without stone.
6 Brugnon, musc taste.
7 Admirable ; Belle of Vitry.
8 The Large Royal.
9 Monstruous Pavie.
10 The Cardinal, very forward.
11 Good Workman.
12 Lêtitia Bonaparte.
13 The Prince's Peach, melting in the mouth.
14 The Prince's Peach from Africa, with large white fruit weighing pound and half each ; hearly, new kind
50 others new kinds of Peach Trees.

PLUM TREES.

1 Plum Lamorte
2 Surpasse Monsieur.
3 Damas with musc taste.
4 Royale of Tonrs.
5 Green Gage, of a violet colour.
6 Large Mirabelle.
7 Green Gage. golded.
8 Imperial, of a violet colour.
9 Empress, of a white colour.
10 Ste-Catherine, zellow, suger taste like.

CHERRY TREES.

1 Cherry from the North.
2 — Royal, gives from 18 to 20 cherries weihing one pound, 4 differentes kinds.
3 Cherry Reina Hortense.
4 — Montmorency.
5 — with thort stalk (Gros-Gobet),
6 — Le Mercier.
7 — Four for a pound.
8 Cherry Beauty of Choicy.
9 — The English.
10 Cherry-Duck
11 — Créole with bunches.
12 — Bigarrot or monster of new Mèzel.

CURRANT TREES.

1 Currant Three with red bunches (grapes).
2 — — with white bunches.
3 Gooseberries of 1st choice. (Raspberries) six kinds of alégery.
4 New kind of currants, of which the grapes are as big as the wine grapes.

GRAPES WINES.

1 Chasselas of Fontainebleau, with large gold grains.
2 Chasselas, black very good.
3 — red, of musc teste.
4 Verdal, the swetest and finest fruit for desert.
5 White Muscadine grape, or of Frontignan.
6 Muscat of Alexandrie, musc taste.
7 Cornichon, white, sweet sugar like, very good.
8 Tokay, red and white.
9 Verjus from Bordeaux, large yellow fruit.
10 St. Peter large and fine fruit.
11 Red Muscadine Graper.
12 Raisin of Malaga.
13 The Celestial Wine Mrec, or the amphibious grain, weighing 2 ounces, the grain of a red and violet colour.

NEW STRAWBERRY PLANTS.

1 The Strawberry Cremont.
2 — the Queen.
3 — monster, new kind.
4 — from Clili.
5 Caperon of a raspberry taste.
6 Scarlat from Venose, very forward plant.
7 Prince Albert, fruit of very greatz beauty.
8 Grinston colalant, very large.
9 Rose-Berry, big fruit and of a long form
10 Bath chery, very good.
11 The Big Chinese Strawberry, weihing 16 to a pound, produce fruit all year round, of the pine apple's taste.
12 Vilmoth full.

NEW FIG TREES OF A MONSTRUOUS SIZE.

1 Diodena white, of a large size.
2 Duchess of Maroc, green fruit.
3 Donne-à-Dieu, blue fruit.
4 La Sanspareille, yellow fruit.

The Perpetual Rapsberry Tree, imported from Indies producing a fruit large as an egg, taste delicious 3 kinds, red, violet and white.

The Rapsberry Tree from Fastolff, red fruit, very good of an extraordinary size, very hearly forward plant.

Cherry Currant Tree, with large bunches, it has a great production. Its numerous and long bunches cover entirely the old wood and looks like grapes ; the fruit of a cherry pink colour is very large and of the best quality.

Asparagus from Africa, new kinds, good to eat the same year of their planting (seeds of two years). 1000 varieties of annual and perpetual flower's grains also of kitchen garden grains.

PAULNOVIA INPERIALIS. Magnificent hardy plant from 12 to 15 yards of higth; its leave come to the size of 75 to 80 centimeter and its fine and larg flowers of a fine blue, gives when the spring comes, a soft and agréable perfume.
Besides these plants the amateur will fine at M. ROUSSET, *stores, a great number of other Plants and Fruit Trees of which would be to long to describe.*

NOTICE.

The admirable and strange plant called *Trompette du Jugement* (The Judgment Trompette), of that name having not yet found its classification.

This marvellous plant was send to us from China by the cleuer and courageous botanist collector M. Fortune, from l'Himalaya, near summet of the Chamalari Macon.

This splendid plant deserves the first rank among all kinds of plant wich the botanical science bas produce till now in spite of all the new discoveries.

This búlbous plant gives several stems on the same subject. It grows to the height of 6 feet. It is furnished with flowers from bottom to top. The bud looks by his from like a big cannon ball of a heavenly blue. The center is of an aurora yellewish colour. The vegetation of that plant is to fouitfull that when it is near to blossom it gives a great heat when tassing it in hand and when the bud opens it produces a naite Similar to a pistole shot. Immediately the vegetation takes fire and burns like alcohol about an hour and half. The flowers succeeding one to the other gives the satisfaction of having flowers during 7 or 8 months.

The most intense cold can not hurt this plant and can be culvivated in pots, in apartments or gpeen houses.

Wa call the public attention to this plant as a great curiosity.

Havre—Printed by F. HUE, rue de Paris, 89.

"But come," said the farmer, " go in; take a drink. Breakfast 'll be ready right smart."

" I do n't want to drink before breakfast, thank you."

" Why not?"

" I'm not accustomed to it, and I do n't think it's wholesome."

Not wholesome to drink before breakfast! That was "a new kink" to our jolly host, and troubled him as much as a new "ism" would an old fogy. Not wholesome? He had always reckoned it warn't very wholesome not to drink before breakfast. He did not expect I had seen a great many healthier men than he was, had I? and he always took a drink before breakfast. If a man just kept himself well strung up, without ever stretching himself right tight, he did n't reckon damps or heat would ever do him much harm. He had never had a sick day since he came to this place, and he reckoned that this was owin' considerable to the good rye whiskey he took. It was a healthy trac' of land, though, he believed, a mighty healthy trac'; every thing seemed

to thrive here. We must see a nigger-gal that he was raisin';
she was just coming five, and would pull up nigh upon a hundred
weight.

"Two year ago," he continued, after taking his dram, as we
sat by the fire in the north room, " when I had a carpenter here
to finish off this house, I told one of my boys he must come in
and help him. I reckoned he would larn quick, if he was a mind
to. So he come in, and a week arterwards he fitted the plank
and laid this floor, and now you just look at it; I do n't believe
any man could do it better. That was two year ago, and now
he 's as good a carpenter as you ever see. I bought him some
tools after the carpenter left, and he can do any thing with 'em—
make a table or a chest of drawers or any thing. I think niggers
is somehow nat'rally ingenious; more so 'n white folks. They is
wonderful apt to any kind of slight."

I took out my pocket-map, and while studying it, asked Yazoo
some questions about the route East. Not having yet studied
geography, as he observed, he could not answer. Our host
inquired where I was going, that way. I said I should go on to
Carolina.

"Expect you 're going to buy a rice-farm, in the Carolinies,
aint you? and I reckon you 're up here speckylating arter nigger
stock, aint you now?"

"Well," said I, "I would n't mind getting that fat girl of
yours, if we can make a trade. How much a pound will you sell
her at?"

"We do n't sell niggers by the pound in this country."

"Well, how much by the lump?"

"Well, I do n't know; reckon I do n't keer about sellin' her
just yet."

After breakfast, I inquired about the management of the farm. He said that he purchased negroes, as he was able, from time to time. He grew rich by the improved salable value of his land, arising in part from their labor, and from their natural increase and improvement, for he bought only such as would be likely to increase in value on his hands. He had been obliged to spend but little money, being able to live and provide most of the food and clothing for his family and his people, by the production of his farm. He made a little cotton, which he had to send some distance to be ginned and baled, and then wagoned it seventy miles to a market; also raised some wheat, which he turned into flour at a neighboring mill, and sent to the same market. This transfer engaged much of the winter labor of his man-slaves.

I said that I supposed the Memphis and Charleston railroad, as it progressed east, would shorten the distance to which it would be necessary to draw his cotton, and so be of much service to him. He did not know that. He did not know as he should ever use it. He expected they would charge pretty high for carrying cotton, and his niggers had n't any thing else to do. It did not really cost him any thing now to send it to Memphis, because he had to board the niggers and the cattle anyhow, and they did not want much more on the road than they did at home.

He made a large crop of corn, which, however, was mainly consumed by his own force, and he killed annually about one hundred and fifty hogs, the bacon of which was all consumed in his own family and by his people, or sold to passing travelers. In the fall, a great many drovers and slave-dealers passed over the road with their stock, and they frequently camped against his house, so as to buy corn and bacon of him. This they cooked themselves.

There were sometimes two hundred negroes brought along together, going South. He did n't always have bacon to spare for them, though he killed one hundred and fifty swine. They were generally bad characters, and had been sold for fault by their owners. Some of the slave-dealers were high-minded, honorable men, he thought; " high-toned gentlemen, as ever he saw, some of 'em, was."

Niggers were great eaters, and wanted more meat than white folks ; and he always gave his as much as they wanted, and more too. The negro cook always got dinner for them, and took what she liked for it; his wife did n't know much about it. She got as much as she liked, and he guessed she did n't spare it. When the field-hands were anywhere within a reasonable distance, they always came up to the house to get their dinner. If they were going to work a great way off, they would carry their dinner with them. They did as they liked about it. When they had n't taken their dinner, the cook called them at twelve o'clock with a conch. They ate in the kitchen, and he had the same dinner that they did, right out of the same frying-pan—it was all the same, only they ate in the kitchen, and he ate in the room we were in, with the door open between them.

I brought up the subject of the cost of labor, North and South. He had no apprehension that there would ever be any want of laborers at the South, and could not understand that the ruling price indicated the state of the demand for them. He thought negroes would increase more rapidly than the need for their labor. " Niggers," said he, " breed faster than white folks, a 'mazin' sight, you know ; they begin younger."

" How young do they begin ?"

"Sometimes at fourteen; sometimes at sixteen, and sometimes at eighteen."

"Do you let them marry so young as that?" I inquired. He laughed, and said, "they do n't very often wait to be married."

"When they marry, do they have a minister to marry them?"

"Yes, generally one of their own preachers."

"Do they with you?" I inquired of Yazoo.

"Yes, sometimes they hev a white minister, and sometimes a black one, and if there ar n't neither handy, they get some of the pious ones to marry 'em. But then very often they only just come and ask our consent, and then go ahead, without any more ceremony. They just call themselves married. But most niggers likes a ceremony, you know, and they generally make out to hev one somehow. They do n't very often get married for good, though, without trying each other, as they say, for two or three weeks, to see how they are going to like each other."

I afterwards asked how far it was to the post office. It was six miles. "One of my boys," said our host, "always gets the paper every week. He goes to visit his wife, and passes by the post office every Sunday. Our paper haint come, though, now, for three weeks. The mail do n't come very regular." All of his negroes, who had wives off the place, left an hour before sunset on Saturday evening. One of them, who had a wife twenty miles away, left at twelve o'clock Saturday, and got back at twelve o'clock Monday.

"We had a nigger once," said Yazoo, "that had a wife fifteen miles away, and he used to do so; but he did some rascality once, and he was afraid to go again. He told us his wife was so far off, 't was too much trouble to go there, and he believed he 'd give her up. We was glad of it. He was a darned rascally nigger—allers getting into scrapes.   One time we sent him to mill, and he went round into town and sold some of the meal.   The storekeeper would n't pay him for 't, 'cause he had n't got an order.   The next time we were in town, the storekeeper just showed us the bag of meal;—said he reckoned 't was stole; so when we got home we just tied him up to the tree and licked him.   He's a right smart nigger; rascally niggers allers is smart.   I'd rather have a rascally nigger than any other—they's so smart allers.   He is about the best nigger we've got."

"I have heard," said I, "that religious negroes were generally the most valuable.   I have been told that a third more would be given for a man if he were religious.   "Well, I never heerd of it before," said he.   Our host thought there was no difference in the market value of sinners and saints.

"Only," observed Yazoo, "the rascalier a nigger is, the better he'll work.   Now that yer nigger I was tellin' you on, he's worth more 'n any other nigger we've got.   He's a yaller nigger."

I asked their opinion as to the comparative value of black and yellow negroes.   Our host had two bright mulatto boys among his—did n't think there was much difference, "but allers reckoned yellow fellows was the best a little; they worked smarter. He would rather have them."   Yazoo would not; he "did n't think but what they'd work as well; but he did n't fancy yellow negroes 'round him; would rather have real black ones."

I asked our host if he had no foreman or driver for his negroes, or if he gave his directions to one of them in particular for all the rest.   He did not.   They all did just as they pleased, and arranged the work among themselves.   They never needed driving.

"If I ever notice one of 'em getting a little slack, I just talk to him ; tell him we must get out of the grass, and I want to hev him stir himself a little more, and then, maybe, I slip a dollar into his hand, and when he gits into the field he'll go ahead, and the rest seeing him, won't let themselves be distanced by him. My niggers never want no lookin' arter. They tek more interest in the crop than I do myself, every one of 'em."

Religious, instructed, and seeking further enlightenment ; industrious, energetic, and self directing ; well fed, respected, and trusted by their master, and this master an illiterate, indolent and careless man! A very different state of things, this, from what I saw on the great cotton planter's estate, where a profit of $100,000 was made in a single year, but where five hundred negroes were constantly kept under the whip, where religion was only a pow-wow or cloak for immorality, and where the negro was considered to be of an inferior race, especially designed by Providence to be kept in the position he there occupied! A very different thing ; and strongly suggesting what a very different thing this negro servitude might be made in general, were the ruling disposition of the South more just, democratic, and sensible.

About half past eleven, a stage coach, which had come earlier in the morning from the East, and had gone on as far as the brook, returned, having had our baggage transferred to it from the one we had left on the other side. In the transfer a portion of my baggage was omitted and never recovered. Up to this time our host had not paid the smallest attention to any work his men were doing, or even looked to see if they had fed the cattle, but had lounged about, sitting upon a fence, chewing tobacco, and talking with us, evidently very glad to have somebody to converse with. He went in once again, after a drink; showed us the bacon he had in his smoke-house, and told a good many stories of his experience in life, about a white man's "dying hard" in the neighborhood, and of a tree falling on a team with which one of his negroes was plowing cotton, "which was lucky"—that is, that it did not kill the negro—and a good deal about "hunting" when he was younger and lighter.

Still embarrassed by an old idea which I had brought to the South with me, I waited, after the coach came in sight, for Yazoo to put the question, which he presently did, boldly enough.

"Well; reckon we're goin' now.   What's the damage?"

"Well; reckon seventy-five cents 'll be right."

CHAPTER IV.

THE INTERIOR COTTON DISTRICTS.

I HAVE considered the condition and prospects of the white race in the South a much more important subject, and one, at this time, much more in want of exposition than that of the African. But the great difference in the mode of life of the slaves when living on large plantations, and when living on farms or in town establishments, or on such small plantations that they are intimately associated with white families, has seemed to me to have been so much overlooked by writers, that I have departed widely from the narrative with which this volume commenced, and drawn from my traveling notes of a previous year, to more fully display it.

Continuing the horseback journey commenced in the rich cotton-bearing soils which border the Mississippi river, I turned eastward, not far above Natchez, and pursued an indirect route towards Tuscaloosa in Alabama. The country grew less fertile, and the plantations smaller. The number of whites (not of negroes), living upon plantations of the class chiefly described thus far in this volume (and in two instances, at length, in my first volume), is, of course, small. The more common sort of plantations and the common middle-class planter, can hardly be seen by a tourist in any other way than that I now pursued, traveling in the interior, away from the rivers and the ordinary lines of communication, and independently of public conveyances; there is consequently ·less general knowledge of them, I apprehend, than of any other portion of the population of the South, yet of the class properly termed "the planters" they constitute probably nine tenths.

The price of "improved" plantation land varies from five to ten dollars per acre, according to its fertility and the vicinity to a market; near large towns only does it command more.*   As the richest soils are in the lowest situations—frequently on the borders of marshes and streams—the most productive plantations are seldom healthy, and their proprietors very generally live for a part of the summer, I am informed, in the neighboring towns, where they constitute congenial society for each other.   Comparatively few of the towns, however, are thus favored; all that I saw in central Mississippi, with the exception of Jackson,† the capital, were forlorn, poverty-stricken collections of shops, groggeries, and lawyers' offices, mingled with unsightly and usually dilapidated dwelling-houses.   Moreover, I found that many a high sounding name (figuring on the same maps in which towns

* "The value of the best cotton plantations on the uplands of Natchez, is about £4 an acre, which is little more than half that which soils of similar quality are worth in Canada West."—*North America: its Agriculture, etc.,* page 271.

† The capital is a rather fine town externally.   At the principal hotel, in some departments of which there is the usual "first-class" regal magnificence, napkins, silver-plated forks and candelabra, there was, at the time of my visit, and, as I learn from a recent traveler, there is still no *cabinet d'aisance.*   On inquiring for it, I was advised by the landlord himself to go to a cypress swamp, perhaps a quarter of a mile distant, and there was evidence enough that this was daily resorted to for the purpose, not only by the other guests of the hotel, but by a large portion of the inhabitants of the town.   The reader need be under no fear of drawing a false inference from this fact, with regard to the degree in which the South generally is possessed of all modern civilized convenience.

of five thousand inhabitants in New England, New York, and
Pennsylvania, are omitted), indicated the locality of merely a
grocery or two, a blacksmith shop, and two or three log cabins.
I passed through two of these map towns without knowing that
I had reached them, and afterwards ascertained that one of them
consisted of a deserted blacksmith shop, and a cabin in which the
post-master lived, and the other, of a single grocery.

The majority of the interior plantations which came under my
observation belong to resident planters, and are from four hundred
to one thousand acres in extent, the average being perhaps six
hundred acres.* The number of negroes on each varies from ten
to forty, more frequently being between twenty and thirty.
Where there are fewer than ten negroes, the owners are frequently seen holding a plow among them ; where there are over
twenty, a white overseer is usually employed, the owner perhaps
directing, but seldom personally superintending, the field labor.

The characteristics of this latter class of cotton-planters vary
much. I shall, I think, be generally rightly understood if I
say that the majority of them possess more dignity of bearing
and manner, that they give a stranger an impression of greater
" respectability" than the middle class of farmers at the North
and in England, while they have less general information and
less active and inquiring minds. The class of farmers in New
England and New York, with whom I compare them, have rarely received any education beyond that of the public schools,
which, in the last generation, afforded a very meager modicum

---

* When the largest share of the labor is not intended to be applied to the
cotton crop, but is divided among various crops, as is usually the case where
less than four hundred acres are held in possession by the proprietor, I term
the enterprise a farm in distinction from a plantation.

of instruction. The planters of whom I speak, I judge to have usually spent a short time at boarding-schools or institutions of a somewhat superior order to the common, or " primary" schools of the country—but their acquisition of knowledge subsequently to their school-days by newspapers and books, and by conversation, has been very small.

It is frequently the case, however, that the planter has started as a poor, and entirely self-dependent young man, the basis of whose present fortune consisted of his savings from the wages earned by him as overseer—these are commonly as illiterate as the very poorest of our northern agricultural laborers. Yet again there are those who, beginning in the same way, have acquired, while so employed, not only a capital with which to purchase land and slaves, but a valuable stock of experience and practical information, and somewhat of gentlemanly bearing from intercourse with their employers. In respect to the enjoyment of material comforts, and the exercise of taste in the arrangement of their houses and grounds, the condition of these planters, while it is superior to that of the Texans, is far below that of northern farmers of one quarter their wealth. But an acquaintance with their style of living can only be obtained from details, and these I shall again give by extracts from my journal, showing how I chanced to be entertained night after night, premising that I took no little pains to select the most comfortable quarters in the neighborhood which I reached at the close of the day. To avoid repetition, I will merely say with regard to diet, that bacon, corn-bread and coffee invariably appeared at every meal ; but, besides this, either at breakfast or supper, a fried fowl, " biscuit" of wheat flour, with butter were added—the biscuit invariably made heavy, doughy and indigestible with shortening (fat), and brought to table in relays, to be eaten as hot as possible with melting butter. Molasses usually, honey frequently, and, as a rare exception, potatoes and green peas were added to the board. Whiskey was seldom offered me, and only once any other beverage except the abominable preparation which passes for coffee.

Until I reached the softly rounded hills, with occasional small prairies, through which flows the Tombigbee, in the eastern part of the State, the scenery was monotonous and somber. The predominating foliage is that of the black-oak, black-jack, and pine, except in the intervale lands, where the profuse and bright-colored vegetation common to the latitude is generally met with in great variety.

Last of May. Yesterday was a raw, cold day, wind north-east, like a dry north-east storm at home. Fortunately I came to the pleasantest house and household I had seen for some time. The proprietor was a native of Maryland, and had traveled in the North; a devout Methodist, and somewhat educated. He first came South, as I understood, for the benefit of his health, his lungs being weak. The climate here is very mild; lung complaints, though not infrequent, not nearly as common as in Maryland. Of a number of northern people whom he had known to come here with consumption, only one or two had recovered. There are several in the country now, he said, young women teaching school. This immediate locality, he considered very healthy; he had a family (including about fifteen negroes) of twenty, and had never been visited by any sickness more serious than chills and fever ; but on lower and richer ground, they suffered much from typhus fever, pneumonia, and malignant typhus.

His first dwelling, a rude log cabin, was still standing, and was occupied by some of his slaves. The new house, a cottage, consisting of four rooms and a hall, stood in a small grove of oaks ; the family were quiet, kind, and sensible.

When I arrived, the oldest boy was at work, holding a plow in the cotton-field, but he left it and came at once, with confident and affable courtesy, to entertain me.

My host had been in Texas, and after exploring it quite thoroughly, concluded that he much preferred to remain where he was. He found no part of that country where good land, timber, and a healthy climate were combined : in the west he did not like the vicinage of the Germans and Mexicans ; moreover, he did n't "fancy" a prairie country. Here, in favorable years, he got a bale of cotton to the acre. Not so much now as formerly. Still, he said, the soil would be good enough for him here, for many years to come.

I said that he was a Methodist ; he was also an extreme proslavery man. He had seen in his religious newspaper an account of Mr. Fillmore's being shown a large Alabama plantation on a Sunday ; Mr. Fillmore had expressed himself highly delighted and surprised with the manner in which the slaves were taken care of, being obliged to attend church, etc. He hoped it would do Mr. Fillmore good. He had been opposed to him in politics, and he doubted now if he could be trusted. They would try to make him President again, he supposed, for they were working hard to make the South think him her friend. There was no knowing about any thing of that kind now. There was New York, my State, who could tell any thing about her now-a-days ? It seemed to him she was controlled by fanatics, demagogues, and foreigners, who were purchased by the highest bidder; she was no more to be depended upon than a weathercock. One year she pointed one way, the next, directly opposite. The South could no more depend on the Democrats than on the Whigs in New York, that was his opinion.

I went five times to the stable without being able to find the servant there. I was always told that "the boy" would feed my horse, and take good care of him, when he came; and so at length I had to go to bed, trusting to this assurance. I went out just before breakfast and found the horse with only ten *dry* cobs in the manger. I searched for the boy; could not find him, but was told that my horse had been fed. I said, "I wish to have him fed more—as much as he will eat." Very well, the boy should give him more. When I went out after breakfast, the boy was leading out the horse. I asked if he had given him corn this morning.

"Oh, yes sir."

"How many ears did you give him?"

"Ten or fifteen—or sixteen, sir; he eats very hearty."

I went into the stable and saw that he had had no more, *i. e.*, after the feed of the evening; there were the same ten cobs (dry) in the manger. I doubted, indeed, from their appearance, if the boy had fed him at all the night before. I fed him with leaves myself, but could not get into the corn crib. The proprietor was, I do not doubt, perfectly honest, but very likely the negro stole the corn for his own hogs and fowls.

The next day I rode more than thirty miles, having secured a good feed of corn for the horse at mid-day. At nightfall I was much fatigued, but had as yet failed to get lodging. It began to rain and grow dark, and I kept the road with difficulty. Finally, about nine o'clock, I came to a large, comfortable house.

An old lady sat in the verandah, of whom I asked if I could be accommodated for the night : " Reckon so," she replied ; then after a few moments' reflection, without rising from her chair she shouted, " Gal !—gal !" Presently a girl came.

" Missis ?"

" Call Tom !"

The girl went off, while I remained, waiting for a more definite answer. At length she returned : " Tom ain't there, missis."

" Who is there ?"

" Old Pete."

" Well, tell him to come and take this gentleman's horse."

Pete came, and I went with him to the gate where I had fastened my horse. Here he called for some younger slave to come and take him down to the pen, while he took off the saddle.

All this time it was raining, but any rapidity of movement was out of the question. Pete continued shouting. " Why not lead the horse to the pen yourself ?" I asked. " I must take care of de saddle and tings, massa ; tote 'em to de house whar dey 'll be safe. Dese niggers is so treacherous can't leave nothin' roun' but dey 'll hook suthing off of it."

Next morning, at dawn of day, I saw honest Pete come into the room where I was in bed and go stealthily to his young master's clothes, probably mistaking them for mine. I moved, and he dropped them, and slunk out to the next room, where he went loudly to making a fire. I managed to see Belshazzar well fed night and morning.

There were three pretty young women in this house, of good manners and well dressed, except for the abundance of rings and jewelry which they displayed at breakfast. I've no doubt they had enjoyed the advantages of some "Institute," where they had been put clean through from "the elementary studies" to "Wax-work and *Watts on the Mind.*" One of them surprised me, therefore, not a little at the table. I had been offered, in succession, fried ham and eggs, sweet potatoes, apple-pie, corn-bread, boiled eggs, and molasses; this last article I declined, and passed it to the young lady opposite, looking to see how it was to be used. She had, on a breakfast plate, fried ham and eggs and apple-pie, and poured molasses between them.

June —. I stopped last evening at the house of a man who was called "Doctor" by his family, but who was, to judge from his language, very illiterate. His son, by whom I was first received, followed me to the stable. He had ordered a negro child to lead my horse, but as I saw the little fellow could n't hold him I went myself. He had no fodder (corn-leaves), and proposed to give the horse some shucks (corn-husks) dipped in salt water, and, as it was now too late to go further, I assented. Belshazzar licked them greedily, but would not eat them, and they seemed to destroy his appetite for corn, for late in the evening, having groped my way into the stable, I found seven small ears of corn, almost un-tasted, in the manger. I got the young man to come out and give him more.

The "Doctor" returned from "a hunt," as he said, with no game but a turtle, which he had taken from a "trot line"—a line, with hooks at intervals, stretched across the river.

The house was large, and in a good-sized parlor or common

room stood a handsome center-table, on which were a few books and papers, mostly Baptist publications. I sat here alone in the evening, straining my eyes to read a wretchedly-printed newspaper, till I was offered a bed. I was very tired and sleepy, having been ill two nights before. A physician, whom I had been obliged to consult, informed me that severe illness was frequently occasioned here by an exposure of the abdomen to the cool night air, an accident to which the irritation of insects must often subject sleepers. The bed was apparently clean, and I embraced it with pleasure.

My host, holding a candle for me to undress by, (there was no candlestick in the house,) called to a boy on the outside to fasten the doors, which he did by setting articles of furniture against them. When I had got into bed he went himself into an inner room, the door of which he closed and fastened in the same manner. No sooner was the light withdrawn than I was attacked by bugs. I was determined, if possible, not to be kept awake by them, but they soon conquered me. I never suffered such incessant and merciless persecution from them before. In half an hour I was nearly frantic, and leaped out of bed. But what to do? There was no use in making a disturbance about it: doubtless every other bed and resting place in the house was full of them. I shook out my day clothes carefully and put them on, and then pushing away the barricade, opened the door and went into the parlor. At first I thought that I would arrange the chairs in a row and sleep on them; but this I found impracticable, for the seats of the chairs were too narrow, and moreover of deerskin, which was sure to be full of fleas if not of bugs. Stiff and sore and weak, I groaningly lay down where the light of the moon came through a broken window, for bugs feed but little except in darkness, and with my saddle-bags for a pillow, again essayed to sleep. Fleas! instantly. I rolled and scratched for hours. There was nothing else to be done; I was too tired to sit up, even if that would have effectually removed the annoyance. Finally I dozed—not long, I think, for I was suddenly awakened by a large insect dropping upon my eye. I struck it off, and at the moment it stung me. My eyelid swelled immediately, and grew painful, but at length I slept in spite of it. I was once more awakened by a large beetle which fell on me from the window; once more I got asleep, till finally at four o'clock I awoke with that dryness of the eyes which indicates a determination of the system to sleep no more. It was daylight, and I was stiff and shivering; the inflammation and pain of the sting in my eyelid had in a great degree subsided. I put on my boots and hat, pushed back the bolt of the outside door-lock with my thumb, and went to the stable. The negroes were already at work in the field. Belshazzar had had nearly as bad a place to sleep in as I; the floor of the stall, being of earth, had been trodden into two hollows at each end, leaving a small rough hillock in the center. Bad as it was, however, it was the best in the stable; only one in four of the stalls having a manger that was not broken down. A little black girl and boy were cleaning their master's horses—mine they were afraid of. They had put some fresh corn in his manger, however, and as he refused to eat I took a curry-comb and brush, and for the next two hours gave him the first thorough grooming he had enjoyed since I owned him. I could not detect the reason of his loss of appetite. I had been advised by an old southern traveler to examine the corn when my horse refused to eat—if corn were high I might find that it had been greased. From the actions of the horse, then and subsequently, I suspect some trick of this kind was here practiced upon me. When I returned to the house and asked to wash, water was given me in a vessel which, though I doubted the right of my host to a medical diploma, certainly smelt strongly of the shop—it was such as is used by apothecaries in mixing drugs. The title of doctor is often popularly given at the South to druggists and venders of popular medicines; very probably he had been one, and had now retired to enjoy the respectability of a planter.

June ——.—I saddled and rode on immediately after breakfast; but as soon as the dew had dried off the grass, and I could find an abandoned plantation, I turned aside from the road and wandered through the old fields till I came upon a thicket of broad-leafed black-jacks, with glades of grass only a little broken by bushes. I then unsaddled, and fastening Belshazzar with a lariat, where he could either graze or lie in the shade of a pine tree, I laid my blanket on the ground among the black-jacks, and in two minutes was rapidly overtaking my lost night's rest.

Awakening suddenly, I find that Belshazzar, his rope stretched to its utmost tension, has got close to me, and stands strongly braced, with nostrils dilated, eyes and ears bent on the swamp below us, where a pack of hounds are rushing past in full frantic cry. Gradually the music dies away in the distance; we see nothing of deer, or fox, or nigger, hounds or huntsmen. Belshazzar returns to feed, and Jude coils down to sleep again upon her form. But I have slept enough; so I wash myself from canteen and get dinner, write up my journal, and am off again.

A PIOUS SLAVE.

Soon I met a very ragged old negro, of whom I asked the way, and at what house within twelve miles I had better stop. He advised me to go to one more than twelve miles distant.

"I suppose," said I, "I can stop at any house along the road here, can't I? They'll all take in travelers?"

"Yes, sir, if you'll take rough fare, such as travelers has to, sometimes. They're all dam'd rascals along dis road, for ten or twelve miles, and you'll git nothin' but rough fare. But I say, massa, rough fare's good enough for dis world; ain't it, massa? Dis world ain't nothin'; dis is hell, dis is, I calls it; hell to what's a comin' arter, ha! ha! Ef you's prepared? you says. I do n't look much 's if I was prepared, does I? nor talk like it, nuther. De Lord he cum to me in my cabin in de night time, in de year '45."

"What?"

"De Lord! massa, de bressed Lord! He cum to me in ae night time, in de year '45, and he says to me, says he, 'I'll spare you yet five year longer, old boy!' So when '50 cum round I thought my time had cum, sure; but as I did n't die, I reckon de Lord has 'cepted of me, and I 'specs I shall be saved, dough I do n't look much like it, ha! ha! ho! ho! de Lord am my rock, and he shall not perwail over me. I will lie down in green pastures and take up my bed in hell, yet will not his mercy circumwent me. Got some tobaccy, master?"

A little after sunset I came to an unusually promising plantation, the dwelling being within a large inclosure, in which there was a well-kept southern sward shaded by fine trees. The house, of the usual form, was painted white, and the large number of neat out-buildings seemed to indicate opulence, and, I thought, unusual good taste in its owner. A lad of sixteen received me, and said I could stay; I might fasten my horse, and when the negroes came up he would have him taken care of. When I had done so, and had brought the saddle to the verandah, he offered me a chair, and at once commenced a conversation in the character of entertainer. Nothing in his tone or manner would have indicated that he was not the father of the family, and proprietor of the establishment. No prince royal could have had more assured and nonchalant dignity. Yet a northern stable-boy, or apprentice, of his age, would seldom be found as ignorant.

"Where do you live, sir, when you are at home?" he asked.

"At New York."

"New York is a big place, I expect?"

"Yes, very big."

'Big as New Orleans, is it?"

"Yes, much bigger."

"Bigger 'n New Orleans? It must be a bully city."

"Yes; the largest in America."

"Sickly there now, sir?"

"No, not now; it is sometimes."

"Like New Orleans, I suppose, sir?"

"No, never so bad as New Orleans sometimes is."

"Right healthy place, I expect?"

"Yes, I believe so, for a place of its size."

"What diseases do you have there, sir?"

"All sorts of diseases—not so much fever, however, as you have here."

"Measles and hooping cough, sometimes, I reckon?"

"Yes, 'most all the time, I dare say."

"All the time! People must die there right smart. Some is dyin' 'most every day, I expect?"

"More than a hundred every day, I suppose."

"Gosh! a hundred every day! Almighty sickly place 't must be?"

"I do n't think it is any more sickly than it is here. It is such a large place, you see—seven hundred thousand people."

"Seven hundred thousand—expect that 's a heap of people, aint it?"

His father, a portly, well-dressed man, soon came in, and learning that I had been in Mexico, said, "I suppose there 's a heap of Americans flocking in and settling up that country along on the line, ain't there, sir?"

"No, sir, very few. I saw none, in fact—only a few Irishmen and Frenchmen, who called themselves Americans. Those were the only foreigners I saw, except negroes."

"Niggers! Where were they from?"

"They were runaways from Texas."

"But their masters go there and get them again, do n't they?"

"No, sir, they can 't."

"Why not?"

"The Mexicans are friendly to the niggers, and protect them."

"But why not go to the government?"

"The government considers them as free, and will not let them be taken back."

"But that 's stealing, that is; just the same as stealing, sir. Why do n't our government make them deliver them up? What good is the government to us if it do n't preserve the rights of property, sir? Niggers are property, ain't they? and if a man steals my property, ain't the government bound to get it for me?

Niggers are property, the same as horses and cattle, and nobody's any more right to help a nigger that's run away than he has to steal a horse."

He spoke very angrily, and was excited. Perhaps he was indirectly addressing me, as a northern man, on the general subject of fugitive slaves. I said that it was necessary to have special treaty stipulations about such matters. The Mexicans lost their *peons*—bounden servants; they ran away to our side, but the United States government never took any measures to restore them, nor did the Mexicans ask it. " But," he answered, in a tone of indignation, " those are not niggers, are they ? They are white people, just as white as the Mexicans themselves, and just as much right to be free."

My horse stood in the yard till quite dark, the negroes not coming in from the cotton-field. I proposed twice to take him to the stable, but was told not to—the niggers would come up soon and attend to him. Just as we were called to supper, the negroes began to make their appearance, getting over a fence with their hoes, and the master called to one to put the horse in the stable, and to " take good care of him." " I want him to have all the corn he'll eat," said I. " Yes, sir—feed him well ; do you hear, there ?"

The house was meagerly furnished within, not nearly as well as the most common New England farm-house. I saw no books and no decorations. The interior wood-work was unpainted.

At supper there were three negro girls in attendance—two children of twelve or fourteen years of age, and an older one, but in a few moments they all disappeared. The mistress called aloud several times, and at length the oldest came bringing in hot biscuit.

" Where 's Suke and Bet ?"

" In the kitchen, missus."

" Tell them both to come to me, right off."

A few minutes afterwards, one of the girls slunk in and stood behind me, at the furthest point from her mistress. Presently she was discovered.

" You, Bet, are you there ? Come here ! come here to me ! close to me ! (*Slap, slap, slap.*) Now, why do n't you stay in here ? (*Slap, slap, slap*, on the side of the head.) I know ! you want to be out in the kitchen with them Indians ! (*Slap, slap, slap.*) Now see if you can stay here." (*Slap !*) The other girl did n't come in at all, and was forgotten.

As soon as supper was over my hostess exclaimed, " Now, you Bet, stop crying there, and do you go right straight home ; mind you run every step of the way, and if you stop one minute in the kitchen you 'd better look out. Begone !" During the time I was in the house she was incessantly scolding the servants, in a manner very disagreeable for me to hear, though they seemed to regard it very little.

The Indians, I learned, lived some miles away, and were hired to hoe cotton. I inquired their wages. " Well, it costs me about four bits (fifty cents) a day," (including food, probably). They worked well for a few days at a time ; were better at picking than at hoeing. " They do n't pick so much in a day as niggers, but do it better." The women said they were good for nothing, and her husband had no business to plant so much cotton that he could n't 'tend it with his own slave hands.

While at table a young man, very dirty and sweaty, with a ragged shirt and no coat on, came in to supper. He was surly and rude in his actions, and did not speak a word ; he left the table before I had finished, and lighting a pipe, laid himself at full length on the floor of the room to smoke. This was the overseer.

Immediately after supper the master told me he was in the habit of going to bed early, and he would now show me to my room. He did so, and left me alone without a candle. It was dark, and I did not know the way to the stables, so I soon went to bed. On a feather bed I did not enjoy much rest, and when I at last awoke and dressed, breakfast was just ready. I said I would go first to look after my horse, and did so, the master following me. I found him standing in a miserable stall, in a sorry state; he had not been cleaned, and there were no cobs or other indications of his having been fed at all since he had been there. I said to my host:

"He has not been fed, sir!"

"I wonder! hain't he? Well, I'll have him fed. I s'pose the overseer forgot him."

But, instead of going to the crib and feeding him at once himself, he returned to the house and blew a horn for a negro; when one came in sight from the cotton-fields, he called to him to go to the overseer for the key of the corn-crib and feed the gentleman's horse, and asked me to now come to breakfast. The overseer soon joined us as at supper; nothing was said to him about my horse, and he was perfectly silent, and conducted himself like an angry or sulky man in all his actions. As before, when he had finished his meal, without waiting for others to leave the table, he lighted a pipe and lay down to rest on the floor. I went to the stable and found my horse had been supplied with seven ears of corn only. I came back to ask for more, but could find neither master nor overseer. While I was packing my saddle-bags preparatory to leaving, I heard my host call a negro to "clean that gentleman's horse and bring him here." As it was late, I did not interpose. While I was putting on the bridle, he took off the musketo tent attached to the saddle and examined it. I told him why I carried it.

"You won't want it any more,"said he; "no musketoes of any account where you are going; you'd better give it to me, sir, I should like to use it when I go a-fishing; musketoes are powerful bad in the swamp." After some further solicitation, as I seldom used it, I gave it to him. Almost immediately afterwards he charged me a dollar for my entertainment, which I paid, notwithstanding the value of the tent was several times that amount. Hospitality to travelers is so entirely a matter of business with the common planters.

I passed the hoe-gang at work in the cotton-field, the overseer lounging among them carrying a whip; there were ten or twelve of them; none looked up at me. Within ten minutes I passed five who were plowing, with no overseer or driver in sight, and every one stopped their plows to gaze at me.

I reached a village before noon, and as I was confident the negro had neglected to feed my horse the evening previous, I stopped' and bought some oats for him, which he ate with great avidity. Oats is a fodder crop here only; no grain is ever threshed out except for seed. A negro in the stable asked if I was "gwine on Tuscaloosy way?"

"Yes."

"Oh, I wish I could go wid you."

"Why, have you friends there?"

"I has dat, both black and white. Does you live in Tuscaloosy, massa?"

" No, I live at the North, in New York."

" At the North ! Oh, dat's de country for to live in. Wish I could go dar wid you, right now. Dat's de country ; a man can live dar, and a nigger too, and no devilishness dar 'cept what a man does to hisself."

He was born in Virginia, owned in Tuscaloosa, and was hired out to a man here. He did not like this place at all, but would rather live here than go any "further down." He seemed to have great dread of going "further down" (South).

" Why ?"

" Niggers does n't have no Sunday dar, massa. Niggers has to work and white folks has muster ; dey drums and fifes de whole bressed day ; dat yer 'll sound strange on a Sunday to a northern man, eh ?"

I told him I did n't think it was so. He did n't know, but so the niggers here had told him. A report of steamboat negroes from New Orleans and the sugar districts, probably.

A MISSISSIPPI SLAVEHOLDING ABOLITIONIST.

Yesterday I met a well-dressed man upon the road, and inquired of him if he could recommend me to a comfortable place to pass the night.

" Yes, I can," said he ; " you stop at John Watson's. He is a real good fellow, and his wife is a nice, tidy woman ; he 's got a good house, and you 'll be as well taken care of there as in any place I know."

" What I am most concerned about is a clean bed," said I.

" Well, you are safe for that, there."

So distinct a recommendation was unusual, and when I reached the house he had described to me, though it was not yet dark, I stopped to solicit entertainment.

In the gallery sat a fine, stalwart man, and a woman who in size and figure matched him well. Some ruddy, fat children were playing on the steps. The man wore a full beard, which is very uncommon in these parts. I rode to a horse-block near the gallery, and asked if I could be accommodated for the night. " Oh, yes, you can stay here if you can get along without any thing to eat ; we do n't have any thing to eat but once a week." " You look as if it agreed with you ; I reckon I 'll try it for one night." " Alight, sir, alight. Why, you came from Texas, did n't you ? Your rig looks like it," he said, as I dismounted. " Yes, I 've just crossed Texas, all the way from the Rio Grande." " Have you, though ? Well, I 'll be right glad to hear something of that country." He threw my saddle and bags across the rail of the gallery, and we walked together to the stable.

" I hear that there are a great many Germans in the western part of Texas," he said presently.

" There are a great many ; west of the Gaudaloupe, more Germans than Americans born."

" Have they got many slaves ?"

" No."

" Well, won't they break off and make a free State down there, by and by ?"

" I should think it not impossible that they might."

" I wish to God they would ; I would like right well to go and settle there if it was free from slavery. You see Kansas and all the free States are too far north for me ; I was raised in Alabama, and I do n't want to move into a colder climate ; but I would like to go into a country where they had not got this curse of slavery."

He said this not knowing that I was a northern man; greatly surprised, I asked, "What are your objections to slavery, sir ?"

"Objections! The first's here," (striking his breast;) " I never could bring myself to like it. Well, sir, I know slavery is wrong, and God'll put an end to it. It's bound to come to an end, and when the end does come, there'll be woe in the land. And, instead of preparing for it, and trying to make it as light as possible, we are doing nothing but make it worse and worse. That's the way it appears to me, and I'd rather get out of these parts before it comes. Then I've another objection to it. I do n't like to have slaves about me. Now, I tell a nigger to go and feed your horse; I never know if he's done it unless I go and see; and if he did n't know I would go and see, and would whip him if I found he had n't fed him, would he feed him ? He 'd let him starve. I 've got as good niggers as anybody, but I never can depend on them; they will lie, and they will steal, and take advantage of me in every way they dare. Of course they will if they are slaves. But lying and stealing are not the worst of it. I 've got a family of children, and I do n't like to have such degraded beings round my house while they are growing up. I know what the consequences are to children, of growing up among slaves."

I here told him that I was a northern man, and asked if he could safely utter such sentiments among the people of this district, who bore the reputation of being among the most extreme and fanatical devotees of slavery. " I 've been told a hundred times I should be killed if I were not more prudent in expressing my opinions, but, when it comes to killing, I 'm as good as the

next man, and they know it. I never came the worst out of a
fight yet since I was a boy. I never am afraid to speak what I
think to anybody. I do n't think I ever shall be."

" Are there many persons here who have as bad an opinion of
slavery as you have ?"

" I reckon you never saw a conscientious man who had been
brought up among slaves who did not think of it pretty much as
I do—did you ?"

" Yes, I think I have, a good many."

" Ah, self-interest warps men's minds wonderfully, but I do n't
believe there are many who do n't think so, sometimes—it 's impossible, I know, that they do n't."

Were there any others in this neighborhood, I asked, who
avowedly hated slavery ? He replied that there were a good
many mechanics, all the mechanics he knew, who felt slavery to
be a great curse to them, and who wanted to see it brought to an
end in some way. The competition in which they were constantly made to feel themselves engaged with slave-labor was degrading to them, and they felt it to be so. He knew a poor, hard-
working man who was lately offered the services of three negroes
for six years each if he would let them learn his trade, but he
refused the proposal with indignation, saying he would starve before he helped a slave to become a mechanic.* There was a

---

* At Wilmington, North Carolina, on the night of the 27th of July (1857,)
the frame-work of a new building was destroyed by a number of persons
and a placard attached to the disjointed lumber, stating that a similar course
would be pursued in all cases, against edifices that should be erected by negro contractors or carpenters, by one of which class of men the house had
been constructed. There was a public meeting called a few days afterwards,
to take this outrage into consideration, which was numerously attended.
Resolutions were adopted, denouncing the act, and the authorities were in-

good deal of talk now among them about getting laws passed to prevent the owners of slaves from having them taught trades, and to prohibit slave-mechanics from being hired out. He could go out to-morrow, he supposed, and in the course of a day get two hundred signatures to a paper alleging that slavery was a curse to the people of Mississippi, and praying the Legislature to take measures to relieve them of it as soon as practicable. (The county contains three times as many slaves as whites.)

He considered a coercive government of the negroes by the whites, forcing them to labor systematically, and restraining them from a reckless destruction of life and property, at present to be necessary. Of course, he did not think it wrong to hold slaves, and the profits of their labor were not more than enough to pay a man for looking after them—not if he did his duty to them. What was wrong, was making slavery so much worse than was necessary. Negroes would improve very rapidly, if they were allowed, in any considerable measure, the ordinary incitements to improvement. He knew hosts of negroes who showed extraordinary talents, considering their opportunities: there were a great many in this part of the country who could read and write, and calculate mentally as well as the general run of white men who had been to schools. There were Colonel ———'s negroes, some fifty of them; he did not suppose there were any fifty

structed to offer a suitable reward for the detection and conviction of the rioters. "The impression was conveyed at the meeting," says the Wilmington Herald, "that the act had been committed by members of an organized association, said to exist here, and to number some two hundred and fifty persons, and possibly more, who, as was alleged, to right what they considered a grievance in the matter of negro competition with white labor, had adopted the illegal course of which the act in question was an illustration." Proceedings of a similar significance have occurred at various points, especially in Virginia.

more contented people in the world; they were not driven hard, and work was stopped three times a day for meals; they had plenty to eat, and good clothes; and through the whole year they had from Friday night to Monday morning to do what they liked with themselves. Saturdays, the men generally worked in their patches (private gardens,) and the women washed and mended clothes. Sundays, they nearly all went to a Sabbath School which the mistress taught, and to meeting, but they were not obliged to go; they could come and go as they pleased all Saturday and Sunday; they were not looked after at all. Only on Monday morning, if there should any one be missing, or any one should come to the field with ragged or dirty clothes, he would be whipped. He had often noticed how much more intelligent and sprightly these negroes all were than the common run; a great many of them had books and could read and write; and on Sundays they were smartly dressed, some of them better than he or his wife ever thought of dressing. These things were purchased with the money they made out of their patches, working Saturdays.

There were two other large plantations near him, in both of which the negroes were turned out to work at half-past three every week-day morning—I might hear the bell ring for them—and frequently they were not stopped till nine o'clock at night, Saturday nights the same as any other. One of them belonged to a very religious lady, and on Sunday mornings at half past nine she had her bell rung for Sunday School, and after Sunday School they had a meeting, and after dinner another religious service. Every negro on the plantation was obliged to attend all these exercises, and if they were not dressed clean they were whipped. They were never allowed to go off the plantation, and if they were caught speaking to a negro from any other place, they were whipped. They could all of them repeat the catechism, he believed, but they were the dullest, and laziest, and most sorrowful looking negroes he ever saw.

As a general rule, the condition of the slaves, as regards their material comfort, had greatly improved within twenty years. He did not know that it had in other respects. It would not be a bit safer to turn them free, to shift for themselves, than it would have been twenty years ago. Of this he was quite confident. Perhaps they were a little more intelligent, knew more, but they were not as capable of self-guidance, not as much accustomed to work and contrive for themselves, as they used to be, when they were not fed and clothed nearly as well as now.

Beyond the excessive labor required of them on some planta-tions, he did not think slaves were often treated with unneces-sary cruelty. It was necessary to use the lash occasionally. Slaves never really felt under any moral obligation to obey their masters. Faithful service was preached to them as a Christian duty, and they pretended to acknowledge it, but the fact was that they were obedient just so far as they saw that they must be to avoid punishment; and punishment was necessary, now and then, to maintain their faith in their master's power. He had seven-teen slaves, and he did not suppose that there had been a hun-dred strokes of the whip on his place for a year past.

He asked if there were many Americans in Texas who were opposed to slavery, and if they were free to express themselves. I said that the wealthy Americans there, were all slaveholders themselves; that their influence all went to encourage the use of slave-labor, and render labor by whites disreputable. " But are there not a good many northern men there ?" he asked. The northern men, I replied, were chiefly merchants or speculators, who had but one idea, which was to make money as fast as they could; and nearly all the little money there was in that country was in the hands of the largest slaveholders.

If that was the way of things there, he said, there could not be much chance of its becoming a free State. I thought the chances were against it, but if the Germans continued to flock into the country, it would rapidly acquire all the characteristic features of a free-labor community, including an abundance and variety of skilled labor, a home market for a variety of crops, denser settlements, and more numerous social, educational and commercial conveniences. There would soon be a large body of small proprietors, not so wealthy that the stimulus to personal and active industry would have been lost, but yet able to indulge in a good many luxuries, to found churches, schools, and railroads, and to attract thither tradesmen, mechanics, professional men and artists. Moreover, the laborers who were not landholders would be intimately blended with them in all their interests; the two classes not living dissociated from each other, as was the case generally at the South, but engaged in a constant fulfillment of reciprocal obligations. I told him that if such a character of society could once be firmly and extensively established before the country was partitioned out into these little independent negro kingdoms, which had existed from the beginning in every other part of the South, I did not think any laws would be necessary to prevent slavery. It might be a slave State, but it would be a free people.

On coming from my room in the morning, my host met me with a hearty grasp of the hand. "I have slept very little with thinking of what you told me about western Texas. I think I shall have to go there. If we could get rid of slavery in this region, I believe we would soon be the most prosperous people in the world. What a disadvantage it must be to have your ground all frozen up and to be obliged to fodder your cattle five months in the year, as you do at the North. I do n't see how you live. I think I should like to buy a small farm near some town where I could send my children to school—a farm that I could take care of with one or two hired men. One thing I wanted to ask you, are the Germans learning English at all?" "Oh, yes; they teach the children English in their schools." "And have they good schools?" "Wherever they have settled at all closely, they have. At New Braunfels, they employ American as well as German teachers, and instruction can be had in the classics, natural history, and the higher mathematics." "Upon my word, I think I must go there," he replied. (Since then, as I hear, an educational institution of a high character, has been established, by German influence, in San Antonio, teachers in which are from Harvard.)

When I left, he mounted a horse and rode on with me some miles, saying he did not often find an intelligent man who liked to converse with him on the question of slavery. It seemed to him there was an epidemic insanity on the subject. It is unnecessary to state his views at length. They were precisely those which used to be common among all respectable men at the South. I have recently received a letter from him, in which, after alluding to the excitement which the Kansas question has produced, he says he thinks a considerable change of sentiment has occurred, in consequence of reading and talking about Kansas difficulties, among his neighbors. He is fully determined to go to western Texas, and reckons as many as ten families and thirty single men would go with him, if there were a prospect that free servants and laborers could be hired there and negroes be kept away.

As we rode, an old negro met and greeted us warmly. My companion hereupon observed that he had never uttered his sentiments in the presence of a slave, but in some way all the slaves in the country had, he thought, been informed what they were, for they all looked to him as their special friend. When they got into trouble, they would often come to him for advice or assistance. This morning, before I was up, a negro came to him from some miles distant, who had been working for a white man on Sundays till he owed him three dollars, which, now that the negro wanted it, he said he could not pay. He had given the negro the three dollars, for he thought he could manage to get it from the white man.

He confirmed the impression I had formed of the purely dramatic and deceptive character of what passed for religion with most of the slaves. One of his slaves was a preacher, and a favorite among them. He sometimes went to plantations twenty miles away—even further—on a Sunday, to preach a funeral sermon, making journeys of fifty miles a day, on foot. After the sermon, a hat would be passed round, and he sometimes brought home as much as ten dollars. He was a notable pedestrian; and once when he had committed some abominable crime for which he knew he would have to be punished, and had ran away, he (Mr. Watson) rode after him almost immediately, often got in sight of him, but did not overtake him until the second day, when starting early in the morning he overhauled him crossing a broad, smooth field. When the run-away parson saw that he could not escape, he jumped up into a tree and called out to him, with an aggravatingly cheerful voice, "I gin ye a good run dis time, did n't I, massa?" He was the most rascally negro, the worst liar, thief, and adulterer on his place. Indeed, when he was preaching, he always made a strong point of his own sinfulness, and would weep and bellow about it like a bull of Bashan, till he got a whole camp meeting into convulsions.

This phrase reminds me of a scene which I witnessed in New Orleans, and as I have not yet described any of the religious services of the negroes, except that observed at a funeral, I will here give an account of it, which was written the same day.

A SLAVE RELIGIOUS SERVICE IN NEW ORLEANS.

Walking this morning through a rather mean neighborhood I was attracted, by a loud chorus singing, to the open door of a chapel or small church. I found a large congregation of negroes assembled within, and the singing being just then concluded, and a negro preacher commencing a sermon, I entered an empty pew near the entrance. I had no sooner taken a seat than a negro usher came to me and, in the most polite manner, whispered,

"Won't you please to let me give you a seat higher up, master, 'long o' tudder white folks?"

I followed him to the uppermost seat, facing the pulpit, where there were three other white persons. One of them was a woman—old, very plain, and not as well dressed as many of the negroes; another looked like a ship's officer, and was probably a member of the police force in undress—what we call a spy when we detect it in Europe; both of these remained diligently and gravely attentive during the service; the third was a foreign-looking person, very flashily dressed, and sporting a yellow-headed walking-stick, and much cheap jewelry.

The remainder of the congregation consisted entirely of colored persons, many of them, however, with light hair and hardly any perceptible indications of having African blood. On the step of the chancel were a number of children, and among these one of the loveliest young girls that I ever saw. She was a light mulatto, and had an expression of unusual intelligence and vivacity. During the service she frequently smiled, I thought derisively, at the emotions and excitement betrayed by the older people about her. She was elegantly dressed, and was accompanied by a younger sister, who was also dressed expensively and in good taste, but who was a shade darker, though much removed from the blackness of the true negro, and of very good features and pleasant expression.

The preacher was nearly black, with close wooly hair. His figure was slight, he seemed to be about thirty years of age, and the expression of his face indicated a refined and delicately sensitive nature. His eye was very fine, bright, deep and clear; his voice and manner generally quiet and impressive.

The text was, "I have fought the good fight, I have kept the faith; henceforth there is laid up for me a crown of glory;" and the sermon was an appropriate and generally correct explanation of the customs of the Olympic games, and a proper and often eloquent application of the figure to the Christian course of life. Much of the language was highly metaphorical; the figures long, strange and complicated, yet sometimes, however, beautiful. Words were frequently misplaced, and their meaning evidently misapprehended, while the grammar and pronunciation were sometimes such as to make the idea intended to be conveyed by the speaker incomprehensible to me. Vulgarisms and slang phrases occasionally occurred, but evidently without any consciousness of impropriety on the part of the speaker or his congregation.

As soon as I had taken my seat, my attention was attracted by an old negro near me, whom I supposed for some time to be suffering under some nervous complaint; he trembled, his teeth chattered, and his face, at intervals, was convulsed. He soon began to respond aloud to the sentiments of the preacher, in such words as these: "Oh, yes!" "That's it, that's it!" "Yes, yes—glory—yes!" and similar expressions could be heard from all parts of the house whenever the speaker's voice was unusually solemn, or his language and manner eloquent or excited.

Sometimes the outcries and responses were not confined to ejaculations of this kind, but shouts, and groans, terrific shrieks, and indescribable expressions of ecstacy—of pleasure or agony—and even stamping, jumping, and clapping of hands, were added. The tumult often resembled that of an excited political meeting; and I was once surprised to find my own muscles all stretched, as if ready for a struggle—my face glowing, and my feet stamping—having been infected unconsciously, as men often are, with instinctive bodily sympathy with the excitement of the crowd. So wholly unintellectual was the basis of this excitement, however, that I could not, when my mind retroverted to itself, find any connection or meaning in the phrases of the speaker that remained in my memory; and I have no doubt it was his "action" rather than his sentiments, that had given rise to the excitement of the congregation.

I took notes as well as I could of a single passage of the sermon. The preacher having said that among the games of the arena, were "raaslin" (wrestling) and boxing, and described how a combatant determined to win the prize, would come boldly up to his adversary and stand square before him, looking him straight in the eyes, and while he guarded himself with one hand, would give him "a lick" with the other, continued in these words : "Then would he stop, and turn away his face, and let the adversary hit back? No, my brethren, no, no! he'd follow up his advantage, and give him another lick; and if he fell back, he'd keep close after him, and not stop!—and not faint!—not be content with merely driving him back!—but he'd *persevere!* (yes, glory!) and hit him again! (that's it, hit him again! hit him again! oh, glory! hi! hi! glory!) drive him into the corner! and never, never stop till he had him *down!* (glory, glory, glory!) and he had got his foot on his neck, and the crown of wild olive leaves was placed upon his head by the lord of the games. (Ha! ha! glory to the Lord! etc.) It was the custom of the Olympian games, my brethren, for the victor to be crowned with a crown of wild olive leaves, but sometimes, after all, it would n't be awarded right, because the lord of the games was a poor, frail, erroneous man, and maybe he could n't see right, or maybe he was n't an honest man, and would have his favorites among the combatants, and if his favorite was beaten, he would not *allow* it, but would declare that he was the victor, and the crown would descend on *his* head (*glory!*) But there ain't no danger of that in our fight with the world, for our Lord is throned in justice. (Glory!—oh, yes! yes!—sweet Lord!

sweet Lord!) He seeth in secret, and he knoweth all things, and there's no chance for a mistake, and if we only will just persevere and conquer, and conquer and persevere (yes, sir! oh, Lord, yes!), and persevere—not for a year, or for two year, or ten year; nor for seventy year, perhaps; but if we persevere— (yes! yes!)—if we persevere—(oh! Lord! help us!)—if we persevere unto the end—(oh! oh! glory! glory! glory!)—until he calls us home! (Frantic shouting.) Henceforth there is laid up for us a crown of immortal glory—(Ha! ha! HA!)—not a crown of wild olive leaves that begin to droop as soon as they touch our brow, (oh! oh! oh!) but a crown of immortal glory! That fadeth not away! Never begins to droop! But is immortal in the heavens!" Tremendous uproar, many of the congregation on their feet, and uttering cries and shrieks impossible to be expressed in letters. The shabby gentleman by my side, who had been asleep, suddenly awakened, dropped his stick, and shouted with all his might, "Glory to the Lord!"

The body of the house was filled by the audience; there were galleries, but few persons were in them; on one side, two or three boys, and on the other, on the seat nearest the pulpit, about a dozen women.

The preacher was drawing his sermon to a close, and offering some sensible and pertinent advice, soberly and calmly, and the congregation was attentive and comparatively quiet, when a small old woman, perfectly black, among those in the gallery, suddenly rose, and began dancing and clapping her hands; at first, with a slow and measured movement, and then with increasing rapidity, at the same time beginning to shout "*ha! ha!*" The women about her arose also, and tried to hold her, as there appeared great danger that she would fall out of the gallery, and those below, left their pews that she might not fall upon them.

The preacher continued his remarks—much the best part of his sermon—but it was plain that they were wasted ; every one was looking at the dancing woman in the gallery, and many were shouting and laughing aloud (in joyful sympathy, I suppose). His eye flashed as he glanced anxiously from the woman to the people, and then stopping in the middle of a sentence, a sad smile came over his face ; he closed the book, and bowed his head upon his hands to the desk. A voice in the congregation struck into a tune, and the whole congregation rose and joined in a roaring song. The woman was still shouting and dancing, her head thrown back and rolling from one side to the other. Gradually her shout became indistinct, she threw her arms wildly about instead of clapping her hands, fell back into the arms of her companions, then threw herself forward and embraced those before her, then tossed herself from side to side, gasping, and finally sunk to the floor, where she remained at the end of the song, kicking, as if acting a death struggle.

Another man now rose in the pulpit, and gave out a hymn, naming number and page, and holding a book before him, though I thought he did not read from it, and I did not see another book in the house. Having recited seven verses, and repeated the number and page of the hymn, he closed the book and commenced to address the congregation. He was a tall, full-blooded negro, very black, and with a disgusting expression of sensuality, cunning and vanity in his countenance, and a pompous, patronizing manner—a striking contrast, in all respects, to the prepossessing quiet and modest young preacher who had preceded him. He was dressed in the loosest form of the fashionable sack overcoat, which he threw off presently, showing a white vest, gaudy cravat, and a tight cut-away coat, linked together at the breast with jet buttons. He commenced by proposing to further elucidate the meaning of the apostle's words; they had an important bearing, he said, which his brother had not had time to bring out adequately before the congregation. At first he leaned carelessly on the pulpit cushion, laughing cunningly, and spoke in a low, deep, hoarse, indistinct and confidential tone, but soon he struck a higher key, drawling his sentences like a street salesman, occasionally breaking out into a yell with all the strength of extraordinarily powerful lungs, at the same time taking a striking attitude and gesturing in an extraordinary manner. This would create a frightful excitement in the people, and be responded to with the loudest and most terrific shouts. I can compare them to nothing else human I ever heard. Sometimes he would turn from the audience and assume a personal opponent to be standing by his side in the pulpit. Then, after battling for a few minutes in an awful and majestic manner with this man of Belial, whom he addressed constantly as " sir !" he would turn again to the admiring congregation, and in a familiar, gratulatory and conversational tone explain the difficulty into which he had got him, and then again suddenly turn back upon him, and in a boxing attitude give an other knock-down reply to his heretical propositions.

His language was in a great part unintelligible to me, but the congregation seemed to enjoy it highly, and encouraged and assisted him in his combat with "Sir" Knight of his imagination most tumultuously, and I soon found that this poor gentleman, over whom he rode his high horse so fiercely, was one of those "who take unto themselves the name of BAPTIST," and that the name of his own charger was "*Perseverance-of-the-Saints.*"

The only intelligible argument that I could discover, was presented under the following circumstances. Having made his supposed adversary assert that "if a man would only just believe and let him bury him under de water, he would be saved,"—he caught up the big pulpit Bible, and using it as a catapult, pretended to hurl from it the reply—"Except ye persevere and fight de good fight unto de end, ye shall be damned!" "That's it, that's it!" shouted the delighted audience. "Yes! you shall be damned! Ah! you've got it now, have ye! Pooh!—Wha's de use o' his tellin' us dat ar?" he continued, turning to the congregation with a laugh; "wha's de use on't, when we know dat a month arter he's buried 'em under de water—whar do we find 'em? Ha? ah ha! Whah? In de grog-shop! (ha! ha! ha! ha!) Yes we do, do n't we? (Yes! yes!) In de rum-hole! (Ha! ha! ha! Yes! yes! oh Lord!) and we know de spirit of rum and de Spirit of God has n't got no 'finities. (Yah! ha! ha! yes! yes! dat's it! dat's it! oh, my Jesus! Oh! oh! glory! glory!) Sut'nly, sah! You may launch out upon de ocean a drop of oil way up to Virginny, and we'll launch annudder one heah to Lusiana, and when dey meets—no matter how far dey been gone—dey'll unite! Why, sah? Because dey's got de 'finities, sah! But de spirit of rum haint got nary sort o' 'finity with de Spirit—" etc.

Three of the congregation threw themselves into hysterics during this harangue, though none were so violent as that of the woman in the gallery. The man I had noticed first from his strange convulsive motions, was shaking as if in a violent ague, and frequently snatched the sleeve of his coat in his teeth as if he would rend it. The speaker at length returned to the hymn, repeated the number and page and the first two lines. These were sung, and he repeated the next, and so on, as in the Scotch Presbyterian service. The congregation sang; I think every one joined, even the children, and the collective sound was wonderful. The voices of one or two women rose above the rest, and one of these soon began to introduce variations, which consisted mainly of shouts of oh! oh! at a piercing height. Many of the singers kept time with their feet, balancing themselves on each alternately, and swinging their bodies accordingly. The reading of the lines would be accompanied also by shouts, as during the previous discourse.

When the preacher had concluded reading the last two lines, as the singing again proceeded, he raised his own voice above all, turned around, clapped his hands, and commenced to dance, and laughed aloud, first with his back, and then with his face to the audience.

The singing ceased, but he continued his movements, leaping, with increasing agility, from one side of the pulpit to the other. The people below laughed and shouted, and the two other preachers who were shut into the pulpit with the dancer, tried hard to keep out of his way, and threw forward their arms or shoulders, to fend off his powerful buffets as he surged about between them. Swinging out his arms at random, with a blow of his fist he knocked the great Bible spinning off the desk, to the great danger of the children below; then threw himself back, jamming the old man, who was trying to restrain him, against the wall.

At the next heave, he pitched headforemost into the young preacher, driving him through the door and falling with him half down the stairs, and after bouncing about a few moments, jerking his arms and legs violently, like a supple-jack, in every direction, and all the time driving his breath with all the noise possible between his set teeth, and trying tó foam at the mouth and act an epileptic fit, there he lay as if dead, the young preacher, with the same sad smile, and something of shame on his face, sitting on the stair holding his head on his shoulder, and grasping one of his hands, while his feet were extended up into the pulpit.

The third man in the pulpit, a short, aged negro, with a smiling face, and a pleasing manner, took the Bible, which was handed up to him by one of the congregation, laid it upon the desk, and, leaning over it, told the people, in a gentle, conversational tone, that the "love feast" would be held at four o'clock; gave some instructions about the tickets of admission, and severely reproved those who were in the habit of coming late, and insisting upon being let in after the doors were locked. He then announced that the doxology would be sung, which accordingly followed, another woman going into hysterics at the close. The prostrate man rose, and released the young preacher, who pronounced the Apostles' blessing, and the congregation slowly passed out, chatting and saluting one another politely as they went, and bearing not the slightest mark of the previous excitement.

The night after leaving Mr. Watson's I was kindly received by a tradesman, who took me, after closing his shop, to his mother's house, a log cabin, but more comfortable than many more pretentious residences at which I passed a night on this journey.

Foɪ the first time in many months tea was offered me. It was coarse Bohea, sweetened with honey, which was stirred into the tea as it boiled in a kettle over the fire, by the old lady herself, whose especial luxury it seemed to be. She asked me if folks ever drank tea at the North, and when I spoke of green tea, said she had never heard of that kind of tea before. They owned a number of slaves, but the young man looked after my horse himself. There was a good assortment of books and newspapers at this house, and the people were quite intelligent and very amiable.

A NIGHT WITH A "POOR WHITE."

The next day, I passed a number of small Indian farms, very badly cultivated—the corn nearly concealed by weeds. The soil became poorer than before, and the cabins of poor people more frequent. I counted about ten plantations, or negro-cultivated farms, in twenty miles. A planter, at whose house I called after sunset, said it was not convenient for him to accommodate me, and I was obliged to ride till it was quite dark. The next house, at which I arrived, was one of the commonest sort of cabins. I had passed twenty like it during the day, and I thought I would take the opportunity to get an interior knowledge of them. The fact that a horse and wagon were kept, and that a considerable area of land in the rear of the cabin was planted with cotton, showed that the family were by no means of the lowest class, yet, as they were not able even to hire a slave, they may be considered to represent very favorably, I believe, the condition of the poor whites of the plantation districts. The whites of the county, I observe, by the census, are three to one of the slaves; in the nearest adjoining county, the proportion is reversed ; and within a few miles the soil was richer, and large plantations occurred.

It was raining, and nearly nine o'clock. The door of the cabin was open, and I rode up and conversed with the occupant as he stood within. He said that he was not in the habit of taking in travelers, and his wife was about sick, but if I was a mind to put up with common fare, he did n't care. Grateful, I dismounted and took the seat he had vacated by the fire, while he led away my horse to an open shed in the rear—his own horse ranging at large, when not in use, during the summer.

The house was all comprised in a single room, twenty-eight by twenty-five feet in area, and open to the roof above. There was a large fireplace at one end and a door on each side—no windows at all. Two bedsteads, a spinning-wheel, a packing-case, which served as a bureau, a cupboard, made of rough hewn slabs, two or three deer-skin seated chairs, a Connecticut clock, and a large poster of Jayne's patent medicines, constituted all the visible furniture either useful or ornamental in purpose. A little girl immediately, without having had any directions to do so, got a frying-pan and a chunk of bacon from the cupboard, and cutting slices from the latter, set it frying for my supper. The woman of the house sat sulkily in a chair tilted back and leaning against the logs, spitting occasionally at the fire, but took no notice of me, barely nodding when I saluted her. A baby lay crying on the floor. I quieted it and amused it with my watch till the little girl, having made " coffee" and put a piece of corn-bread on the table with the bacon, took charge of it.

I hoped the woman was not very ill.

"Got the headache right bad," she answered. " Have the headache a heap, I do. Knew I should have it to-night. Been cuttin' brush in the cotton this arternoon. Knew 't would bring on my headache. Told him so when I begun."

As soon as I had finished my supper and fed Jude, the little girl put the fragments and the dishes in the cupboard, shoved the table into a corner, and dragged a quantity of quilts from one of the bedsteads, which she spread upon the floor, and presently crawled among them out of sight for the night. The woman picked up the child—which, though still a suckling, she said was twenty-two months old—and nursed it, retaking her old position. The man sat with me by the fire, his back towards her. The baby having fallen asleep was laid away somewhere, and the woman dragged off another lot of quilts from the beds, spreading them upon the floor. Then taking a deep tin-pan, she filled it with alternate layers of corn-cobs and hot embers from the fire. This she placed upon a large block, which was evidently used habitually for the purpose, in the center of the cabin. A furious smoke arose from it, and we soon began to cough. "Most *too* much smoke," observed the man. "Hope 't will drive out all the gnats, then," replied the woman. (There is a very minute flying insect here, the bite of which is excessively sharp.)

The woman suddenly dropped off her outer garment and stepped from the midst of its folds, in her petticoat; then, taking the baby from the place where she had deposited it, lay down and covered herself with the quilts upon the floor. The man told me that I could take the bed which remained on one of the bedsteads, and kicking off his shoes only, rolled himself into a blanket by the side of his wife. I ventured to take off my cravat and stockings, as well as my boots, but almost immediately put my stockings on again, drawing their tops over my pantaloons. The advantage of this arrangement was that, although

my face, eyes, ears, neck, and hands, were immediately attacked,
the vermin did not reach my legs for two or three hours. Just
after the clock struck two, I distinctly heard the man and the
woman, and the girl and the dog scratching, and the horse out in
the shed stamping and gnawing himself. Soon afterward the
man exclaimed, " Good God Almighty—mighty! mighty!
mighty!" and jumping up, pulled off one of his stockings, shook
it, scratched his foot vehemently, put on the stocking, and lay
down again with a groan. The two doors were open, and
through the logs and the openings in the roof, I saw the clouds
divide, and the moon and stars reveal themselves. The woman,
after having been nearly smothered by the smoke from the pan
which she had originally placed close to her own pillow, rose and
placed it on the sill of the windward door, where it burned feebly
and smoked lustily, like an altar to the Lares, all night. Fortunately the cabin was so open that it gave us little annoyance,
while it seemed to answer the purpose of keeping all flying
insects at a distance.

When, on rising in the morning, I said that I would like to
wash my face, water was given me for the purpose in an earthen
pie-dish. Just as breakfast, which was of exactly the same materials as my supper, was ready, rain again began to fall, presently
in such a smart shower as to put the fire out and compel us to
move the table under the least leaky part of the roof.

At breakfast occurred the following conversation :

" Are there many niggers in New York?"

" Very few."

" How do you get your work done?"

" There are many Irish and German people constantly coming
there who are glad to get work to do."

" Oh, and you have them for slaves?"

" They want money and are willing to work for it. A great many American-born work for wages, too."

" What do you have to pay ?"

" Ten or twelve dollars a month."

" There was a heap of Irishmen to work on the railroad ; they was paid a dollar a day ; there was a good many Americans, too, but mostly they had little carts and mules, and hauled dirt and sich like. They was paid twenty-five or thirty dollars a month and found."

" What did they find them ?"

" Oh, blanket and shoes, I expect ; they put up kind o' tents like for 'em to sleep in all together."

" What food did they find them ?"

" Oh, common food ; bacon and meal."

" What do they generally give the niggers on the plantations here ?"

" A peck of meal and three pound of bacon is what they call 'lowance, in general, I believe. It takes a heap o' meat on a big plantation. I was on one of William R. King's plantations over in Alabamy, where there was about fifty niggers, one Sunday last summer, and I see 'em weighin' outen the meat Tell you, it took a powerful heap on it. They had an old nigger to weigh it out, and he warn't no ways partickler about the weight. He just took and chopped it off, middlins, in chunks, and he'd throw 'em into the scales, and if a piece weighed a pound or two over he would n't mind it ; he never took none back. Ain't niggers all-fired sassy at the North ?"

" No, not particularly."

" Aint they all free, there ? I hearn so."

" Yes."

" Well, how do they get along when they 's free ?"

" I never have seen a great many, to know their circumstances very well. Right about where I live they seem to me to live quite comfortably ; more so than the niggers on these big plantations do, I should think."

" O ! They have a mighty hard time on the big plantations. I 'd ruther be dead than to be a nigger on one of these big plantations."

" Why, I thought they were pretty well taken care of on them."

The man and his wife both looked at me as if surprised, and smiled.

" Why, they are well fed, are they not ?"

" Oh, but they work 'em so hard. My God, sir, in pickin' time on these big plantations they start 'em to work 'fore light, and they do n't give 'em time to eat."

" I supposed they generally gave them an hour or two at noon."

" No, sir ; they just carry a piece of bread and meat in their pockets and they eat it when they can, standin' up. They have a hard life on 't, that 's a fact. I reckon you can get along about as well withouten slaves as with 'em, can't you, in New York ?"

" In New York there is not nearly so large a proportion of very rich men as here. There are very few people who farm over three hundred acres, and the greater number—nineteen out of twenty, I suppose—work themselves with the hands they employ. Yes, I think it 's better than it is here, for all concerned, a great deal. Folks that can't afford to buy niggers get along a great deal better in the free States, I think ; and I guess that those who could afford to have niggers get along better without them."

"I no doubt that's so. I wish there warn't no niggers here. They are a great cuss to this country, I expect. But 't would n't do to free 'em ; that would n't do no how !"

GET RID OF THE NIGGERS.

"Are there many people here who think slavery a curse to the country ?"

"Oh, yes, a great many. I reckon the majority would be right glad if we could get rid of the niggers. But it would n't never do to free 'em and leave 'em here. I do n't know anybody, hardly, in favor of that. Make 'em free and leave 'em here and they'd steal every thing we made. Nobody could n't live here then."

These views of slavery seem to be universal among people of this class. They were repeated to me at least a dozen times.

NIGGER PANICS.

"Where I used to live, [Alabama] I remember when I was a boy—must ha' been about twenty years ago—folks was dreadful frightened about the niggers. I remember they built pens in the woods where they could hide, and Christmas time they went and got into the pens, 'fraid the niggers was risin'.'"

"I remember the same time where we was in South Carolina," said his wife ; "we had all our things put up in bags, so we could tote 'em, if we heerd they was comin' our way."

They did not suppose the niggers ever thought of rising now, but could give no better reason for not supposing so than that "everybody said there warn't no danger on 't now."

Hereabouts the plantations were generally small, ten to twenty negroes on each ; sometimes thirty or forty. Where he used to live they were big ones—forty or fifty, sometimes a hundred on each. He had lived here ten years. I could not make out why he had not accumulated wealth, so small a family and such an inexpensive style of living as he had. He generally planted twenty to thirty acres, he said; this year he had sixteen in cotton and about ten, he thought, in corn. Decently cultivated, this planting should have produced him five hundred dollars' worth of cotton, besides supplying him with bread and bacon—his chief expense, apparently. I suggested that this was a very large planting for his little family; he would need some help in picking time. He ought to have some now, he said ; grass and bushes were all overgrowing him ; he had to work just like a nigger ; this durnation rain would just make the weeds jump, and he did n't expect he should have any cotton at all. There warn't much use in a man's trying to get along by himself; every thing seemed to set in agin him. He 'd been trying to hire somebody, but he could n't, and his wife was a sickly kind of a woman.

His wife reckoned he might hire some help if he 'd look round sharp.

My horse and dog were as well cared for as possible, and a "snack" of bacon and corn-bread was offered me for noon, which has been unusual in Mississippi. When I asked what I should pay, the man hesitated and said he reckoned what I had had, was n't worth much of any thing ; he was sorry he could not have accommodated me better. I offered him a dollar, for which he thanked me warmly. It is the first instance of hesitation in charging for a lodging which I have met with from a stranger at the South.

CHAPTER V.

THE PIEDMONT COTTON DISTRICT.

NORTHERN ALABAMA.

ÓMITTING a portion of my journey, in which the general characteristics of the country through which I passed, differed not
materially from those of the district described in the last chapter, I resume my narrative at the point where, in my progress
northward, it was first evident that cotton was no longer the all-
important object of agricultural interest, other crops receiving, at
least, equal attention.

June —. I have to-day reached a more distinctly hilly country—somewhat rocky and rugged, but with inviting dells. The
soil is sandy and less frequently fertile; cotton-fields are seen only
at long intervals, the crops on the small proportion of cultivated
land being chiefly corn and oats. I notice also that white men
are more commonly at work in the fields than negroes, and this
as well in the cultivation of cotton as of corn.

The larger number of the dwellings are rude log huts, of only
one room, and that unwholesomely crowded. I saw in and
about one of them, not more than fifteen feet square, five grown
persons, and as many children. Occasionally, however, the mo-
notony of these huts is agreeably varied by neat, white, frame
houses. At one such, I dined to-day, and was comfortably entertained. The owner held a number of slaves, but made no cot-

ton. He owned a saw mill, was the postmaster of the neighborhood, and had been in the Legislature.

I asked him why the capital had been changed from Tuscaloosa to Montgomery. He did not know. "Because Montgomery is more central and easy of access, probably," I suggested.
"No, I do n't think that had any thing to do with it." "Is Tuscaloosa an unhealthy place?" "No, sir; healthier than Montgomery, I reckon." "Was it then simply because the people of
the southern districts were stronger, and used their power to
make the capital more convenient of access to themselves?"
"Well, no, I do n't think that was it, exactly. The fact is, sir,
the people here are not like you northern people; they do n't
reason out every thing so. They are fond of change, and they
got tired of Tuscaloosa; the Montgomery folks wanted it there
and offered to pay for moving it, so they let 'em have it; 't was
just for a change." "If there really was no better reason, was it
not rather wasteful to give up all the public buildings at Tuscaloosa?" "Oh, the Montgomery people wanted it so bad they
promised to pay for building a new State House; so it did not
cost any thing."

Quite on a par with the economics of southern commercial
conventions.

COTTON-GROWING FARMERS.

I passed the night at the second framed house that I saw during the day, stopping early in order to avail myself of its
promise of comfort. It was attractively situated on a hill-top,
with a peach orchard near it. The proprietor owned a dozen
slaves, and "made cotton," he said, "with other crops." He

had some of his neighbors at tea and at breakfast; sociable,
kindly people, satisfied with themselves and their circumstances,
which I judged from their conversation had been recently improving. One coming in, remarked that he had discharged a
white laborer whom he had employed for some time past;
the others congratulated him on being " shet" of him ; all
seemed to have noticed him as a bad, lazy man; he had often
been seen lounging in the field, rapping the negroes with his hoe
if they did n't work to suit him. " He was about the meanest
white man I ever see," said a woman ; " he was a heap meaner 'n
niggers. I reckon niggers would come somewhere between white
folks and such as he." " The first thing I tell a man," said another, " when I hire him, is, ' if there 's any whippin' to be done
on this place I want to do it myself.' If I saw a man rappin'
my niggers with a hoe-handle, as I see him, durned if I would n't
rap him—the lazy whelp."

One of the negroes complimented my horse. " Dar's a heap
of genus in dat yar hoss's head !" The proprietor looked after
the feeding himself.

These people were extremely kind ; inquiring with the simplest
good feeling about my domestic relations, and the purpose of my
journey. When I left, one of them walked a quarter of a mile
to make sure that I went upon the right road. The charge for
entertainment, though it was unusually good, was a quarter of a
dollar less than I have paid before, which I mention, not as Mr.
De Bow would suppose,* out of gratitude for the moderation,
but as an indication of the habits of the people, showing, as it
may, either closer calculation, or that the district grows its own

* See De Bow's Review, for August, 1857, p. 117.

supplies, and can furnish food cheaper than those in which attention is more exclusively given to cotton.

June —. The country continues hilly, and is well populated by farmers, living in log huts, while every mile or two,
on the more level and fertile land, there is a larger farm,
with ten or twenty negroes at work. A few whites are usually
working near them, in the same field, generally plowing while
the negroes hoe.

WARM WORK FOR WOMAN-KIND.

About noon, my attention was attracted towards a person upon
a ledge, a little above the road, who was throwing up earth and
stone with a shovel. I stopped to see what the purpose of
this work might be, and perceived that the shoveler was a
woman, who, presently discovering me, stopped and called to
others behind her, and immediately a stout girl and two younger
children, with a man, came to the edge and looked at me.
The woman was bare-headed, and otherwise half-naked, as
perhaps needed to be, for her work would have been thought
hard by our stoutest laborers, and it was the hottest weather
of the summer, in the latitude of Charleston, and on a hill-
side in the full face of the noon sun. I pushed my horse up
the hill until I reached them, when another man appeared, and in
answer to my inquiries told me that they were getting out iron
ore. One was picking in a vein, having excavated a short adit;
the other man picked looser ore exterior to the vein. The
women and children shoveled out the ore and piled it on kilns of
timber, where they roasted it to make it crumble. It was then
carted to a forge, and they were paid for it by the load. They
were all clothed very meanly and scantily. The woman worked,

so far as I could see, as hard as the men. The children, too, even
to the youngest—a boy of eight or ten—were carrying large
lumps of ore, and heaving them into the kiln, and shoveling the
finer into a screen to separate the earth from it.

Immediately after leaving them I found a good spot for noon-
ing. I roped my horse out to graze, and spread my blanket in a
deep shade. I noticed that the noise of their work had ceased,
and about fifteen minutes afterwards, Jude suddenly barking, I
saw one of the men peering at me through the trees, several rods
distant. I called to him to come up. He approached rather
slowly and timidly, examined the rope with which my horse was
fastened, eyed me vigilantly, and at length asked if I was resting
myself. I replied that I was; and he said that he did not know
but I might be sick, and had come to see me. I thanked him,
and offered him a seat on my blanket, which he declined. Presently he took up a newspaper that I had been reading, looked at
it a moment, then told me he could n't read. "Folks do n't care
much for edication round here; it would be better for 'em, I
expect, if they did." He then began to question me closely
about my circumstances—where I came from, whither I was going, etc.

When his curiosity was partially appeased he suddenly laughed
in a silly manner, and said that the people he had been working
with had watched me after I left them; they saw me ride up the
hill and stop, ride on again, and finally take off my saddle, turn
my horse loose and tote my saddle away, and they were much
frightened, thinking I must be crazy at least. When he started
to come toward me they told him he would n't dare to go to me,
but he saw how it was, well enough—I was just resting myself.

" If I should run down hill now," said he, " they'd start right

off and would n't stop for ten mile, reckoning you was arter me.
That would be fun; oh, we have some good fun here sometimes
with these green folks.   There 's an amazin' ignorant set round
here."

I asked if they were foreigners.

"Oh, no; they are common, no account people; they used to
live over the hill, here; they come right nigh starvin' thar, I expect."

They had not been able to get any work to do, and had been
"powerful poor," until he got them to come here.   They had
taken an old cabin, worked with him, and were doing right well
now. He did n't let them work in the vein—he kept that for himself—but they worked all around, and some days they made a
dollar and a half—the man, woman and children together.   They
had one other girl, but she had to stay at home to take care of
the baby and keep cattle and hogs out of their "gardien." He
had known the woman when she was a girl; "she was always a
good one to work. She 'd got a voice like a bull, and she was as
smart as a wildcat; but the man warn't no account."

He had himself followed this business (mining) since he was a
young man, and could earn three dollars a day by it if he tried;
he had a large family and owned a small farm; never laid up
any thing, always kept himself a little in debt at the store.

He asked if I had not found the people "more friendly like"
up in this country to what they were down below, and assured me
that I would find them grow more friendly as I went further
north, so at least he had heard, and he knew where he first came
from (Tennessee) the people were more friendly than they were
here.   "The richer a man is," he continued, pursuing a natural
association of ideas, "and the more niggers he 's got, the poorer

he seems to live. If you want to fare well in this country you
stop to poor folks' housen; they try to enjoy what they've got,
while they ken, but these yer big planters they do n't care for
nothin' but to save. Now, I never calculate to save any thing; I
tell my wife I work. hard and I mean to enjoy what I earn as
fast as it comes."

Sometimes he "took up bee-huntin' for a spell," and made
money by collecting wild honey. He described his manner of
finding the hives and securing the honey, and, with a hushed
voice, told me a "secret," which was, that if you carried three
leaves, each of a different tree (?) in your hand, there was never
a bee would dare to sting you.

I asked about his children. He had one grown-up son, who
was doing very well; he was hired by the gentleman who owned
the forge, to cart ore. He had nothing to do but to drive a team;
he did n't have to load, and he had a nigger to take care of the
horses when his day's teaming was done.

ARTICLES OF FEMININE LUXURY.

His wages were seven dollars a month, and board for himself
and wife. They ate at the same table with the gentleman, and
had good living, beside having something out of the store, "tobacco and so on—tobacco for both on 'em, and two people uses
a good deal of tobacco, you know; so that's pretty good wages
—seven dollars a month, beside their keep and tobacco." Irishmen, he informed me, had been employed occasionally at the
forge. "They do well at first, only they is apt to get into fights
all the time; but after they've been here a year or two, they get
to feel so independent and keerless-like, you can't get along with
'em." He remained about half an hour, and not till he returned

did I hear again the noise of picking and shoveling, and cutting timber.

At the forges, I was told, slave labor is mainly employed—the slaves being owned by the proprietors of the forges.

"PLEASE TO REMEMBER," ETC.

I spent that night at a large inn in a village. In the morning as I sat waiting in my room, a boy opened the door. Without looking up I asked, "Well?"

"I did n't say nuthin', sar." with a great grin.

"What are you waiting there for?" "Please, massa, I b'leve you's owin' me suthin', sar." "Owing you something? What do you mean?" "For drying yer clothes for yer, sar, last night." I had ordered him immediately after tea to go up stairs and get my clothes, which had been drenched in a shower, and hang them by the kitchen fire, that they might be dry if I should wish to leave early in the morning. When I went to my bedroom at nine o'clock I found the clothes where I had left them. I went down and reported it to the landlord, who directly sent the boy for them. In the morning, when I got them again I found they were not dry except where they were burned. I told him to be gone; but with the door half open, he stood putting in his head, bowing and grinning. "Please, sar, massa sent me out of an errand, and I was afeard you would be gone before I got back; dat's the reason why I mention it, sar; dat's all, sar; I hope you'll skuse me, sar."

A SPORTING FARMER AND NIGGER-HUNTING.

During the afternoon I rode on through a valley, narrow and apparently fertile, but the crops indifferent. The general social characteristics were the same that I met with yesterday.

At night I stopped at a large house having an unusual number of negro cabins and stables about it. The proprietor, a hearty old farmer, boasted much of his pack of hounds, saying they had pulled down five deer before he had had a shot at them. He was much interested to hear about Texas, the Indians and the game. He reckoned there was "a heap of big varmint out thar."

His crop of cotton did not average two bales to the hand, and corn not twenty bushels to the acre.

He amused me much with a humorous account of an oyster supper to which he had been invited in town, and his attempts to eat the "nasty things" without appearing disconcerted before the ladies.

An old negro took my horse when I arrived, and half an hour afterward, came to me and asked if I wanted to see him fed. As we walked toward the stables, he told me that he always took care not to forget gentlemen's hosses, and to treat them well; "then," he said, bowing and with emphasis, "they looks out and do n't forget to treat me well."

The same negro was called to serve me as a candlestick at bedtime. He held the candle till I got into bed. As he retired I closed my eyes, but directly afterward, perceiving the light return, I opened them. Uncle Abram was bending over me, holding the candle, grinning with his toothless gums, winking and shaking his head in a most mysterious manner.

"Hush! massa," he whispered. "You hain't got something to drink, in dem saddle-bags has you, sar?"

My host wanted much to buy or borrow Jude of me; offering to return her to me in New York, with the best pup, and without expense to me, if I would let him get a litter from her.

I have been asked for my dog at every house in which I have stopped on the road, and, on an average, twice a day beside, since I left Natchez. Gentlemen inquire respectfully : " Would not you like to give away that dog, sir ?" Negroes : " Do n't you want to gib me dat dog, sar ?" Boys : " Please, sir; gin me that dog, sir ?" and children, black and white, demand it peremptorily : " Gim me dat dog."

The farmer told me something about " nigger dogs ;" they did n't use foxhounds, but bloodhounds—not pure, he thought, but a cross of the Spanish bloodhound with the common hounds or curs. There were many men, he said, in the country below here, who made a business of nigger-hunting, and they had their horses trained, as well as the dogs, to go over any common fence or if they could n't leap it, to break it down. Dogs were trained, when pups, to follow a nigger—not allowed to catch one, however, unless they were quite young, so that they could n't hurt him much, and they were always taught to hate a negro, never being permitted to see one except to be put in chase of him. He believed that only two of a pack were kept kenneled all the time—these were old, keen ones, who led the rest when they were out ; they were always kept coupled together with a chain, except when trailing. He had seen a pack of thirteen who would follow a trail two days and a half old, if rain had not fallen in the mean time. When it rained immediately after a negro got off, they had to scour the country where they supposed he might be, till they scented him.

When hard pushed, a negro always took to a tree ; sometimes however, they would catch him in an open field. When this was the case the hunter called off the dogs as soon as he could, unless the negro fought—" that generally makes 'em mad (the hunters), and they 'll let 'em tear him a spell. The owners do n't mind having them kind o' niggers tore a good deal ; runaways ain't much account no how, and it makes the rest more afraid to run away, when they see how they are sarved." If they caught the runaway within two or three days, they got from $10 to $20 ; if it took a longer time, they were paid more than that ; sometimes $200. They asked their own price ; if an owner should think it exorbitant, he supposed, he said in reply to an inquiry, they 'd turn the nigger loose, order him to make off, and tell his master to catch his own niggers.

HILL-FOLKS ON SUNDAY.

June —, *Sunday.*—I rode on, during the cool of the morning, about eight miles, and stopped for the day, at a house pleasantly situated by a small stream, among wooded hills. During the forenoon, seven men and three women, with their children, gathered at the house. All of them, I concluded, were non-slaveholders, as was our host himself; though, as one told me, " with his five boys he makes a heap more crop than Mrs. ——, who 's got forty niggers." " How is that?" " Well, she 's a woman, and she can 't make the niggers work ; she won't have an overseer, and niggers won't work, you know, unless there 's somebody to drive 'em."

Our host, when I arrived, had just been pulling weeds out of his potato patch, which he mentioned as an apology for not being a little clean, like the rest.

Beside the company I have mentioned, and the large family of the house, there was another traveler and myself to dinner, and three bountiful tables were spread, one after another.

The traveler was said to be a Methodist preacher, but gave no indication of it, except that he said grace before meat, and used the Hebrew word for Sunday. He was, however, a man of superior intelligence to the others, who were ignorant and stupid, though friendly and communicative. One asked me "what a good nigger man could be bought for in New York;" he did n't seem surprised, or make any further inquiry, when I told him we had no slaves there. Some asked me much about crops, and when I told them that my crops of wheat for six years had averaged twenty-eight bushels, and that I had once reaped forty from a single acre, they were amazed beyond expression, and anxious to know how I "put it in." I described the process minutely, which astonished them still more; and one man said he had often thought they might get more wheat if they put it in differently; he had thought that perhaps more wheat would grow if more seed were sown, but he never tried it. The general practice, they told me, was to sow wheat on ground from which they had taken maize, without removing the maize stumps, or plowing it at all; they sowed three pecks of wheat to the acre, and then plowed it in—that was all. They used the cradle, but had never heard of reaping machines; the crop was from five to ten bushels an acre; ten bushels was extraordinary, six was not thought bad. Of cotton, the ordinary crop was five hundred pounds to the acre, or from one to two bales to a hand. Of maize, usually from ten to twenty bushels to the acre; last year not over ten; this year they thought it would be twenty-five on the best land.

HUNTING TALES.

The general admiration of Jude brought up the topic of negro dogs again, and the clergyman told a story of a man who hunted niggers near where he lived. He was out once with another man, when, after a long search, they found the dogs barking up a big cottonwood tree. They examined the tree closely without finding any negro, and concluded that the dogs must have been foiled, and they were about to go away, when Mr. ——, from some distance off, thought he saw a negro's leg very high up in the tree, where the leaves and moss were thick enough to hide a man lying on the top of a limb with his feet against the trunk. He called out, as if he really saw a man, telling him to come down, but nothing stirred. He sent for an ax, and called out again, saying he would cut the tree to the ground if he did n't come down. There was no reply. He then cut half through the tree on one side, and was beginning on the other, when the negro halloed out that if he would stop he would come down. He stopped cutting, and the negro descended to the lowest limb, which was still far from the ground, and asked the hunter to take away his dogs, and promise they should n't tear him. But the hunter swore he 'd make no conditions with him after having been made to cut the tree almost down.

The negro said no more, but retained his position until the tree was nearly cut in two. When it began to totter, he slid down the trunk, the dogs springing upon him as soon as he was within their reach. He fought them hard, and got hold of one by the ear; that made them fiercer, and they tore him till the hunter was afraid they 'd kill him, and stopped them.

I asked if dogs were often allowed to tear the negroes when they caught them?

" When the hunters come up they always call them off, unless the nigger fights. If the nigger fights 'em that makes 'em mad, and they let 'em tear him good," said the clergyman.

There were two or three young women present, and the young men were sparking with them in the house, sitting on the beds for want of sofas, the chairs being all in use outside ; the rest of the company sat on the gallery most of the time, but there was little conversation. It was twice remarked to me, " Sunday's a dull day—nothing to do."

As the Methodist and I were reading after dinner, I noticed that two or three were persuading the others to go with them somewhere, and I asked where they proposed to go. They said they wanted to go over the mountain to hunt a bull.

" To shoot him ?"

" Oh, no, it's a working bull ; they got his mate yesterday. There ain't but one pair of cattle in this neighborhood, and they do all the hauling for nine families." They belonged, together with their wagon, to one man, and the rest borrowed of him. They wanted them this week to cart in their oats. The stray bull was driven in toward night, yoked with another to a wagon, and one of the women, with her family, got into the wagon and was carried home. The bulls were fractious and had to be led by one man, while another urged them forward with a cudgel.

Last night a neighbor came into the house of Uncle Abram's master, and in the course of conversation about crops, said that on Sunday he went over to John Brown's to get him to come out and help him at his harvesting. He found four others there for the same purpose, but John said he did n't feel well, and he reckoned he could n't work. He offered him a dollar and a half a day to cradle for him, but when he tried to persuade him, John spoke out plainly and said, " he 'd be d—d if he was going to work anyhow ;" so he said to the others, " Come, boys, we may as well go; you can't make a lazy man work when he's determined he won't." He supposed that remark made him mad, for on Thursday John came running across his cotton patch, where he was plowing. He did n't speak a word to him, but cut along over to his neighbor's house, and told him that he had shot two deer, and wanted his hounds to catch 'em, promising to give him half the venison if he succeeded. He did catch one of them, and kept his promise.

This man Brown, they told me, had a large family and lived in a little cabin on the mountain. He pretended to plant a corn patch, but he never worked it, and did n't make any corn. They reckoned he lived pretty much on what corn and hogs he could steal, and on game. The children were described as pitiably, "scrawny," half-starved little wretches. Last summer his wife had come to one of them, saying they had no corn, and she wanted to pick cotton to earn some. He had let her go in with the niggers and pick. She kept at it for two days, and took her pay in corn. Afterward he saw her little boy "toting" it to the mill to be ground—much too heavy a load for him.

I asked if there were many such vagabonds.

"Yes, a great many on the mountain, and they make a heap of trouble. There is a law by which they might be taken up [if it could be proved that they have no 'visible means of support'] and made to work to support their families; but the law is never used."

Speaking of another man, one said: "He'll be here to breakfast, at your house to dinner, and at Dr. ——'s to supper, leaving his family to live as they best can." They "reckoned" he got most of his living in that way, while his family had to get theirs by stealing. He never did any work except hunting, and they "reckoned" he killed about as many shoats and yearlings as deer and turkeys.

They said that this sort of people were not often intemperate; they had no money to buy liquor with ; now and then, when they 'd sold some game or done a little work to raise money, they 'd have a spree; but they were more apt to gamble it off or spend it for fine clothes and things to trick out their wives.

June —. To-day, I am passing through a valley of thin, sandy soil, thickly populated by poor farmers. Negroes are rare, but occasionally neat, new houses, with other improvements, show the increasing prosperity of the district. The majority of the dwellings are small log cabins of one room, with another separate cabin for a kitchen; each house has a well, and a garden inclosed with palings. Cows, goats, mules and swine, fowls and doves are abundant. The people are more social than those of the lower country, falling readily into friendly conversation with a traveler. They are very ignorant; the agriculture is wretched and the work hard. I have seen three white women hoeing field crops to-day. A spinning-wheel is heard in every house, and frequently a loom is clanging in the gallery, always worked by women ; every one wears homespun. The negroes have much more individual freedom than in the planting country, and are not unfrequently heard singing or whistling at their work.

CHAPTER VI.

THE HIGHLANDERS.

THE northernmost cotton-fields, which I observed, were near the Tennessee line. This marks a climactic division of the country, which, however, is determined by change of elevation rather than of latitude. For a week or more afterwards, my course was easterly, through parts of Tennessee and Georgia into North Carolina, then northward, and by various courses back into Tennessee, when, having finally crossed the Apalachians for the fourth time, I came again to the tobacco plantations of the Atlantic slope in Virginia.

AGRICULTURAL NOTES IN THE HIGHLANDS.

The climate of this mountain region appears not to differ very greatly from that of Long Island, southern New Jersey and Pennsylvania. It is perhaps more variable, but the extremes both of heat and cold are less than are reached in those more northern and less elevated regions. The usual crops are the same, those of most consequence being corn, rye, oats, and grass. Fruit is a more precarious crop, from a greater liability to severe frosts after the swelling of buds in the spring. The apple-crop has been thus totally destroyed in the year of my journey, so that in considerable orchards I did not see a single apple. Snow had fallen several inches in depth in April, and a severe freezing night following, even young shoots, which had begun to grow, forest trees, and leaves which had expanded, were withered.

The summer pasture continues about six months. The hills generally afford an excellent range, and the mast is usually good, much being provided by the chestnut, as well as the oak, and smaller nut-bearing trees. The soil of the hills is a rich dark vegetable deposit, and they are cultivated upon very steep slopes. It is said to wash and gully but little, being very absorptive. The valleys, and gaps across the mountain ranges, are closely settled, and all the feasible level ground that I saw in three weeks was fenced, and either under tillage or producing grass for hay. The agricultural management is nearly as bad as possible. Corn, planted without any manure, even by farmers who have large stocks of cattle, is cultivated for a long series of years on the same ground ; the usual crop being from twenty to thirty bushels to the acre. Where it fails very materially, it is thought to be a good plan to shift to rye. Rye is sown in July, broadcast, among the growing corn, and incidentally covered with a plow and hoes at the "lay by" cultivation of the corn. It is reaped early in July the following year with cradles, an acre yielding from five to fifteen bushels. The following crop of corn is said to be much the better for the interpolation. Oats, and in the eastern parts, buckwheat, are sowed in fallow land, and the crops appeared to be excellent, but I could learn of never a measurement. Herds-grass (*agrostis vulgaris*), is sown on the valley lands, (rarely on the steep slopes of the mountains,) with oats, and the crop, without any further labor, pays for mowing and making into hay for from four to eight years afterward. Where it becomes mossy, weedy, and thin, it is often improved by harrowing or scarifying with a small "bull-tongue," or coulter-plow, and meadows thus made and occasionally assisted, are considered "permanent." The hay from them soon becomes in large part, however, coarse, weedy and bushy.

Natural meadows are formed on level land in the valleys, which is too wet for cultivation, by felling the timber and cutting up the bushes as close to the ground as practicable, in August. The grass is cut the following year in June, and again in August or September, at which time the new growth of bushes yield to the scythe. The sprouts cease to spring after the second or third year. Clover is a rare crop, but appears well, and is in some localities a spontaneous production. Hay is stored but little in barns, the larger part being stacked in fields. The hay fields are pastured closely, and with evident bad effect, in the spring and autumn.

Horses, mules, cattle, and swine, are raised extensively, and sheep and goats in small numbers, throughout the mountains, and afford almost the only articles of agricultural export. Although the mountains are covered during three months of the winter with snow several inches in depth, and sometimes (though but rarely) to the depth of a foot or more, and the nights, at least, are nearly always freezing, I never saw any sort of shelter prepared for neat stock. In the severest weather they are only fed occasionally, hay or corn being served out upon the ground, but this is not done daily, or as a regular thing, even by the better class of farmers. One of these, who informed me that his neighbor had four hundred head that were never fed at all, and never came off the mountain, in consequence of which "heaps of them" were starved and frozen to death every year, said that he himself gave his stock a feed "every few days," sometimes not oftener than "once in a week or two." The cattle are of course small, coarse, and "raw-boned." They are usually sold to drovers from Tennessee when three years old, and are driven by them to better lowland pastures, and more provident farmers, by whom they are fattened for the New York market. During the past five or six years, in consequence of the increasing competition, the drovers have purchased also the two year olds.

No dairy products are sold. I saw no cheese; but butter of better quality than I found elsewhere at the South, is made by all farmers for their own tables. Mules are raised largely. The mares with foals are usually provided with a pen and shed, and fed with corn, cut oats, (the grain and straw chopped together), and hay, daily during winter. This is done by no means universally, however. In no single case did I find stabling and really comfortable shelter prepared for a stock of mules; as a consequence, the mules are inferior in size and constitution to those of Kentucky, Tennessee and Missouri, and command less prices when driven to the plantations of South Carolina and Georgia—the market for which they are raised.

The business of raising hogs for the same market, which has formerly been a chief source of revenue to the mountain region, has greatly decreased under the competition it has latterly met with from Tennessee and Kentucky. It is now a matter of inferior concern except in certain places where the chestnut mast is remarkably fine. The swine at large in the mountains, look much better than I saw them anywhere else at the South. It is said that they will fatten on the mast alone, and the pork thus made is of superior taste to that made with corn, but lacks firmness. It is the custom to pen the swine and feed them with corn for from three to six weeks before it is intended to kill them. In some parts of the mountains the young swine are killed a great deal by bears. Twenty neighbors, residing within a distance of three miles, being met at a corn-shucking, last winter, at a house in which I spent the night in North Carolina, account had been taken of the number of swine each supposed himself to have lost by this enemy, during the previous two months, and it amounted to three hundred.

Bears, wolves, panthers, and wild-cats are numerous, and all kill young stock of every description. Domestic dogs should also be mentioned among the beasts of prey, as it is the general opinion of the farmers that more sheep are killed by dogs than by all other animals. Sheep raising and wool growing should be, I think, the chief business of the mountains. If provided with food in deep snows, a hardy race of sheep could be wintered on the mountains with comfort. At present no sheep are kept with profit. I have no doubt they might be, were shepherds and dogs kept with them constantly, and were they always folded at night. Eagles are numerous, and prey upon very young lambs and pigs.

Many of the farmers keep small stocks of goats, for the manageable quantity of excellent fresh meat the kids afford them, when killed in summer. Their milk is seldom made use of. They require some feeding in winter, and the new-born kids, no adequate shelter ever being provided for them, are often frozen to death. Goats, in all parts of the South, are more generally kept by farmers than at the North.

The agricultural implements employed are rude and inconvenient. A low sled is used in drawing home the crops of small grain. As it is evident that large loads may be moved with a sled across declivities where it would be impracticable to use a cart or wagon, hill-side farmers, elsewhere, might frequently find it advantageous to adopt the plan.

Slaves, I was often told, were "unprofitable property" in the mountains, except as they increase and improve in salable value. Two men, on different occasions, in mentioning the sources of revenue of the farmers in their respective districts, spoke of the sale of negroes in the same sentence with that of cattle and swine. "A nigger," said one of them, "that would n't bring over $300, seven years ago, will fetch $1000, cash, quick, this year; but now, hogs, they ain't worth so much as they used to be; there's so many of 'em driven through here from Tennessee, they've brought the price down."

Of the people who get their living entirely by agriculture, few own negroes; the slaveholders being chiefly professional men, shop-keepers, and men in office, who are also land owners, and give a divided attention to farming.

The disadvantages attendant upon slave-labor are more obvious where slaves are employed in small numbers together, because the proportion of the labor of the agricultural establishment which requires discretion and trustiness on the part of the laborer or vigilant superintendence, and "driving," at many different points at the same moment, on that of the overseer, is much smaller on a farm than on a plantation. A man can compel the uninterrupted labor of a gang of fifty cotton-hoers almost as absolutely as he can that of a gang of five, and it takes scarcely more superintendence to make sure of the proper feeding of thirty mules, when they are collected in their stable, than of three. For this reason, the bad economy of slavery is more obvious to the unthinking people, where it exists in the mild and segregated form in which it is found, when found at all, in these highland districts, than in the large properties of the cotton and sugar districts. The direct moral evils of slavery,

however, are less—even less proportionately to the number of
slaves, because the slaves being of necessity less closely superintended, and their labor being directed to a greater variety of
employments, their habits more resemble those of ordinary free
laborers, they exercise more responsibility, and both in soul and
intellect they are more elevated ; and this may be said generally
of the slaves of the northern or farming, as compared with those
of the southern or planting slave States.

The condition of a slave, however, must always carry with it
the strongest temptations to falsehood and eye-service, and slavery, in its mildest character, must be prejudicial to the morals
and to the prosperity of the country in which it exists. How
this appears in the highland region I can easily show.

In a valley of unusual breadth and fertility, where the farmers
were wealthier and the slaves more numerous than usual, I came,
one afternoon, upon a herd of uncommonly fine cattle, as they
were being turned out of a field by a negro woman. She had
given herself the trouble to let down but two of the seven bars
of the fence, and they were obliged to leap over a barrier at
least four feet high. Last of all came, very unwillingly, a handsome heifer, heavy with calf; the woman urged her with a cudgel and she jumped, but lodging on her belly, as I came up she
lay bent, and, as it seemed, helplessly hung upon the top bar. I
was about to dismount to help her, when the woman struck her
severely, and with a painful effort she boggled over. I spent the
night at the best farm, and with the best educated man I met in
all the mountain region—this, indeed, was rather below the
mountain district proper, in a valley of the eastern Piedmont
region. He spoke with some pride of the improvement in the
quality of the stock and agriculture of the neighborhood, and

asked if I had not seen some fine cattle during the afternoon. I replied that I had, and at the same time mentioned the incident I have just related. " Ha ! yes," said he, " that 's just a piece of nigger-work. She ought to have had fifty given her right off. But a nigger always will be lazy and careless." " But," said his son, a young man of eighteen, " niggers can be made to do right." " No, they can not," returned the father, " they can never be trusted to do right. I never had a nigger that would even plow to suit me unless while I was standing right over him. And who wants to spend all his life in scolding ?" Then to me, " If I could get such hired men as you can in New York, I 'd never have another nigger on my place ; but the white men here who will labor, are not a bit better than negroes. You have got to stand right over them all the time, just the same ; and then, if I should ask, now, one of my white men to go and take care of your horse, he 'd be very apt to tell me to do it myself, or, if he obeyed, he would take pains to do so in some way that would make me sorry I asked him ; then if I should scold him, he would ask me if I thought he was a nigger, and refuse to work for me any more."

Wherever there are slaves, I have found that farmers universally testify that white laborers adopt their careless habits, and that they are even more indifferent than negroes to the interests of their employers. Southerners, sometimes, deny that "slavery degrades labor," or prevents industry among the free, and I have been shown individual instances of hard-working white men to prove this. Perhaps it would be more strictly correct to say that slavery breeds unfaithful, meretricious, inexact and non-persistent habits of working. This influence of slavery extends to the mountains, although the people are much more industrious than those of the low lands. It continued to be my custom to bivouac in the woods during the hottest part of the day. One fine morning, in July, I stopped about ten o'clock, at a fork in the road, to inquire my way of a couple of young men who were binding grain in an adjoining field. They both left their work and came to the fence before answering me, but as soon as I could with civility interrupt the conversation they desired, I rode on. Just beyond the fork, a brook, having a grassy bank, and a hill crowned by a forest upon one side, crossed the road. The view down the valley was fine, and thinking I was unlikely to find a pleasanter spot later, I rode into the woods until I reached a shaded opening, took off my saddle, and soon brought my horse back to the brook crossing to graze. I then returned down the brook till I found a deep, clear pool, where I bathed ; then coming back toward my horse I saw that the men had followed me all this time. I went on to my saddle, and presently saw them approach and lie down near the horse. I walked towards them, but before I came within speaking distance, they rose and returned to their work. Half an hour later, I was awakened by Jude, and found they had again left the field, and were coming toward me. I restrained the dog and they approached ; one whittling a stick, but aimlessly, and to no purpose or shape, unlike a Yankee. Whittling away, he addressed me :

" 'Low yer minin'." (Searching for ore-beds.)

" No, sir."

" 'Low yer travelin'."

" Yes."

" 'Lowed yer was."

" 'Low that hoss was raised in the mountings," said the other.

"No; he was raised in Texas."

"What sort of a dog you call that?"

"A bull terrier."

"'Lowed 't was a sort of a bully dog," and so on. They were very ignorant. Reckoned if I was going to New York, I would not come back here—people that went that way hardly ever did: I asked if many went from here to New York. "There was a heap gone to the Texies," they said; "but they allowed New York was beyond the Texies." (Texas.)

They remained standing fully an hour near me. At length I went to the horse to give him a little corn; they followed me down, and I left them watching him eat it. Before they again returned to their work, they had lost not less than three hours of the finest harvesting morning of the season; and this is a fair illustration of the way in which the poor white farmers of the slave States are generally found to attend to their business.

Extreme poverty is rare in the mountains, but a smaller proportion of the people live in a style corresponding to that customary among what are called in New England "fore-handed folks," than in any other part of the civilized world which I have visited. The number who can be classed as moderately well-informed, using the New England rural standard, is extremely small. I did not meet in a whole month more than two or three natives who seemed to have enjoyed equal advantages of education with the lowest class of New England (native) working people. Each of those above the average in this respect I shall speak of distinctly.

The great majority live in small and comfortless log huts, two detached cabins usually forming the habitation of a family. These are rarely provided with glass windows, many are even without a port; yet the winter is more severe than that of England. The interior of one frame house, in which I spent a night, forty by thirty feet in dimensions, and two stories in height, occupied by a family of much more than the usual wealth, received light in the lower story only by the door and the occasional interstices of the boarding, and in the upper, by two loopholes, unfurnished with shutters.

The table is usually abundantly provided, its only marked difference from that of the lower country being the occasional presence of unleavened rye bread, made with saleratus and fat, unlike any rye bread I have eaten elsewhere, but more palatable to me than the usual corn bread. Butter is always offered in the mountains, and is usually good.

The women, as well as the men, generally smoke, and tobacco is grown for home use. They are more industrious than the men, often being seen at work in the fields, and at spinning wheels and hand-looms in almost every house. I was less troubled by vermin than in the low country, yet so much so that I adopted the habit of passing the night on the floor of the cabins, rather than in their beds. The furniture of the cabins is rather less meager than that of a similar class of habitations in the lower region. In the northern parts, it is common to see a square frame in which are piled a dozen bed quilts. Notwithstanding the ignorance of the people, books are more common than even in the houses of the slave owners of the planting districts. They seemed fond of reading aloud, those who were able—in a rather doleful and jolting manner. Their books are generally the cheapest and tawdriest of religious holiday books, as Mr. Sears' publications, Fox's "Martyrs," the "Biography of Distinguished Divines," with such others as "The Alarm to the

Unconverted" and "The Cause and Cure of Infidelity;" not such as *Pilgrim's Progress*, or *Robinson Crusoe*, neither of which did I ever meet with.

The generally open-hearted, frank, and kindly character of the people, the always agreeable scenery, usually picturesque, and in some parts grandly beautiful, and the salubrious atmosphere, cool at night, and though very hot, rarely at all enervating at mid-day, made this part of my journey extraordinarily pleasant. I would have been willing to continue it for months. My horse and dog, now almost every day bountifully fed on suitable food, were in good condition and spirits, and resting on Sundays, I could calculate to make twenty-six miles a day. The dog, notwithstanding the roads were much more stony and hotter than in the low country, was now never foot-sore, which I attribute to the frequency of mountain streams in which she could cool herself. Nor did my horse, though climbing and descending mountains, get seriously saddle-galled. The only precaution I took against this danger, was to wash his back twice a day with cold water, and to be sure that the saddle-blanket was laid on smoothly, and was quite clean even from dust. My expenses were not over one dollar a day, the usual charge for a night being from fifty to seventy-five cents, or little more than half that charged me by Mississippi planters for much poorer entertainment.

I resume the narrative of my journey, chiefly in the form of extracts from my diary, as before.

June 29. At nightfall I entered a broader and more populous valley than I had seen before during the day, but for sometime there were only small single-room log cabins, at which I was loth to apply for lodging. At length I reached a large and substantial log house with negro cabins. The master sat in the stoop. I asked if he could accommodate me.

"What do you want?"

"Something to eat for myself and horse, and room to sleep under your roof."

"The wust on 't is," he said, getting up and coming toward me, "we have n't got much for your horse."

"You 've got corn, I suppose."

"No, haint got no corn but a little that we want for ourselves, only just enough to bread us till corn comes again."

"Well, you have oats?"

"Haint got an oat."

"Have n't you hay?"

"No."

"Then I must go further, for my horse can't travel on fodder."

"Haint got nary fodder nuther."

A TENNESSEE SQUIRE.

Fortunately I did not have to go much further before I came to the best house I had seen during the day, a large, neat, white house, with negro shanties, and an open log cabin in the front yard. A stout, elderly, fine-looking woman, in a cool white muslin dress sat upon the gallery, fanning herself. Two little negroes had just brought a pail of fresh water, and she was drinking of it with a gourd, as I came to the gate. I asked if it would be convenient for her to accommodate me for the night, doubtingly, for I had learned to distrust the accommodations of the wealthy slaveholders.

"Oh yes, get down, fasten your horse there, and the niggers will take care of him when they come from their work. Come up here and take a seat."

I brought in my saddle-bags.

"Bring them in here, into the parlor," she said, "where they 'll be safe."

The interior of the house was furnished with unusual comfort. "The parlor," however, had a bed in it. As we came out she locked the door.

We had not sat long, talking about the weather, (she was suffering much from the heat), when her husband came. He was very hot also, though dressed coolly enough in merely a pair of short-legged, unbleached cotton trowsers, and a shirt with the bosom spread open—no shoes nor stockings. He took his seat before speaking to me, and after telling his wife it was the hottest day he ever saw, squared his chair toward me, threw it back so as to recline against a post, and said gruffly, "Good evening, sir; you going to stay here to-night?"

I replied, and he looked at me a few moments without speaking. He was in fact so hot that he spoke with difficulty. At length he got breath and asked abruptly: "You a mechanic, sir, or a dentist, eh—or what?"

I presently asked what railroad it was that I had crossed about six miles east of Chatanooga. I had not expected to find any railroad in this direction. He answered pompously that it was "the Atlantic and Pacific railroad. It began at Charleston and ended at Chatanooga, but was to be carried across to a place called Francisco in California."

Valuable information, but hardly as interesting as that which the old lady gave me soon afterward. We had been talking of Texas and the emigration. She said "there was a new country they had got annexed to the United States now, and she reckoned people would all be for going to that, now it was annexed. They called it Nebrasky ; she did n't know much about it, but she reckoned it must be a powerful fine country, they'd taken so much trouble to get possession of it."

Supper was cooked by two young women, daughters of the master of the house, assisted by the two little negro boys. The cabin in front of the house was the kitchen, and when the bacon was dished up, one of the boys struck an iron triangle at the door. "Come to supper," said the host, and led the way to the kitchen, which was also the supper room, One of the young ladies took the foot of the table, the other seated herself apart by the fire, and actually waited on the table, though the two negro boys stood at the head and foot, nominally waiters, but always anticipated by the Cinderella, when any thing was wanted.

A big lout of a youth who came from the field with the negroes, looked in, but seeing me, retired. His father called, but his mother said, "'t would n't do no good—he was so bashful."

Speaking of the climate of the country, I was informed that a majority of the folks went barefoot all winter, though they had snow much of the time four or five inches deep, and the man said he did n't think most of the men about here had more than one coat, and they never wore any in winter except on holidays. "That was the healthiest way," he reckoned, "just to toughen yourself and not wear no coat ; no matter how cold it was, he did n't wear no coat."

The master held a candle for me while I undressed, in a large room above stairs; and gave me my choice of the four beds in it. I found one straw bed (with, as usual, but one sheet), on which I slept comfortably. At midnight I was awakened by some one coming in. I rustled my straw, and a voice said, " Who is there in this room?"

" A stranger passing the night; who are you?"

" All right; I belong here. I 've been away and have just come home."

He did not take his clothes off to sleep. He turned out to be an older son who had been fifty miles away, looking after a stray horse. When I went down stairs in the morning, having been wakened early by flies, and the dawn of day through an open window, I saw the master lying on his bed in the " parlor," still asleep in the clothes he wore at supper. His wife was washing herself on the gallery, being already dressed for the day; after drying her face on the family towel, she went into the kitchen, but soon returned, smoking a pipe, to her chair in the doorway.

Yet every thing betokened an opulent and prosperous farmer— rich land, extensive field crops, a number of negroes, and considerable herds of cattle and horses. He also had capital invested in mines and railroads, he told me. His elder son spoke of him as " the squire."

A negro woman assisted in preparing breakfast (she had probably been employed in the field labor the night before), and both the young ladies were at the table. The squire observed to me that he supposed we could buy hands very cheap in New York. I said we could hire them there at moderate wages. He asked if we could n't buy as many as we wanted, by sending to Ireland for them and paying their passage. He had supposed we could buy them and hold them as slaves for a term of years, by paying the freight on them. When I had corrected him, he said, a little hesitatingly, "You do n't have no black slaves in New York?" "No, sir." "There's niggers there, ain't there, only they're all free?" "Yes, sir." "Well, how do they get along so?" "So far as I know, the most of them live pretty comfortably." (I have changed my standard of comfort lately, and am inclined to believe that the majority of the negroes at the North live more comfortably than the majority of whites at the South.) "I would n't like that," said the old lady. "I would n't like to live where niggers was free, they are bad enough when they are slaves : it's hard enough to get along with them here, they're so bad. I reckon that niggers are the meanest critters on earth ; they are so mean and nasty" (she expressed disgust and indignation very strongly in her face). "If they was to think themselves equal to we, I do n't think white folks could abide it—they're such vile saucy things." A negro woman and two boys were in the room as she said this.

At night I was again troubled to find a house at which my horse could be suitably fed, and was finally directed to a place at some distance off my direct road. To reach it, I followed a cart path up a pretty brook in a mountain glen, till I came to an irregular-shaped cattle yard, in the midst of which was a rather picturesque cabin, the roof being secured by logs laid across it and held in place by long upright pins. The interior consisted of one large "living-room," and a "lean-to," used as a kitchen, with a sleeping loft over half the living-room. For furniture, there were two bedsteads, which occupied one-third of the room ; a large and a small table, on the latter of which lay a big Bible, and other books ; several hide-bottomed chairs, two chests, shelves, with crockery, and a framed lithographic portrait of Washington on the white horse. Women's dresses hung as a curtain along the foot of one bed; hides, hams, and bunches of candles from the rafters. An old man and his wife, with one hired man, were the occupants; they had come to this place from North Carolina two years before. They were very good, simple people; social and talkative, but at frequent intervals the old man, often in the midst of conversation, interrupting a reply to a question put by himself, would groan aloud and sigh out, "Glory to God!" "Oh, my blessed Lord!" "Lord, have mercy on us!" or something of the sort, and the old woman would respond with a groan, and then there would be silence for reflection for a few moments, as if a dead man were in the house, and it had been forgotten for a time. They talked with great geniality and kindness, however, and learning that I was from New York, said that I had reminded them, "by the way I talked," of some New York people who had moved near to where they had lived in North Carolina, and whom they seemed to have much liked. "They was well larned people," the old man said; "though they warn't rich, they was as well larned as any, but they was the most friendly people I ever see. Most of our country folks, when they is well larned, is too proud, they won't hardly speak civil to the common; but these Yorkers was n't so, the least bit; they was the civilest people I ever seed. When I seed the gals coming over to our housen, I nat'rally rejoiced; they always made it so pleasant. I never see no peo· ple who could talk so well."

He and his wife frequently referred to them afterwards, and complimented me by saying that "they should have known me for a Yorker by my speeching so like them."

I said, in answer to their inquiry, that I had found the people of this part of the country remarkably friendly and sociable. The old man said he had " always heard this was so, and it was nat'ral it should be. There warn't no niggers here; where there was niggers, people could n't help getting a cross habit of speaking." He asked if New York were not a free State, and how I liked that. I answered, and he said he 'd always wished there had n't been any niggers here (the old woman called out from the other room, that she wished so, too), but he would n't like to have them free. As they had got them here, he did n't think there was any better way of getting along with them than that they had. There were very few in this district, but where they came from there were more niggers than whites. They had had three themselves; when they decided to move up here into the mountains, the niggers did n't want to come with them, and they sold them to a speculator.

I asked if it was possible they would prefer to be sold to a trader, who might take them off and sell them to a cotton planter.

" O, yes, they had a great fear of the mountains; they would rather, they said, be sent to a cotton farm, or a rice or sugar farm—any thing else; so we sold them to the first nigger-speculator that come along." The old woman called out again, that she wished they had n't, for after all they was a great help to her, and it was very hard sometimes to do all the work she had to do, alone. "Those Yorkers did n't like slaves neither," she continued, coming into the room, "they said they could n't bear to have 'em do any thing for 'em, they was so shacklin and lazy, but one of the gals married a man who owned a heap of niggers, for all that."

Their notions of geography were amusing. They thought Virginia lay to the southward, and was a cotton-growing State, and they supposed that one reason their niggers were willing to be sold, was that their mother came from Virginia, and they had heard her talk of it, and that they thought they might be sold to go back there upon a cotton farm. New York, they thought, lay west of Georgia, and between them and Texas. They asked about Indiana, and said that I must have passed through it coming from Texas, confusing it, probably, with Louisiana; and they asked if New York were not the country the Yankees came from—" the people that used to come peddling." They supposed also that New York had a much warmer climate than Georgia. The younger man informed me that " the United States had lately annexed a new country that was called Nebrisky. It was large enough to make thirteen States, and they had had a great commotion as to whether it should be free or slave States. The people here all wanted it to be slave States, because they might want to move out there, and a fellow might get a nigger and have to sell him. If a man moved into a free State, he 'd have to sell his niggers; if he did n't, they 'd be free as soon as he took 'em in. He did n't think that was right; a man ought to be able to take his property wherever he pleased."

I replied that it would be a great deal better place for non-slaveholders to move to, if slaves were excluded, to which he made no reply.

We had for supper, cold corn bread, cold bacon and hot coffee. The old woman remarked she had got so warm she could n't eat any thing, but she drank much coffee. I was a good deal fatigued; about eight o'clock I intimated that I would like to go to bed. The old man lighted a candle, for until then, we had been sitting by the firelight in the chimney, and after groaning aloud for the space of ten minutes, began to read in a very slow, monotonous manner, spelling out the hard words, from the Bible. After continuing this exercise for half an hour, he took a hymn book, read two lines and commenced to sing, and thus went on reading and singing, the other two joining him at the second verse, when we all rose. Thirteen verses were sung, and then, after blowing out the candle, he kneeled for prayer. He prayed with great fervor, much assisted by the ejaculatory responses of his wife, for more than half an hour. When we rose, the old woman took a single clean sheet from a chest, spread it on one of the beds, and told me that I could take that one. I began to undress, and she stepped out of doors till I was under the counterpane. The young man climbed into the loft, and the two old people took the other bed. There was no window at all in the house; they closed both doors and left a considerable fire burning on the hearth. There did not, however, appear to be any want of ventilation, the logs and roof being sufficiently open. It was the first time, with only one exception, in more than a month, that I had been furnished with a clean sheet. (The luxury of two sheets I have never had in a private house since crossing the Mississippi;) and I slept better than I have done before, for weeks.

When I came to breakfast, the old woman was much disappointed that I declined coffee. She had thought I would like it sweet, and had taken pains to boil in some sweetenin' (molasses) on my account; she said she did not think I could have strength to travel such hot weather without it. I replied that I thought that I had found that in hot weather, after a little while, its effect was rather debilitating. "Perhaps it was so," she said,

" and that was the reason she felt so weak and sleepy in the afternoon. They did n't have no coffee for dinner, and she had thought she ought to have it, because in the afternoon she was always so tired and sleepy she could hardly drag about till supper time, and at supper she always drank a lot of coffee just to keep from going to sleep till after prayers. She did n't feel as though she could live without coffee."

She had taken much pains otherwise to get a good breakfast—thick griddle cakes of Indian meal, which I could really praise with a good conscience. This greatly elevated her, and she told me in a confidential whisper, " there were none of her neighbors ever had any thing nice, not even for company, because they did n't any of 'em know how to cook beyond the common."

Molasses they always used as if in the plural number (like oats), urging me to take " them molasses—but perhaps I would n't like them with my bacon."

My horse was well cared for, voluntarily, by the hired man; cleaned and fed generously with corn, fodder, hay and sheaf oats. Charge for all, including two of the notable Indian slap-jacks, which I carried away in my haversack, sixty-two and a half cents. When I wanted to wash, I was directed to "'the spring," the old woman having the wash basin in use. In fact, she was mixing the cakes in it.

TENNESSEE COPPER MINING.

I have been visiting the mining region, which I approached through the pretty valley of the ———, where, for the first time in this journey, I met with hemlocks and laurels growing in great perfection.

The first discovery of ore was made ten years ago, soon after which, specimens were taken to New York, but no mining was done, and nothing was known of it here, until a New York company bought a tract of land three years ago, and immediately commenced operations. New veins were soon found and new companies formed, and the excitement continues, new discoveries being made up to this time. At the public house were ten or twelve gentlemen of wealth, who had come to sell or buy copper land, or to learn "the signs" that they might look for them on their own land elsewhere.

The mines in operation at present are owned almost entirely in New York and London. The miners employed are mostly white North Carolinians, who are paid twenty to twenty-five dollars a month, when digging perpendicular shafts, and twenty-five to thirty dollars, when working horizontally. There are here, however, several hundred Cornish men ("London miners," a native told me), and more are constantly coming. They are engaged in Cornwall, and have their expenses out paid, and forty dollars a month wages. They are said, at these wages, to be much more profitably employed than the natives. Two, whom I found at work together, one hundred and fifty feet from the surface, told me that they had been here about six weeks, and were well pleased. They each got forty dollars a month ; in England, they had earned respectively but three and four pounds. Board costs here at the boarding houses seven dollars a month, but they thought that a man living "in a cottage" by himself, could live cheaper than in England. Corn-bread (though Cornish men), they had not yet eaten, and they did not believe that they should ever come to it. They must have wheaten bread. The only thing they much missed was ale ; the people here did not know what it was, but drank whiskey. They would rather have one draught of Cornish swipes than a gallon of this whiskey.

Some of the miners, including some of the Cornish men, had been getting ready a pole, which they were to erect, and hoist a flag upon, on the fourth of July. I heard a report the day before I reached the mines, that the Englishmen at the mines were going to hoist the English flag and hurrah for the Queen on the fourth of July. The country people were much excited by this report, and on the third I met a great many of them, armed with rifles, coming in " to see about it." I could not persuade them that the Englishmen were intending in good faith to celebrate the day, so strong was their belief in the continued hostility of the English people to American independence.

There were few settlers here when the mines were discovered. At present, the population is reported to be many thousand. If so, it must be remarkably scattered, for there is nothing like a village; the only houses, with two or three exceptions, being small log cabins. I stopped at what is considered the best public house. When I asked for a bed, I was pointed to a room in which there were seven beds, and told that I could take my pick. Two gentlemen immediately called out to inform me which of the beds they had used the night before, hoping that I would respect their claim to hold them. All the beds had been slept in by others, without change of sheet. Being the first to withdraw from the bar room, I had my choice, and found one straw bed among them, which, of course, I appropriated. Fortunately, I had no bed-fellow; the other beds were mostly doubly occupied.

At a public house, a few nights before, I heard the landlord, while conducting two men to their sleeping room, observe, that he supposed that they would like to sleep both in the same bed, as they came together, and I afterwards saw them together in a feather bed, notwithstanding there were several vacant beds in the same room. It was almost the hottest night I ever experienced out of the East Indies, and I sweltered upon the floor.

A SMART YANKEE.

Everybody at the mines took me for either a shrewd speculator, or a mineralogist who had come to make examinations for a speculator. I was several times stopped and asked if I did not wish to look at a good piece of mineral land, and often requested to give my opinion of specimens, nor could I make myself believed when I said I knew nothing about the matter. After I returned from visiting some of the mines, there was a room full of people at the public house. One asked me if I would tell them what I thought about those I had seen. I assured him that I was not in the least able to judge of their value, probably not half so much so as he was himself. He laughed, and another, laughing, asked, " What do you carry in that thing at your side ?" and every body smiled.

" In this pouch, do you mean ?"

" Yes, if it 's no offense—no offense meant, no offense taken, you know."

" Certainly not ; I 'll tell you exactly what I 've got in it." I opened it and looking in, as it were, read the contents, " a pair of gloves, a knife, a corkscrew, a fleam, a tooth brush, a box of tapers, and a ball of twine." All laughed aloud, being quite sure in their minds that the pouch contained a blow-pipe, tests, and specimens of ore, and that I was a very knowing fellow, who could keep his own counsel.

July 5th.—Last evening I rode several miles, constantly saying to myself, as I passed the miserable huts, "that, I can't put up with," and still going on to try further for something better, until, just as it was getting dark, I came to some larger cabins, one of which had creepers trained over a porch, for which sign of taste I selected it. It was occupied by a family, possessing a number of negro servants, and living in more comfort than I have seen for some time. My horse being brought out in the morning covered with mire, I asked the negro if he would not clean him. He picked up a piece of corn cob and began scraping him. "Had n't he got a curry comb or card?" I asked, but he did not know what I meant, and laughed when I explained it to him, as you would laugh at some little article of pure foppery.

I passed through Murphy to-day, a pretty, shady town, surrounded by lovely scenery. I was a little surprised at the sight of a pillory and stocks, and to learn that a white man had been recently stripped, whipped, and branded with a red hot iron for some petty crime, by the officers of the law, in the presence of my informant, and of all of the inhabitants who could be called together to witness this solemn testimony of the legislative barbarism of their State.

While I stopped under a tree near a house as a heavy rain cloud was passing, a white man came out, and after greeting me with a single word, began calling: "Duke, Clary, Tom, Joe," etc., finally collecting seven little negroes and three white children; "Just look a here! here's a reg'lar nigger dog; have it to ketch niggers when they run away, or do n't behave." (He got a piece of bread and threw it to Jude.) "There! did you see that! See what teeth she's got, she'd just snap a nigger's leg off. If you do n't mind I'll get one—you Jule, if I hear you crying any more, I'll get this gentleman to send me one. See how strong its jaws be; he says all he's got to do when a nigger do n't behave, is just to say the word, and it'll snap a nigger's head right off, just as easy as you'd take a chicken's head off with an ax." (The niggers look with dismay at Jude, who is watching them very closely expecting some more bread. The white children laugh foolishly.)

July 6.—I have to-day crossed the Tomahila mountain, having spent the night at an unusually comfortable house, known throughout all the country as " Walker's," situated at its western base. Apparently it is a house which the wealthy planters from the low country make a halting station on their journey to certain sulphur springs further north and east. There were plenty of negroes, under unusually good government, and the table supply was abundant and various. Yet every thing was greasy; even what we call simple dishes, such as boiled rice, and toast, were served soaking in a sauce of melted fat. I gave the stable boy a quarter of a dollar for thoroughly cleaning my horse, but rode away with less than usual scrutiny of the harness, and when I came to climb a steep pitch of the mountain, discovered that the rascal had unbuckled and kept the preventer-girth.

The road, which is excellent, and which was built by aid of a State appropriation, follows for some distance the slopes of a water course, and then, tack and tack, up a steep mountain-side, until, at about twelve miles from Walker's, a small plateau and clearing is reached, on which stands a cabin occupied by a man, who, as he told me, gets his living by turning bed-posts of maple, which grows here abundantly and is scarce below.

After leaving this place, the road descends into a shallow valley in which flows the Tomahila river, a stream some twenty yards across, then follows for several miles along the crest of a deep dark gorge, at the bottom of which the river roars in frequent cascades, and then mounts another high ridge. From the summit there is a grand prospect, to the eastward. Directly below is a deep valley, surrounded on all sides by a succession of mountain peaks. With the exception of one bald prominence towering up on the left, these are all, notwithstanding their great height, densely wooded. Those directly opposite are some forty miles distant, and are among the highest elevations on the continent.

While I was resting my horse and looking at these distant summits, some thunder clouds drifted around and collected before them, and then floated forward, hovering over the minor peaks and pouring copious showers upon them. The thunder grew constantly more threatening, and I began to descend hastily. A zigzag road has been made with great labor, so that by traveling two miles upon a descending slope, never more rapidly than at the rate of perhaps six feet in one hundred, you accomplish with entire ease what would be, in a direct course down the steep side of the mountain, not more than a thousand feet. The entire distance to the valley is six miles.

A little boy on a mule, carrying a mail-bag, here overtook me. He said that he carried the mail from Ashville to Murphy, one hundred and fourteen miles, traveling each way once a week. He starts from Ashville Monday morning and returns there Saturday night, rests on Sunday, but during the week travels an average of nearly forty miles a day on a mule's back. Last winter, he said, the snow was often up to the mule's shoulders on the mountain; but he did not fail to accomplish his stated journey every day. When I asked him how old he was, he said " he be-

lieved that he should be about fifteen in three or four months."
He had two mules, but only changed from one to the other on
alternate weeks. He was paid $5 a month, and board.

Speaking of mountains, he asked if I "had ever been on Old
Balsam?" He had; he was up on the top of it one morning at
sunrise. I asked how he could sleep there—was there a cabin?
No, but he had been coon hunting with some fellows all night,
and toward daylight they got to running a wild-cat, for they had
a dog that would kill any wild-cat if it could catch it. They
did not succeed, however, and just at sunrise they gave it up and
found themselves close to the top of Old Balsam. Then he had
to go down the mountain and get up his mule, and ride forty
miles with the mail before he could go to sleep. It was as much
as he could do to keep awake that day.

Hearing that I belonged in New York, he asked if I knew a
man there by the name of Poillon. Yes, I did; he lived a little
out of New York city, though—in the country. "The man I
mean lives in New York center—right in the village itself," he
replied. I knew that there was a man there of that name, I
said. "Well he went from Ashville." "Yes, perhaps so." "Oh
he did, he went from there two year ago. Do you know a man
there by the name of Ogee?"

"No."

"There was a man at Ashville, came from somewhere in that
country—Charleston, I believe 't was—by that name."

"Charleston is not very near New York."

"Ain't it? well, 't was Charleston he said, I believe; Charleston or New York, or some place out there."

Another man near Waynesville in this region, asked me if I

knew Mr. White, of New York. I did not. "Why, he belongs in New York."

"Very likely, but New York is a large place. There are probably a hundred people of the name of White there, but I do n't happen to know one of them."

"Reckon you 'd know this man if he came from there, for he 's a man of talent; must be one of the first men; I never see a man who knew so much about all sorts of things, and who could explain every thing out to you, as well as he. Expect he must have come from some other place. I thought he said he was raised in New York, too."

"Very possibly he was, but I know but very few indeed of all the men of talent in New York. You do n't consider how many people there are there."

"It 's a right smart business place, I know; it must be. You know Mr. ——, do n't you?"

"Who is he?"

"Why the little man that keeps store in Waynesville; reckon you know him, he goes to New York every spring to buy goods; seen him there, hain't you?"

"I do n't think that I have; you see, there are seven hundred thousand people in New York, and there are thousands and tens of thousands whom I never saw. It would be impossible for me to see one in a thousand of the people who come there every year. In fact, though I have lived in New York some years, I have but very few acquaintances there, not nearly as many as you have in this county probably."

"Such a big place; I suppose there 's some people been living there all their lives that do n't know each other, and never spoke to one another once yet in their lives, ain't there?"

"Certainly—thousands of them."

"'T ain't so here; people's more friendly, this country."

Ashville, July 11*th.*—This is a beautiful place among the hills, with a number of pretty country-seats about it, which, I suppose are summer residences of South Carolina planters. A great many of these "Southerners," as they are called here, are now traveling farther north, to spend the heat of summer at the numerous sulphur springs and other pleasure haunts, where good boarding houses have been established for them along the cool region of the Blue Ridge. I passed one of these, a sulphur spring, yesterday. It was a white, wooden building, with a long piazza for smokers, loungers, and flirters, and a bowling alley and shuffle board; with coaches and trotting wagons at the stable; poor women picking blackberries, poor men bringing fowls, school girls studiously climbing romantic rocks and otherwise making themselves as pretty as possible, children fighting their black nurses, and old gold spectacles stopping me to inquire if I was the mail, and if I had not got a newspaper.

It is very odd, by the way, what old news one keeps getting in these places far from telegraphs. I inquired here for a late paper, and the clerk of the hotel went to a store to get one. It was the Ashville News, with the same articles copied from New York papers, which I had read a month before. All this country is to be netted by railroads soon, however, that is, as soon as they can be built after an appropriation to assist them passes Congress. I have crossed engineers' stakes every day, I believe, since I left Jackson, Mississippi, and generally, when I stop at night, the farmer tells me that a railroad, which will be *the* link which is wanting, either in a direct communication between the Atlantic and the Mississippi, or between New York and New Orleans, is to pass between his house and his corn-crib, and that in consequence land about him has lately become of great value, that is, from four to ten dollars an acre. He is in great perplexity, too, to conclude how much he can make the railroad company pay for damages.

Day before yesterday I ascended "Balsam Mountain," said to have been recently ascertained to be the highest peak of the Apalachian chain. A barometrical measurement of Professor W. D. Jones, of Tennessee, makes it ten thousand and three hundred feet above the sea, or one hundred and five feet higher than Black Mountain, which has always had the reputation of being the highest. I was told that the ascent was easy, and could be made on horseback to within less than a quarter of a mile of the top. I was offered a guide, but preferred to go alone, leaving Belshazzar to rest and recruit below.

The mountain is one of a very lofty range, and the gap between it and the next peak is crossed by a (State) turnpike road. The distance to the top from this road is about four miles, and its elevation above the road, four thousand feet. A very rank growth of weeds and grass covers the ground on nearly all parts of the mountain to the top, which is all used as a range for cattle, horses and hogs, and would be very profitably employed in this way but for the havoc committed on young cattle, and especially on swine and sheep, by bears, wolves and panthers.

The horses and cattle make so many paths that I was soon led astray from the one which leads directly to the top (if there is any such), and had to shape my course by the sun, and the apparent feasibility of the ground in different directions before me. The mountain, to within less than a mile from the top, is entirely shaded by a forest of large trees, the chestnut predominating.

The only change found as you ascend, is in their height; the trunks continually becoming shorter and sturdier. At perhaps half a mile from the summit, the trees appear gradually more scattered; at length there is a nearly bald zone, covered, however, with grass and weeds waist high. Above this, at a quarter of a mile from the top, begins a forest of balsam firs (popularly called "balsams"). In the interval, between the two forests, the ascent was steep and fatiguing. Whether owing to the exertion of climbing altogether, or somewhat to the rarity of the atmosphere, I was obliged to stop frequently to rest, to relieve myself from a rush of blood to the head. The moment I entered the balsam forest, I was freed from this. These balsams are thirty or forty feet high, and under their shelter flourish a variety of smaller trees and shrubs. A great many of these trees have fallen down, and the nearer I came to the top the steeper became the ascent, the more frequent the prostrate trees, and the thicker and more impenetrable the undergrowth, a large part of it being blackberry briars. I crept under and climbed over, and pulled myself along slowly, and at length came to a knob or pinnacle, across and upon which, trees and shrubs, and stumps, with the roots uppermost, seemed to have been hurled by a whirlwind. Supposing this to be the summit itself, I climbed among the roots and briars, the best way I could, until I got my head above the wreck. It was very dark from the shade of the standing trees, and I perceived that the rocks rose still higher beyond. I worked my way down again and continued climbing, until I reached a comparatively level surface of several yards in extent, from which a number of trees had been cut away so as to open a view in two or three directions. A dense cloud hung in a circle all around the peak, and though it was quite clear in the cen-

ter where I stood, I could not see beyond it at all. Overhead, at
a still vast apparent distance, were striæ, through which, at
length, the sun came out for a few minutes, but the only effect
was to give the cumulus below me a more mist-like and steamy
appearance. At length came a slight breeze, and set it in rapid
motion, and rent and lifted, and lowered it, so that I got a few
glimpses across the neighboring mountains, and saw their tops
rising above rolling thunder heads, one of which was dark, and
probably discharging rain. I heard thunder, and conjectured that
at a distance, the cloud within which I stood would appear to be
a thunder cloud, wooly and snowy, and gilded when the sun
shone, and dark and rainy below.

The peculiarity of this mountain-top, distinguishing it from all
others I know, of nearly equal height, is its moderate temperature and consequent abundant vegetation. It was so warm (it
was half past one), that, heated as I became by my exertions, I
felt no necessity for putting on my coat. The air was soft and
agreeable. The ground, a dark, rich soil, with rocks protruding
and shaly stones, bore luxuriant coarse herbage. Beside the
thick growth of firs, I noticed black birch, chestnut, mountain
ash, wild currant, whortleberry, blackberry, honeysuckle, and a
variety of cherry, all growing on the highest point. The air was
of coarse moist, and every thing damp, and this was evidently its
usual condition. All the dead and broken down trees, and the
rocks were covered thickly with mosses and lichens, which were
charged with water like a soaked sponge.

I remained half an hour, hoping the cloud would clear away,
but it only grew denser and darker. Beginning to descend, I
found a path and endeavored to follow it, but as it soon ran into
forks, branching out in every direction, I determined to pursue a

direct course down the mountain to the edge of the balsam forest, and then follow its lower line until I came to the path, or to the ridge along which I knew the path or way usually followed, led. I got lost, however, in the cloud, and descended at a point where the lower forest extended up so as to meet the firs. I could not see out, but turning to the left, continued descending diagonally. The slope was very steep, and the ground covered with shelving stones, so that it was difficult to keep my feet. At length, on an inclination of about thirty-five degrees, I slipped, caught myself with a quick motion of my foot, but at the next step, tripped on a protruding root or tangle of weeds, balanced for a moment and was then thrown down headlong. I was severely bruised, and for some minutes could not rise. Fortunately, at no great distance, I found a deep gully with a stream of cold water; after bathing in which, I entirely recovered my strength, though it was not till after several days that the contusions I received ceased to be inconvenient. I soon reached a more moderate slope, with a rich soil, bearing large trees, and very luxuriant tangled herbage.

Meanwhile the cloud on the pinnacle was muttering thunder, and growing darker and more threatening. As I hastened on, I saw at no great distance, waddling off through the weeds, two black bears, but was so fortunate as to meet no snakes, and nothing else at all memorable. At about half past six I reached the foot of the mountain, and shortly afterward the cloud on its summit swept downward and onward with heavy thunder and copious rain.

I was about five hours descending and reaching the house whence I started. The farmer said that he went nearly to the top to salt his cattle once a week, and he could go up and back again by his path in two hours. In going up I went leisurely, stopping to sketch, and made a very good course until I got to the firs; but in coming down I missed my way, and probably traveled over four times as much ground as was necessary. It was from carelessness or indifference at the start—I was willing to make a day of it.

The view from under the cloud was very beautiful. The general character of the scenery is less grand than that of the White Mountains, but it has impressive sublimity and repose. All the mountains are covered with trees, which, with the luxuriant herbage beneath them, secures softness of outline. Brooks of clear water are frequent. The mountain sides are often very steep, but actual precipices or even large ledges or masses of rock, I have not seen. These mountains would therefore be more pleasant to ramble over than the White Mountains, and will probably, when railroads are completed in their neighborhood, be much resorted to for pleasure. At present there is no public conveyance to any point within thirty-five miles of the base of " Balsam Mountain."

Mr. Buckley, a New York botanist, gives the following facts with regard to the mountains of this vicinity :

" The following are the heights of some mountains, and places among the mountains of North Carolina, south and west of Ashville. These heights were ascertained by me with two of Green's standard barometers. Professor J. Le Conte, of Columbia, South Carolina, observed the stationary barometer at Waynesville, for the measurement of the highest Smoky mountains, and being called away by the duties of his professorship, Miss S. Cathey, with the same barometer, made observations at the Forks of Pigeon, Haywood county, while I was with another barometer on the tops of the other mountains measured. The highest are in the Great Smoky or Unaka range of mountains, on the line between the States of North Carolina and Tennessee, near the head waters of the Oconaluftee and Little Pigeon rivers. You will observe that there are twelve peaks higher than Mount Washington, and two higher than Mount Mitchell, 6711 feet high, which has long been considered the highest east of the Rocky Mountains, viz. : Mount Le Conte, 6670 ; Mount Guyot, 6734 ; Mount Buckley, 6755 ; Clingman's Peak, 6941.

" Those high mountains show us why western North Carolina and eastern Tennessee have a northern climate in a southern latitude.

" These late measurements show us that the highest mountains at the South are not at the sources of the largest rivers, as has generally been supposed.

" The highest mountains are covered with Abies Nigra and Abies Fraseri, which are rarely found growing beneath an elevation of four thousand feet—the first being called by the inhabitants the he-balsam, and the latter the she-balsam. The Abies balsamica is not found there as stated by Michaux. A large moss (Hypnum splendens), often dotted with oxalis acetosella and Mitchella repens, almost invariably forms a thick, soft carpet beneath these balsam trees. Our little red squirrel (Sciurus Hudsonius), there called the mountain buma, sports and chatters among these balsam trees, feeding on their cones. He rarely descends to the base of the mountains."

July 13.—I rode late last night, there being no cabins for several miles in which I was willing to spend the night, until I came to one of larger size than usual, with a gallery on the side toward the road and a good stable opposite it. A man on the

gallery was about to answer (as I judged from his countenance),
" I reckon you can," to my inquiry if I could stay, when the
cracked voice of a worryful woman screeched out from within,
" We do n't foller takin' in people."

" No, sir," said the man, " we do n't foller it."

" How far shall I have to go ?"

" There 's another house a little better than three quarters of a
mile further on."

To this house I proceeded—a cabin of one room and a loft,
with a kitchen in a separate cabin. The owner said he never
turned anybody away, and I was welcome. He did not say that
he had no corn, until after supper, when I asked for it to feed my
horse. The family were good-natured, intelligent people, but
very ignorant. The man and his wife and the daughters slept
below, the boys and I in the cock-loft. Supper and breakfast
were eaten in the detached kitchen. Yet they were by no
means poor people. The man told me that he had over a thousand acres of rich tillable land, besides a large extent of mountain range, the most of which latter he had bought from time to
time as he was able, to prevent the settlement of squatters near
his valley-land. " There were people who would be bad neighbors I knew," he said, " that would settle on most any kind of
place, and every body wants to keep such as far away from them
as they can." (When I took my bridle off, I hung it up by the
stable door ; he took it down and said he 'd hang it in a safer
place. " He 'd never had any thing stolen from here, and he
did n't mean to have—it was just as well not to put temptation
before people," and he took it into the house and put it under his
bed.)

Besides this large tract of land here, he owned another tract

of two hundred acres with a house upon it, rented for one third
the produce, and another smaller farm, similarly rented ; he also
owned a grist mill, which he rented to a miller for half the tolls.
He had also a considerable stock of cattle and large crops of
grain, so that he must be considered a very respectable capitalist
for a mountaineer. He told me that he had thought a good deal
formerly of moving to new countries, but he had been doing
pretty well and had staid here now so long, he did n't much think
he should ever budge. He reckoned he 'd got enough to make
him a living for the rest of his life, and he did n't know any use
a man had for more 'n that.

I did not see a single book in the house, nor do I think that
any of the family could read. He said that many people here
were talking about Iowa and Indiana; "was Iowa (Hiaway) beyond the Texies ?" I opened my map to show him where it was,
but he said he "was n't scollar'd enough" to understand it, and I
could not induce him to look at it. I asked him if the people here
preferred Iowa and Indiana to Missouri at all because they were
free States. "I reckon," he replied, "they do n't have no allu-
sion to that. Slavery is a great cuss, though, I think, the greatest there is in these United States. There ain't no account of
slaves up here in the west, but down in the east part of this State
about Fayetteville, there 's as many as there is in South Carolina.
That 's the reason the West and the East do n't agree in this
State ; people out here hates the eastern people."

" Why is that ?"

" Why you see they vote on the slave basis, and there 's some
of them nigger counties where there ain't more 'n four or five
hundred white folks, that has just as much power in the Legisla-

ture as any of our mountain counties where there 'll be some thousand voters."

He made further remarks against slavery and against slave-holders. When I told him that I entirely agreed with him, and said further that poor white people were usually far better off in the free States than in the slave, he seemed a little surprised and said, " New York ain't a free State, is it ?"

Laborers' wages here, he stated, were from fifty cents to one dollar a day, or eight dollars a month. " How much by the year ?" " They 's never hired by the year."

" Would it be $75 a year ?"

" 'T would n't be over that, any how, but 't ain't general for people to hire here only for harvest time; fact is, a man could n't earn his board, let alone his wages, for six months in the year."

" But what do these men who hire out during harvest time do during the rest of the year; do they have to earn enough in those two or three months to live on for the other eight or nine ?"

" Well they gets jobs sometimes, and they goes from one place to another."

" But in winter time, when you say there 's not work enough to pay their board ?"

" Well, they keeps a goin' round from one place to another, and gets their living somehow."

" The fact on 't is," he said at length, as I pressed the enquiry, " there ain't anybody that ever means to work any in this coun-try, except just along in harvest—folks do n't keep working here as they do in your country, I expect."

" But they must put in their crops ?"

" Yes, folks that have farms of their own, they do put in their craps and tend 'em, but these fellows that do n't have farms, they won't work except in harvest, when they can get high wages [$8 a month]. I hired a fellow last spring for six months; I wanted him to help me plant and tend my corn. You see I had a short crap last year, and this spring I had to pay fifty cents a bushel for corn for bread, and I did n't want to get caught so again, not this year, so I gin this fellow $6 a month for six months—$36 I gin him in hard silver."

" Paid it to him in advance ?"

" Yes, he would n't come 'less I 'd pay him right then. Well, he worked one month, and maybe eight days—no, I do n't think it was more than six days over a month, and then he went away, and I hain't seen a sight on him since. I expect I shall lose my money—reckon he do n't ever intend to come back; he knows I 'm right in harvest, and want him now, if ever I do."

" What did he go away for ?"

" Why he said he was sick, but if he was, he got well mighty easy after he stopped working."

" Do you know where he is now ?"

" Oh, yes, he 's going round here."

" What is he doing ?"

" Well, he 's just goin' round."

" Is he at work for any one else ?"

" Reckon not—no, he 's just goin' round from one place to another."

At supper and breakfast surprise was expressed that I declined coffee, and more still that I drank water instead of milk. The woman observed, " 't was cheap boarding me." The man said he must get home a couple more cows; they ought to drink milk more, coffee was so high now, and he believed milk would be just as healthy. The woman asked the price of coffee in

New York; I could not tell her, but said I believed it was uncommonly high; the crops had been short. She asked how coffee grew. I told her as well as I was able, but concluded by saying I had never seen it growing. "Don't you raise coffee in New York?" she asked; "I thought that was where it came from."

The butter was excellent. I said so, and asked if they never made any for sale. The woman said she could make "as good butter as any ever was made in the yarth, but she couldn't get any thing for it; there warn't many of the merchants would buy it, and those that did, would only take it at eight cents a pound for goods." The man said the only thing he could ever sell for ready money was cattle. Drovers bought them for the New York market, and lately they were very high—four cents a pound. He had driven cattle all the way to Charleston himself, to sell them, and only got four cents a pound there. He had sold corn here for twelve and a half cents a bushel.

Although the man could not read, he had honored letters by calling one of his children "Washington Irving," another was known as Matterson (Madison?). He had never tried manuring land for crops, but said, "I do believe it is a good plan, and if I live I mean to try it sometime."

A COLONIZATIONIST.

July 16*th.*—I stopped last night at the pleasantest house I have yet seen in the mountain; a framed house, painted white, with a log kitchen attached. The owner was a man of superior standing. I judged from the public documents and law books on his table, that he had either been in the Legislature of the State, or that he was a justice of the peace. There

were also a good many other books and newspapers, chiefly of a
religious character. He used, however, some singularly uncouth
phrases common here. He had a store, and carried on farming and stock raising. After a conversation about his agriculture, I remarked that there were but few slaves in this part of
the country. He wished that there were fewer. They were not
profitable property here, I presumed. They were not, he said,
except to raise for sale; but there were a good many people here
who would not have them if they were profitable, and yet who
were abundantly able to buy them. They were horrid things, he
thought; he would not take one to keep it if it should be given
to him. 'T would be a great deal better for the country, he believed, if there was not a slave in it. He supposed it would not
be right to take them away from those who had acquired property
in them, without any remuneration, but he wished they could all
be sent out of the country—sent to Liberia. That was what
ought to be done with them. I said it was evident that where
there were no slaves, other things being equal, there was greater
prosperity than where slavery supplied the labor. He did n't
care so much for that, he said; there was a greater objection to
slavery than that, in his mind. He was afraid that there was
many a man who had gone to the bad world, who would n't have
gone there if he had n't had any slaves. He had been down in
the nigger counties a good deal, and he had seen how it worked
on the white people. It made the rich people, who owned the
niggers, passionate, and proud and ugly, and it made the poor
people mean. "People that own niggers are always mad with
them about something; half their time is spent in swearing and
yelling at them."

"I see you have 'Uncle Tom's Cabin' here," said I; "have you read it?"

"Oh, yes."

"And what do you think of it?"

"Think of it? I think well of it."

"Do most of the people here in the mountains think as you do about slavery?"

"Well, there's some thinks one way and some another, but there's hardly any one here that do n't think slavery's a curse to our country, or who would n't be glad to get rid of it."

I asked what the people about here thought of the Nebraska Bill. He could n't say what the majority thought. Would people moving from here to Nebraska now, be likely to vote for the admission of slavery there? He thought not; "most people would much rather live in a free State." He told me that he knew personally several persons who had gone to California, and taken slaves with them, who had not been able to bring them back. There were one or two cases where the negroes had been induced to return, and these instances had been made much of in the papers, as evidence that the slaves were contented.

"That's a great lie," he said; "they are not content, and nine tenths of 'em would do 'most any thing to be free. It's only now and then that slaves, who are treated unusual kind, and made a great deal of, will choose to remain in slavery if freedom is put in their way." He knew one man (giving his name), who tried to bring two slaves back from California, and had got started with them when some white people suspecting it, went on board the ship and told him it was against the law to hold negroes as slaves in California, and his negroes should n't go back with him unless they were willing to. Then they went to the slaves and told them they need not return, if they preferred to stay, and the slaves said they had wanted very much to go back to North Carolina, yet they would rather remain in California, if they could be free, and so they took them ashore. He had heard the slave-owner himself relating this and cursing the men who interfered. He had told him that they did no more than Christians were obliged to do.

I overtook upon the road, to-day, three young men of the poorest class. Speaking of the price of land and the profit of farming, one of them said, believing me to be a southerner,

"We are all poor folks here; do n't hardly make enough to keep us in liquor. Anybody can raise as much corn and hogs on the mountains as he'll want to live on, but there ain't no rich people here. Nobody's got any black ones—only three or four; no one's got fifty or a hundred, like as they have down in the East." "It would be better," interrupted another, somewhat fiercely, "there warn't any at all; that's my mind about it; they're no business here; they ought to be in their own country and take care of themselves, that's what I believe, and I do n't care who hears it." But let the reader not be deceived by these expressions; they indicate simply the weakness and cowardice of the class represented by these men. It is not slavery they detest; it is simply the negro competition, and the monopoly of the opportunities to make money by negro owners, which they feel and but dimly comprehend.

HOW THEY TALK.

A man said to me to-day, "It's a heap warm."

The hail here, as in Texas, is "Travelin'?" after which:

"Traveled a good piece?" "What parts you been to?" etc.

If you meet a man without stopping, the salutation always is, "How d' ye do, sir?" never "Good morning;" and on parting it is, "I wish you well, sir," more frequently than "Good bye." You are always commanded to appear at the table, as elsewhere throughout the South, in a rough, peremptory tone, as if your host feared you would try to excuse yourself.

"Come in to supper." "Take a seat. Some of the fry! Help yourself to any thing you see that you can eat."

They ask your name, but do not often call you by it, but hail you "Stranger," or "Friend."

Texas is always spoken of in the plural—"the Texies."

"Bean't the Texies powerful sickly?"

"Ill" is used for "vicious." "Is your horse ill?" "Not that I am aware of. Does he appear so?" "No; but some horses will bite a stranger. if he goes to handling on 'em."

"Is your horse ill?" "No, I believe not." "I see he kind o' drapt his ears when I came up, 'zif he was playful."

Everybody I've met in the last three counties—after ascertaining what parts I came from, and which parts I 'm going to, where I got my horse, what he cost, and of what breed he is, what breed the dog is, and whether she 's followed me all the way from the Texies, if her feet ain't worn out, and if I do n't think I 'll have to tote her if I go much further, and if I do n't want to give her away, how I like the Texies, etc.—has asked me whether I did n't see a man by the name of Baker in the Texies, who was sheriff of ———— county, and did n't behave exactly the gentleman, or another fellow by the name of ————, who ran away from the same county and cut to the Texies. I 've been asked if they had done fighting yet in the Texies, referring to the war with Mexico.

HIGHWAYS AND BYWAYS.

"The prosperity of a country can be best estimated from the character of its roads."—*Bushnell.* (?)

Elizabethton (pronounced Lizzi Bethton), *Tenn., July* 15th.— You will be surprised to find me dating from Tennessee again. I have made a very crooked course. My only guide in planning out my route ahead has been "Mitchell's Traveler's Guide." For the last month I have had my eye fixed upon a long stretch of straight road, running parallel to the North Carolina and Tennessee line, between Bakersville, N. C., and Greensville, Va. I was forced, after giving up the road by Knoxville, to go as far east as Ashville, North Carolina, whence, according to my map, there was a road by the French Broad to Bakersville. But I was advised that the regular road-route to Bakersville was further to the eastward, by Burnsville, so I fetched a course by Burns- ville. Here, people disagreed about the road to Bakersville, and, as to Greensville, they had never heard of it. I found my way to Bakersville, however, the third day after leaving Ashville, by a difficult road—found, I should say, the guide posts to Bakers- ville. Finally, reading "Bakersville, 1 M.," I rode the mile, but could see no town; there were only three log cabins within a distance of a quarter of a mile. I asked a boy at the first of these, "how far is it to Bakersville?" "It's right up there." "How far?" "Oh, right up there." I passed the two other cabins, and just beyond them meeting two great Tennessee bacon wagons, I asked the driver of one how far it was to Bakersville. He had never heard of the place; had seen no vil- lage in twenty miles. I rode back to the last of the three cabins, but it was unoccupied, the door being fastened by a stake thrust into the ground and pressed against it. I went to the next cabin where I found an old man, of whom I asked,

" Is this house Bakersville ?"

"Yes, sir" (with gravity). He knew of no such place as Greensville; there was no road running hence northwardly. There did use to be, he added, on second thoughts, a horsepath over the mountain to what was called the "Fields of Tow," but it had n't been used much for a long time, and he doubted if it could be found now. Beyond the *Fields of Tow*, he knew of no track at all to the northward. The shortest way into Virginia, he thought, was to cross Iron mountain into Tennessee. My map (thus agreeing with his advice,) showed a road to Elizabethton, thence a straight road to Greensville. So I followed the road over the mountain, and soon found mile posts reading thus,

TOEBIOM.

(*i. e.*, To Eliza-Bethton, 10 miles). Here I find myself at fault again, there being no such road as is shown in the map, to Greensville; at least, the post-master, the inn keeper and two merchants of the place, know of none. There is said to be a plain road, leading to Abington in Virginia, which, as it is the only road to the northward, I must, of course, follow.

SLAVE AND FREE IN THE HOUSEHOLD.

North-Eastern Tennessee, ——.—Night before last I spent at the residence of a man who had six slaves; last night, at the home of a farmer without slaves. Both houses were of the best class common in this region; two-story framed buildings, large, and with many beds, to accommodate drovers and wagoners, who, at some seasons, fill the houses which are known to be prepared with stabling, corn, and beds for them. The slaveholder was much the wealthier of the two, and his house originally was the finer, but he lived in much less comfort than the other. His house was in great need of repair, and was much disordered; it was dirty, and the bed given me to sleep in was disgusting. He and his wife made the signs of pious people, but were very morose or sadly silent, when not scolding and re-ordering their servants. Their son, a boy of twelve, was alternately crying and bullying his mother all the evening till bed-time, because his father had refused to give him something that he wanted. He slept in the same room with me, but did not come to bed until after I had once been asleep, and then he brought another boy to sleep with him. He left the candle burning on the floor, and when, in five minutes after he had got into bed, a girl came after it, he cursed her with a shocking volubility of filthy blackguardism, demand-ing why she had not come sooner. She replied gently and entreatingly, "I didn't think you'd have more'n got into bed yet, master John." The boys were talking and whispering ob-scenity till I fell asleep again. The white women of the house were very negligent and sluttish in their attire; the food at the table badly cooked, and badly served by negroes.

The house of the farmer without slaves, though not in good repair, was much neater, and every thing within was well-ordered and unusually comfortable. The women and girls were clean and neatly dressed; every one was cheerful and kind. There was no servant. The table was abundantly supplied with the most wholesome food—I might almost say the first wholesome food—I have had set before me since I was at the hotel at Natchez—loaf bread for the first time, chickens, stewed instead of fried, potatoes without fat, two sorts of simple preserved fruit, and whortleberry and blackberry pies. (The first time I have had any of these articles at a private house since I was in Western Texas.) All the work, both within and without the house, was carried on regularly and easily, and it was well done, because done by parties interested in the result, not by servants interested only to escape reproof or punishment.

Doubtless two extreme cases were thus brought together, but similar, if less striking, contrasts are found the general rule, according to my experience. It is a common saying with the drovers and wagoners of this country, that if you wish to be well taken care of, you must not stop at houses where they have slaves.

THE METHODISTS OF THE NORTHERN SOUTH.

The man of the last described house was intelligent and an ardent Methodist. The room in which I slept was papered with the "Christian Advocate and Journal," the Methodist paper of New York.* At the slaveholder's house, my bedroom was partially papered with "Lottery Schemes."

The free laboring farmer remarked, that, although there were few slaves in this part of the country, he had often said to his wife that he would rather be living where there were none. He thought slavery wrong in itself, and deplorable in its effects upon

---

* RELIGION IN VIRGINIA.—A mass meeting of citizens of Taylor county, Virginia, was held at Boothesville recently, at which the following, among other resolutions, was passed unanimously :

"That the five *Christian Advocates*, published in the cities of New York, Pittsburg, Cincinnati, St. Louis, and Chicago, having become Abolition sheets of the rankest character, we ask our commonwealth's attorneys and post-masters to examine them, and, if found to be of an unlawful character, to deal with them and their agents as the laws of our State direct."—*Washington Republic.*

the white people. Of all the Methodists whom he knew in north-eastern Tennessee and south-western Virginia, he believed that fully three fourths would be glad to join the Methodist Church North, if it were "convenient." They generally thought slavery wrong, and believed it the duty of the church to favor measures to bring it to an end. He was not an Abolitionist, he said; he did n't think slaves could be set free at once, but they ought to be sent back to their own country, and while they were here they ought to be educated. He had perceived that great injustice was done by the people both of the North and South, towards each other. At the South, people were very apt to believe that the northerners were wanting not only to deprive them of their property, but also to incite the slaves to barbarity and murder. At the North, people thought that the negroes were all very inhumanely treated. That was not the case, at least hereabouts, it was n't. If I would go with him to a camp meeting here, or to one of the common Sunday meetings, I would see that the negroes were generally better dressed than the whites. He believed that they were always well fed, and they were not punished severely. They did not work hard, not nearly as hard as many of the white folks; they were fat and cheerful. I said that I had perceived this, and it was so generally, to a great degree, throughout the country; yet I was sure that on the large plantations it was necessary to treat the slaves with great severity. He "expected" it was so, for he had heard people say, who had been on the great rice and cotton plantations in South Carolina, that the negroes were treated very hard, and he knew there was a man down here on the railroad, a contractor, who had some sixty hands which he had hired in Old Virginny ("that's what we call eastern Virginia here"), and everybody who saw them at work, said he drove them till they could hardly stand, and did not give them half what they ought to have to eat. He was opposed to the Nebraska bill, he said, and to any further extension of slavery, on any pretext; the North would not do its Christian duty if it allowed slavery to be extended; he wished that it could be abolished in Tennessee. He thought that many of the people who went hence to Kansas would vote to exclude slavery, but he was n't sure that they would do it generally, because they would consider themselves southerners, and would not like to go against other southerners. A large part of the emigration from this part of the country went to Indiana, Illinois, and Iowa; those States being preferred to Missouri, because they were free States. There were fewer slaves hereabouts now, than there were when he was a boy. The people all thought slavery wrong, except, he supposed, some slaveholders who, because they had property in slaves, would try to make out to themselves that it was right. He knew one rich man who had owned a great many slaves. He thought slavery was wrong, and he had a family of boys growing up, and he knew they would n't be good for any thing as long as he brought them up with slaves; so he had told his slaves that if they wanted to be free, he would free them, send them to Liberia, and give them a hundred dollars to start with, and they had all accepted the offer. He himself never owned a slave, and never would own one for his own benefit, if it were given to him, "first, because it was wrong; and secondly, because he did n't think they ever did a man much good."

I noticed that the neighbors of this man on each side owned slaves; and that their houses and establishments were much poorer than his.

SOUTH-WESTERN VIRGINIA.

Abington, Va., July 17*th.*—Abington is a compact little town, with a good deal of wealth. The country all about here, this side of the Virginia line, is rich and beautiful. The surface is rolling, with fine oak woods, clear of undergrowth, good pastures, luxuriant corn, and tolerable grain crops, good clover and grass. Land of the best, within three miles of the town, is worth $100; ten miles out, $25 an acre. The Virginia and Tennessee railroad is being constructed through this place. The hotel seems to be pretty well kept; every thing is tolerable, except the beds. While I was washing myself from head to foot, a white man suddenly opened the door, and looked at me for a minute in silence, till I faced him.

" What yer doin' ?"

" What am I doing ?"

" Yes, what yer doin' ?" (laughing.)

" Why, sir, can't you see ?"

" Washin' on yer, he! he!"

" Yes."

" Yes, humph !" and he withdrew, laughing foolishly.

July, 18*th.*—Left Abington. The country continues beautiful, rich and productive, much like central New York. There are more slaves here than I have seen before for several weeks. Negroes and whites seem to be about equally employed in agricultural labor. I saw this morning seven cradlers together. The leader was a negro, the second man a white, then four negroes, and a white at the foot. They were followed, as long as I could see them, by the owner or overseer, who walked close behind them with a stick in his hand. An old man, whom I overtook

riding upon the road, told me that niggers had all been hired
to work on the railroad, at $200 a year. White laborers were
paid $10 a month. " But," said he, " they do n't do so much
work here as they do in the north country. They say nobody
works so hard here as they do where you come from ; neither
niggers nor white men will do more than half as much in a day,
so they say."

I passed upon the road two large flocks of sheep. The drivers
said they had brought them from western Tennessee, where they
cost $1 a head on an average. They intended to drive them two
hundred miles further, into " the valley of Virginia," where they
would be sold to farmers who would fatten them on meal, and
sell them to drovers for the New York markets. They expected
to get $2 to $3 a head. This sort of business is fast increasing
in Virginia ; fatting cattle being found in most localities much
more profitable than grain growing.

Agriculture in all northern Virginia is, I apprehend, in a tran-
sition state, from pure grain, to what the English writers call
" convertible husbandry," and the change is likely to progress,
and I think will be unfavorable to slavery.

I stopped for the night at a large, handsome house ; the owner
a well-informed, thoughtful gentleman, was evidently an excellent
manager and master. In contrast with what I have recently
seen, the house was extremely clean and well-ordered, as were
also the gardens, stables, and other surroundings ; the servants
were attentive, and I heard but one reproof of them while I was
in the house. The table was neat, the food wholesome and well
cooked. I compared notes with the gentleman upon crops and
farm economy. He said the average crop of the country was
not over eight bushels of wheat to the acre ; his own crop last

year was twenty-seven (on a farm of four hundred acres tillage land). The difference was principally owing to more careful cultivation. He plowed ten inches deep, with three horses to a plow. His usual crop of corn was forty to fifty bushels to the acre, sometimes much more.

He asked if I did not think as he did, that their climate here was more favorable to profitable agriculture than that of New York. I thought that it was so for all purposes of agriculture, except for the small grains. "But," rejoined he, "you have one great advantage over us. If I could get good laborers as easily as you can in New York, I would never have another negro on my place; it's a part of the evil we suffer from slavery that it spoils our white men. Our white hands are not, in general, a bit better than the negroes." He employed several white hands, and paid them ten dollars a month; and they wanted the same whether they were hired by the year or only for the summer. They did n't care to work for any great length of time without a change. They were very stupid at work, almost as much so as the negroes, and could not be set to do any thing that required the least exercise of judgment, unless he stood over them constantly. Yet he believed that the white men, whom he had this year at $120 a year wages, were worth more to him than the negroes who were hired for $140. One of the latter was almost useless, and this entirely from laziness and stupid indifference, for he was strong enough; he hardly paid for his bread. Still there was much that was inconvenient and unpleasant in employing white men, especially where they were employed with negroes.

His white hands all were seated with us at the breakfast table; coarse, dirty, silent, embarrassed, and embarrassing men.

He afterwards observed that if they could get rid of slaves,

and obtain a sufficient number of white laborers to do their field
work, they would still have to employ negro girls for the kitchen
and household labor. The white girls who would go out to work
were worse than the men, much worse than the negroes. He
did not know a white girl who would hire out, whose habits
were such that he could endure to have her in his house. In
fact, no girl hereabouts, whose character was good, would ever
hire out to do menial service. There were some Maine gentlemen whom he knew, who were professors in Emery and Henry
College. They thought slavery wrong, and they would n't buy
slaves, and had tried to get along with white girls, but they were
obliged to give it up, and pay owners for the use of their slaves,
as cooks and maids.

Abolition of slavery he thought impracticable. The slaves
could not take care of themselves. If they were freed and
allowed to remain here, they would ruin the country. Every
one knew, he said, that the State would be far more prosperous
if the slaves were out of it. No doubt the State would be richer
if they were all taken out of it without being paid for. He
wished they might be.

July 19*th*.—Last night I spent with the family of a farmer
who owned three or four negroes, and lived in a superior sort of
log cabin quite comfortably. Indeed, a higher degree of comfort is generally evident since I entered Virginia. Although
they had slaves, and there was a daughter, eighteen or twenty
years old, I observed that they had a slovenly and very ugly
white girl (possibly a very light mulatto), who seemed to be a
servant, and who did not come to the table with the family, but
gave the negroes their breakfast in the kitchen while we ate in
an adjoining room with the door between the rooms open.

On a small table in the parlor were some books, the " Revival Miscellanies," and the " Alarm to the Unconverted," two Methodist Hymn Books, a large Bible, and a North Carolina Almanac, of the year before. The mother of the family, a very kindly fat old lady, officiated at family prayers.

"What yer done with yer gun?" inquired the mother; "see you 've got your shot pouch."

" No, madam, it is not shot I carry in this pouch."

" No. 'Lowed 't wan't shot."

Silence and universal gravity, the eyes of the whole family bent on my leather pocket for the next five minutes. At length, a young man asks if I got much gold in Texas. He had heard say there was powerful good mines there. I told him there were no gold mines in operation in Texas; perhaps it was California he meant. He did n't know but it was; it was either Texas or California; he was sure he 'd heard people say there was heaps of gold got out there.

These people told me that they had heard that some Yankees ("that 's what they called people who came from that part of the country," they parenthesized—New Jersey Yankees,) had come down into Virginia somewhere to raise stuff for New York. " They come here because it is so much hotter, and they can raise things earlier than they can about New York, and then they take 'em on to New York. The New Yorkers is so fond of novels that they 'll pay high for 'em to come a little earlier."

July 20*th.*—After two farmers had declined to receive me, because, as they said, they had not got any corn and were not prepared for travelers, and did not like to take them in unless they could treat them well, I stopped, near nine o'clock, at a house to which they had recommended me, as the best within some miles. It was a boarded log house, of four rooms and a gallery. The owner was a farmer, with two hired white hands besides his sons; the whole family coarse, ignorant people. As I took a seat for my supper, the mother placed herself opposite to me, resting her two red scabby arms on the table, smoking a pipe, and in the most good-natured way, inquired into all the particulars of my life as far as possible; whether I were married or not, what "persuasion" (religious sect) my father and mother belonged to, etc., etc. She had had some notion of moving to Texas. A woman who went out from here and settled there, wrote home that she had n't got any cows of her own yet, but she could have the milking of twenty, if she wanted, that belonged to the planters around ; and she made butter and sold it at 37½ cents a pound to the very men who owned the cows. They were too lazy to make butter for themselves, but they liked it so well they would pay 37½ cents a pound for it. The old woman thought if she could get 37½ cents a pound for making butter, it would n't take long for her to get rich, and "I 'd like to be rich," said she, "not so rich as Wade Hampton, but so rich I need n't do any more work." There had been several others from hereabout, however, who went out to Texas and did n't like it. There were two young men came back last spring. They said 't was a right level flat country, and 't was all of such deep, sticky mud, that it took five pair of mules to haul a load of corn, and it was dreadful sickly there, and there was n't any water at all; all that people had to drink was rain water that they caught and kept. These men had, it appeared, landed at Galveston or Indianola, gone back only a few miles from the coast, lived there through a summer, and then returned disgusted with Texas, as well they might be if that were all of it.

Although there were four rooms in the house, six of us, including a girl of fifteen, were bedded in one tight room. There were no sheets at all on my bed, and what, with the irritation of the feathers and the blanket, the impurity of the air, and a crying child, I did not fall asleep till near daylight.

Notwithstanding it was the middle of the harvest season, and they had mentioned to me that their oats had been struck with rust, and would lose value very rapidly every additional hour they remained uncut, there seemed to be no hurry about getting to work in the morning. I hastened them all I could, in order to ride while the day was tolerably cool, but the sun was three hours high before breakfast was ready, and even when I rode away after it was finished, all the men and boys were lounging on the gallery, waiting to see me start, before they went afield ; nothing at all out of doors having been done before breakfast, not even the grinding of scythes.

The following day I descended the eastern slope of the Blue Ridge and came to that part of Virginia which was considered in the first volume of this work.

Richmond, where I arrived a week later, somewhat surprised me by its substance, show and gardens, and I was inclined to think that in coming to it directly from New York and Philadelphia, I had been led to rather underrate its quality at my first visit.* There are only six towns, having a town-like character, in the slave States—New Orleans, Mobile, Louisville, St. Louis, Charleston, and Richmond. Savannah, and all the other "places" having, like it, in winter, a population for a town, are simply overgrown villages in appearance, and in convenience ; half the streets tolerably good pastures, the other half intolerable cart-

* Seaboard Slave States, p. 19.

roads; the best mansions, clap-board, Americo-moresque cottages; the best gardens in a setting of picket fence; the public squares mere camp grounds, with weedy walks and sedge-grass lawns; the majority of the shops selling raisins, nailrods and nigger cloth, from the same counter with silks, and school books and " bitters." Richmond, by contrast, is a metropolis, having some substantial qualities, having a history, and something prepared for a future as well. Compared with northern towns of the same population, there is much that is quaint, provincial and excessively slovenly, especially in whatever connects directly with the country, such as the marketing. It is only the mills and warehouses, a few shops and a few private residences and hotels, that show real enterprise or real and permanent wealth.

The Crawford Washington Monument is much the highest attainment of American plastic art, and would be a glory to any town or country, but it points to the past. What a failure has there been in the promises of the past!

That, at last, is what impresses one most in Richmond. It is a metropolis, and, of course, the tide of modern life elsewhere reaches it, stirs it, and here and there possesses it, but yet it is plainly the metropolis of Virginia, of a people who have been dragged along in the grand march of the rest of the world, but who have had, for a long time and yet have, a disposition within themselves only to step backward.

Revolting from the generous and noble theories of Jefferson the essential difficulty with Virginians of to-day is want of faith in the capacity of men individually, white and black. Wealth, knowledge, and morality, are practically regarded as the accidents of men, not as their earnings. Slavery, and the laziness and faithlessness of the poor whites, are deplored, especially through out the west, but every one says, and every one feels, it is hopeless to contend with these evils. " Slavery makes our poor whites worthless laborers ; even slaves are better. The country languishes for want of laborers. No one then must be allowed to think of our dispensing with slaves." They thus acknowledge the cause of the evil ; but show that they have not a spark of faith in the capacity of their poor whites to improve, even on the removal of this cause. This is what they mean, when they say, " It is impossible to abolish slavery ;"—it is impossible to live without somebody can be made to work. In every neighborhood, I found hope to center in something to come from without A railroad or canal, which the Governor had recommended the State to aid; a copper or coal mine, or salt works, which some New Yorkers were talking about establishing ; a new college, which some religious body proposed to found. But, lately, in the extreme West, where slaves are no direct impediment, a new hope seems to have got a lodgment, and where, even on the frontier, a newspaper can not be prevented from giving utterance to it, in such a manner as is done in the following paragraph from the Wheeling Intelligencer, it is impossible that it shall not bring with it at least a negative faith. A faith that will not resist, if it may not encourage, an infusion of such elements of improvement, as will make the obstruction which slavery presents to wealth, more and more obvious to all, at the same time that the possibility of dispensing with it is demonstrated.

" The present great and pressing want of our State, like that of the United States, is cultivation and improvement, not enlargement or annexation, and the obvious and the only mode of a rapid growth of our State or city, is such a change of public policy as shall invite to our aid and coöperation our Caucasian cousins, the intelligent, moral and industrious artizans, mechanics, miners, manufacturers, farmers, and commercial men of Europe and the northern States, to share our taxation, develop our resources, and make ours a white man's country, with all the energy, education, love of order, of freedom, and of progress characteristic of the Anglo-Saxon race. The history of the world, and especially of the States of this Union, shows most conclusively that public prosperity bears an almost mathematical proportion to the degree of freedom enjoyed by all the inhabitants of the State. Men will always work better for the cash than for the lash. The free laborer will produce and save as much, and consume and waste as little as he can. The slave, on the contrary, will produce and save as little, and consume and waste as much as possible. Hence States and counties filled with the former class must necessarily flourish and increase in population, arts, manufactures, wealth, and education, because they are animated and incited by all the vigor of the will; while States filled with the latter class must exhibit comparative stagnation, because it is the universal law of nature that force and fear end in ruin and decay."

CHAPTER VII.

PATRIARCHAL LIFE IN VIRGINIA, AND IN GENERAL.

JAMES RIVER CHAT.

From Richmond I went with my horse and dog direct to New York by the steamer. There were but few first-class passengers; the majority of those who did not leave at the river landings, or at Norfolk, being Northern men, or men of Northern birth doing business at the South, and going North with their families for the remainder of the summer.

Of the project of a line of "mammoth steamships," to be established between Richmond and Antwerp, with the assistance of mail patronage from the United States, and loans from the Belgian and Virginian governments, which, when I was last on James River, was the exciting topic of conversation, I now no longer heard a word spoken. The party of progress, however, represented by six gentlemen in black, with gold-headed walking-sticks, sitting in caucus around a spittoon by the side of the wheel-house, as we were carefully floated in ballast over the shoals, were equally animated in the confidence of some new scheme, which it was deemed equally safe and respectable to discuss publicly, and which it was held with equal confidence would be the sure salvation of old Virginia.

My room-mate proved to be a Mississippian, lazy and amiable, a sort of smouldering fire-eater. He sneered at the Virginians and their speculations, and held men to be little better than fools who would keep niggers to make corn and tobacco, when by moving them to his own region, and setting them to make cotton, they might easily double their incomes. But they did not keep them to make corn, he said, they kept them to breed and raise young ones. It was folly to pretend that they did not. A man might not raise a nigger with a well-considered plan to sell him eighteen years after he was born; he might never sell a nigger, but for all that, it was the readiness with which he could command a thousand dollars for every likely boy he had, if he should ever need it, that made him stay here and be bothered with taking care of a gang of niggers who barely earned enough to enable his family to live decently. He did not sell them, because he thought they were a good investment to hold, and men were proud of being able to hold a big lot of niggers. There were not many men here, either, who did not sell their niggers off, some of them, every year or two; whenever they wanted money. Some pretended that they only sold the rascals, but the rascals they sold were generally likely boys, just the thing for cotton pickers, and would bring more money than the slow men and the women whom they kept. If they did not sell them off, why were not the stocks larger? There were a few men here who owned a hundred or two niggers, but not nearly as many as in Mississippi, and yet every body knew a nigger stock would naturally increase twice as fast here as it would in Mississippi. What became of them if they were not sold? He had never sold a nigger in his life, but he had bought a good many, and two-thirds of them were fresh from Virginia. He had one boy who said that the man who raised him had sold him to get the money to pay for a piano which he had bought for his daughter. A gentleman would never think of doing such a thing as that in Mississippi. He would always calculate to pay from his crop.

I have more than once observed that the rich men of the Southwest feel themselves rather a superior class to the Virginians, somewhat as the rich Virginia country-gentlemen look upon Northern farmers—as if agriculture in a free-labor country were necessarily a small and rather mean business. The following passage from an article in the Brandon Republican, a Mississippi newspaper, manifests the general incredulity with regard to the assertion that slaves are not bred for commercial purposes in Virginia and the adjoining States, which it is impossible to resist in regions where half the population of a county often consists of negroes who have been sold from that State:

"Now let us consider the probable consequences of drawing upon the savage and barbarous hordes of Africa for slaves to compete with our own, and most likely eventually drive out of Southern markets the slave breeders of the South. Are there not, including South Carolina—although for the last eight or ten years she has thrown upon us more slaves than any one of the old slave States—six States that must hereafter derive profit from breeding slaves for the Southern States or derive no profit from the institution? We mean Delaware, Maryland, Virginia, North Carolina, Kentucky and Missouri. Nearly one third of the population of these States are slaves. If slave labor can not be made to pay there—and we hear it continually asserted that this labor can not be advantageously employed in grain growing countries—then what are they to do with their slaves if this policy is inaugurated and they are excluded from Southern markets, they being forced to retain in their hands property which can make no adequate return for the expenses of feeding, clothing, etc? Do you think, reader, that any surer means could be employed to call into existence an abolition sentiment there than that of forcing these States to retain in their territory a large and expensive body of slaves that they can not find remunerative employment for? No practical man will believe that they will keep them when the time comes that they can not be turned to profit. Should they be shut out from the Southern markets, with their heavy slave population to 'harass them and eat out their substance,' and almost unproductive and rapidly producing, how can they keep them? Let it come to this, and we predict that their owners will get rid of

them, even if they are compelled to incur the expenses of their ship-
ment to Africa. Allow them still. to find a profit in slave breeding,
and their affection for the institution will remain as fixed as ' Ixion on
his wheel."

To the same effect is the following admission of the Charleston Standard in an article on agricultural improvement at the
South :

"The Virginia journalists have repeatedly borne witness to the fact,
that in many districts, where large estates have been divided and sold
to small farmers, the land is turning off from three to six times as much
produce as it did a few years ago."*

This is much the same as saying, that from certain limited
districts of Virginia, where slavery has been practically abandoned (the slaves having been sold off by the sheriff in most
cases) the contribution of the earth to the comfort of the human
race has almost immediately been increased four fold.

Once again, during the afternoon, I had the pleasure of wit-
nessing a scene similar to those described in the first volume, in
the same locality, the joyful welcome of white people, returning
to their plantation, by their house-servants ; and again I noticed
the comparative indifference of the field-hands or common slaves,
who barely touched their tatterred hats and grinned, before lifting on to each other's heads the trunks which were to be thus
carried to the house after the carriage which bore the whites
and upper servants altogether. This humbler kind did not say
one word to their master or mistress, and only grinned in sympathy with the excitement of the young people, nor were they
spoken to at all, so far as I observed.

I am here reminded that I may seem to have hitherto too
much overlooked a certain view of Southern life, much delighted

* Charleston Standard, August 17, 1854.

in by novelists and poets, and not usually neglected by travelers.
I mean that which, in debates, is commonly alluded to when the
terms, patriarchal, paternal, filial, tutellary and pupilage, are
used, the two latter terms being less frequently heard of late
years than in the early days of the republic.

The truth is, that I have made, as all travelers are inclined to
make, the most I honestly could of every instance or indication of
such a relation as these terms express, that I have seen. Anything of the kind is always interesting, and gratifying to read of
and to write of, as it is to witness. Would I then have it inferred
that Slavery has been too much honored in this respect ? I must
say that such is my conviction.

Will the reader consider how many poets and novelists, and
what is of more consequence, how many apparently matter-of-fact
travelers speak of our Yankee tars otherwise than as gallant, jolly
and generous fellows, or of the red Indian otherwise than as the
calm, sad, dignified child of nature—" the noble savage." And
yet the reader probably knows, if he has taken the trouble to look
the facts in the face, regardless of traditions and predispositions,
that American seamen, (sea-going,) as a class, are more wretched,
and are governed more by threats of force than any other civilized
laborers of the world. There are exceptions. There are ports
from which when ships are manned the rule is otherwise. But
at our great ports, New York, Philadelphia, Baltimore, the sailor
of sea-going ships, nine times out of ten, when sober and not led
to do otherwise by vanity or a desire to satisfy your romantic
interest, will tell you that he hates the sight of blue water, that
he habitually hates his ship, hates his officers, hates his mess-
mates and despises himself. And as for the red man of nature,
when found in a state of nature, what, in fact, is he ? Nine

times out of ten experience will say that the description which
in the second volume of this work* I quoted, as best expressing
my own obversation among the most natural and the most warlike, that is, the most murderous and every way detestable tribes
on the continent, is no libel;—"a conceited, tiresome, bloodthirsty
monotonous humbug."

Civilization is, in fact, the best condition of mankind, and the
steps by which mankind have arrived at civilization do not need
to be retraced to find morality, respectability or happiness.

The supposition of a master's occupying the position of a
father toward his slaves and of the slaves accepting this relation,
affectionately, faithfully and confidingly, is an improbable one.
Imagine a household consisting of first a man and wife, second
an ordinary family of sons and daughters, for whom the parents
must have a special affection, and who must be favored and
petted, as compared with—third, twenty to fifty additional sons
and daughters, of all ages, the majority being adults, however, but
all subject in all their movements, not to the influence and advice
merely, but absolutely and abjectly, to the will, of their parents,
not being able to eat or drink, or to dress, or to engage in any
business, or to pursue any inclination of taste, or to marry, except
with the approval of their father, not even after marriage to be
any more independent than before. There is not one man among
millions whose household under such circumstances would not be
a pandemonium. The slaves are not their master's children; he
is not affected in his government of them by the instinctive regard
for their happiness which a parent might have.

The patriarchal condition of society is, in fact, an exceedingly

* Journey in Texas, p. 289.

rude, uncomfortable and low state of society, only endurable by indolent, wandering men, who are obliged for purposes of defense to remain attached, on any terms which may be required, to the most convenient nucleus of combined strength which is offered them. If a solitary wanderer on the great plains without arms or food should be overtaken by a family of wanderers, and the father should offer to supply him with food, and to furnish him with means of defense, on condition that he would obey his orders and attach his fortunes to those of the family, he would probably accept the proposal, and would remain in irksome dependence so long as the family were subject to the dangers of the wilderness, but as soon as the opportunity of fixed settlements and a peaceable organization of many independent families made it possible, he would form other and various associations and direct his movements according to his own judgment, for his own good, and it would doubtless be for the best good of all concerned that he should do so.

The patriarchal condition is a transitional one. If long maintained it must be by an abuse of intelligence and at the expense of comfort and morality. It then ceases to be paternal and becomes oppressive; becomes degrading, both in patriarch and patriarchate. The true teaching of history is clearly expressed in the following passage from Mill's Political Economy :*

" The theory of dependence and protection is an idealization, grounded on the character and conduct of here and there an individual. All privileged and powerful classes, as such, have used their power in the interest of their own selfishness, and have used their self-importance in despising and not in lovingly caring for those who were, in their estimation, degraded, by being under the necessity of working for their benefit. I do not affirm that what has always been always must be,

* Principles of Political Economy, II., 325.

or that human improvement has no tendency to correct the intensely selfish feelings engendered by power; but though the evil may be lessened, it cannot be eradicated until the power itself is withdrawn. This, at least, seems to me undeniable, that long before the superior classes could be sufficiently improved to govern in the tutelary manner supposed, the inferior classes w ud be too much improved to be governed."

This, written with no reference to Slavery, is, in my experience, the lesson taught at all points by Slavery, to-day, in our nation.

CHAPTER VIII.

SLAVERY EXTENSION; SOUTHERN COMMERCE AND COTTON SUPPLY; PRESENT CONDITION AND CHARACTER OF THE CITIZENS OF THE SOUTH; THE CAUSES AND THE REMEDY.

To observe the condition and character of the citizens, was my principal object while traveling in the slave States; to contribute toward a study of the practical workings of the system of which their condition and character must be the truest exponent is the principal object of these volumes. That system, while it rests on slavery, is not simply slavery, but is slavery of the peculiar kind which exists alone in our republic, including especially the various laws, habits and political and social customs which are designed to secure its inviolability and perpetuity, and by which any modification, improvement or different arrangement, is resisted. American slavery is not merely a system for the subjection and government, under individual masters, of a certain number of slaves. It is, for instance, a system of colonization as well.

Most of the citizens of the slave States appear to believe that the continuance of slavery depends upon the continual and rapid territorial dispersion of the slave-holding community. Whether they are right or not, such a movement is at present a distinguishing and essential fact of American slavery. If an American slave-holding community could be other than a very loosely organized community, American slavery would be, in that community, a different thing from what it is now everywhere found to be. In Virginia itself, an essentially frontier condition of society prevails to this day. Beasts and birds of prey, forests and marshes are increasing; bridges, schools, churches and shops diminishing in number, where slavery has existed longest. The habits of the people correspond.

There are various other circumstances at present peculiar and essential to the system of American slavery, which might be changed, and yet slavery remain, but such slavery would not be the system which is now discussed, nor would its effects be the same. When speaking of the slavery of our slave States, then, I mean not slavery simply, but all those habits, customs and laws, which at present invariably accompany, and are peculiarly connected with the slave system as it at present exists in our own country.

The slave States are vast territorially. There are, independently of slavery, important circumstances acting in their different parts, hence a study of the condition of the people must be an extended and tedious one, nor can facts or phenomena in sufficient number to enable the reader to form an estimate for himself, of the effects which it is right to ascribe simply to slavery and the customs, habits and laws, which at present belong to the slave system, be given otherwise than in a long and circumstantial narrative.

In previous volumes, the grand divisions of old settlement and of recent settlement, have been separately considered. In the present volume, my experience and observations with regard to two distinct divisions have been narrated. The first, a region which, independently of slavery, is unquestionably able to yield a larger money value for agricultural labor than any other in the world, it being the favored soil, in the favored climate, with the cheapest natural facilities of transportation to a market, of that production, for which there is the most urgent commercial demand; the second, widely different, being distant from markets, with no peculiar agricultural productions, and offering but small rewards for agricultural labor.

In the latter, the mountainous region, the people are poor, and there are but few slaves. It is true that nearly all have either themselves been educated in the slave-holding districts, or are the direct descendants, and but one or two generations removed from persons so educated; but slavery at present exercises scarcely any direct effect upon them. Whether in consequence of this exemption or not, they differ noticeably in character, customs and habits from the people of the slave-holding districts. Their own impression that the absence or scarcity of slaves is the cause of this difference, and that this is a matter of congratulation, was expressed to me every day while I was among them, nor was any doubt of it even once intimated to me. Compared with the slaveholders, these people are more cheerful, more amiable, more sociable, and more liberal. Compared with the non-slaveholders of the slave-holding districts, they are also more hopeful, more ambitious, more intelligent, more provident, and more comfortable. Their general poverty can not be thought to result from the absence of slaves. Rather it is the small reward for labor which agriculture in the mountains offers, and their consequent inability to accumulate capital, which prevents them from possessing slaves. Such difference as is most obvious and general between them and the people of the mountain regions in the free States may be confidently attributed to their distance from markets (including markets of intelligence) and the consequent want of variety in their occupation.

The distinguishing element of the condition of the other region considered in this volume, is the extraordinary value which attaches to labor within it, in consequence of the peculiar favorableness of the soil and climate for the production of cotton.

It is quite plain, notwithstanding all the drawbacks attending the employment of forced labor, and notwithstanding the high price of slaves, that slave labor is employed profitably by the large planters in Mississippi, and in certain other parts of the South, in the culture of cotton. That the profit, in this case, is not only large compared with the profit of slave labor employed elsewhere, and in other occupations, but that it is moderately good, at least, compared with the profit of other investments of capital and enterprise at the North and in Europe, must also be admitted. There are few enterprises to which capital lends itself more freely than to speculation in slaves, when the seeker for it is already a large cotton planter.

Is slave labor, then, profitable?

To certain individuals, unquestionably.

Nor do I think myself warranted in denying that the production of cotton per acre on many Mississippi plantations may not be as large as it can be economically made with land as low and slaves as high in price as is at present the case.

Is not then this slave agriculture economically conducted?

To the ends had in view by the planter it certainly is.

I answer thus distinctly, because assertions to the same effect have been addressed to me, evidently with the supposition that they invalidated the argument on the economy of Virginia, and of other parts of my first volume. That argument was intended to lead to the conclusions that the cost of such labor as is usually performed by slaves in Virginia, is more than double, in that State, what it is in New York. That in consequence of this excessive cost of labor, the profits of agriculture are much less than they would be if free trade in the commodity of labor could be established. That it is a consequence also of this high cost of labor that enterprise and capital avoid Virginia, especially avoid agriculture in Virginia, and that, as might therefore be supposed, agriculture in Virginia is a wretchedly conducted business, and among the agricultural class, niggardness, surliness and bigoted·ignorance much more prevail than among the farmers of the free States. In short, that slavery, by unnecessarily adding to the cost of making natural wealth, or the resources of the country, available, and by causing a wasteful use of natural wealth, has the effect of impoverishing and degrading Virginia.

The difference between Virginia and Mississippi is mainly found in the fact that in the latter State cotton grows luxuriantly and matures perfectly. The demand for cotton is such, and the soil on which it can be grown is so limited, that wherever it can be produced with facility a given investment in land, tools and labor will be much better rewarded than a similar investment can be rewarded in any agricultural enterprise in Virginia. What is true with regard to Virginia, I believe to be true with regard to Mississippi, with only this difference, that in Mississippi there is one description of natural wealth available with so little labor (having regard to its value in the world) that even with the disadvantages of slavery, capital appears for a time to be well invested in developing it, hence agriculture; that is to say, cotton

culture, in Mississippi attract capital, enterprise and skill, as corn
culture would in Virginia if the value of corn bore the same relation to the cost of the labor employed in its production.

The cost of labor merely, is as much increased by slavery in
Mississippi as it is in Virginia; the cost of production, the barrier
to wealth, is as much more than it needs to be in Mississippi as it
is in Virginia. The necessary loss appears to me to be larger in
Mississippi, indeed. Substitute a free trade of labor in Mississippi
for the present system, and I suppose that you will have, as you
would in Virginia, a fourfold value of land, a fourfold economy.

I repeat: Slave labor is to-day undoubtedly profitable to certain
owners of slaves in Mississippi.

It was undoubtedly profitable to roll tobacco in casks one
hundred miles to market, at one time, in Virginia.

It would probably be profitable in Illinois to reap wheat with
sickles, and thrash it with flails, and market it by wagons, if there
were no horse reaping machines and horse thrashing machines,
and steam locomotive machines, engaged in supplying the demand for wheat, but there is many hundredfold the wealth in
Illinois to-day that there would have been had sickles, flails and
wagon trains been held to there with the same bigotry as is
slavery in Mississippi; and if it could be made certain that ten
years hence the present labor system of Mississippi would be
superseded by the free labor system, I have little doubt that
twenty years hence the wealth of Mississippi would be at least
tenfold what, under the present system, it is likely to be, and the
whole country and the whole world be some degrees happier than
it is now likely to be.

But this is conjectural. What is the actual condition of the
people of Mississippi to-day?

In Mississippi (and in the rich lowland cotton regions generally of the slave States) the social phenomena are found most
satisfactory in districts wherein a fixed community has for many
years been established, and the fertility of the soil not yet largely
exhausted. Evidences of wealth, of education, religion and refinement will never be wanting among the citizens of such a
district, nor evidences of a bantling civilization and of a certain
degree of rude comfort among the other part of the people.
Among the citizens there may, indeed, be but few indigent or uninstructed; possibly on several square miles not one such family
will be resident. At no great distance, however, there may, I
believe, invariably be found some tract of sterile or less fertile
land, a large majority of the inhabitants of which are extremely
poor and ignorant whites, stupidly contented, helpless and hopeless in their ignorance and poverty.

I have on my desk, as I write, and I write only after seeing
how fully the judgment to which I am compelled from my own
scrutiny of the ground is confirmed by it, evidence published by
many partisans of the extension of slavery enough to half fill this
volume, of which, to corroborate the sweeping assertion just made,
I need give here but a single example :

" I am not aware that the relative number of these two classes has
ever been ascertained in any of the States, but I am satisfied that the
non-slaveholders far outnumber the slaveholders, perhaps by three to
one.*   In the more southern portion of this region ['the south-west,'
of which Mississippi is the center], the non-slaveholders possess generally
but very small means, and the land which they possess is almost universally poor, and so sterile that a scanty subsistence is all that can be derived from its cultivation, and the more fertile soil, being in the hands
of the slaveholder, must ever remain out of the power of those who

* It was not long since estimated in the Legislature of Kentucky as seven
to one in that State.

have none. * * * And I lament to say that I have observed of late years that an evident deterioration is taking place in this part of the population, the younger portion of it being less educated, less industrious, and, in every point of view, less respectable than their ancestors."*

And, for the present, I ask that what is said by this writer of the material condition of two thirds of the whole population of his own quarter, which, in its natural resources, is the very richest region at this moment in the known world, may be assumed to be true of the majority of the people of the South, as, I believe, no ingenuous southern gentleman will deny that it is.

Is their condition the result of poverty caused merely by a poor return for labor which is yielded by such a soil? I say that it is not, because I know that the occupants of similar soils at the North are far superior to them in nearly every quality, habit and attainment which civilized men respect and value. Is their condition the result of climate? The conviction in my mind that it is not, has been formed from innumerable personal observations and some personal experience. The recent German settlers in Texas and in South Carolina, the whites on steamboats and railroads and in trade, the white workmen in New Orleans, as well as thousands of exceptional, hardworking and successful laboring Southerners testify that the climate is no preventive of persevering toil by the white race in any part of the slave States. I have, in fact, seen more white native American women at work in the hottest sunshine in a single month, and that near midsummer, in Mississippi and Alabama than in all my life in the free States, not on account of an emergency, as in harvesting, either, but in the regular cultivation of cotton and of corn, chiefly of cotton.

* De Bow's Resources of the South and West, vol. ii., p. 106.

Further evidence leading to the same conclusion, I find in the fact, that men born, nurtured and trained in the South show no lack of strength or endurance when engaged in athletic exercise which is immediately gratifying to their ambition, passions, or their tastes. The climate prohibits no sort of labor, except such as would be generally productive of wealth, to the white man of the South."* How is this to be explained?

In part, at least, thus, is it not? (I ask, and I hope the reader will not neglect to answer according as he is well persuaded.) All mankind have an intuitive respect for strength or power. Slavery is the most palpable evidence of weakness or the involuntary subjection of strength in the slave. That is the meaning of slavery. The condition of a slave, therefore, as compared with that of a man independent of another's will, so far as that condition of him is alone concerned, is universally regarded with the absence of respect, with something of contempt or pity. Whatever is associated with the slave as having been peculiarly attached to his condition is regarded with a certain degree of similar feeling. Manual agricultural labor is the chief employment of slaves in the South. For manual agricultural labor, therefore, the free man looking on, has a contempt, and for its necessity in himself, if such necessity exists, a pity quite beyond that of the man under whose observation it has been free from such an association of ideas.

Slaves are not wholly confined to agricultural labor, it is true, but it is equally true that in proportion as they are engaged in other

---

* See the evidence of Mr. Darby and others, p. 586 and onward, Seaboard Slave States. See also pp. 182, 187, 279, 281. 358, 359 and 360, Texas Journey. Additional testimony on this point from southern experts may be found further on.

employments are the whites who are also engaged in these employments found to be generally indolent, careless, untrustworthy
and unsuccessful.   That such persons are conscious of the degradation which attaches to the employment of slaves is manifested
in the fierce hostility of white mechanics to the instruction of
slaves in their crafts, for this opposition is not at all relative or
proportionate to the effect of such use of slaves in reducing their
wages.   It is not the mere competition of slaves in the market
which throws white men out of it.   If it were, labor contracts
could be made at a lower rate in the slave than in the adjoining
free States, whereas the contrary is the case.*   " The poor white
man," Mr. De Bow tells us, " will endure the evils of pinching

---

* Of course I do not refer to contracts for the *time* of laborers or workmen, which, owing to their indolence and unskillfulness, are frequently lower
for whites at the South than at the North. So few southerners hesitate to
admit this effect of slavery, and it has been so forcibly set forth by Jefferson
and most other statesmen of the South, that it may seem supererogatory to
argue its existence or importance. I observe, however, that of late not a few
Democratic journalists of the North have shown a disposition to discredit it,
and nearly all to make light of it. A friend of Senator Douglas, for instance,
said recently in the " Mattoon Gazette:"

" We are one of those that utterly discredit the idea that the presence of
slaves works an injury to the whites. * * * We candidly and firmly
believe to-day that if Illinois were a slave State the best men of Kentucky,
Virginia, Tennessee, and even States further South, would be here as soon
as they could remove their families, and the prairies of Illinois would be
made to smile as a lovely garden. We have seen the best class of men come
to our State, admire it with enthusiasm, but return to their homes because
they could not bring their whole families with them."

Judge Nichols, of Kentucky, whose opportunity of observation was probably better than this gentleman's, and whose character and position entitle his
views to particular respect, said, in a speech in 1837 : " The deliberate con-
victions of my most matured consideration are, that the institution of slavery
is a most serious injury to the habits, manners and morals of our white population ; that it leads to sloth, indolence, dissipation and vice."

poverty rather than engage in servile labor;"* and the white woman would, "however humble in the scale of society, consider such services a degree of degradation to which she could not condescend, and she has, therefore, no resource but to suffer the pangs of want and wretchedness." And J. H. Taylor, Esq., of Charleston, in defending an effort to employ whites in manufactories in South Carolina against the charge that it might tend to injure the value of slaves, says :

"The poor man has a vote as well as the rich man, and in our State the number of the former will largely overbalance the latter. So long as these poor but industrious people could see no mode of living except by a degrading operation of work with the negro upon the plantation, they were content to endure life in its most discouraging forms, satisfied they were *above* the slave, though faring often worse than he."†

Many writers attempt, in my opinion, to attach an entirely undeserved "honor to labor." Mere plodding manual labor is not in itself honorable. Dexterity, ingenuity in the application of labor, industry and perseverance are honorable traits in all men, but labor in itself is not honorable. On the other hand, in no enlightened free community is labor in itself practically degrading, because hireling labor is everywhere the stepping-stone from poverty and mediocrity to comfort and a position of usefulness. But in the South the step has become, if we are to believe Mr. De Bow, (as quoted above,) a degradation which the poorest white considers more grievous than the "pangs of want and wretchedness."

It is sometimes said that this feeling of degradation only exists when the free laborer works in the same gang or the same

* Resources of the South, vol. i., p. 241.
† De Bow's Review, January, 1850.

field with slaves, or that at furthest it extends only to hired laborers working under the direction of their employers, that it does not lesson the industry of men working on their own account. The observation above quoted from Mr. De Bow may be intended to be so restricted. In view of notorious facts, of which many have been already cited in this work from other and equally respectable advocates of the slave social system the reader may judge how far this theory is philosophically probable. I will only say here that I have seen nothing in the South to lead me to entertain it.

Not that I have seen no industrious white men at the South, I have seen many, and seen them side by side with slaves. There are incentives to industry acting counter to this influence of slavery, which in certain situations can not fail to be in some degree effective, for there is probably no country in the world where nature offers a better reward for intelligent labor than in some parts of the slave States. When, indeed, this is considered, the mere popular degradation of labor arising from its association with the idea of subjection and submission to the will of a master, does not seem adequate to account for the actual excessive indolence, folly and poverty of the majority of the people of the South. Nor does it, for that would be a result of slavery simply, of any slavery. American slavery, as at present advocated, American slavery, as it is desired to be perpetuated, nourished, protected and extended, has an influence far more cruel, more strenuously repressive upon the mass of free citizens than slavery elsewhere ever did; than slavery in itself at all needs to have; than, with all possible safety, with all reasonable profitableness to the owners of slaves, it is my judgment that it needs to have.

I hope that those who have read what I, as an eye-witness have described, in this and the preceeding volumes, will have acquired, if they did not otherwise possess, some understanding of the manner in which slavery, as it is now maintained in our slave States, operates very generally to put a limit, and a very short limit upon the natural motives which should impel a free man to live industriously. No theoretic explanation can be sufficient, if the facts, the abundant facts, which no intelligent traveler who has really penetrated the South has failed to acquire, which no sincere patriot of the South attempts to disguise, are not strongly impressed upon the mind of the investigator.

The accidental discovery of a palliative sometimes indicates unerringly the true nature of a disease and makes its remedy simple. I think that I always felt the poverty of the whites of the South, in the midst of so much inert wealth, to be somewhat mysterious; I had no such prejudice against American slavery that I felt satisfied with it as the sole cause, until I caught sight of a fragment of the annual report of the president of a South Carolina manufacturing company. This presiding manufacturer is not a Massachusetts spinner, nor a New York merchant, but a well-known and a much and worthily respected citizen of Charleston, William H. Gregg, Esq. In his report, Mr. Gregg, in a manner characteristic of his class and his education, withdraws the attention of his directors as soon as practicable from the mere commercial view of their enterprise, and shows its higher interest as a social experiment. I quote:

"The population of Graniteville is made up mainly from the poor of Edgefield, Barnwell and Lexington districts."

Before going further, it is well that it should be known that

the "poor" of these districts are by no means more destitute of educational and religious privileges than the poor men, on an average,
within the planting regions. By reference to the census returns I
find that they are provided with public schools at the rate of one
to less than thirty square miles, while within the State of South
Carolina, inclusive of its several towns, there is but one public
school, on an average, to every forty square miles. There are
churches within these districts, one to about seventeen square
miles; throughout the State, including Charleston and its other
cities, one to every twenty-five square miles. In Georgia the average is one to thirty-two square miles. With the condition of
the newer cotton States, in these respects, that of Edgefield,
Barnwell and Lexington would be found to compare still more
favorably for the poor. In Lexington there is even a theological
seminary. Nevertheless, even in these districts, there must have
been not a little destitution and ignorance, for Mr. Gregg goes
on congratulating the stockholders on what their enterprise has
accomplished :

"From extreme poverty and want, they have become a thrifty,
happy, and contented people. When they were first brought together, the *seventy-nine* out of a hundred grown girls who could neither read nor write were a by-word around the country ; that re-
proach has long since been removed. We have night, Sunday and
week-day schools. Singing-masters, music-teachers, writing-masters,
and itinerant lecturers all find patronage in Graniteville where the
people can easily earn all the necessaries of life, and are in the enjoyment of the usual luxuries of country life." * * *
"To get a steady supply of workmen, a population must be collected
which will regard themselves as a community, and two essential elements
are necessary to the building up, moral growth and stability of such a
collection of people, namely, a church and a school-house." * * *

The truth of these views Mr. Gregg establishes by the failure
of manufacturing enterprises at the South in which they have

been disregarded. From these failures the opinion has obtained that the poor whites were not available as laborers, and that in all industrial enterprises the capitalists would be obliged to employ slave labor. Mr. Gregg combats this view energetically, and says :

I can safely say that it is only necessary to make comfortable homes in order to procure families that will afford laborers of the best kind. A large manufacturing establishment located anywhere in the State, away from a town and in a healthy situation, will soon collect around it a population who, however poor, with proper moral restraints thrown around them, will soon develop all the elements of good society. Self-respect and attachment to the place will soon find their way into the minds of such, while intelligence, morality, and well directed industry, will not fail to acquire position."

To relieve the extreme poverty and want of the South it is necessary, according to the teaching of this report, to lead those who suffer "to regard themselves as a community," for this purpose the nuclei of "a church and a schoolhouse" are essential, to which will be added, as the work develops, such other stimulants as "singing and writing schools, itinerant lecturers," etc., etc. In short, the power of obtaining, as the result of their labor, "the necessaries of life," "the usual luxuries of country life," or, in two words, which cover and include church, school, music and lecture, as well as bread, cleanliness, luxuries and necessities, "comfortable homes."

Mr. Gregg has here indicated, in my opinion, not only the truest test of a prosperous people, but the essential condition of prosperity with any people. The mass of men must have in their minds the idea and the hope of a comfortable home as a starting point of respectable industry ; must have secured some degree of home comfort as a condition of continued success in their industry.

The present system of American slavery prevents the people at large from having " comfortable homes," in the sense intended by Mr. Gregg. For nine tenths of the citizens, comfortable homes, as the words would be understood by the mass of citizens of the North and of England, as well as by Mr. Gregg, are impossible, and are rendered impossible by the system of slavery.

How ?

I believe that all political economists agree in the opinion that either a varied industry within the limits of any given country or district must exist, or that it must enjoy a large export trade, to support a prosperous and happy people. The slave States would appear to be in the latter condition. Their export of cotton is of great value. It should make comfortable homes for their people. It does not, because their slavery system interposes to prevent the demand of commerce from having its legitimate effect upon the mass of the people.

Examine almost any rural district of the South, study its history, and it will be seen how it does so.

Take, in the first instance, one of entirely rich soil. Suppose it to be of twenty square miles, with a population of six hundred, all told, and with an ordinarily convenient access by river navigation to market. The whole of the available cotton land in this case will probably be owned by three or four men, and on these men the demand of commerce will have had, let us suppose, its full effect. Their tillage land will be comparatively well cultivated. Their houses will be comfortable, their furniture and their food luxurious. They will, moreover, not only have secured the best land on which to apply their labor, but the best brute force, the best tools, and the best machinery for ginning and pressing, all superintended by the best class of overseers. The cotton of each will be shipped at the best season, perhaps all at once, on a boat or by trains expressly engaged at the lowest rates of freight. It will everywhere receive special attention and care, because it forms together a parcel of great value. The merchants will watch the markets closely to get the best prices for it, and when sold the cash returns to each proprietor will be enormously large. As the expense of raising and marketing cotton are in inverse ratio to the number of hands employed, planters nearly always immediately reinvest their surplus funds in slaves; and as there is a sufficient number of large capitalists engaged in cotton-growing to make a strong competition for the limited number of slaves which the breeding States can supply, it is evident that the price of a slave will always be as high as the product of his labor, under the best management, on the most valuable land, and with every economical advantage which money can procure, will warrant.

But suppose that there are in the district besides these three or four large planters, their families and their slaves, a certain number, say twenty white families, who do not own slaves. The fact of their being non-slaveholders is evidence that they are as yet without capital. In this case one of two tendencies must soon be developed. Either being stimulated by the high price of cotton they will grow industrious, will accumulate capital and purchase slaves, and owning slaves will require a larger amount of land upon which to work them than they require for their own labor alone, thus being led to buy out one of the other planters, or to move elsewhere themselves before they have acquired an established improvement of character from their prosperity; or, secondly, they will not purchase slaves, but either expend currently for their own comfort, or hoard the results of their labor.

If they hoard they will acquire no increase of comfort or improvement of character on account of the demand. If they
spend all their earnings, these will not be sufficient, however
profitable their cotton culture may be supposed, to purchase
luxuries much superior to those furnished to the slaves of the
planters, because the local demand, being limited to some fifty
white families, old and young, in the whole district of twenty
square miles, is not enough to draw luxuries to the neighborhood, unless they are brought by special order, and at great expense from the nearest shipping port. Nor is it possible for so
small a number of whites to maintain a church or a newspaper,
nor yet a school, unless it is one established by a planter, or two
or three planters, and really of a private and very expensive
character.

Of course, this is a somewhat extreme case. As a general rule,
accidents of settlement, divisions by inheritance, the resistance
of moral or social to economical forces, or other irregular circumstances, will modify in a greater or less degree what is nevertheless the ruling tendency.

Suppose, again, another district in which either the land is
generally less productive or the market less easy of access than
in the last, or that both is the case. The stimulus of the cotton demand is, of course, proportionately lessened. In this case,
equally with the last, the richest soils, and those most convenient to the river or the railroad, if there happens to be much
choice in this respect, will assuredly be possessed by the largest
capitalists, that is, the largest slaveholders, who may nevertheless
be men of but moderate wealth and limited information. If so,
their standard of comfort will yet be low, and their demand will
consequently take effect very slowly in increasing the means of

comfort, and rendering facilities for obtaining instruction more accessible to their neighbors. But suppose, notwithstanding the disadvantages of the district in its distance from market, that their sales of cotton, the sole export of the district, are very profitable, and that the demand for cotton is constantly increasing. A similar condition with regard to the chief export of a free labor community would inevitably tend to foster the intelligence and industry of a large number of people. It has this effect with only a very limited number of the inhabitants of a plantation district consisting in large part as they must of slaves. These laborers may be driven to work harder, and may be furnished with better tools for the purpose of increasing the value of cotton which is to be exchanged for the luxuries which the planter is learning to demand for himself, but it is for himself and for his family alone that these luxuries will be demanded. The wages—or means of demanding home comfort—of the workmen are not at all influenced by the cotton demand, the effect, therefore, in enlarging and cheapening the local supply of the means of home comfort will be almost inappreciable, while the impulse generated in the planter's mind is almost wholly directed toward increasing the cotton crop through the labor of his slaves alone. His demand upon the whites of the district is not materially enlarged in any way. The slave population of the district will be increased in number, and its labor more energetically directed, and soon the planters will find the soil they possess growing less productive from their increasing drafts upon it. There is plenty of rich unoccupied land to be had for a dollar an acre a few hundred miles to the West, still it is no trifling matter to move all the stock, human, equine and bovine, and all the implements and machinery of a large plantation. Hence, at the same time, perhaps, with an importation from Virginia of purchased slaves, there will be an active demand among the slaveholders for all the remaining land in the district on which cotton can be profitably grown. Then sooner or later, and with a rapidity proportionate to the effect of the cotton demand, the white population of the district divides, one part, consisting of a few slaveholders, obtains possession of all the valuable cotton land, and monopolizes for a few white families all the advantages of the cotton demand. A second part removes with its slaves, if it possess any, from the district, while a third continues to occupy the sand hills, or sometimes perhaps takes possession of the exhausted land which has been vacated by the large planters, because they, with all their superior skill and advantages of capital, could not cultivate it longer with profit.

This class, still ignorant of all luxury, having no higher aim than to procure the bare means of subsistence, is doomed to remain in a condition thus described in De Bow's Review by a writer " whose name," says the editor, " has long been illustrious for the services he has rendered the South :"

" All of you must be aware of the condition of the class of people I allude to.   What progress have they made in the last hundred years, and what is to be their future condition, unless some mode of employment be devised to improve it ?   A noble race of people ! reduced to a condition but little above the wild Indian of the forest, or the European gipsy, without education, and, in many instances, unable to procure the food necessary to develop the natural man. They seem to be the only class of people in our State who are not disposed to emigrate to other countries, while our wealthy and intelligent citizens are leaving us by scores, taking with them the treasures which have been accumulated by mercantile thrift, as well as by the growth of cotton and the consequent exhaustion of the soil."*

* Vol. xviii., p. 790.

The population of the district, then, will consist of the large land owners and slave owners, who are now so few in number as to be unnoticeable either as producers or consumers; of their slaves, who are producers but not consumers (to any important extent), and of this forlorn hope of poor whites, who are, in the eyes of the commercial world, neither producers nor consumers.*

To set forth their condition more clearly than I have done in the quotations from southern writers already given in this chapter, is possible only by obtaining the actual statistics of population and trade of a district the soil of which is in great part naturally unproductive, or which has become so through the process I have described. This is difficult, owing not only to the neglect of all the slave States to obtain statistics of the character now generally reqr.'ed by the legislatures of the free States as a basis of legislative judgment, but owing to the difficulty of finding a region in which the elements of fertility correspond at all closely with the political divisions under which all extant statistics are classified. It would perhaps be desired that I chose for this purpose the counties referred to by Mr. Gregg, but the meagre returns of the National Census appear to be peculiarly untrustworthy with regard to South Carolina, and I prefer to take cor-

---

* Mr. Mills' remarks on the condition of India apply, with very slight changes, to portions of the slave States: "The implements and processes of agriculture are, however, so wretched that the produce of the soil, in spite of its great natural fertility, and a climate highly favorable to vegetation, is miserably small; and the land might be made to yield food in abundance for many more than the present number of inhabitants, without departing from the system of small holdings. But to this the *stimulus* is wanting, which a large town population would afford. That town population again does not grow up because *the few wants and unaspiring spirit* of the cultivators prevent them from attempting to become consumers of *town produce.*"

responding counties in Georgia, chiefly because there is a volume of statistics compiled in this State, a special section of which is devoted to the condition of trade in each of its counties, while a comparison is also attempted to be given, from the personal observation of the compiler, of the comparative social, moral and religious properties of their people. Thus, so far as the plan has been thoroughly executed, an estimate is presented, not only of the ordinary commercial demand of the citizens, but, so to speak, of the state of their intellectual and moral market. I refer to " WHITE'S STATISTICS OF GEORGIA," a large octavo volume of 700 pages.

The compiler's standard of manners and morals is a local one, and the northern reader must not understand his language in all cases as he would if it were used by a northern writer, but taken relatively to one another, the terms by which the people in the different counties are characterized afford significant indications of their condition.

The counties referred to by Mr. Gregg are in the second tier from the sea in South Carolina. I shall give statistics from Mr. White, and other authorities named in the note*, with regard to all the second tier counties of Georgia. What of good soil to be brought into cultivation, without a heavy expenditure at starting, there was originally in these counties begun to be first oc-

---

* The population, following Mr. White, is given in round numbers, from the State census of 1845 ; average personal estate, per family of citizens, reckoned from an official return, published in the "Soil of the South" (Columbus, Georgia, 1852, p. 210), the amount given for each county being divided by one fifth the number of its population (for families). Observations on education and the character of the people, from White's Statistics of Georgia (generally in quotations). School, library and church statistics, in figures, from official United States Census, 1850.

cupied by whites about 1740. It was not till nearly twenty
years after this that slavery obtained the slightest footing in
them, and it was not till about thirty years ago that they had
begun to seriously deteriorate in production. There is yet some
rich land upon the alluvial bottoms of the numerous rivers, which,
rising above, pass through these counties toward the ocean ; and
here many wealthy planters still remain, owning a large number
of slaves, and there has been recently a considerable increase of
production of some parts owing to the employment of capital in
draining marshes, the riches of which have previously been considered impregnable.* In general, however, this whole range of
country is now quite barren, and most of the land at present cultivated will not probably yield one third as large a crop for the
same expenditure of labor as would fair Mississippi cotton land.
The slaves formerly owned here have therefore been very largely
transferred westward, and the land they have worn out is left for
the non-slaveholding whites to make the best of.

As an instructive contrast, I place in an adjoining column with
the statistics of these counties those of the counties which bound
each of them on the east. In these there is a much larger proportion of rich alluvial soil, and they contain the famous " sea
island" cotton plantations, as well as the Georgian rice plantations. The valuable soil is still entirely possessed, as will be evi-

* The presence of these few planters, with their valuable human property,
makes the average nominal wealth of each white family, at first sight, appear
large. If, however, the slaves had been appraised at only $500 each, which
would be low, they would alone amount in value in some counties to the
sum assigned for the whole personal property of the citizens. This item is not,
therefore, trustworthy, but, in comparing the coast and second tier counties,
it serves to show the great difference in the average wealth of the citizens of
each. A similar division of personal estate, as officially returned for the city
of New York, would give $4,660 to each family.

dent, by large planters and slave owners, the usual monopolizing effect of slavery being in this instance increased by the peculiar local insalubrity of the coast.

SECOND TIER COUNTIES.

Bullock County. (The Central Railroad, the best conducted road in all the South, passes either through this county or close beside its northern boundary, for a distance of fifty miles. It is watered by the Ogeechee and Connauchee and a number of smaller rivers. On the larger rivers there is yet a considerable amount of productive land.)

Population. Whites, 2,000; slaves, 1,000. Average amount of property to each white family, $1,570. State tax for each white family, $2 95.

Mr. White omits his usual statistics of trade. Both in this and the adjoining coast county of Bryan, the poor people, as well as the planters, are in the habit of dealing directly with Savannah, as described in Seaboard Slave States, p. 414, and there are probably no established tradesmen in either.

The *soil* is described by Mr. White as generally poor, with some productive "hummock" and river tracts.

Education. "No newspapers are taken, and few books read. The school fund was once sufficient to educate many poor children, but owing to bad management it has become exhausted."

COAST COUNTIES.

Bryan County, adjoining Bullock county, on the coast.

Population. Whites, 1,000; slaves, 2,400. Average amount of property to each white family, $5,302, (fourfold what it is in Bullock county.) State tax to each white family, $7.

No statistics of trade, again.

Soil. "The soil, under the present system of culture, can not, without rest and manure, be made to produce more than one half as much as when new." This appears to refer particularly to the rice plantations.

Education. There is no academy, and there are no schools, except those supported by the "Poor School Fund," (a State provision for the children of indigent parents.) "The children of the

SECOND TIER COUNTIES.

COAST COUNTIES.

Thus says Mr. White. The census returns show, however, a public school expenditure of $150 per annum, and a private expenditure of $3,000, divided among fifteen schools, which is one for eighty square miles. This is so much better than usual, that, with Mr. White's remarks, I am inclined to think it an error.

Character of the people. "By industry and economy, they manage to supply their wants, which, however, are few. Many rely a great deal on game. * * * As far as temperance is concerned, they are behind the times. Whiskey has its votaries. Those who have attempted to show the citizens the folly and ill consequences of intemperance have been insulted and threatened. Even ministers of our holy religion have publicly denounced the motives and efforts of those who have attempted to form temperancce societies."

Religion. "The most numerous [sects] are the Anti-Missionary [hard shell?] Baptists." Ten church edifices; average value, $145. No Sunday school or other public libraries.

wealthy are either educated by private teachers or sent to school in the more favored portions of the country ; [the vicinity of Savannah, where there is a celebrated and well endowed academy, and of Liberty, where there are others, accounts for this ;] the population is too sparse to furnish pupils enough to sustain a regular school," (large tracts of land being held by the planters, though wholly unproductive, to prevent the settlement of poor whites near their negroes, as one in this county informed me.) According to the census returns, there were eight schools (one to twenty-five square miles) of all kinds, with an average of twelve pupils each. Total expenditure for each school, $38 per annum.

Character of the people. No remarks.

Religion. The county contains eleven church edifices ; average value, $500. No Sunday school or other public libraries.

SECOND TIER COUNTIES.

COAST COUNTIES.

Tatnall County.

Population. Whites, 2,000; slaves, 600. Average amount of property to each white family, $901.

Capital invested in trade, $4,200.

Soil. "Light and sandy, except on the streams, which is stiff."

Education. "Education is neglected." Eight public schools, (1 to 148 square miles,) with sixteen pupils each. Annual cost of maintenance of each school, $150. No other schools; no Sunday school or other libraries.

Liberty County.

Population. Whites, 2,000; slaves, 6,000. Average amount of property to each white family, $6,330.

State tax to each white family, $10.

Capital invested in trade, $3,850.

Soil. "The practice has been to wear out the virgin soils, and clear new lands. * * * Much waste land."

Education. "Excellent schools are found. * * * And it is believed that a greater number of young men from Liberty county graduate from our *colleges* than from any other section of Georgia." There are five "academies," with an average of nineteen pupils each. Five public schools, (1 to 160 square miles,) maintained at an average expenditure of $15.40 per annum each. No libraries found in the census canvass of 1849. Mr. White states that the Medway and Newport Library Society had, in 1845, "about seven hundred volumes, in a very bad state of preservation." This library was established by some New England immigrants before the prohibition of slavery was annulled in the province. The early settlers of the county were chiefly from Massachusetts.

Character of the people. "Generally upright and virtuous, and they are unsurpassed for the great attention paid to the duties of religion."

Religion. Ten church edifices; average value, $1,200.

Character of the people. "Sober, industrious and hospitable," (phrases applied to every county not specially noted as conspicuous for some vice or virtue of its inhabitants.)

Religion. Sixteen church edifices, valued at $938 each. According to Mr. White, however,

SECOND TIER COUNTIES.

there are "about thirty churches" in the county.

Wayne County.

Population. Whites, 930 ; slaves, 350. Average amount of property for each white family, $898.

State tax, $1 23.
Capital invested in trade, $4,200.
Soil. "Generally poor, barren pine land ; when manured, will produce about twenty bushels of corn per acre."
Education. "Few schools ;" two academies, (one Baptist, and the other Methodist, probably,) with thirteen pupils between them. Four public schools, (1 to 148 square miles,) averaging ten pupils each ; expense of maintenance not returned.

Character of the people. "High for morality and hospitality ;" "poor, but honest." At the seat of justice "are many beautiful pine hills, affording delightful summer residences to the wealthy planters of Glynn," (hence the academical advantages.)
Religion. Eight church edifices; average value, $240.

Ware County. (About one fifth of this county is occupied by the Okefenokee Swamp.)

Population. Whites, 2,000 ; slaves, 300. Average amount of personal property for each white family, $480.

COAST COUNTIES.

McIntosh County, broadest on the sea.
Population. Whites, 1,300 ; slaves, 4,400. Average amount of property for each white family, $7,287, or eight times as much as in Wayne.
State tax, $2 77.
Capital invested in trade, $1,200.
Soil. Poor turpentine pine land in the rear ; on the Altamaha, "of inexhaustible fertility."
Education. One academy, with thirty-eight scholars ; four public schools, twelve and a half miles apart, averaging twenty pupils each. Expense of maintaining each school, $78 per annum. "The wealthier classes are highly educated ; but, generally, little interest is felt in the subject of education."
Character of the people. "Like all parts of lower Georgia, the citizens of McIntosh are generally intelligent and hospitable."

Religion. Twelve church edifices; average value, $1,041.

Camden County. Much the largest part of this county, which is L shaped, with but one arm on the sea, is inland, and unfertile.
Population. Whites, 3,000 ; slaves, 4,000. Average amount of personal property for each white family, $4,428.

SECOND TIER COUNTIES.

State tax, $4 05.
Stock in trade, $2,200.

Soil; "light and tolerably productive."

Education. "Very little interest is taken in the subject of edution." No academies; six public schools, (1 to 485 square miles,) sixteen pupils each. Wages of teachers, etc., yearly, $41· each school. No Sunday school or other libraries.

Character of the people. "The citizens are said to be hardy, industrious and honest." "Much good might be done by the organization of temperances societies."

Religion. Fifteen church edifices, fourteen miles apart, each accommodating one hundred sitters, and valued at $56 each.

COAST COUNTIES.

State tax, $13.

"Amount of business done at St. Mary's is about $30,000 per annum," nearly all in lumber, and done by New Englanders. No other trade statistics.

Soil; "of celebrated fertility."

Education. No remarks on education or character by Mr. White. Four public schools, (1 to 280 square miles,) with seventeen pupils each, maintained at an average expenditure of $290 per annum. Two academies, with forty-five pupils. Five Sunday school libraries, with one hundred and ten volumes each.

Character of the people. No remarks.

Religion. Ten churches, (five of which are in the town of St. Mary's, a beautiful and healthy village, resorted to by consumptives;) average value, $850.

I have purposely omitted Effingham county in the above arrangement, because the adjoining coast county of Chatham contains the city of Savannah, an aggregate agency of northern and foreign merchants, through which is effected the commercial exchanges of a great extent of back country, the population of which can therefore afford no indication as to the point under consideration. Effingham, the county above Chatham, and one of the second tier, is worthy of notice, from some other important exceptional features of its constitution. Owing to the amount of rich soil in the county, along the Savannah river, there is a larger proportion of slaves to the whole population than is usual in the second tier, their number being sixteen hundred against only eighteen hundred whites; the non-slaveholders, however, appear to possess unusual privileges. There is an academy, with fifty pupils, which Mr. White describes as "a fine school." The public schools, eight in number, are less than eight miles apart, with an average attendance of sixteen pupils. Each school costs one hundred and twelve dollars a year. There are twenty-one churches, less than five miles apart, and valued at over twelve hundred dollars apiece. Mr. White says that honesty and industry are leading characteristics of the people, who, notwithstanding the poverty of the soil, are generally in comfortable circumstances.

The reason of this is partially the close vicinity of Savannah, affording a cash market for a variety of productions and household manutures, among which, as distinguishing the county from any other in the State, are mentioned fruits, silk, fishing lines and cow-bells, "the latter," Mr. White is told, "superior to any manufactured in the North or in Europe." But an equally important reason for the better character and condition of the people is to be found in the fact that ¬ majority of them* are descendants and heirs of the land of those very early settlers who most strenuously and to the last resisted the introduction of slaves into the colony, being convinced that, if permitted, it would, as they said in their memorials, "prove a scourge" to the poor people who were persuaded to petition for it.† It is most gratifying to perceive that all traces of the habits of industry, honesty and manly self-reliance, in which they thus educated their children, are not wholly lost in the lapse of a century.

To recapitulate the more exact of these statistics :

A large majority of the whole white population resides within the barren counties, of which the slave population is less than one fourteenth that of the aggregate slave population of the whole.

The personal estate of the whites of these upper counties is, on an average, less than one sixth that of the others.

As the wealthy are independent of public schools, *the means of education* are scarcely more available for those who are not rich in one than the other, the school houses being, on an average, ten and a half miles apart in the less populous, thirteen and three quarters miles apart in the more populous.

It is widely otherwise as to *churches*. In the planting counties, there is a house of worship for every twenty-nine white families; in the poor white counties, one for every one hundred and sixty-

---

* White's Statistics, p. 224.
† Hewitt, —; Seaboard Slave States, p. 528.

two white families. Notwithstanding the fact, that to accommodate all, the latter should be six times as large, their average
value is less than one tenth that of the others; the one being
eight hundred and ninety-eight dollars, the other eighty-nine
dollars. So wholly do the planters, in whose hands is the
wealth, depend on their factors for direct supplies from without,
the capital invested in trade, in the coast counties, is but thirty-
seven and a half cents to each inhabitant, and in the upper counties it is but one dollar and fifty cents. From the remarks on
temperance, it would seem that the most of this capital must be
held in the form of whiskey. One "store" in Liberty county,
which I myself entered, contained, so far as I could see, nothing
but casks, demijohns, decanters, a bag of coffee, a case of tobacco,
and some powder and lead, and I believe that nine tenths of the
stock in trade referred to in these statistics is of this character.
It was mentioned to me by a gentleman who had examined this
district with a commercial purpose, that, off the plantations, there
was no money in the country—almost literally, no money. The
dealings even of the merchants or tradesmen seemed to be entirely by barter. He believed there were many full grown men
who had never seen so much as a dollar in money in their lives.

What inducement has capital in railroads or shops or books or
tools to move into districts like this, or which are to become like
this? Why, rather, I shall be asked, does it not withdraw more
completely? Why do not all, who are able, remove from a region
so desolate? Why was not its impoverishment more complete,
more simultaneous? How is it that any slaveholders yet remain?
Mr. Ruffin, president of the Virginia State Agricultural Society,
shall answer:*

* Address before the South Carolina Institute.

"The causes are not all in action at once, and in equal progress. The labors of exhausting culture, also, are necessarily suspended as each of the cultivators' fields is successively worn out. And when tillage so ceases, and any space is thus left at rest, nature immediately goes to work to recruit and replace as much as possible of the wasted fertility, until another destroyer, after many years, shall return, again to waste and in much shorter time than before, the smaller stock of fertility so renewed. Thus the whole territory, so scourged, is not destroyed at one operation. But though these changes and partial recoveries are continually, to some extent, counteracting the labors for destruction, still the latter work is in general progress. It may require, (as it did in my native region,) more than two hundred years, from the first settlement, to reach the lowest degradation. But that final result is not the less certainly to be produced by the continued action of the causes."

As to the extent to which the process is carried, Mr. Gregg says :*

"I think it would be within bounds to assume that the planting capital withdrawn within that period [the last twenty-five years] would, judiciously applied, have drained every acre of swamp land in South Carolina, besides resuscitating the old, worn out land, and doubling the crops—thus more than quadrupling the productive power of the agriculture of the State."

It would be consoling to hope that this planters' capital in the new region to which it is driven were used to better results. Does the average condition of the people of Mississippi and Texas justify such a hope? When we consider the form in which this capital exists, and the change in the mode of its investment which is accomplished when it is transferred from South Carolina, we perceive why it does not.

If we are told that the value of one hundred thousand dollars has been recently transferred from Massachusetts to a certain young township of Illinois, we reasonably infer that the people of this township will be considerably benefited thereby. We

* Fifth Annual Report to Directors of Graniteville Company.

think what an excellent saw mill and grist mill, what an assortment of wares, what a good inn, what a good school, what fine breeding stock, what excellent seeds and fruit trees, what superior machinery and implements, they will be able to obtain there now, and we know that some of these or other sources of profit, convenience and comfort to a neighborhood, are almost certain to exist in all capital so transferred. In the capital transferred from South Carolina, there is no such virtue—none of consequence. In a hundred thousand dollars of it there will not be found a single mill, nor a wagon load of "store goods;" it will hardly introduce to the neighborhood whither it goes a single improvement, convenience or comfort. At least ninety thousand dollars of it will consist in slaves, and if their owners go with them it is hard to see in what respect their real home comfort is greater.

We must admit, it is true, that they are generally better satisfied, else this transfer would not be so unremitting as it is. The motive is the same at the North as at the South, the prospect of a better interest from the capital, and if this did not exist it would not be transferred. Let us suppose that, at starting, the ends of the capitalist are obtained equally in both cases, that a sale of produce is made, bringing in cash twenty thousand dollars; suppose that five thousand dollars of this is used in each case for the home comfort of the owners, and that as much immediate comfort is attainable with it in the one case as in the other. What, then, is done with the fifteen thousand dollars? At the South, it goes to pay for a further transfer of slaves purchased in the East, a trifle also for new tools. At the North, nearly all of it will go to improvement of machinery of some kind, machinery of transfer or trade, if not of manufacture, to the improvement

of the productive value of whatever the original capital had been
invested in, much of it to the remuneration of talent, which is
thus enabled to be employed for the benefit of many people
other than these capitalists—for the home comfort of many people. If five thousand dollars purchased no more comfort in the
one case than the other, at starting, in a few years it will purchase
double as much. For the fifteen thousand dollars which has gone
East in the one case to pay for more labor, will, in the other,
have procured good roads and cheap transportation of comforts,
or shops and machinery, and thus the cheap manufacture of comforts on the spot where they are demanded. But they who sell
the reinforcement of slaves, and to whom comes the fifteen thousand dollars, do they have no increase of home comfort? Taking
into consideration the gradual destruction of all the elements of
home comfort which the rearing and holding of those slaves has
occasioned in the district from which they are sold, it may be
doubtful if, in the end, they do. Whither, then, does this capital
go? The money comes to the country from those who buy cotton, and somebody must have a benefit of it. Who? Every one
at the South says, when you ask this, it is the northern merchant,
who, in the end, gets it into his own hands, and it is only him
and his whom it benefits. Mr. Gregg apparently believes this.
He says, after the sentence last quoted from him, describing the
transfer of capital to the West from South Carolina :

"But this is not all. Let us look for a moment at the course of
things among our mercantile classes. We shall not have to go much
further back than twenty-five years to count up twenty-five millions
of capital accumulated in Charleston, and which has left us with its
enterprising owners, who have principally located in northern cities.
This sum would build factories enough to spin and weave every pound
of cotton made in the State, besides making railroads to intersect
every portion of the up-country, giving business facilities to the re-
motest points."

How comes this capital, the return made by the world for the
cotton of the South, to be so largely in the hands of northern
men? The true answer is, that what these get is simply their fair
commercial remuneration for the trouble of transporting cotton,
transporting money, transporting the total amount of home comfort, little as it is, which the South gets for its cotton, from one
part of the country to the other, (chiefly cotton to the coast, and
goods returned instead of money from the coast to the plantations.) Is this service over paid? If so, why do not the planters transfer capital and energy to it from the plantations? It is
not so. Dispersed and costly labor makes the cost of trade or
transfer enormous, (as it does the cost of cotton producing.) It
is only when this wealth is transferrred to the free States or to
Europe that it gives great results to human comfort. The
South, as a whole, has at present no advantage from cotton,
even planters but little. The chief result of the demand for
it, as far as they are concerned, is to give a fictitious value to
slaves.

Throughout the Southwest I found men, who either told me
themselves or of whom it was said by others, that they settled
where I found them, ten or fifteen years ago, with scarcely any
property beyond half a dozen negroes, who were then indeed
heavily in debt, but who were now quite rich men, having from
twenty to fifty negroes. Nor is this at all surprising, when it is
considered that cotton costs nothing but labor, the value of the
land, however rich, being too inconsiderable to be taken into account, and that the price of cotton has doubled in ten years. But
in what else beside negroes were these rich men better off than
when they called themselves poor? Their real comfort, unless
in the sense of security against extreme want, or immunity from

the necessity of personal labor to sustain life, could scarcely have been increased in the least. There was, at any rate, the same bacon and corn, the same slough of a wagon channel through the forest, the same bare walls in their dwellings, the same absence of taste and art and literature, the same distance from schools and churches and educated advisers, and—on account of the distance of tolerable mechanics, and the difficulty of moving without destruction, through such a rough country, anything elaborate or finely finished—the same make-shift furniture. There were, to be sure, plows and hoes, and gins and presses, and there were scores of very "likely negroes." Whoever sold such of these negroes as had been bought must have been the richer, it will be said. But let us see :

A large proportion of the negroes were probably bought by traders at forced sales in the older States, sales forced by merchants who had supplied the previous owners of the negroes, and who had given them credit, not on account of the productive value of their property as then situated, but in view of its cash value for sale, that is, of the value which it would realize when applied to cotton on the new soils of the Southwest.

The planters of the Southwest are then, in fact, supplying the deficit of eastern production, taking their pay almost entirely in negroes. The free West fills the deficit of the free eastern cereal production, but takes its pay in the manufactured goods, the fish, the oil, the butter and the importations of the free East.

Virginia planters owning twenty to forty slaves, and nominally worth as many thousand dollars, often seem to live generously, but, according to northern standards, I do not think that they possess at all equal comforts and advantages for a rationally happy life, with the average of northern farmers of half that wealth. If they do, they are either supplying slaves for the new cotton fields or living on credit—credit based on an anticipation of supplying that market.

Of course, it can not be maintained that no one, while living at the South, is actually richer from the effects of the cotton demand. There are a great many very wealthy men at the South, and of planters, as well as land dealers, negro dealers and general merchants, but, except in or near those towns which are, practically, colonies of free labor, having constant direct communication and intimate relationship with free countries, the wealth of these more fortunate people secures to them but a small proportion of the advantages which belong to the same nominal wealth anywhere in the free States, while their number is so small that they must be held of no account at all in estimating the condition of the people, when it is compared with the number of those who are exceedingly destitute, and at whose expense, quite as much as at the expense of their slaves, the wealth of the richer class has been accumulated.

This can not be rightly deemed extravagant or unjust language. I should not use it if I did not feel satisfied that it was warranted, not only by my own personal observations, but by the testimony of persons whose regard for the pride of the South, whose sympathy with wealthy planters, and whose disposition not to underrate the good results of slavery, if not more sincere than mine, is more certain not to be doubted. I quote, for instance, a single passage from the observations of Mr. Russell, an English gentleman, who, traveling with a special view of studying the agricultural condition and prospects of the country, was, nevertheless, so much limited in time that he was obliged to trust, in a great degree, to the observations of planters for his facts.

"In traveling through a fertile district in any of the southern States, the appearance of things forms a great contrast to that in similar districts in the free States. During two days' sail on the Alabama river from Mobile to Montgomery, I did not see so many houses standing together in any one spot as could be dignified with the appellation of village :* but I may possibly have passed some at night. There were many places where cotton was shipped and provisions were landed, still there were no signs of enterprise to indicate that we were in the heart of a rich cotton region. *   *   *   The planters supply themselves directly through agents in the large towns, and comparatively little of the money drawn for the cotton crop is spent in the southern States. Many of the planters spend their incomes by traveling with their families in the northern States or in Europe during the summer, and a large sum is required to pay the hog-raiser in Ohio, the mule-breeder in Kentucky, and, above all, the northern capitalists who have vast sums of money on mortgage over the estates. Dr. Cloud, the editor of the Cotton Plant, [Alabama,] assured me that after all these items are paid out of the money received for the whole cotton crop and sugar crops of the South, there did not remain one fourth part of it to be spent in the southern States. Hence, the slave States soon attain a comparatively stationary condition, and, further, the progress they make is in proportion to the increase of freemen, whose labor is rendered comparatively unproductive, seeing that the most fertile land is occupied by slaveholders."†

I questioned the agent of a large land speculation in Mississippi with regard to the success of small farmers. In reply he made the following statement, allowing me to take notes of it. I quote from these in order to show that what is true of the Atlantic shore and of the banks of the Alabama is also true of more western and interior districts.

* Mr. Russell uses the language of England. There are several collections of houses on this river bank, the inhabitants of which would consider it an insult if they should hear such an humble term as "village" applied to their pseudo towns and cities.

† North America; Its Agriculture and Climate, p. 290.

"The majority of our purchasers have been men without capital. To such we usually sell one hundred and sixty acres of land, at from two to three dollars an acre, the agreement being to pay in one, two and three years, with six per cent. interest. It is very rare that the payments are made when due, and much the largest proportion of this class fail even to pay their interest punctually. Many fail altogether, and quit their farms in about ten years. When crops are generally good, and planters in the same neighborhood make seven bales to a hand, poor people will not make over two bales, with their whole family. There is ―――― ――――, in ―――― county, for instance. We sold him one hundred and sixty acres of land in 1843. He has a family of good sized boys—young men now. For ten years he was never able to pay his interest. He sold from two to four bales a year, but he did not get much for it, and after taking out the cost of bagging and rope, and ginning and pressing, he scarcely ever had two hundred dollars a year coming to him, of which he had to pay his store bills, chiefly for coffee and molasses, sometimes a little clothing—some years none at all. They made their own cloth mostly in the house, but bought sheeting sometimes. He has made one payment on the principal, from a sale of hogs. Almost the only poor people who have kept up to their agreement have been some near ――――, since the cotton factory was started there. It is wonderful what a difference that has made, though it's but a picayune affair. People who have no negroes in this country generally raise corn enough to bread them through the year, and have hogs enough ranging in the swamps to supply them with bacon. They do not often buy anything except coffee and molasses and tobacco. They are not generally drunkards, but the men will spend all the money they may have, and get gloriously drunk once or twice a year, at elections or at court time, when they go to the county town. I think that two bales of cotton a year is as much as is generally made by people who do not own negroes. They are doing well if they net over fifty dollars a year from their labor, besides supplying themselves with corn. A real smart man, who tends his crop well, and who knows how it ought to be managed, can make five bales, almost always. Five bales are worth two hundred and fifty dollars, but it's very rare that a white man makes that. They have not got the right kind of tools, and they don't know how. Their crops are never half tended. If folks generally tended their crops as some do, there would be more than twice as much cotton raised as there is."

With regard to the enlargement of estates by successful planters, having stated what were my impressions, the same gentleman replied that I was entirely right, and gave an instance, as follows, from his personal knowledge:

"J. B. moved into ——— county within my recollection. He has bought out, one after another, and mainly since 1850, more than twenty small land owners, some of them small slaveholders, and they have moved away from the vicinity. I do not know how many negroes he has now, but several hundred, certainly. His surplus must have averaged twenty thousand dollars a year for several years, and, as far as I know, the whole is expended in purchasing negroes or land. He spends no money for anything else in the county, I am sure. It is a common thing to hear a man say, 'J. B. has bought up next to me, and I shall have to quit soon.' He never gets the land alongside of a man that within two years he does not buy him out. In the last ten years I know of but one exception, and that is a man who has shot two of B.'s niggers who were stealing his corn. This man swears he wont sell at any price, and that he will shoot any of J. B.'s niggers whom he catches coming on his place. B.'s niggers are afraid of him, and let him alone. J. B. will pay more for land than its worth to anybody else, and his negroes are such thieves that nobody can live in comfort on any place adjoining one of his. There are two other men in the county who are constantly buying up the land around there. The white population of the county is diminishing, and the trade of the place [the county town] is not as good as it was ten years ago."

I am not at liberty to give the name of the above quoted observer. I will state, however, that he was a southerner born, and if his narration needs authentication with any reader, I refer to the Hon. C. C. Clay, whose observations, (given at p. 576, Seaboard Slave States,) will be found to confirm it in all essential particulars, especially in those describing the absorption of small landed properties in large slave estates.

The following description of the social construction of the western cotton districts I find among the selected matter of a country newspaper. The author is unknown to me, but it is apparent from the context that he writes from personal observation. I quote it, not so much for the additional testimony it offers as for the clearer statement it affords of the tendency I have asserted to exist throughout the rich cotton districts.

"The cotton-growing portion of the valley of the Mississippi, the very garden of the Union, is year by year being wrested from the hands of the small farmer and delivered over to the great capitalists. The white yeoman, the class which has contributed more of the blood and devotion, and good sense and enterprise which have made this country what it is than any other, are either forced into the sandy pine-hills or are driven West to clear and prepare the soil for the army of negroes and negro-drivers which forever presses on their heels, to make their industry unprofitable, and their life intolerable.

"All the great cotton lands were first opened up by industrious settlers, with small means and much energy. No sooner is their clearing made, and their homestead growing into comfort, than the great planter comes up from the East, with his black horde, settles down on the district, and absorbs and overruns everything. This is precisely the process which is going on, day by day, over the greater portion of Louisiana and Mississippi. The small farmers, that is to say, the mass of the white population, are fast disappearing. The rich bottom lands of that glorious valley are being concentrated in the hands of large planters, with from one hundred to one thousand negroes. The average number of negroes and average quantity of land belonging to single proprietors is yearly increasing. The wealthier the proprietor himself, the less does he reside on his property, and the more disposed is he to commit it to the care of overseers. In some counties in Mississippi the negroes are twenty times more numerous than the citizens. Whole districts are solely peopled by black 'merchandise,' and some half dozen white drovers. The real 'people' are thus not only deprived of the patrimony which our abolition of the laws of entail and primogeniture was specially intended to secure them; are not only driven off the fairest portions of the soil, like the Scotch Highlanders and the Irish peasantry, but literature and religion are fast disappearing in that portion of this continent on which Providence seems to have intended them to flourish most."

THE DIFFICULTY OF POPULAR EDUCATION.

The last sentence, it will be observed, only confirms the opinion quoted from the Superintendent of the Census, at p. 298, an opinion which I have not ventured to express as my own.

In the Seaboard Slave States, I declared the impracticability of Mr. Wise's redeeming certain promises he was, when that book was written, freely making to the people of Virginia with regard to the education of the poor whites, unless he was prepared to adopt the emancipation system of Mr. Jefferson with regard to the blacks. I quoted, in evidence of this impracticability, from the county reports printed in the General Report of the year to the Governor with regard to the working of the then existing educational system of the State. Mr. Wise was elected on those promises. He has occupied the gubernatorial chair four years, and I now take from the report made to Governor Wise himself, November, 1859, extracts of the same kind then given, for several of the considerable slaveholding counties. They are from the remarks of the local commissioners or the superintendents having charge of the expenditure for the education of the indigent. Comparatively few make any report at all, especially in the slaveholding counties—not nearly as many as in 1852. I copy all reports with regard to the large slave counties in full, and some instructive notes from counties containing but few slaves. These are chiefly in the mountain region, and show the influence of the advantages possessed everywhere by the mountain people, as described in the beginning of this chapter, over those living immediately adjoining plantations, yet the effect upon them of State laws adapted to the necessities of slaveholders is obvious.

BEDFORD.
Whites, 13,536; slaves, 10,061.

" The superintendent states that the benefits of the fund have been extended to a larger number of children than in previous years, but that much remains yet to be done to give to the system the efficiency of which it is capable; that his observation leads him to believe that a large number of the teachers employed are miserably incompetent, and perhaps better qualified for some other vocation than that of directing the education of the young, and that some other plan ought to be adopted for the examination of teachers as to their competency before they are employed."

BRUNSWICK.
Whites, 4,885; slaves, 8,456.

" The superintendent regrets that he can not present in his annual account a full view of the school operations for the year. He has repeatedly urged upon the commissioners the importance of requiring the teachers in their respective districts to render their accounts on or before the 30th of September, but the attainment of that desirable object has not as yet been effected. He can bear cheerful testimony to the capacity, competency and faithfulness of most of the teachers who are employed to instruct the indigent, and believes that the progress of the pupils is as satisfactory as could be expected under the existing circumstances.

"The present primary school system, whatever may be its defects, has accomplished much good in this county. The benefits conferred thereby on many of the poorer classes of people are not only great but incalculable. The system may be amended; but as long as southern society remains as at present constituted, and the white population of the State continues to be sparse, any system that may be devised for the education of the poor will in a great measure prove inefficient."

CULPEPPER.

Whites, 5,112 ; slaves, 6,683.

"The superintendent states that he has received no synopsis of reports of the commissioners, and he believes that they do not visit the schools very often. Consequently, he has no authority to notice their visits or their observations of the working of the system. The commissioners, however, have promptly attended the meetings of the board, and examined accounts before payment. The superintendent (individually) thinks the system far from being perfect, yet, for the amount expended, it does perhaps as well as any other. To improve the system, would require an immense additional expenditure to agents, for which the State treasury is but little prepared at the present time."

CUMBERLAND.

Whites, 3,082 ; slaves, 6,339.

"The commissioners report that they have found much difficulty in securing the attendance of the children at school; that many of the teachers are disinclined to take the indigent children, in consequence of the inadequacy of the compensation, and they recommend an increase of the maximum rate of compensation to ten cents a day."

FAIRFAX.

Whites, 6,835; slaves, 8,250.

"The superintendent states, that in some of the districts the teachers refused to dismiss the children when notified of the exhaustion of the district apportionment. In other districts, the commissioners failed to notify the teachers of the insufficiency of funds to continue the children—which must operate a loss to the teachers, though a benefit to the children."

FAYETTE.

Whites, 3,780; slaves, 156.

"The board report, that the appropriation from the treasury is insufficient to aid in the education of all that really stand in need of assistance from the fund. Those who are the most needy, and at the same time most punctual in their attendance, are the ones for whose benefit we endeavor to apply the funds."

"The superintendent, in his report to the board of school commissioners, says: "While I would recommend to the board the propriety of having all teachers who apply for schools examined as to their qualifications, I am aware that they are compelled to send to such teachers as are employed by the paying patrons of the school; but really some plan ought to be adopted to prevent unqualified persons from teaching; for it is evident, if I be permitted to judge from the accounts presented for payment, that we have many teachers who would not be injured by taking a few lessons in penmanship and orthography themselves; but I am happy to say to the board that we have some teachers who are eminently qualified to teach. So far as I have been able to observe, there is certainly an increased interest manifested by parents and children on the subject of education, and a visible amount of good has been accomplished under the present system. The shortness of the session is one of the greatest objections to the schools. I would, so far as my experience both as teacher and commissioner extends, recommend a general system of free schools; *for while the county is large, and upon first thought one would think sparsely settled, yet the people are generally settled in neighborhoods or settlements sufficiently large and compact to justify the system;*" [a mountain county—observe the small proportion of slaves;] "and upon the adoption of such a system, I think it would be best for the first few years to teach about six months in the year, including the winter months; and under proper restrictions, I have no doubt but that it would be crowned with success."

SPOTSYLVANIA.

Whites, 6,894; slaves, 7,481.

"The board report that the appropriation from the treasury would not be sufficient, if all the indigent children were sent to school and attended regularly. Some of those entered attend regularly—others not at all. The fault lies in the parents and guardians."

FRANKLIN.

Whites, 11,638; slaves, 5,736.

"The superintendent regrets to say that it is a difficult thing to get suitable persons to undertake to act as school commissioners, and the duties, when undertaken, are not attended to as they should be; that if a small compensation were allowed, perhaps they would be fulfilled in a better manner."

GLOUCESTER.

Whites, 4,290; slaves, 5,887.

"The board report that the schools have been visited by some of the commissioners, and that many of the children have improved very much. The teachers are generally qualified and attentive to their schools. The amount allowed and received for the school fund is entirely insufficient to send all the children entitled to the said fund to school. That they are pleased to say that they have no difficulty now as heretofore in getting the parents to send their children; hence the large number that attended school the past year."

HANOVER.

Whites, 6,539; slaves, 8,393.

"The board report that they have unshaken confidence in the value of our school system, and would earnestly call upon the Legislature to do all they can constitutionally to increase the fund for this purpose."

"The superintendent reports: The important duty of visiting the districts, inspecting the schools, and making the proper returns to the superintendent, are almost entirely neglected; and we believe, that partly in consequence of this neglect, the proper discrimination between those children who are really proper objects of the State's bounty and those who are not, is lost sight of. I have no hesitation in saying that the small amount of money laid out in our county schools does more good than the same amount expended in any other way, or in any other form of education. There are returns from thirty-four schools, and the teachers are generally believed to be competent."

HENRY.

Whites, 5,524; slaves, 3,340.

"The superintendent states: It will be seen from the foregoing report of the board that there are several blanks which remain unfilled. These blanks can not be filled with any accuracy, as the commissioners say, which is very true, that they get nothing for their services, and they do not intend to trouble themselves in getting such information as will enable us to fill the blanks in the report. We are, therefore, under the necessity of forwarding a report which can not be considered complete."

"I would further remark, that while the commissioners are somewhat remiss in furnishing reports, I do not suppose the children of the county suffer any from that cause, as the teachers' accounts show that the commissioners all send to school fully to the amount allotted their respective districts; so that the children of the county are getting the full benefit of the fund. The only difficulty is, that the fund is by no means sufficient to educate the indigent children of this county.'

HENRICO,

Whites, 23,826; slaves, 16,109.

" The superintendent states that he takes pleasure in reporting the fact that the false pride which has in former years prevented many poor parents from sending their children to school, to be paid for by the State, has been broken down, and that at the present price allowed by the law, most of the teachers in the county are not only willing but anxious to teach the children—so that now the main obstacle in the way of more extended usefulness is the want of sufficient funds. He is of the opinion that nearly double the amount now appropriated might and could be judiciously expended by the board. He thinks the present system is working well, and knows it has and is doing good, and that he has no alteration to suggest except an increase of funds."

ISLE OF WIGHT.

Whites, 4,710; slaves, 3,395.

"The superintendent states that the average attendance of the children at school for the year appears to be only thirty-two and a quarter days, yet were the outstanding claims all paid, it would show quite a different state of things. Those accounts would exhibit an increase of the number of days, while the number of children would only be the same. He has on two or three occasions visited two of the three schools in his district, and was much pleased with the operations of those schools—the teachers being fully competent to the discharge of the important duties devolving on them. Had the funds been sufficient, nearly every child in the district could have attended school through the year."

LANCASTER.

Whites, 1,802; slaves, 2,640.

" The board report that, as a general thing, the schools of the county are of a higher grade than formerly, and few teachers will take pupils for the price (five cents per day) allowed by the school commissioners. The difference between their charge for tuition and the amount paid by the commissioners is therefore charged to the parents, guardians or other friends of the indigent children. A few very ordinary teachers may be found who will take pupils at the price allowed by law out of the funds of the State and county."

MONROE.

Whites, 9,062; slaves, 1,061.

" The committee appointed to report the transactions of the school commissioners, state that the commissioners have done as much to promote the interest of the indigent children as was in their power, laboring as they do under many disadvantages."

MONTGOMERY.

Whites, 6,822; slaves, 1,491.

" The superintendent has for years complained of the incompetency of teachers, and he has to regret that the evil is growing rather than diminishing. The visiting of schools by the commissioners has become obsolete."

NANSEMOND.

Whites, 5,424; slaves, 4,715.

" The commissioners have visited their schools during the year, and are satisfied with the qualifications of their teachers. The children make very fair improvement. Children from eight to eighteen years of age have been admitted to school, without regard to sex. The commissioners have not established any new schools, but have sent to those established in different neighborhoods by the people. They have authorized the superintendent to furnish books, paper, etc. The school quota for this county is not sufficient for the education of the indigent children by three or four thousand dollars, if they could be induced to attend school."

NOTTOWAY.

Whites, 2,234; slaves, 6,050.

" The superintendent is under the necessity of reporting the great want of attention paid to the requirements of the law on the part of school commissioners. Having to make out his account and report almost entirely from teachers' accounts, he is unable consequently to say how many poor children there are in the county who do not attend school, but, from the best information he can get, thinks there are at least sixty or seventy."

TUCKER.

Whites,   ; slaves,

" The board report that the insufficiency of the appropriation from the treasury precludes the education of all the poor children of the county, and it is only the most needy that can be sent to school."

WYTHE.

Whites, 9,618; slaves, 2,185.

" The board report that the funds are insufficient to send all the poor children for the whole time; that their object has been to send all a greater or less time, proportioned to their means."

WOOD.

Whites, 9,008; slaves, 375.

" The superintendent congratulates the board upon the advanced condition of the schools of the county generally."

"In reference to the general system of education, as pursued under the present arrangement of Virginia, although it is liable to some defects and objections, yet if properly and efficiently attended to and carried out by the commissioners, in selecting good and competent teachers, and in a just and equitable distribution of the funds for the education of the indigent children in all the neighborhoods of the county, it is the best that can be devised."

THE QUESTION OF COTTON SUPPLY.

Mr. Russell, although he clearly sees the calamity of the South, fully accepts the cotton planter's opinion, that, after all, the system of slavery is a necessary evil attending upon the great good of cheap cotton. He says: " If the climate had admitted of the growing of cotton on the banks of the Ohio, we should have seen that slavery possessed as great advantages over free labor in the raising of this crop as it does in that of tobacco." If this is so, it is important that it should be well understood why it is so as precisely as possible.

In his Notes on Maryland, Mr. Russell (p. 141) says : " Though a slave may, under very favorable circumstances, cultivate twenty acres of wheat and twenty acres of Indian corn, he can not manage more than two acres of tobacco. The cultivation of tobacco, therefore, admits of the concentration of labor, and thus the superintendence and management of a tobacco plantation will be more perfect and less expensive than a corn one." And this is the only explanation he offers of the supposed advantage of slave labor in the cultivation of tobacco, (and of consequence in the cultivation of cotton.) The chief expense of raising corn is chargeable to planting and tillage, that of tobacco to the seed-bed, the transplanting and nursing of the young plants, (which is precisely similar to the same operation with cabbages,) the hand-weeding, the hoeing after the plant has "become too large to work without injuring the leaves by the swingle-trees of a horse plow;"* "the topping," "the suckering," the selection and re-moval of valueless leaves, and "the worming," all of them, except hoeing, being operations which can be performed by children and child-bearing women, as they usually are in Virginia.†

The chief expense of raising cotton, as of corn, is that of planting and tillage. The principal difference between the method of tillage of cotton and that of corn is occasioned by the greater luxuriance of weeds in the southern climate and the slow growth of the cotton plant in its early stages, which obliges the tillage process to be more carefully and more frequently performed. For this reason, the area of cotton cultivated by each laborer is less than of corn. The area of corn land to a hand is, however, very much over-estimated, in my opinion, by Mr. Russell. On the other hand, the only mention he makes of the area of cotton land to a hand (being the statement of a negro) would lead to the conclusion that it is often not over three acres, and that five acres is extra-ordinary. Mr. De Bow says,‡ in an argument to prove that the average production per acre is over-estimated, "In the real cotton region, perhaps the average number of acres per hand is ten."

* De Bow, vol. iii., p. 342.   † See De Bow's "Resources," art. Tobacco.
‡ Vol. i., p. 175, "Resources"

Mr. Russell observes of worming and leafing tobacco : " These operations can be done as well, and consequently as cheaply, by women and children as by full grown men." (Page 142.) After reading Mr. Russell's views, I placed myself, through the kindness of Governor Chase, in communication with the Ohio Board of Agriculture, from which I have obtained elaborate statistics, together with reports on the subject from twelve presidents or secretaries of county agricultural societies, as well as from others. These gentlemen generally say that a certain amount of labor given to corn will be much better repaid than if given to tobacco. " Men are worth too much for growing corn to be employed in strolling through tobacco fields, looking for worms, and even women can, as our farmers think, find something better to do about the house." Children, too, are thought to be, and doubtless are, better employed at school in preparing themselves for more profitable duties, and this is probably the chief reason why coarse tobacco* can not be cultivated with as much profit as corn in Ohio, while the want of intelligent, self-interested labor, is the reason why the corn field, among the broad blades of which a man will work during much of its growth in comparative obscurity, can not be cultivated with as much profit on soils of the same quality in Virginia as in Ohio. In short, a class of laborers,

---

* In my Notes on Eastern Virginia, it was mentioned that a tobacco planter informed me that he could not raise the finer sorts of tobacco with profit, because he could not make his slaves take pains enough with it; and in certain localities in Ohio, having a favorable soil for the production of fine or high priced tobacco, it appears that free labor is engaged more profitably in the cultivation of tobacco than in the cultivation of corn. It is the same in parts of Connecticut and of Massachusetts. Except in these limited districts, however, it is found that the labor of Ohio, as of Connecticut and Massachusetts, is more profitably directed to the cultivation of corn (maize) and other crops than of tobacco.

which are good for nothing else, and which but for this would be an intolerable burden upon those who are obliged to support them, can be put to some use in raising tobacco, and, therefore, coarse tobacco continues to be cultivated in some of the principal slave-holding counties of Virginia. But this class of laborers is of no more value in cotton culture than in corn culture. Mr. De Bow says: "The Southwest, the great cotton region, is newly settled, and the number of children, out of all proportion, less than in negroes [regions?] peopled by a natural growth of population.* Weak women and weak children are, in fact, not at all in demand for cotton culture, the cotton planter's inquiry being only for 'prime boys,' or ' A. 1. field hands.' "

Thus, in every way, cotton culture, in my judgment, more resembles corn culture than it does tobacco culture. The production of corn is larger in the aggregate, is considerably larger per man engaged in its cultivation, and is far larger per acre in Ohio than in Virginia.† I should, therefore, be inclined to reverse Mr.

* "Resources," p. 175.

† Virginia, with 10,360,135 acres of improved land, produced, according to the last census returns,

> 35,254,319 bushels of corn,
> 56,803,227 pounds of tobacco.

Ohio, with 9,851,493 acres of improved land, produced

> 59,078,695 bushels of corn,
> 10,454,449 pounds of tobacco.

The aggregate value of these two products alone, at present New York prices, would be

> Ohio........$5,127,223,565
> Virginia.....$3,564,639,385

Actual crops per acre, on the average, as returned by the marshals for 1849-50 (Census Compilation, p. 178):

	Corn.	Tobacco.
Ohio	36 bushels	730 pounds.
Virginia	18 "	630 "

Russell's statement, and to say that if the climate had admitted of the growing of cotton on both banks of the Ohio, we should have seen that free labor possessed as great advantages over slavery in the cultivation of cotton as of corn.

Mr. Russell echoes also the opinion, which every cotton planter is in the habit of urging, that the production of cotton would have been comparatively insignificant in the United States if it had not been for slave labor. He likewise restricts the true cotton region within much narrower limits than are usually given to it, and holds that the slave population must soon in a great measure be concentrated within it. As these conclusions of a scientific traveler unintentionally support a view which has been lately systematically pressed upon manufacturers and merchants both in Great Britain and the free States, namely, that the perpetuation of slavery in its present form is necessary to the perpetuation of a liberal cotton supply, and also that the limit of production in the United States must be rapidly approaching, and consequently that the tendency of prices must be rapidly upward, the grounds on which they rest should be carefully scrutinized.

Mr. Russell says, in a paragraph succeeding the words just now quoted with regard to the supposed advantages of slave labor in raising tobacco :

" The rich upland soils of the cotton region afford a profitable investment for capital, even when cultivated by slaves left to the care of overseers. The natural increase of the slaves, from two to six per cent., goes far to pay the interest of the money invested in them. The richest soils of the uplands are invariably occupied by the largest plantations, and the alluvial lands on the banks of the rivers are so unhealthy for white laborers that the slave owners occupy them without competition. Thus the banks of the western rivers are now becoming the great cotton-producing districts. Taking these facts into consideration, it appears that the quantity of cotton which would have been raised without slave labor in the United States would have been comparatively insignificant to the present supply."*

* North America, its Climate, etc., p. 286.

The advantages of slave labor for cotton culture seem from this to have been predicated mainly upon the unwholesomeness to free or white laborers of the best cotton lands, especially of the alluvial lands on the banks of rivers. Reference is made particularly to " the county of Washington, Mississippi State, [which] lies between the Yazoo and Mississippi rivers. * * * The soil is chiefly alluvial, though a considerable portion is swampy and liable to be flooded."

Mr. Russell evidently considers that it is to this swampy condition, and to stagnant water left by floods, that the supposed insalubrity of this region is to be chiefly attributed. How would he explain, then, the undoubted salubrity of the bottom lands in Louisiana, which are lower than those of the Mississippi, exposed to a more southern sun, more swampy, and which were originally much more frequently flooded, but having been dyked and "leveed," are now inhabited by a white population of several hundred thousand. I will refer to the evidence of an expert:

"Heat, moisture, animal and vegetable matter, are said to be the elements which produce the diseases of the South, and yet the testimony in proof of the health of the banks of the lower portion of the Mississippi river is too strong to be doubted. Here is a perfectly flat alluvial country, covering several hundred miles, interspersed with interminable lakes, lagunes and jungles, and still we are informed by Dr. Cartwright, one of the most acute observers of the day, that this country is exempt from miasmatic disorders, and is extremely healthy. His assertion has been confirmed to me by hundreds of witnesses, and we know, from our own observation, that the population presents a robust and healthy appearance." (Statistics are given to prove a greater average length of life for the white race in the South than in the North.)—ESSAY ON THE VALUE OF LIFE IN THE SOUTH, by Dr. J. C. Nott, of Alabama.

The unacclimated whites on the sea coast and on the river and bayou banks of the low country, between which and the sea coast there is much inter-communication, suffer greatly from cer-

* De Bow's "Resources." See "Seaboard Slave States," pp. 463 and 586, for further southern evidence.

tain epidemic, contagious and infectious pestilences. This, however, only renders the fact that dense settlements of whites have been firmly established upon them, and that they are remarkably exempt from miasmatic disease, one of more value in evidence of the practicability of white occupation of the upper bottom lands. There are strong grounds for doubting the common opinion that the negroes at the South suffer less from local causes of disease than whites. (See "Seaboard Slave States," p. 647.) They may be less subject to epidemic and infectious diseases, and yet be more liable to other fatal disorders than whites. The worst climate for unacclimated whites of any town in the United States is that of Charleston. (This, together with the whole of the rice coast, is clearly exceptional in respect to salubrity for whites.) It happens fortunately that the most trustworthy and complete vital statistics of the South are those of Charleston. Dr. Nott, commenting upon these, says that the average mortality, during six years, has been, of blacks alone, one in forty-four; of whites, alone, one in fifty-eight. "This mortality," he adds, "is perhaps not an unfair test, as the population during the last six years has been undisturbed by emigration, and acclimated in greater proportion than at any previous period." If the comparison had been made between native negroes and native or acclimated whites alone, it would doubtless show the climate to be still more unfavorable to negroes.*

---

* Dr. Barton, of New Orleans, in a paper read before the Academy of Science of that city, says: "The class of diseases most fatal in the South are mainly of a '*preventible* nature,' and embraces fevers and intestinal diseases, and depends mostly on conditions under the control of man, as drainage, the removal of forest growth—of personal exposure and private hygiene. The climate further north is too rigid the greater part of the year for personal exposure to the open air, so essential to the enjoyment of health, and when the extremes are great and rapid, another class of maladies predominate—

Upon the very district to which Mr. Russell refers, as offering an extreme case, I quote the testimony of a Mississippi statistician :

"The cotton planters, deserting the rolling land, are fast pouring in upon the 'swamp.' Indeed, the impression of the sickliness of the South generally has been rapidly losing ground, [i. e. among the whites of the South] for some years back, and that blessing [health] is now sought with as much confidence on the swamp lands of the Yazoo and the Mississippi as among the hills and plains of Carolina and Virginia."— (De Bow's "Resources," vol. ii., p. 43.)

Dr. Barton says :

", In another place I have shown that the direct temperature of the sun is not near so great in the South, (during the summer,) as it is at the North. I shall recur to this hereafter. In fact, the climate is much more endurable, all the year round, with our refreshing breezes, and particularly in some of the more elevated parts of it, or within one hundred miles of the coast, both in and out of doors, at the South than at the North, which shows most conspicuously the folly of the annual summer migrations, to pursue an imaginary mildness of temperature, which is left at home."

Mr. Russell assumes that slave labor tends, as a matter of course, to the formation of large plantations, and that free labor can only be applied to agricultural operations of a limited scope. Of slaves, he says : "Their numbers admit of that organization and division of labor which renders slavery so serviceable in the culture of cotton." I find no reason given for this assumption, except that he did not himself see any large agricultural enterprises conducted with free labor, while he did see many plantations of fifty to one hundred slave hands. The explanation, in my judgment, is that the cultivation of the crops generally grown in the free States has hitherto been most profitable when conducted on the

the pulmonary, as well as others arising from crowding, defective ventilation and filth—exacting preventive measures from the public authorities with as much urgency as the worst fevers of the South."

"small holding" system ;* the cultivation of cotton is, as a general rule, more profitable upon the "large holding" system.† Undoubtedly there is a point below which it becomes disadvantageous to reduce the farm in the free States, and this varies with local circumstances. There is equally a limit beyond which it is acknowledged to be unprofitable to enlarge the body of slaves engaged in cotton cultivation under one head. If cotton were to be cultivated by free labor, it is probable that this number would be somewhat reduced. I have no doubt that the number of men on each plantation, in any case, would, on an average, much nearer approach that which would be most economical, in a free labor cotton growing country than in a country on which the whole dependence of each proprietor was on slaves. Is not this conclusion irresistible when we consider that the planter, if he needs an additional slave hand to those he possesses, even if temporarily, for harvesting his crop, must, in most cases, employ at least a thousand dollars of capital to obtain it ?

Mr. Russell has himself observed that—

"The quantity of cotton which can be produced on a [slave-worked] plantation is limited by the number of hands it can turn into the field during the picking or harvesting of the crop. Like some other agricultural operations, this is a simple one, though it does not admit of being done by machinery, as a certain amount of intelligence must direct the hand."

The same is true of a wheat farm, except that much more can be done by machinery, and consequently the extraordinary demand for labor at the wheat harvest is much less than it is on a

* Corn has been considered an exception, and there are probably larger corn fields in Indiana than cotton fields in Mississippi.

† I believe that plantations or agricultural operations devoted to a single crop are, as a general rule, profitable in proportion to their size in the free States, unless indeed the market is a small one and easily overstocked, which is never the case with the cotton market.

cotton plantation. I have several times been on the Mississippi
plantations during picking time, and have seen how every thing
black, with hands, was then pressed into severe service; but, after
all, I have often seen negroes breaking down, in preparation for
re-plowing the ground for the next crop, acres of cotton plants,
upon which what appeared to me to be a tolerable crop of wool
still hung, because it had been impossible to pick it. I have seen
what was confesssed to be many hundred dollars' worth of cotton
thus wasted on a single Red River plantation. I much doubt if
the harvest demand of the principal cotton districts of Mississippi adds five per cent. to their field hand force. In Ohio, there
is a far larger population ordinarily engaged in other pursuits
which responds to the harvest demand. A temporary increase of
the number of agricultural laborers thus occurs of not less than
forty per cent. during the most critical period.

An analogous case is that of the vintage in the wine districts
of France. In some of these the "small holding" or *parcellement*
system is carried to an unfortunate extreme under the influence
of what are perhaps injudicious laws. The parcels of land are
much smaller, on an average, than the smallest class of farms
ordinarily cultivated by free labor in the United States. But can
any one suppose that if the slave labor system, as it exists in the
United States, prevailed in those districts, that is to say, if the
proprietors depended solely on themselves, their families and their
regular servants, as those of Mississippi must, at the picking time,
there would not be a disastrous falling off in the commerce of those
districts? Substitute the French system, unfortunate as in some
respects it is, for the Mississippi system in cotton growing, and
who will doubt that the commerce of the United States would be
greatly increased?

Hop picking and cotton picking are very similar operations. The former is the more laborious, and requires the greater skill. What would the planters of Kent do if they had no one but their regular laborers to call upon at their harvest season? As it is, the population in many parishes in Kent I suppose to be quadrupled in picking time.

I observed this advantage of the free labor system exemplified in Western Texas, the cotton fields in the vicinity of the German village of New Braunfels having been picked, when I saw them, far closer than any I had before seen, in fact, perfectly clean, having been undoubtedly gleaned by the poor emigrants. I was told that some mechanics made more in a day, by going into the field of a slave owner and picking side by side with his slaves, being paid by measure, than they could earn at their regular work in a week. The degree of intelligence and of practice required to pick to advantage was found to be very slight, less very much than in any single operation of wheat harvesters. One woman was pointed out to me who had, in the first year she had ever seen a cotton field, picked more cotton in a day than any slave in the county.

I am reminded, as this page is about to be stereotyped, by observing the letter of a cotton planter in the New Orleans Price Current, of another disadvantage for cotton production, of slave labor, or rather of the system which slavery induces. In the Texas journey, I stated that I was informed by a merchant that the cotton picked by the free labor of the Germans was worth from one to two cents a pound more than that picked by slaves in the same township, by reason of its greater cleanliness. From the letter referred to, I make the following extracts:

"DEAR SIR: * * * There are probably no·set of men engaged in any business of life who take as little pains and care to inform themselves with regard to the character and quality of their marketable produce as the cotton planter. Not one in a thousand knows, nor cares to know, whether the cotton he sends to market is ordinary, good ordinary, or middling. Not one in a hundred spends one hour of each day at his gin in ginning season; never sees the cotton after it is gathered, unless he happens to ride near the scaffold and looks from a distance of a hundred yards, and declares the specimen very white and clean, when, perhaps, it, on the contrary, may be very leafy and dirty. * * *

"I have often seen the hands on plantations picking cotton with sacks that would hardly hold stalks, they were so torn and full of holes; these sacks dragging on the ground and gathering up pounds of dirt at every few steps. The baskets, too, were with scarcely any bottoms remaining, having been literally worn out, the cotton lying on the ground. Indeed, some overseers do not forbid the hands emptying their cotton on the ground when their sacks are full, and they some distance from their baskets. When this cotton is taken up, some dirt must necessarily come with it. When gathering in wet weather, the hands get into their baskets with muddy feet, and thus toss in some pounds of dirt, in this way making their task easier. These things 'are never, or rarely, seen by the proprietor; and, consequently, when his merchant writes him that his cotton is a little dusty, he says how can it be? you are surely mistaken.

"Now, sir, for all this there is one simple, plain remedy; let the planter spend his time in ginning season at his gin; let him see every load of cotton as it comes from the field and before it goes through the gin. But, says the man of leisure, the gin is a dirty, dusty place. Yes, sir, and always will be so, until you remedy the evil by staying there yourself. You say your overseer is hired to do this dirty work. *Your overseer is after quantity, sir, and the more extra weight he gets in your cotton, the more bales he will have to brag of having made at the end of the year. Don't trust him at the gin.* * * *

"Probably he has a conditional contract with his employer: *gets so many dollars for all he makes over a certain number of bales; thus having every inducement to put up as much leaf and dirt, or, if he is one of the dishonest kind, he may add stones, if they should abound in the neighborhood.*

"Why will not the cotton planter take pride in his own production? The merchant prides himself on his wares; the mechanic on the work of his hands. All seem to pride themselves on the result of their labor except the cotton planter." * * *

It can not be admitted that the absence in the free States of that organization and division of labor in agriculture which is found on a large slave-worked plantation is a necessity attending the use of free labor. Why should it be any more impossible to employ an army of free laborers in moving the ground with an agricultural design than with the intention of constructing a canal or a road, if it were profitable to so employ the necessary capital? A railroad contractor in one of the best cotton districts of the United States told me, that having begun his work with negroes, he was substituting Irish and German laborers for them as rapidly as possible, with great advantage, (and this near midsummer.) But if I were convinced with Mr. Russell upon this point, I should still be inclined to think that the advantages which are possessed in a free labor state of society equally by the great hop planters at picking time and the *petits propriétaires* at vintage, which are also found in our own new States by the wheat farmer, and which are not found under the present system anywhere at the South, for cotton picking, would of themselves be sufficient to turn the scale in favor of the free labor cotton grower.

The errors of the assumptions upon which the opinion is based by Mr. Russell, that slave labor is essential or important to sustain cotton production in the United States, is, I trust, apparent. The more common and popular opinion is, that the necessary labor of cotton tillage is too severe for white men in the cotton-growing climate. As I have said before, I do not find the slightest weight of fact to sustain this opinion. The necessary labor and causes of fatigue and vital exhaustion attending any part or all of the process of cotton culture does not compare with that of our July harvesting; it is not greater than attends the cultivation of Indian corn in the usual New England method. I have seen a weakly white woman the worse for her labor in the cotton field, but never a white man, and I have seen hundreds of them at work in cotton fields under the most unfavorable circumstances, miserable, dispirited wretches, and of weak muscle, subsisting mainly, as they do, on corn bread. Mr. De Bow estimates one hundred thousand white men now engaged in the cultivation of cotton, being one ninth of the whole cotton force (numerically) of the country.* I have just seen a commercial letter from San Antonio, which estimates that the handful of Germans in Western Texas will send ten thousand bales of cotton, the production of their own labor, to market this season. If it should prove to be half this, it must be considered a liberal contribution to the needed supply of the year, by those who, following Mr. Russell, have considered Western Texas out of the true cotton region, and taking the truth of the common planters' assertion for granted, have thought Africans, working under physical compulsion, the only means of meeting the demand which could be looked to in the future of the United States.

It would not surprise me to learn that the cultivation of cotton by the German settlers in Texas had not, after all, been as profitable as its cultivation by the planters employing slaves in the vicinity. I should attribute the superior profits of the planter, if any there be, however, not to the fitness of the climate for negro labor, and its unfitness for white labor, but to the fact that his expenses for fencing, on account of his larger fields and larger estate, are several hundred per cent. less than those of the farmer; to the fact that his expenses for tillage, having mules and plows and other instruments to use at the opportune moment, are less than those of the farmer, who, in many cases, can not afford to own a single team; to the fact that he has, from experience, a better knowledge of the most successful method of cultivation; to the fact that he has a gin and a press of his own in the midst of his

* Vol. i., p. 175, "Resources."

cotton fields, to which he can carry his wool at one transfer from the picking; by which he can put it in order for market expeditiously, and at an expense much below that falling upon the farmer, who must first store his wool, then send it to the planter's gin and press and have it prepared at the planter's convenience, paying, perhaps, exorbitantly therefor; and, finally, to the fact that the planter deals directly with the exporter, while the farmer, the whole profit of whose crop would not pay his expenses in a journey to the coast, must transfer his bale or two to the exporter through two or three middle-men, carrying it one bale at a time, to the local purchaser. Merchants will never give as good prices for small lots as for large. There are reasons for this which I need not now explain. I consider, in short, that the disadvantages of the farmer in growing cotton are of the same nature as I have before explained (p. 122) with those which long ago made fire-wood of hand-looms, and paupers of those who could be nothing else but hand-loom weavers, in Massachusetts. Exactly how much is gained by the application of labor with the advantage of capital and combination of numbers over its isolated application as directed by individuals without capital in a slaveholding region, I can not estimate, but no one will doubt that it is considerable. Nevertheless, in all the cotton climate of the United States, if a white farmer has made money without slaves, it will be found that it has been, in most cases, obtained exclusively from the sale of cotton. If cotton is a plant the cultivation of which by free or white labor is especially difficult, how is it that, with the additional embarrassments arising from a lack of capital, his gains are almost exclusively derived from his cotton crop?

But I may be asked, if combination is what is needed to make cotton a source of more general prosperity at the South, why is there no such thing as a joint-stock cotton plantation in Mississippi, as there are joint-stock cotton mills in Massachusetts, the stock in which is in large part owned by those employed in them? I ask, in reply, how is it that the common way of obtaining breadstuffs in northern Alabama is to sow three pecks of seed wheat on hard stubble ground, plow it under with unbroken bullocks, led with a rope, and a bull-tongue plow, and finally to garner rarely so much as six bushels from an acre. How is it that while in Ohio the spinning-wheel and hand-loom are curiosities, and homespun would be a conspicuous and noticeable material of clothing, half the white population of Mississippi still dress in homespun, and at every second house the wheel and loom are found in operation? The same influences which condemn the majority of free laborers in Alabama to hand-looms, homespun, and three hundred pounds of wheat to the acre as the limit of production, also condemn them to isolated labor, poor soil, poor tools, bad management, "bad luck," small crops and small profits in cotton culture.

The following passages from a letter published in the "New York Times" present convincing evidence that it is no peculiarity of the Western Texas climate, but only the exceptional social condition with which its people are favored, that enables free white labor to be employed in increasing the cotton production of the country. I have ascertained that the author of the letter is known to the editor of the Times, and is esteemed a gentleman of veracity and trustworthy judgment.

"I am well acquinted with eastern Mississippi, south of Monroe county, and there are few settlements where my name or face is unknown in the following counties, over the greater part of which I have ridden on horseback, to wit: Loundes, Oktibleha, Choctaw, Carroll, Attalla, Winston, Noxubee, Kemper, Nashoba, Leake, Scott, Newton,

Lauderdale, Clarke, Smith and Jasper. After four years' travel through these counties, transacting business with great numbers of their inhabitants, stopping at their houses, conversing much with them, and viewing their mode of living, I unhesitatingly answer that white men can and do labor in the cotton field, from Christmas to Christmas following; and that there, as elsewhere, prudence, industry and energy find their universal reward, success and wealth.

"In the counties of Choctaw, Winston, Nashoba, Newton and Smith, there are very few large plantations; most of those having slaves holding but two or three, while those who own none are in the majority; yet these are all cotton-growing counties, and the staple of their cotton, poor as their lands are, is equal to the average sold in the Mobile market. Where the young farmer is enterprising and go-ahead, his cotton is usually superior. * * *

"The rich lands where white labor, even in small numbers, might be profitable, are either in the hands of large planters, or too heavily timbered for a single man. The only thing now preventing any poor white man in the South from gaining a fair competence, and even attaining wealth, is his own laziness, shiftlessness and ignorance; for the small planters in the counties I have mentioned are deplorably ignorant. * * *

"There is one case I remember, which is to the point; the man lives in Choctaw county, and was born in Georgia. He does not own a negro, but has two boys, one sixteen, the other twelve. With the assistance of these boys, and the most imperfect agricultural implements, he made twenty-two bales of cotton, year before last, plenty of corn, and sufficient small grain for himself and family, although the season was more than ordinarily bad in his neighborhood, while many of his neighbors, with five or six slaves, did not exceed him, and some made even less. He went on to his place without ten dollars in his pocket, gave his notes for eight hundred dollars, payable in one, two and three years' time, with interest at six per cent. per annum, and the ensuing year he purchased another one hundred and sixty acres for seven hundred and fifty dollars, also on time. This man is, however, far more intelligent and progressive in farming than those about him; he does not plant as did his grandfather, because his father did so, but endeavors to improve, and is willing to try an experiment occasionally.

"In my own county, in Alabama, there is a woman whose husband died shortly after the crop was planted, leaving her without a single servant, and no assistance except from a little son of twelve years of age; yet she went into the field, plowed and picked her cotton, prepared her ground for the coming crop, and raised a second crop thereon."

My conclusion, from the various evidences to which I have referred, would be a widely different one from Mr. Russell's, from that which is generally thought to prevail with our leading capitalists, merchants and manufacturers, and from that which seems to have been accepted by the Cotton Supply Associations of Liverpool and Manchester. It is this: that there is no physical obstacle in the way of our country's supplying ten bales of cotton where it now does one. All that is necessary for this purpose is to direct to the cotton-producing region an adequate number of laborers, either black or white, or both. No amalgamation, no association on equality, no violent disruption of present relations is necessary. It is not even requisite that both black and white should work in the cotton fields. It is necessary that there should be more objects of industry, more varied enterprises, more general intelligence among the people, and especially that they should become or should desire to become richer, more comfortable, than they are.

The simple truth is, that even if we view in the brightest light of Fourth of July patriotism, the character of the whites of the cotton-producing region, and the condition of the slaves, we can not help seeing that, commercially speaking, they are but in a very small part a civilized people. Undoubtedly a large number of merchants have a profitable business in supplying civilized luxuries and conveniences to the South. The same is true of Mexico, of Turkey, of Egypt, and of Russia. Silk, cloth and calico, shoes, gloves and gold watches, were sold in some quantity in California before its golden coffers were forcibly opened ten years ago. The southern supply to commerce and the southern demand of commerce is no more what it should be, comparing the resources of the South with those of other lands occupied by an active civilized community, than is that of any half civilized community, than was that of California. Give the South a people moderately close settled, moderately well-informed, moderately ambitious and moderately industrious, somewhat approaching that of Ohio, for instance, and what a business it would have! Twenty double-track railroads from the Gulf to the lakes, and twenty lines of ocean steamers, would not sufficiently meet its requirements. Who doubts, let him study the present business of Ohio, and ask upon what in the natural resources of Ohio, or its position, could, forty years ago, a prediction of its present wealth and business have been made, of its present supply and its present demand have been made, which would compare in value with the commercial resources and advantages of position possessed to-day by any one of the western cotton States?*

REMEDIAL MEASURES.

Mr. Gregg's scheme, which I have before described, is a simple, common sense method of palliating the wretchedness of the poor of his own district, by endeavoring to make practicable to them the acquisition of "home comforts." That it can afford only a palliation will be obvious if we consider how much capital would be needed to make it a remedy, having a general application. So large a part of the whole population consists of slaves, whose demand for manufactured goods would be supplied by a small number of operatives, the factories would be required to send their goods to a distance for Purchasers. Mr. Gregg acknowledges that the manufacture of the coarse goods, such as are

* Some one can render a service to civilization by publishing precisely what feudal rights, so called, were abolished in large parts of Germany and Hungary in 1848, and what results to the commerce of the districts affected the greater freedom and impulse to industry arising therefrom has had. If I am rightly informed, trade, in many cases, both export and import, has already much more than quadrupled in value, thousands of peasants now demanding numerous articles and being able to pay for them, which before only a few score or hundred proprietors were expected to buy.

chiefly required by slaves, and which near the factory displace
the common home-spun and woven cloth formerly worn by the
majority of the free people, has been already over-done. He estimates the white population of South Carolina alone, "who
ought to work and who do not, or who are so employed as to be
wholly unproductive to the State," at one hundred and twenty-
five thousand. If they were all collected, as he proposes, they
would operate (upon his own data) five million spindles. In
Massachusetts, with all its railroads, foundries, quarries, and
machine shops, it is usual to reckon the plant cost of a factory of
the character proposed by Mr. Gregg at twenty-five dollars a
spindle. Thus, to put at work, on Mr. Gregg's plan, merely that
portion of the population of South Carolina who at present are
pure vagrants, and attempting nothing directly for those who
barely earn their own means of subsistence, a capital would be
required, at the lowest estimate, of one hundred and twenty-five
million dollars, or more than six times the estimated value of all
the landed property in the State.

But suppose that this capital could be profitably used in cotton manufacturing, would this be the best way of applying it?

Mr. Gregg says that three fourths of the eight hundred adults
whom he has collected at Graniteville are not able to read or to
write their names. "With the aid of ministers of the gospel on
the spot to preach to them and lecture them on the subject, we
have obtained but about sixty children for our school, of about
a hundred which are in the place. We are satisfied that
nothing but time and patience will enable us to bring them all
out. * * * Notwithstanding our rule that no one can be
permitted to occupy our houses who does not send all his children to school that are between the ages of six and twelve, it

was with some difficulty, at first, that we could make up even a small school."*

Mr. Taylor, a co-laborer of Mr. Gregg, says : "The question has often been asked, Will southern operatives equal northern in their ability to accomplish factory work ? As a general answer, I would reply in the affirmative; but at the same time it may with justice be said they can not at present, even in our best factories, accomplish as much as is usual in northern mills. The habitude of our people has been to anything but close application to manual labor, and it requires time to bring the whole habits of a person into a new train."†

As affording an argument against establishing factories in towns, Mr. Gregg refers to the history of manufacturing in Augusta. I myself had a singular confirmation of the correctness of his views in this respect in the information given me by the landlord of a hotel in Augusta, who said, in answer to my inquiries, that the hands employed in the factories were country people who had been induced by a promise of fixed cash wages to move into town, but who were so lazy that only an immediate necessity to keep them from starvation would induce them to work. The president or foreman of the mills had been to him and implored him never to give them food when they came begging for it, as he had sometimes done, because it increased the difficulty of making them work. "If you ride past the factory," he added, "you will see them loafing about, and I reckon you never saw a meaner looking set of people anywhere. If they were niggers, they would not sell for five hundred dollars a head."

* Address to South Carolina Institute.
† De Bow's Review, January, 1850.

Of one of the manufacturing villages of Georgia, Tobler's Creek, the Rev. Mr. White, (Statistics, p. 575,) says : " The character of the operatives is marked by the usual traits which distinguish the poor uneducated class of this country. Of the whole population of the village, which amounts to two hundred and forty, there are not twenty who can either read or write. * * * Nearly all the families residing here are those who have been driven by necessity to engage their children to work in the mills, whose toil on some worn out or barren piece of land was not sufficient to supply their wants." Yet the same authority says elsewhere (p. 576) : " No one can visit this section of the country without forming a favorable opinion of the character of its population, the greater part are snug farmers, out of debt."

I have previously shown that the population from which Mr. Gregg's operatives are drawn is a rather superior one to that of other parts of the State.

Is it not obvious that the capital required to have the slightest remedial effect would be much better employed in transferring the raw cotton to a free country and there manufacturing it, or that it would be far more economical to transport, en masse, a body of decent, intelligent, disciplined and industrious work-people to South Carolina, than to enlist, drill and educate to the necessary degree of intelligence for effective operatives, the wretched starvelings and wild men of the pine woods, who have grown up under the educational influence of slavery? It may be replied that the labor of these latter may be procured at half the price per day of the more intelligent and industrious class. But how long would they be content with these low wages after they had become sufficiently intelligent to earn them? Knowing that, on free soil, as it would be impossible long to prevent their knowing, the same degree of intelligence and the same amount of labor would earn twice the amount of comfort, how long would it be before Mr. Gregg's "communities" would take themselves to free soil, or— make free soil of South Carolina? It will help us to an answer to look for an instant at Missouri.

In 1849, in Missouri, only fourteen counties out of one hundred were returned as sending above twenty per cent. of their whole population to school. Seven years afterwards came the presidential election, and the next year a State election, hotly canvassed, in which the representative of the administration party declared the question between himself and his opponent to be between the fortification of slavery and emancipation. His opponent courageously accepted it, and was denounced by that name so odious to ignorant southern citizens, abolitionist. What did the administration party gain by it in those counties where education had been least obstructed? In six of these counties but three hundred and twenty-eight votes, while in eight of these counties the vote against it was increased over that of the presidential election fourteen hundred and forty-six votes.

It is, however, as impracticable, as it would be unsafe to the present system, to introduce white operatives in large numbers from free soil. Impracticable, because, except at greatly enhanced wages, they will not endure the necessary discomfort of the life of working people in a slave State; unsafe, because, with their intelligence, the antagonism of slavery to their interests could not be concealed from them. They are naturally, in the words of a South Carolina editor before quoted, "enemies to the peculiar institution," or, as De Bow says, "European [or intelligent, in contradistinction to African or ignorant] labor * * * has not taken foothold in our limits, evidencing thus an incapacity to adapt itself to our condition." It is from the admission of German laborers into Missouri that the agitation for emancipation in that State has arisen. The southern gentlemen could not occupy the land with their forces, not even with a single slave family to a square mile in many parts. They could not afford to "take up" or hold all they left unoccupied and have not the slightest production from it. Much as the Germans disliked the proximity of slaves, they could not resist the temptation to buy this rich unoccupied land at a fourth part of the value of similar soil in the adjoining free States; government could not refuse to sell it them, and so came the catastrophe of popular education and of discussion of the value of slavery right in the midst of a slaveholding state.

How can such a process be prevented from going on, or from recurring?

The Charleston Mercury says: "Traveling in any direction, broad uncultivated lands and beds of mineral wealth, still unopened, lie before you. Settlement and cultivation mark only the most fertile spots. In South Carolina, one of the oldest States, thousands upon thousands of acres of surpassing richness stretch along her rivers, crowned with the unshorn forest. * * * These remarks have a much stronger application to the newer States of the South. Florida, Alabama, Mississippi, Arkansas, and Texas, exhibit this want of labor in far more startling degrees."

Mr. Spratt, writing from Charleston to the editor of the New Orleans Delta, (September, 1859,) upon the settlement of Kansas, which the South then expected to make a slave State before 1860:

"Without slaves, there will be little advantage in having it nominally a slave State. * * * The State of Delaware is nominally a slave State, but it were madness to rely on Delaware for aid; and Missouri even, which has ninety thousand slaves, has an abolition party to contest for power.

"So circumstanced, it is to be doubted whether Kansas can ever acquire the slaves to make her in fact a slave State; but should she do so, she must take them from Maryland, Virginia, Kentucky, Tennessee, or Missouri—no one of which has slaves enough now to sustain the perfect integrity of a slave system. Maryland reels upon the line between slavery and the isms, and cast her vote for Fillmore in the late election. Virginia is threatened with a colony of New Englanders to cultivate a space she can not cover with slave labor.

"In Kentucky it has been proposed to manumit the slaves. Tennessee is aghast at the mention of the slave trade, and Missouri, as I have said, has an abolition party to contest for power. It can never strengthen slavery to take slaves from those States to Kansas, and perhaps there is no place in the Union where one hundred thousand slaves could be so profitably planted as upon the soil of the brave old State of Virginia."

Thus, while we are every year presented with new projects from southern politicians for an increase of territory, are called upon to further stimulate the expanding and dispersing tendency, some answer must be given at home to the question: What are we going to do with it? "While we have millions of acres open to slave occupation, yet a perfect wilderness, while some of the longest settled parts of our present territory are every year regaining more and more of their original wilderness condition, from the dispersion of our labor over new wildernesses, when it is certain that civilized laborers will not come upon our territory, or that if they do they will wrest it from us, what can we do with more territory? What can we do with that we have?"

Mr. De Bow says: "To one who has observed the signs of the times, the evidence is irresistible, that the question of labor supply is at this moment attracting in every part of the South and of the Southwest a degree of attention which has never been accorded to it before, stimulated as the question is by the almost boundless and now but partially occupied domain in our possession *or within our reach*, adapted to rich and productive cultivation; by the increasing demand and enhanced prices obtained for every description of product peculiar to that domain, and by the unprecedented rise in the value of the only species of labor which it is capable of employing."*

It will profit us to observe how the South, becoming, in these last few years, gradually aware of the dilemma into which its policy of extension has carried it, goes to work to relieve itself. Up to this time it is only at a few points, in the vicinity of commercial centers, where the contact of men with each other is most frequent, that the dread of entering upon any discussion is not the strongest feeling manifested. The more impetuous only as yet have propounded a remedy, and this they advocate not earnestly but frantically; thus:

FROM THE CHARLESTON MERCURY.

"The alternative to the South is, whether she will continue to depend solely upon the natural increase of her slaves, for development and colonization, wholly inadequate as it is for either, or, despising for once and for ever the whinings of fanaticism, she will brush from her path its flimsy obstacles, and demand that the original and true source of her labor shall be no longer closed—that Africa and America shall be free to reciprocate blessings? If, when slavery was deemed an evil, southern men consented to the abolition of the slave trade, as the precursor of emancipation, will they adhere to the same policy when slavery is proved to be a blessing—nay, the very heart blood of the South? Are they still advocates of emancipation? Do they not perceive that by such a course they are preparing the way of abolition? Is it worthy of a free people to consent to absolute restrictions upon their legitimate progress, when progress is to them, more than to all others, the very necessity of their existence? Shall the North be permitted to supply her demand for labor, wherewith to usurp the common territories, and abolitionize the government by an emigration, attended with all the horrors of the slave trade, while the South is tied hand and foot? Will

* Letter to W. L. Yancey, published generally in Southern newspapers, July, 1859.

she perpetuate a policy which stigmatizes her civilization, betrays her cause into the silliest inconsistencies, and tends to her complete annihilation? Will she permit her vast and splendid resources to be wasted, because fanaticism and political rivalry demand the sacrifice?"

FROM THE SAME.

"If it benefits the African, and benefits the southern planter, and benefits the trader who brings over the slaves, who is there to be injured by it? We are to be content with the answer that there is a pack of fools and Pharisees in England and the Northern States, whose feelings are hurt by the horrors of the slave trade, and that the general assembly of French philosophers have decided that man can rightfully have no property in man."

FROM THE CHARLESTON STANDARD.

"It is first necessary to see that we are right, to look at this great question of the slave trade, and see if, in fact, we require its establishment, and, if so, we will demand its reëstablishment within the Union, or we will reëstablish it to ourselves."

FROM THE STATES RIGHT LOUISIANIAN.

"Unless the slave trade be reëstablished, slavery, instead of increasing, must necessarily diminish its borders, and, after a certain length of time, be extinguished. Slaveholders, for the present, have no other interest than to strengthen and defend it in all places where it already exists, and where it is an essential and integrant part of the domestic institutions."

FROM THE MOBILE REGISTER.

We can not people a country with blacks or whites, without a *people* to do it with, and the simple truth is, the South has not the black labor to spare for any such an enterprise.

"We can not hold our own in such a race until we increase the slave population, and that can only be done with effective rapidity by transferring them from the great hive of barbarian slavery in Africa to the scene of humanized and Christianized slavery in America. If the South desires to maintain the conflict, so far against her in its results, for an equality of rights in the territories, and for the preservation of an equilibrium of political power in the Union, we know of no other way to do it but to go to work at once in an effort to repeal the laws of the Union which prohibit the African slave trade. This is a powerful, active, and vital issue; and pushed to the wall by her fanatical enemies, we see no course open to the South but to strip it of all meretricious surroundings of prejudice and cant, and to discuss and meet it boldly on its merits."

For heaven's sake, do not propose anything so startling, is the first reply; for the discussion which it must provoke will be ruinous to us.

And to this time, therefore, the advocates of the slave trade are chiefly engaged in arguing, not the feasibility of their scheme, but the safety of arguing its feasibility. Mr. De Bow, for one, believes "it is an idle assumption that the discussion will divide and distract the South. The division, at most," he contends, "will prove to be of no more importance than such as already exists in regard to cardinal matters of State and federal policy; (in saying which he can only refer to the naturalization question, which has been the base of the only party divisions of the South in the last six years;) "and which," continues Mr. De Bow, "is at any moment ready to be sacrificed when the common interest is menaced. We must trust our fellow-citizens thus far, and they in return will suspect us [who?] neither of distrust or of treason."*

It is clear that the majority are, at the opening, against the African party, that is to say, are against discussion, but it is equally clear that the African party can not be silenced, and that a practical agreement will be arrived at, is in many parts already arrived at, as follows:

The question shall be argued, and the South given over to discussion, upon these conditions : That it shall always be taken for granted on both sides—First, that free society is full of morbid and dangerous elements, not respectable, irreligious, and altogether offensive to a true Southerner. Second, that slavery, under our present laws, is a Bible institution, and the most effective agent of freedom, Christianity, Democracy, civilization, and

* Letter to Hon. Wm. L. Yancey.

wealth. Third, that any man who proposes measures which involve an amelioration of the condition of the slaves, or which look in the slightest toward the possibility of any portion of them or of their descendants being allowed to take care of themselves, shall be called an abolitionist, and as such shall be publicly entertained. Fourth, that the man who shows the greatest regard for slavery is the truest Democrat and truest Christian, and shall be held to deserve best of his country.

Wherever the main question is yet at all discussed, these conditions are rigidly adhered to. South of Washington, not a single newspaper article, not a single pamphlet, not a single sermon or address has been published, since the scheme was suggested, in which these conditions have been in the slightest degree infringed.

The opponents of importation may manage to postpone a general engagement upon the final issue, but it is impossible that it shall be more than postponed, and when they can no longer avoid it, they will have to fight on ground upon which the African party will be irresistible.

For who can object to this scheme, and on what grounds can he object to it, that will not, as soon as the battle is at all hot, stamp him an enemy to the South, a traitor, an infidel? Immorality? It would not be well for a man to suggest that line of argument. "Either slavery is right or it is wrong, and it is a greater and more unmitigated wrong in him who keeps the negro to that sad condition than in him who originally fastened the yoke upon him." Thus replies in advance the Charleston Standard, and who dare rejoin with the Charleston mob, to maintain the fundamental conditions of the discussion, before him?

The only resistance to be feared at the South is from those ignorant citizens whose ruling passion is hatred not of slavery, but of negroes, and who with some difficulty are now restrained from demanding measures which will deport them all from their own vicinity. Nevertheless, they can be managed. Assure them that an importation of the original savage stock is a measure directed against those who would like to give the negroes who have come of families two hundred years under American training a chance to better themselves when they can, without fighting or breaking laws, and they will yield their prejudices.

Is evidence needed of how the plan carries, by its mere statement, conviction to those who give it a hearing, it is found in confessions like the following,* the writer of which opens his letter with expressions of doubt. The measure is a little too startling—impracticable—he fears; but he presently adds:

"I can go thus far with you, however. I have some two thousand acres of land that will now sell for about six dollars an acre, and which, when twenty or even ten thousand slaves are brought into the country from Africa, or any other quarter, will sell for thirty dollars an acre. I think I could find it in my breast to pocket the difference of forty-eight thousand dollars, and trust to casuists to determine whether I came honestly by it. I am not sure but I could go a little further. I have an interest in a gold mine, whose work requires no very great intelligence, and which yields from two to four dollars a day to the hand. I am now purchasing negroes at from eight hundred to eleven hundred dollars each. If I could have an opportunity of purchasing some one or two thousand at about two hundred dollars each, I am not certain that I should insist upon their having been torn from their families either in this or the adjoining States, but could even find it in my heart to take them with a knowledge of the fact that they had come from Africa. We want labor, and only labor, to a most rapid and astonishing development of wealth, but our sources of supply are limited. What we get is limited. What we get is taken from some other employments in our own vicinity. The gain at one point is to be dimin-

* Published in the Charleston Standard.

ished by the loss at another, and there is no other way of it but that we must set to work and laboriously breed the labor by which the golden harvest of our country is to be ultimately gathered."

Another, writing to the same editor from the State Capitol of South Carolina, says:

"There are many gentlemen of character and standing in the State who daily tell me that they are not ashamed of slavery, [the man would be a hero, indeed, who dare speak otherwise in that locality, but what follows?] *or the means by which it was established.* They confess the want of labor to every interest in the country, and express the assurance that the only kind of labor we are capable of receiving, without a disturbance of existing relations, is in the form of slavery."

The domestic slave trade, slave auctions, the forcible separation of husbands and wives, of parents and children; the compulsion to adultery of members of Christian churches, without legal remedy; and a commerce (the internal slave trade) once characterized by John Randolph, of Roanoke, on the floor of Congress, as "the infernal traffic," has been maintained by convincing men who objected to it, on the score of morality and humanity, of its necessity for the "safety" of the South, that is (as assumed by those interested) of the political equality in power of the slaveholding minority with the non-slaveholding majority of the republic.* It can not be doubted that the African slave

---

* It is an infamous libel which we by our partisanship have fastened upon ourselves, that the North has an aggressive spirit towards the South. It has always been directly otherwise. Mr. Webster, in his plea for the compromise on the 7th of March, 1850, said these true words:

"The honorable member from South Carolina, (Mr. Calhoun,) observed there has been a majority all along in favor of the North. If that be true, sir, the North has acted either very liberally and kindly, or very weakly; for they never exercised that majority efficiently five times in the history of this government, when a division or trial of strength arose. Never. Whether they were out-generalled, or whether it was owing to other causes, I shall not stop to consider; but no man acquainted with the history of the

trade is, at this time, a much more obvious and immediately pressing necessity for that purpose than the domestic slave trade has ever been. And the moral objections to it are to be more easily overcome. As, therefore, a South Carolinian quoted elsewhere says,* "*If men are to make a fuss about it, they will have to begin with the internal slave trade.*"

After all, then, the difficulty is at the North; the North can never be convinced or brought to consent to the reopening of the foreign slave trade.

Why not?

Evidently there would be no difficulty, if the same conditions of discussion could be imposed at the North—even in parts of the North. There are spots where this might be hoped for. If a party at the North could be got to accept those conditions of discussion—could be got to take ground that slavery must be

Union can deny that the general lead in the politics of the country, for three fourths of the period that has elapsed since the adoption of the Constitution has been a southern lead."

The Charleston Courier, commenting on a discourse delivered in South Carolina, against the immediate secession of that great Power from our Union, to which the Courier itself is yet kindly opposed, says it "truthfully as well as strongly, details and depicts the various occasions on which southern interests have obtained the mastery in Congress, or, at least, important advantages, which are well worthy of the consideration of all who erroneously suppose that the action of the general government has been, on the whole, adverse to slavery. The truth is that our government, although hostile in its incipiency [that is, until after the administration of Jefferson] to domestic slavery, and starting into political being with a strong bent toward abolition, yet afterwards so changed its policy that its action for the most part, and with only a few exceptions, has fostered the slaveholding interest, and swelled it from six to fifteen states, and from a feeble and sparse population to one of ten millions.

* Sea-Board Slave States, p. 522.

considered a good thing for low people, or for niggers alone, and could be kept in ascendency in a few States, or a few parts of States, that would be sufficient; the South being united to control Congress and the navy, and remove the present difficulties.*

Not to directly and avowedly legalize the traffic; that would be too much to hope of this generation. The friends of the institution at the North could hardly be asked to advocate that. It would be too much for the South to demand that, except to make a less advanced position appear more tenable—except to prepare the way for a new "compromise." But the friends of slavery at the North can be brought to adopt measures in the interest of the South, which, if carried, will soon involve the African slave trade as a necessity—a necessity of that kind which knows no law, which cares for no law, which will evade or overcome all law and all legal force that seeks to prevent the profits which would soon attend the supply of labor to the insatiable demand of capitalists for the South.

"The course we propose to be pursued is this : Let each southern State say, through her legislature, that the importation—immigration if you prefer—of the African race to the South, is the means appointed of heaven for their civilization, and that as their coming will be mu-

---

* "We took occasion to notice, a few days since, the resolution reported by Mr. Slidell, from the Committee on Foreign Relations, proposing to give to England and France notice of the abrogation of the treaty stipulations by which we are bound to keep a naval force upon the African coast for the suppression of the slave trade. We stated then our approbation of this measure, from the conviction that it is onerous to our country, destructive to our seamen engaged in this service, and utterly inefficient for the purpose intended. We also approve of it for another reason, which we will state with perfect frankness to the people of this country. We have no sympathy in the purposes of this convention, and no wish for its success."—*Charleston Standard.*

tually beneficial both to us and to them, hereafter it shall be lawful for all ships having such *passengers* on board, freely to land them at any port or harbor in the State; that the sheriff of the district in which the port may be situated shall lodge such passengers at the expense of the State, until they can find employment, and shall moreover pay to the captain of the ship bringing them liberal passage money, to be charged against the State in the first instance, and provided for in any subsequent contract respecting their service and employment."—*Pee Dee Times.*

Governor Moore, of Alabama, being a candidate for reëlection, and addressed on the subject of the slave trade, says that " he is in favor of *modifying* the laws which make it piracy, and discriminating among the different grades of the offense, but thinks that neither this nor any other question should be allowed to divide the South in the crisis of the approaching presidential campaign."

This indicates the policy of the mischief-makers. Insist that it is a mistake to suppose that slavery is an evil, and wait for a chance to demand, with some show of force, as a matter of courtesy and of safety to the Union, the modification of the laws against the African slave trade. Then the Cuba game.

The Florida jury, which lately had a slaver captain in their hands, published a card in which they pledged themselves to labor unremittingly for a "repeal of all laws which directly or indirectly condemn" the institution of slavery, or "those who have inherited or maintained it." They denominated the prejudice which has existed against the business of importing Africans " a sickly sentiment of pretended philanthropy."

Undoubtedly the African slave trade is yet protested against by many. It would be unjust and unkind to say that the leading politicians of the South had adopted it, and were only restrained from openly advocating it from a fear that by so doing they would open ground upon which a conservative party could rally.

It is not unjust to say; it is certainly true that there is a necessity upon the South—a pressing necessity—a necessity of constantly increasing pressure, which, if not in some other way met, must inevitably lead to the renewed importation of Africans.

Says a Virginian, addressing Elihu Burritt:

"Europe needs it; every steamer brings us intelligence that efforts are to be made to produce more cotton. Tropical and semi-tropical products—some of them articles of prime necessity—are constantly increasing in price. Already sugar is so high that its consumption in Europe is becoming a luxury. Cotton is rising daily; and no sugar or cotton lands are brought into cultivation. Nor can they. There is a want of labor to cultivate these lands. Give us more of the only kind of labor that will enable us to keep up the supply of the raw material, and the free labor of Europe and the North can find employment, and consequently bread in its manufacture. Diminish the supply of cotton, or let it not increase to keep pace with the demand, and you throw thousands out of employment, and bring starvation upon all manufacturing communities."

"America needs it. The North needs it, as Western Europe does, for clothing, to furnish the raw material for manufacture. The South needs it to bring more land into cultivation."

This is the plain truth, and there is no avoiding it. The African slave trade may easily be made a more pressing necessity than it is at present by an enlargement of the field of slave occupation but it is already, to-day, a necessity more urgent than the Dred Scott decision was yesterday, than the repeal of the Missouri Compromise was the day before yesterday, than the Fugitive Slave Law was the day before that; a necessity more imperative and obvious than the internal slave trade ever has been; a necessity less sincerely resisted, and by far less logically, less convincingly, by the politicians of the South to-day, than the inter-State slave trade was by those of the last generation.*

For the politicians of the South it is a necessity which can no more be avoided than agitation can be avoided by those of the North. As, says Mr. Spratt, in concluding the article on the settlement of Kansas, from which I recently quoted : " The foreign slave trade is the certain road to power [with the three fifths rule] for the South, and the *only road to power* within the Union."†

Is dissolution or the slave trade, to be the next alternative presented us by the politicians of the South?

I see not how any man in his senses, comprehensively viewing the whole ground, can escape from the conclusion, that, if not the next, it is but a few steps beyond it.

Is there no ground on which a Union party can permanently stand at the South?

* "Both South Carolina and Georgia have at different times passed acts to prevent the internal slave trade. Governor Williams, of South Carolina, in his annual message to the Legislature of that State (1817) spoke of it as a 'remorseless and merciless traffic, a ceaseless dragging along the highways of a crowd of suffering beings to minister to insatiable avarice, condemned alike by enlightened humanity, wise policy, and the prayers of the just.' "— *Hildreth*, vol. vi., p. 614.

† "It may be said that the slave trade can never be re-established within this Union. This may be true, perhaps, and we would regret the alternative thus presented to us. We have, with the northern States, a common independence, a common government and a common history, and we would regret the necessity for a separation ; but if we have a separate existence to defend, we must have the means by which we are to defend it ; if we have war within this Union for the preservation of our institutions, we must have within this Union the right to use our own natural implements of warfare, or we must leave it. It is first necessary to see that we are right, to look at this great question of the slave trade, and see if, in fact, we require its reëstablishment, and if so, we will demand its reëstablishment within this Union, or we will reëstablish it to ourselves."—*Charleston Standard.*

There is.

"Slavery shall, by general consent, be hereafter confined within its present limits."

There is no other.

Is this ruin to the South?

Ruin to the present ruling politicians of the South, it per haps is.

WHAT MIGHT BE ANTICIPATED FROM A TERRITORIAL RESTRICTION OF SLAVERY.

The necessity of the South really demands only cheaper labor and cheaper means of exchanging the results of labor. To restrict the region within which slave labor may be employed, would, after the varying demands for labor of different parts within the region had been equalized, check the further emigration of slaves from any particular district. As the natural increase of negroes would then in a great measure remain where it was born, any given district would soon be better supplied than at present with laborers. (This tendency might be increased by legal restrictions on the transfer, or State exportation of slaves.) With a better provision of laborers, land would increase in production. With an increased production of each district, new facilities of transportation to the consumer would be required from that district. With a diminished cost of labor, these facilities could be more cheaply obtained; with a larger amount to carry, more effective means of carriage could be provided with profit. With the cost of exportation, the cost of importation would be lessened. Articles of use, comfort and luxury, including tools and machinery, and the results of study in improved methods of agriculture, and in all industry, would be made more accessible, cheaper and more common. This would act further, and constantly further and further, to lessen the cost of the labor necessary to obtain a given value of cotton or of any other production of the soil.

The present facility of acquiring land in the cotton States, the capital needed for its purchase not exceeding, for fresh soil, on an average, three dollars an acre, and the large outlay of capital needed to obtain labor, necessarily induces that mode of agriculture which has desolated so large a portion of the seaboard slave States. Twenty slave laborers cost over twenty thousand dollars.* They will cultivate four hundred acres of land, which costs less than a tenth of that sum. Knowing that he can buy as much more as he wants, at an equally low rate, why, when the production of his land decreases, should the slave owner drain. it, or manure it, or "rest" it, or vary his crops, to prevent further exhaustion? It will cost twenty dollars' worth of labor to manure an acre. Why make this expenditure when he can obtain other land at five dollars an acre, (fenced and ready for the plow,) which, without manure, will return just as much cotton for the same amount of labor (in cultivation merely) as this with it? Why, when on fresh soil he can get three hundred dollars' worth of cotton a year for each slave employed in cultivating it, should he apply that labor to some other crop on his old land which would return him not more than a hundred dollars for each slave

---

* The following paragraph, from a North Carolina newspaper, gives the latest quotations:

"We learn, through a friend, that on Monday last the following property was sold in Salisbury at the prices annexed: Leve, $1,600; George, $1,895; Charlotte and two children, $1,600; Henry, $1,476; Alick, $1,600; and Hiram, $2,130. The above prices show that negro property is not depreciating in value."

employed? Why, in these circumstances, should he arrange to remain half his life on the same spot? and if he is not expecting to remain, why should he expend his costly labor on houses and roads and bridges and fruit trees, or on schools and churches, or on railroads and wharves? Fifteen years hence his land will no longer be worth cultivating for cotton, and it will then afford no business to a railroad or a steamboat, and in the mean time the difference between wagoning and railing or boating his cotton to the merchant would do but little toward defraying the cost of a railroad or establishing a steamboat route.

"In 1825, Madison County, [Alabama,] cast 3,000 votes; now, [1855,] it can not cast exceeding 2,500. * * The freshness of its agricultural glory is gone; the vigor of its youth is extinct, and the spirit of desolation seems brooding over it." These are what the Hon. C. C. Clay, member of Congress from Alabama, describes as "memorials of the artless and exhausting culture of cotton" in the State he represents. But why thus artless and exhausting? He himself gives the answer: "Our small planters, after taking the cream off their lands, * * * are going further West and South, in search of other virgin lands, which they will despoil and impoverish in a similar manner." And when they have done this, they fully anticipate going still further and further, and again and again repeating the process. Can the men who do this and who have these anticipations be expected to build railroads, or bridges, or schools, or churches? Can they, wanting nothing but corn, coffee, hogs, niggers, and camp furniture, support mechanics or merchants? Can they form by themselves a prosperous or respectable community? Will the annexation of Sonora, of the whole of Mexico, Nicaraugua, Cuba, and the Amazon region enable them to do so?

Except the African slave trade is reëstablished, it will have—
and every southern gentleman knows it and will acknowledge
it—directly the contrary influence. The first thing necessary to
the prosperity of the South is, to make possible to its citizens
the comforts of civilized life. To this is first essential the civilized idea of home; and this will not be gained while the nomadic
and vagabond propensities of its petty patriarchs continue to be
stimulated by our government as they have been hitherto.

OBJECTIONS.

Practically, I have heard but one urged: that the danger of
insurrection would increase. This supposes that a portion of the
non-slaveholding population would remove to free territory, or
at least that the slave population would increase more rapidly
than the free.

I believe that the counteracting element would soon be
obvious, in the incoming of a "town population" of whites,
which would follow from the greater abundance of raw material—
the production of unskilled labor—and the better markets which
an increasing density even of a plantation population would
occasion. This could be insured, if thought necessary, by laws,
for a time, prohibiting slave labor to be employed for any other
purpose than the production of raw materials and in domestic
duties, thus obliging planters to give employment to free,
instead of using, as at present, slave mechanics.

No one apprehends that a plan of general insurrection will be
devised and successfully executed by negroes over a large extent
of country. The danger is that the slaves will rise and make a
temporarily successful stand in some of those districts in which
the proportion of white inhabitants is the smallest, (it being now

one man to a hundred slaves of both sexes, in some parts,) and that from such a success an insurrectionary contagion will be communicated to adjoining districts, in which the strength of the whites is otherwise sufficient to leave no room for apprehension.

There is now a law in several of the slave States, perhaps in all, which requires that there shall be at least one white man resident on every plantation. This law, while it recognizes the principle that each owner of slaves should be required to maintain any arrangement that is deemed necessary by the legislature for the safe control of his property, is very inadequate to its purpose, for precisely under the circumstances where danger is most to be apprehended, it posts the weakest guard. I have seen four adjoining plantations, the aggregate slave population of which was close upon one thousand, with but one overseer living on each, and these, together with one other, the only white men within several hours' ride; all the land in the vicinity being, in fact, engrossed in these great plantations. In a region of small plantations there are not only more whites on the plantations themselves, proportionately to the number of blacks, but almost always resident, some families of non-slaveholding whites.

Suppose that, instead of this inefficient law, it should be enacted that each owner of a plantation on which lived twenty-five slaves, should either himself reside, or should cause a white overseer to reside on each such plantation, and that for every twenty-five slaves, additional to the first twenty-five, he should cause another white man, as overseer or assistant overseer, to reside. Further: that each such owner or overseer, (one only for each plantation, however large,) should be held responsible to

the magistrates of the county for the prudent guardianship of
said slaves; that he should be required to report at stated intervals the number he had in charge, and any other particulars
necessary to give confidence that a sufficient guard was maintained. It would not be necessary that the assistants should be
employed as overseers. They might be mechanics; they
might be any poor whites already resident in the vicinity, who
could be depended upon to be always within reach if wanted by
the responsible overseer.

Such a law would not only be far more effective than the present one, for the present circumstances, it would be equally so
for a slave population of ten times the present average density ;
because even though the white population should not increase
proportionately, those classes of it which are now mainly relied
upon to prevent insurrection, would be stronger, and more effec-
tively stationed for the purpose.*

It is, however, the opinion of students on the subject whose
judgment is most respected at the South, that the slave
population, if densely settled, would be less dangerous and more
efficiently managed than as at present, even without any such
precaution as I have suggested, and this opinion seems reasonable. The following is from a Memoir on Negro Slavery,
written by Chancellor Harper, of South Carolina, edited by Mr.

---

* If to such a law there should be added a provision requiring that no one
should be deemed an overseer, within the meaning of the act, who had not
been certified by specified authorities to be a man of good character and
of adequate intelligence and information for the legal duties to be imposed
upon him, it would not only be a humane act toward the slaves, but would
practically embody a well-distributed and trustworthy police force, vastly
better for its purpose, and costing the community less than the present rural
patrols.

De Bow, of Louisiana, in which state it was published not ten years ago, while it is yet exposed for sale by booksellers in Mobile and Charleston, without causing their expulsion. Hence it may be inferred that the mob as yet really hold the same opinions:

"President Dew," (whose writings have also escaped being placed on the Index Expurgatorium,) "President Dew," says Chancellor Harper, endorsed as to safety by Commissioner De Bow, "has very fully shown how utterly vain are the fears of those who, though there may be no danger for the present, yet apprehend great danger for the future, when the number of slaves shall be greatly increased. He has shown that the larger and more condensed society becomes, the easier it will be to maintain subordination, supposing the relative numbers of the different classes to remain the same, or even if there should be a very disproportionate increase of the enslaved class."

＊　　＊　　＊　　＊　　＊　　＊　　＊　　＊

"When the demand for agricultural labor shall be fully supplied, then of course the labor of slaves will be directed to other employments and enterprises. Already it begins to be found that, in some instances, it may be used as profitably in works of public improvement. As it becomes cheaper, it will be applied to more various purposes, and combined in larger masses. It may be commanded and combined with more facility than any other sort of labor, and the laborer, kept in strict subordination, will be less dangerous to the security of society than in any other country which is crowded and overstocked with a class of what are called free laborers. Let it be remembered that all the great and enduring monuments of human art and industry—the wonders of Egypt, the everlasting works of Rome, were created by the labor of slaves."*

But the Egyptians and the Romans enjoyed the advantage of an unimpeded importation of slaves, when engaged in these works. It was a DENSE slave population only which made them possible; and if the South is to rival them it must reopen the African slave trade, or put a check upon the dispersion of its laborers, which is thus shown to be as much a measure of safety as of glory.

* Resources, Vol. ii., p. 233.

The alleged danger, on which is based the plea of the necessity of the South to extend slavery, I propose to yet further consider in the last chapter. I will now simply add that the advantages and the safety of a restriction of the territorial field of slave labor, and of other measures which, as I have suggested, might be employed for the same purposes, will be found much more fully and clearly set forth in any of the many able papers which have been published in South Carolina since the last presidential election in advocacy of the African slave trade.

CHAPTER IX.

CHARACTER AND MANNERS.

FORMULA FOR JUSTIFYING SLAVERY.

Since the growth of the cotton demand has doubled the value of slave labor, and with it the pecuniary inducement to prevent negroes from taking care of themselves, hypotheses and easy methods for justifying their continued slavery have been multiplied. I have not often conversed with a planter about the condition of the slaves, that he did not soon make it evident, that a number of these were on service in his own mind, naively falling back from one to another, if a few inquiries about matters of fact were addressed him without obvious argumentative purpose. The beneficence of slavery is commonly urged by an exposition not only of the diet, and the dwellings, and the jollity, and the devotional eloquence of the negroes, but also by demonstrations of the high mental attainments to which individuals are already found to be arriving. Thus there is always at hand some negro mathematician, who is not merely held to be far in advance of the native Africans, but who beats most white men in his quickness and accuracy in calculation, and who is at the same time considered to be so thoroughly trustworthy, that he is constantly employed by his master as an accountant and collecting agent; or some negro whose reputation for ingenuity and skill in the management and repair of engines, sugar-mills, cotton presses,

or other machinery, is so well established that his services are more
highly valued, throughout a considerable district, than any white
man's; or some negro who really manages his owner's plantation,
his agricultural judgment being deferred to, as superior to that
of any overseer or planter in the county.   Scarcely a plantation
did I visit on which some such representative black man was
not acknowledged and made a matter of boasting by the owner,
who, calling attention perhaps to the expression of intelligence
and mien of self-confidence which distinguished his premium
specimen, would cheerfully give me a history of the known special
circumstances, practically constituting a special mental feeding,
by which the phenomenon was to be explained.   Yet it might
happen that the same planter would presently ask, pointing to
the brute-like countenance of a moping field hand, what good
would freedom be to such a creature?   And this would be one
who had been provided from childhood with food, and shelter,
and clothing with as little consideration of his own therefor as
for the air he breathed; who had not been allowed to determine
for himself with whom he should associate; with what tools and
to what purpose he should labor; who had had no care on
account of his children; who had no need to provide for old
age; who had never had need to count five-and-twenty; the
highest demand upon whose faculties had been to discrimi-
nate between cotton and crop-grass, and to strike one with a
hoe without hitting the other; to whose intelligence, though
living in a civilized land, the pen and the press, the mail and the
the telegraph, had contributed nothing; who had no schooling
as a boy; no higher duty as a man than to pick a given quantity of cotton between dawn and dark; and of whom, under this
training and these confinements, it might well be wondered that

he was found able to understand and to speak the language of
human intelligence any more than a horse.

Again, one would assure me that he had witnessed in his own
time an obvious advance in the quality of the slaves generally;
they were more active, less stupid, employed a larger and more
exact vocabulary, and were less superstitious, obstinate, and perverse in their habits of mind than when he was himself a boy;
but I had only to presume that, with this rapid improvement,
the negroes would soon be safely allowed to take some step
toward freedom, to be assured with much more apparent confidence than before, that in the special quality which originally
made the negro a slave, there had been no gain; that indeed it
was constantly becoming more evident that he was naturally
too deficient in forecasting capacity to be able to learn how to
take civilized care of himself.

As a rule, when the beneficence of slavery is argued by southerners, an advancing intellectual as well as moral condition of
the mass of negroes is assumed, and the high attainments of
individuals are pointed to as evidence of what is to be expected
of the mass, if the system is not disturbed. Suggest that
any modification of the system would enlarge its beneficence,
however, and an exception to the general rule, as regards the
single quality of providence, is at once alleged, and in such a
manner, that one can not but get the impression that, in this
quality, the negro is believed to be retrograding as surely as he
is advancing in everything else; and this is one method by which
the unconditional perpetuation of the system, as it is, is justified.
Such a justification must of course involve the supposition that
in the tenth generation of an unremitted training, discipline,
education, and custom in abject dependence upon a voluntary

provision by others, for every wish of which the gratification is permitted, white men would be able, as a rule, to gain in the quality of providence and capacity for independent self-support.

As to the real state of the case, I find, in my own observation, no reason for doubting, what must be expected of those interested, that the general improvement of the slave is usually somewhat overrated, and his forecasting ability underrated. Measures intended to prevent a man from following his natural inclinations often have the effect of stimulating those inclinations; and I believe that the system which is designed not merely to relieve the negro from having any care for himself, but, as far as practicable, to forcibly prevent him from taking care of himself, in many particulars to which he has more or less instinctive inclination, instead of gradually suppressing this inclination, to some extent stimulates it, so that the southern negro of to-day, however depraved in his desires, and however badly instructed, is really a man of more cunning, shrewdness, reticence, and persistence in what he does undertake for himself than his father was. The healthful use of these qualities (which would constitute providence) is, however, in general, successfully opposed by slavery, and, as far as the slave is concerned, nothing worse than this can be said of the system.

Admitting that, in this view, slavery is not beneficent, or is no longer beneficent, or can be but for a time beneficent to the slave, the present attitude of the South still finds a mode of justification with many minds, in the broad assertion that the negro is not of the nature of mankind, therefore can not be a subject of inhumanity. This, of course, sweeps the field, if it does anything : thus, (from the Day-Book,)

"The wide-spread delusion that southern institutions are an evil, and their extension dangerous—the notion so prevalent at the North that there is a real antagonism, or that the system of the South is hostile to northern interests; the weakened union sentiment, and the utter debauchment, the absolute traitorism of a portion of the northern people, not only to the Union, but to Democratic institutions, and to the cause of civilization on this continent; all these, with the minor and most innumerable mischiefs that this mighty world-wide imposture has engendered or drags in its midst, rest upon the dogma, the single assumption, the sole elementary foundation falsehood, that a negro is a black man."

This bold ground is not as often taken at the South as by desperate bidders for southern confidence among ourselves. I have heard Christian men, however, when pushed for a justification of the sealing up of the printed Bible, of the legal disregard of marriage, of giving power to rascally traders to forcibly separate families, and so on, refer to it as a hypothesis not at all to be scouted under such circumstances. Yet, as they did so, there stood behind their chairs, slaves, in whose veins ran more Anglo-Saxon blood than of any African race's blood, and among their other slaves, it is probable there were many descendants of Nubians, Moors, Egyptians, and Indians, all interbred with white and true negro tribes, so that it would be doubtful if there remained one single absolutely pure negro, to which animal alone their argument would strictly apply. If the right or expediency of denying the means of preparing themselves for freedom to these beings could even be held to be coexistent with the evident preponderance in them of certain qualities of form, color, etc., the number of those who are held unjustly or inexpediently in the bonds of a perpetual slavery is already quite large in the South, and is gradually but surely increasing—is increasing much more rapidly than are their means of cultivating habits which are necessary to be cultivated, before the manliest child of white men is capable of enjoying freedom.

There are but two methods of vindicating the habit of depending on the labor of slaves for the development of wealth in the land, which appear to me, on the face of them, entitled to be treated gravely. One of these, assuming the beings held in slavery to be as yet, generally incompetent to take care of themselves in a civilized manner, and dangerous to the life as well as to the wealth of the civilized people who hold them in slavery, argues that it is necessary for their humane maintenance, and to prevent them from acquiring an increase of the disposition and strength of mind and will which has always been felt a source of danger to the well-being of their masters, that all the present laws for their mental repression should be rigidly maintained. It is not to be denied, I think, that there is some ground for this assumption. Inasmuch as it is also argued that the same necessity requires that these beings, and with them all these laws, should be carried on to territory now free from them, we are called upon to give a sober consideration to the argument which is based upon it. This I shall do in the last chapter. The other method to which I refer assumes that by having a well-defined class set apart for drudging and servile labor, the remainder of a community may be preserved free from the demeaning habits and traits of character which, it is alleged, servile and menial obligations and the necessity of a constant devotion to labor are sure to fix upon those who are subject to them. Hence a peculiar advantage in morals and in manners is believed to belong to the superior class of a community so divided. I am inclined to think that there is no method of justifying slavery, which is more warmly cherished by those interested to maintain it, than this. I am sure that there is none which planters are more ready to suggest to their guests.*

No sensible man among us shuts his eyes to the ignorance, meanness, vice, and misery which accompanies our general prosperity; no class of statesmen, no politicians or demagogues, no writers deny or ignore it. It is canvassed, published, studied, struggled with, by all honest men, and this not in our closets alone, but in our churches, our legislatures, our colleges, our newspapers, our families. We are constantly urging, constantly using means for discovering it and setting it forth plainly. We commission able men to make a business of bringing it to the light, and we publish the statistics which their labors supply as legislative documents to be circulated at the general expense, in order that our misfortune may be as well known and as exactly comprehended as possible.

* From an "*Address on Climatology*," before the Academy of Science, by Dr. Barton, of New Orleans:—

"The institution of slavery operates by contrast and comparison; it elevates the tone of the superior, adds to its refinement, allows more time to cultivate the mind, exalts the standard in morals, manners, and intellectual endowments, operates as a safety-valve for the evil disposed, leaving the upper race purer, while it really preserves from degradation, in the scale of civilization, the inferior, which we see is their uniform destiny when left to themselves. The slaves constitute essentially the lowest class, and society is immeasurably benefited by having this class, which constitutes the offensive fungus—the great cancer of civilized life—a vast burthen and expense to every community, under surveillance and control; and not only so, but under direction as an efficient agent to promote the general welfare and increase the wealth of the community. The history of the world furnishes no institution under similar management, where so much good actually results to the governors and the governed as this in the southern States of North America."

"It is by the existence of slavery, exempting so large a portion of our citizens from labor, that we have leisure for intellectual pursuits."—*Governor Hammond, in South. Literary Mess.*

From much of all this, which so painfully and anxiously con-
cerns us, we are told that the South is free.   We are told that
what we bewail is seen at the South to be the result of a mistaken social system; that the South escapes that result by
slavery.   We do not deny, we daily acknowledge that there are
mistakes in our system; we endeavor to remedy them; and we
not unfrequently have to acknowledge that in doing so, we have
made some of our bad things worse.   Does slavery relieve all?
And without compensation?   We often find, upon a thorough
review, that our expedients, while they have for a time seemed
to produce very valuable results, have in fact corrected one evil
by creating or enhancing another.   We have borrowed from
Peter to pay Paul.   In this way we find investigation and discussion to be constantly essential to prevent errors and mistakes
from being exaggerated and persevered in unnecessarily.   Thus
we—our honestly humane part at least—are ever calling for
facts, ever publishing, proclaiming, discussing the facts of our
evil.   It is only those whose selfish interest is thought by themselves to be served by negligence, who resist investigation and
publication, who avoid discussion.   Thus we come to habitually
associate much activity of discussion, much consideration, much
publication with improvement—often no doubt erroneously—
still it is natural and rational that when we find no discussion of
facts, no publication, no consideration, where we find general
consideration and general discussion practically prevented by a
forcible resistance to publication, we can not but suspect there is
something sadly needing to be made better.   And this last we do
find to be the case at the South, and with regard to slavery.
Why, if their system has such tangible evidence of its advantages within the personal knowledge of any citizen, do they

object to its alleged disadvantages being set forth for consideration, and, if it should happen, discussion? True, we may be
wrong, we may be mistaken in supposing that this, our constant
publication and challenge to discussion is a good thing.
Perhaps if we were better, we should talk less, know less of
what evil remained to be gradually grown out of. It might be
found that the constant consideration of our evil had had a bad
effect upon us. But I have not found that the people of the
South are inclined to shut their eyes, and close their ears, and
bar their imaginations to the same evil. With the misery which
prevails among us, southerners generally appear to be, indeed,
more familiar than the most industrious of our home philan-
thropists. Great as it is, it is really overestimated at the South—
overestimated in the aggregate at least—for it is perhaps impossible to overestimate the sufferings of individuals. South of Virginia, an intelligent man or woman is rarely met who does not
maintain, with the utmost apparent confidence, that the people
who do the work of the North are, on the whole, harder driven,
worse fed, and more destitute of comfort than are the slaves at
the South, taking an average of both classes; and this I heard
assumed by gentlemen, the yearly cost of maintaining whose own
slaves, according to their statement to me, would not equal the
average monthly expenses of an equal number of the poorest
class of laborers I have ever known at the North. I have heard
it assumed by planters, who not only did not themselves enjoy,
but who never imagined or aspired to a tithe of the comfort to
which most journeymen mechanics whom I have known are
habituated. I have heard it assumed by gentlemen, nine-
tenths of whose neighbors for a hundred miles around them
lived in a manner which, if witnessed at the North, would

lave made them objects of compassion to the majority of our day-laborers.

A gentleman coming up the Mississippi, just after a recent "Southern Commercial Convention" at Memphis, says:

"For three days I have been sitting at a table three times a day opposite four of the fire-eaters. * * * It was evident that they were sincere; for they declared to one another the belief that Providence was directing the South to recommence the importation of Africans, that she might lead the world to civilization and Christianity through its dependence upon her soil for cotton. All their conversation was consistent with this. They believed the South the center of Christianity and the hope of the world, while they had not the slightest doubt that the large majority of the people of the North were much more to be pitied than their own negroes. Exclusive of merchants, manufacturers, lawyers, and politicians, they evidently imagined the whole population of the North to be quite similar to the poor white population of the South. Yet they had traveled in the North, it appeared. I could only conclude that their observation of northern working men had been confined to the Irish operatives of some half-finished western railroad, living in temporary shanties along the route."

I have even found that conservative men, who frankly acknowledged the many bad effects of slavery, and confessed the conviction that the northern slave States were ruined by it; men who expressed admiration of Cassius Clay's course, and acknowledged no little sympathy with his views, and who spoke with more contempt of their own fanatics than of the Abolitionists themselves; that such men were inclined to apologize for slavery, and for their own course in acting politically for its extension and perpetuation, by assuming certain social advantages to exist where it prevailed. "There is a higher tone in southern society than at the North," they would say, "which is, no doubt, due to the greater leisure which slavery secures to us. There is less anxiety for wealth, consequently more honesty. This also leads to the habit of more generous living and of hospitality, which is so characteristic of the South."

I think that there is a type of character resulting in a secondary way from slavery, of which Mr. Clay is himself a noble example, which attracts admiration and affection in a rare manner. I shall explain this secondary action of slavery by and by. I have come to the conclusion that whatever may be the good results of slavery in the way I shall then describe, this so constantly asserted, so generally conceded, of inducing a "higher tone" of breeding, and especially of nourishing the virtue of hospitality, is chimerical.

Some reader may at once be inclined to say that the southerners whom he has met are unquestionably better bred people than are common at the North, and that they state as their experience that they do not find that hospitality, that honesty, that guilelessness of dealing one with another among the people of the North, to which they are accustomed at home. It would remain a question, whether the southerners whom the reader has ᴍᴇᴛ are of a common or an exceptional class; whether it is to slavery, or to some other circumstance, they owe their breeding; whether this other circumstance is dependent on slavery, or whether it may exist (and, if so, whether, when it does exist, it produces the same fruit), quite independently of slavery. It can not be said that there are no gentlemen and gentlewomen of first water in free countries. A comparison, then, must be a comparison of numbers. I shall, by and by, offer the reader some assistance in making a comparison of this kind. And if, as we hear, free-labor society is still an experiment, and one of the results of that experiment is to be found in the low condition of portions of our community, and   by comparing this result with the condition of the whites of the South that we must judge of the success of the experiment; it may again be a question of numbers. As to experience of hospitality, that is not a question of quantity or of quality merely. I should wish to ask the reader's southern authorities, " where and with whom has your experience been, North and South ?" And if with a similar class and in similar circumstances, I should wish to ask further, " what do you mean by hospitality ?"

In the previous chapter, I have shown that slavery does not prevent a condition of destitution of what at the North are deemed the ordinary comforts of civilized life, with a large part of the race supposed to be benefited especially by slavery; whether it secures to it the supposed advantage in morals and manners remains to be considered.

I think that the error which prevails in the South, with regard to the general condition of our working people, is much strengthened by the fact that a different standard of comfort is used by most persons at the South from that known at the North, and that used by northern writers. People at the South are content and happy with a condition which few accept at the North unless with great complaint, or with expressions of resignation such as are the peculiar property of slaves at the South. If, reader, you had been traveling all day through a country of the highest agricultural capability, settled more than twenty years ago, and toward nightfall should be advised by a considerate stranger to ride five miles further, in order to reach the residence of Mr. Brown, because Mr. Brown, being a well-to-do man, and a right good fellow, had built an uncommonly good house, and got it well furnished, had a score of servants, and being at a distance from neighbors, was always glad to enter-

tain a respectable stranger—after hearing this, as you continued
your ride somewhat impatiently in the evening chill, what con-
solations would your imagination find in the prospect before you?
My New England and New York experience would not forbid
the hope of a private room, where I could, in the first place,
wash off the dust of the road, and make some change of clothing
before being admitted to a family apartment. This family room
would be curtained and carpeted, and glowing softly with the
light of sperm candles or a shaded lamp. When I entered it, I
could expect that a couch or an arm-chair, and a fragrant cup
of tea, with refined sugar, and wholesome bread of wheaten flour,
leavened, would be offered me. I should think it likely that I
should then have the snatch of Tannhauser or Trovatore, which
had been running faintly in my head all day, fingered clearly
out to my entire satisfaction upon a piano-forte. I should then
look with perfect confidence to being able to refer to Shakespeare,
or Longfellow, or Dickens, if anything I had seen or thought
during the day had haply led me to wish to do so. I should
expect, as a matter of course, a clean, sweet bed, where I could
sleep alone and undisturbed, until possibly in the morning a jug
of hot water should be placed at my door, to aid the removal of
a traveler's rigid beard. I should expect to draw a curtain from
before a window, to lift the sash without effort, to look into a garden, and fill my lungs with fragrant air; and I should be certain
when I came down of a royal breakfast. A man of these circumstances in this rich country, he will be asking my opinion of
his fruits. A man of his disposition can not exist in the country
without ladies, and ladies can not exist in the country without
flowers; and might I not hope for the refinement which decks
even the table with them? and that   breakfast would be a

meal as well as a feed—an institution of mental and moral sustenance as well as of palatable nourishment to the body? My horse I need harldly look after if he be a sound brute;—good stables, litter, oats, hay, and water, grooming, and discretion in their use, will never be wanting in such a man's house in the country.

In what civilized region, after such advice, would such thoughts be preposterous, unless in the slave States? Not but that such men and such houses, such families and home comforts may be found in the South. I have found them—a dozen of them, delightful homes. But then in a hundred cases where I received such advice, and heard houses and men so described, I did not find one of the things imagined above, nor anything ranging with them. Between the Mississippi and the upper James River, I saw not only none of those things, received none of those attentions, but I saw and met nothing of the kind. Nine times out of ten at least, after such a promise, I slept in a room with others, in a bed which stank, supplied with but one sheet, if with any; I washed with utensils common to the whole household; I found no garden, no flowers, no fruit, no tea, no cream, no sugar, no bread; (for corn pone, let me assert, in parenthesis, though possibly, as tastes differ, a very good thing of its kind for ostriches, is not bread: neither does even flour, salt, fat, and water, stirred together and warmed, constitute bread;) no curtains, no lifting windows (three times out of four absolutely no windows), no couch—if one reclined in the family room it was on the bare floor—for there were no carpets or mats. For all that the house swarmed with vermin. There was no hay, no straw, no oats (but mouldy corn and leaves of maize), no discretion, no care, no honesty at the —— there was no   ble, but a log-pen; and besides this, no other out-house but a smoke-house, a corn-house, and a range of nigger-houses.

I do not exaggerate; I can not but err, if at all, from a wish to avoid all possibility of exaggeration. I say nothing more, I am sure, than is unquestionably and undeniably true, and exactly true, on this subject. I have avoided generalizations, which would cover more ground than I can speak of with confidence from personal experience. As to causes, we may differ; as to facts, we can not; for if the reader should be incredulous, I will presently give him the means of satisfying himself, that after the experience and observation of others, who can not be supposed prejudiced unfavorably to the condition and character of the people of the slave country, there is nothing improbable in what I say, namely : that in nine tenths of the houses south of Virginia, in which I was obliged, making all reasonable endeavor to find the best, to spend the night, there were none of these things. And most of these houses had been recommended to me by disinterested persons on the road as being better than ordinary—houses where they "sot up for travelers and had things." From the banks of the Mississippi to the banks of James, I did not (that I remember) see, except perhaps in one or two towns, a thermometer, nor a book of Shakespeare, nor a piano-forte or sheet of music; nor the light of a carcel or other good center-table or reading-lamp, nor an engraving, or a copy of any kind, of a work of art of the slightest merit.

Most of these houses were, I should also say, the mansions of "planters," "slave owners," "cotton lords" of the "southern aristocracy." But I need not ring the changes. If the word "planter" comes with the same associations to the reader which it would have formerly brought to my ind, I need say no more of the different ideas which may be attached to the same words in the same great country. For when has the word "planter," in popular usage, been allowed to stand without the company of certain other words which hardly prepare most of us at the North for simple bacon and greens, pone and "coffee;" which naked log-walls, swarming with bugs; which naked "puncheon" floors; which feather beds, with but one sheet, in July, and windows without glass, in January, hardly satisfy with men and women who have got above rag-picking or charcoal-burning for their means of living at the North. It is my experience that the majority of "planters," however broad, generous, lavish, bountiful and luxurious may be their open-handed hospitality of character, know of nothing better to which they can lift open their creaking doors in welcome to the stranger guest.

Yet it is the popular opinion of the South, that the people who do the work of the North have less experience of comfort, not to say luxury, than these planters' "niggers."

Now, if the reader finds my statements of the planters' real poverty incredible, or if he imagines my experience a strangely unfortunate and exceptional one, I must beg him to review in connection the quotations given in full from southern authorities, and chiefly from the most determined defenders of slavery and advocates of its extension, southern born and southern bred, at pp. 166, 167, 172, 173, 274, 280, 289, 295, 506, 510, 511, 514, 518, 520, 533, 538, 544, 576, 707, 708, 709, 710, "Seaboard Slave States." Compared with these he will find that my statements have been made cautiously and with intentional moderation, that my happenings were fortunate, my experience favorable. Let him also consult Sir Charles Lyell, or the journal of any traveler who has ventured beyond hotels without letters to "first family" planters.

I will here call upon just one more witness, whose evidence I cite at this point not merely because, in very few words, having reference to the very heart of the planter's prosperity, it practically endorses all I have said, but for another reason which will presently appear.

"If one unacquainted with the condition of the Southwest were told that the cotton-growing district alone had sold the crop for fifty millions dollars for the last twenty years, he would naturally conclude that this must be the richest community in the world. * * * But what would be his surprise when told that so far from living in palaces, many of these planters dwell in habitations of the most primitive construction, and these so inartificially built as to be incapable of defending the inmates from the winds and rains of heaven. That instead of any artistical improvement, this rude dwelling was surrounded by cotton fields, or probably by fields exhausted, washed into gullies, and abandoned; that instead of canals, the navigable streams remain unimproved, to the great detriment of transportation; that the common roads of the country were scarcely passable; that the edifices erected for the purposes of learning and religion were frequently built of logs and covered [roofed] with boards."—J. O. B. De Bow, *Resources of the South*, vol. ii. p. 113.

Do a majority of northern working men dwell in habitations having no more elements of comfort, even taking difference of climate into consideration, than Mr. De Bow ascribes to the residences of the slaves' owners? No northern man can for a moment hold such an opinion. What, then, becomes of the theory by which the planters justify slavery to themselves and recommend it to us? If the ennobling luxuries which the institution of sla-very secures to the "superior class," and by which it is supposed to be "qualified for the higher duties of citizenship," are, at the most, sugar, instead of molasses, in its coffee; butter, with its pone; cabbage, with its bacon, and two sheets to its bed—and the traveler who goes where I traveled, month after month, with the same experience, can not help learning to regard these as luxuries indeed, —if "freedom from sordid and petty cares," and "leisure for intel-

lectual pursuits," means a condition approaching in comfort that
of the keeper of a light-ship on an outer-bar, what is the exact
value of such words as "hospitality," "generosity," and "gallantry." What is to be understood from phrases in such common
use as "high toned," "well bred," "generous," "hospitable," and
so on, when used in argument to prove the beneficence of slavery
and to advocate its extension?

OF SOUTHERN HOSPITALITY.

"Mr. Frederick Law Olmsted, after signalizing himself by two very
wordy volumes, abounding in bitterness and prejudice of every sort,
and misrepresentations upon the 'Seaboard Slave States,' finding how
profitable such literature is in a pecuniary point of view, and what a
run is being made upon it throughout the entire limits of abolitiondom,
vouchsafes us now another volume, entitled a 'Journey through Texas,
or a Saddle-trip on the Southwestern Frontier.' Here, again, the opportunity is too tempting to be resisted to revile and abuse the men
and the society whose open hospitality he undoubtedly enjoyed, and
whom we have no doubt, like every other of his tribe traveling at the
South, he found it convenient at the time to flatter and approve. We
have now grown accustomed to this, and it is not at all surprising that
here and there it is producing its effect in some violent exhibition of
feeling like that displayed by our worthy old friend Dr. Brewer, of
Montgomery county, Maryland, who persistently refuses, on all occasions, to allow a Yankee even to cross his fields, or like that of John
Randolph, who said in the House, 'Mr. Speaker, I would not allow
one of my servants to buy as much as a toot-horn from one of these
people.' * * *
"Somewhat further on the parties rest for the night. 'For this the
charge was $1.25 to each person, including breakfast and horse-feed.'
At the end of every page or two our tourist repeats these growlings
over the enormous exactions. It is the refrain from one corner of the
book to the other. What a series of martyrdoms. Could such a journey by any possibility be made 'to pay?' Perhaps, friend traveler,
you had heard of the lavish hospitality of the South, and imagined that
people there moved out upon the high road for the sole purpose of
sharing the society which gentlemen, like yourself, could furnish, believing every arrival to be an act of special providence! When you
offered to pay the woman on Red River, and 'feared she was offended
by your offering her money for her hospitality,' you paid the highest
compliment to the South, for heaven knows you would have had no
such apprehension on the banks of the Connecticut."

I can not but be gratified that so much importance should have been attached to the preceding volume of this work as to induce the Superintendent of the Census to devote to its consideration a leading article in the first economico-political review of the country, and I can feel nothing but regret that he should be obliged to attribute to an unworthy motive even those of my labors the result of which he does me the honor to designate as valuable and trustworthy. I have often had occasion to refer to Mr. De Bow, and I believe have always done so in a manner consistent with the respect which I feel for the class of men among whom he has had the honorable ambition to rank himself. That a man while occupying a position which properly belongs to the most able and just-minded statistician in the country, should think it proper to write under his own name in the manner of which the above extracts are a sample, about a work which assumes to relate calmly and methodically, the result of a personal study of the condition of the people of a certain State, is a note-worthy circumstance in illustration of the present political history of our country. I cite them now, however, chiefly to show what need there is for a discussion upon which I propose to enter myself, little further than is necessary to enable me to clearly set forth certain facts, in their more important significance, the right of publishing which can hardly be denied me, in view of the insinuations made by Mr. De Bow, who in this follows what has got to be a general custom of southern reviewers and journalists toward travelers with whose expressed judgments upon any matter observed within the slave States they differ. There are numerous homes in the South the memory of which I cherish tenderly. There are numbers of men in the South for whom I have a warm admiration, to whom I feel grateful, whose respect

I wish not to lose. There are others for whom I have a quite different feeling. Of a single individual of neither class have I spoken in these three volumes, I believe, by his true name, or in such a manner that he could be recognized, or his home pointed out by any one who had not been previously familiar with it and with him, being, as a rule, careful to so far differ from the actual order of the events of my journey in narrating them, that facts of private life could not be readily localized. From this rule I do not intend now to depart further than is necessary to exhibit the whole truth of the facts to which I have referred, but since the charge of ingratitude and indelicacy is publicly made against me, as it has frequently been of late against better men, on similar grounds, I propose to examine those grounds in the light of certain actual experiences of myself and others, and let it be judged whether there must always exist a peculiar moral obligation upon travelers to be mealy-mouthed as to the habits of the people of the South, either on account of hospitality or in reciprocation of the delicate reserve which, from the tenor of Mr. De Bow's remarks, it might be supposed was habitually exercised in the South with regard to the habits of their own people. These experiences shall be both special and general. What immediately follows is of the former class, but, in the end, it will be found to have a general significance.

IN OLD VIRGINIA.

On a hot morning in July a northern traveler left the town of Lynchburg, the chief market-town of Virginia tobacco, and rode eastwardly toward Farmville. Suddenly taken severely ill, and no house being in sight, he turned from the road into the shade of the wood, dismounted, reclined against a sturdy trunk, took an anodyne, which he fortunately had with him, and at length found relief in sleep. Late in the day he awoke, somewhat recovered, but with a sharp headache and much debilitated. He managed, however, to mount, and rode slowly on to find a shelter for the night. In half an hour the welcome sight of an old plantation mansion greeted his eyes. There was a large court, with shade trees and shrubbery between the road and the house, and in the corner of this court, facing the road, a small warehouse or barn, in and around which were a number of negroes moving casks of tobacco. A white man, evidently their owner, was superintending their labor, and to him the traveler applied for lodging for the night.

" We don't take in strangers."

The traveler informed the planter of his illness and inability to ride further.

" You'll have to try to ride as far as the next house, sir ; we don't take in travelers here," was the reply.

" Really I don't feel able. I should not like to put you to inconvenience, sir, but I am weak and faint. My horse, too, has eaten nothing since early in the morning."

" Sorry for you, but we have no accommodations for travelers here," was the only reply, and the planter stepped to the other side of a tobacco cask.

The traveler rode on. About half an hour afterward he came in sight of another house. It was at a distance from the road, and to reach it he was obliged to let down and put up again three different sets of fence-bars. The owner was not at home, and his wife said that they were not accustomed to take in strangers. " It was not far to the next house," she added, as the traveler hesitated.

He reached, at length, the next house, which proved to be the residence of another large tobacco planter, who sat smoking in its veranda, as the traveler rode near and made his petition.

" We don't take in travelers," was again his answer.

The sick man stated his special claims to kindness, and the planter good-naturedly inquired the particulars, asked how far he had ridden, where he got his horse and his dog, whither he was bound, and so on (did not ask where he was born or what were his politics). The traveler again stated that he was ill, unable to ride further, and begged permission to remain for the night under the planter's roof, and again the planter carelessly replied that they didn't take in travelers; anon, asked how crops were looking further west, and talked of guano, the war news, and the prospect for peaches. It became dusk while the traveler lingered, and the negroes came in with their hoes over their shoulders from the fields across the road, but the planter continued chatting and smoking, not even offering the traveler a cigar, till at length the latter said, " If you really can not keep me to-night I must go on, sir; I can not keep my horse much longer, I fear."

" It is not far to the next house."

" But I have already called at three houses to-night, sir."

" Well, you see, since the railroad was done, people here don't reckon to take in travelers as they once did. So few come along they don't find their account in being ready for them."

The traveler asked for a drink of water, which a negro brought in a calabash, bade good night to the planter, and rode on through the woods. Night presently set in; the road crossed a swamp and was difficult to follow, and for more than an hour he rode on—seeing no house—without stopping. Then crossing water, he deliberated whether he should not bivouac for the night where he was. He had with him a few biscuits and some dried figs. He had not eaten hitherto, hoping constantly to come to a habitation where it might happen he could get a cup of tea, of which he felt more particularly in need. He stopped, took some nourishment, the first he had tasted in fifteen hours, and taking also a little brandy, gained strength and courage to continue his journey. A bright light soon cheered him, and after a time he made his way to a large white house, in the rear of which was an old negro woman stirring the contents of a cauldron which stood over the fire, by which he had been guided. The old woman had the appearance of a house servant, and he requested her to ask her master if he would favor him with lodging for the night.

"Her master did not take in travelers," she said, "besides, he was gone to bed;" and she stirred on, hardly looking at the traveler till he put his hand in his pocket, and, holding forth silver, said,

"Now, aunty, mind what I tell you. Do you go in to your master and say to him, 'There is a gentleman outside who says he is sick, and that his horse is tired and has had nothing to eat to-day; that he is a stranger and has been benighted, don't know the roads, is not well enough to ride further, and wants to know if you won't be so kind as to let him stay here to-night.' "

"Yes, massa, I'll tell him; twon't do no good, though, and he'll be almighty cross."

She went in, returned after a few minutes, seized her paddle, and began stirring before she uttered the words,

"Says yer ken go on to de store, he reckon."

It was after ten o'clock when the traveler reached the next house. It stood close upon the road, and the voice of a woman answered a knock upon the door, and in reply to the demand, said it was not far to the store, and she reckoned they accommodated travelers there.

Finally, at the store, the traveler succeeded in getting admittance, was comfortably lodged and well entertained by an amiable family. Their kindness was of such a character that he felt in the position of an invited guest, unable to demand and unwilling to suggest any unvolunteered service. There was no indication that the house was an inn, yet the traveler's experience left him little room to hesitate to offer money, nor was there the slightest hesitation on the part of the storekeeper in naming the amount due for the entertainment he had, or in taking it.

If the reader will accept the traveler's judgment of himself, he will assume that there was nothing in his countenance, his dress, his language, or his bearing, by which he could readily be distinguished from a gentleman of southern birth and education, and that he was not imagined to be anything else, certainly not on his first inquiry, at any one of the plantations where he was thus refused shelter.

So far as this inhospitality (for this is, I think, what even the southern reader will be inclined to call it) needed explanation, it was supposed to be sufficiently given in the fact that the region had, by the recent construction of a railroad through it, approximated the condition of a well-settled and organized community, in which the movements of travelers are so systematized, that the business of providing for their wants, as a matter of pecuniary profit, can no longer be made a mere supplement of another business, but becomes a distinct occupation.

This, then, but a small part of the whole land being thus

affected by railroads, was an exception in the South.   True; but what is the rule to which this is the exception ?

Mr. De Bow says, that the traveler would have had no apprehension that the offer of money for chance entertainment for the night furnished him at a house on the banks of the Connecticut, would give offense; yet in the Connecticut valley, among people having no servants, and not a tithe of the nominal wealth of the Red River planter, or of one of these Virginia planters, such has been a frequent experience of the same traveler.   Nor has he ever, when calling benighted at a house, anywhere in the State of Connecticut, far from a public house, escaped being invited with cordial frankness to enjoy such accommodation as it afforded; and this, he is fully convinced, without any thought in the majority of cases of pecuniary remuneration.   In several instances a remuneration in money has been refused in a manner which conveyed a reproof of the offer of it as indelicate; and it thus happens that it was a common experience of that, of the possibility of which Mr. De Bow is unable to conceive, that led in no small degree to the hesitation upon which this very comment was made.

This simple faith in the meanness of the people of the North, and especially of New England, is no eccentricity of Mr. De Bow's.   It is in accordance with the general tone of literature and of conversation at the South, that penuriousness, disingenuousness, knavish cunning, cant, and hypocrisy, are assumed to be the prevailing traits by which they are distinguished from the people of the South—not the poor people of New England from the planters of the South, but the people generally from the people generally.   Not the tone of the political literature and of the lower class of the South, but of its wealthy class, very gen-

erally, really of its " better class."   Mr. De Bow is himself the
associate of gentlemen as well informed and as free from narrow
prejudices as any in the South.   No New England man, who has
traveled at the South, would be surprised, indeed, if, at a table
at which he were a guest, such an assumption as that of Mr.
De Bow should be apparent in all the conversation ; that the gist
of it should be supposed to be so well understood and generally conceded, that he could not be annoyed by its plainest
statement.

I need hardly say that this reference to Mr. De Bow is continued, not for the purpose of vindicating the North any more
than myself from a mistaken criticism.   I wish only to demonstrate how necessary it must soon be to find other means for
saving the Union than these common-place flatteries of southern
conceit and apologies for southern folly, to which we have not
only become so accustomed ourselves, as to hardly believe our
eyes when we are obliged to meet the facts (as was my own
case), but by which we have so successfully imposed upon our
friends, that a man like Mr. De Bow actually supposes that the
common planters of the teeming and sunny South, are, as a rule,
a more open-handed, liberal, and hospitable class than the hard-
working farmers of the bleak and sterile hills of New England;
so much so, that he feels warranted not merely in stating facts
within his personal knowledge, illustrating the character of the
latter and arguing the causes, but in incidentally referring to
their penuriousness as a matter of proverbial contempt.   Against
this mistake, which, I doubt not, is accomplishing constant mischief to our nation, I merely oppose the facts of actual experience.   I wish to do so with true respect for the good sense of
the South.

IN GENERAL.

Presenting myself and known only in the character of a chance traveler, most likely to be in search of health, entertainment and information, usually taken for and treated as a southerner, until I stated that I was not one, I journeyed nearly six months at one time (my second journey) through the South. During all this journey, I came not oftener than once a week, on an average, to public houses, and was thus generally forced to seek lodging and sustenance at private houses. Often it was refused me; not unfrequently rudely refused. But once did I meet with what northern readers could suppose Mr. De Bow to mean by the term (used in the same article), "free road-side hospitality." Not once with the slightest appearance of what Noah Webster defines hospitality, the "practice of receiving or entertaining strangers without reward,"

Only twice, in a journey of four thousand miles, made independently of public conveyances, did I receive a night's lodging or a repast from a native southerner, without having the exact price in money which I was expected to pay for it stated to me by those at whose hands I received it.

If what I have just narrated had been reported to me before I traveled in the manner I did in my second journey at the South, I should have had serious doubts of either the honesty or the sanity of the reporter. I know, therefore, to what I subject myself in now giving my own name to it. I could not but hesitate to do this, as one would be cautious in acknowledging that he believed himself to have seen the sea-serpent, or had discovered a new motive power. By drawing out the confidence of other travelers, who had chanced to move through the South in a manner at all similar, however, I have had the satisfaction of finding that I am not altogether solitary in my experience. Even this day I met one fresh from the Southwest, to whom, after due approach, I gave the article which is the text of these observations, asking to be told how he had found it in New England and in Mississippi. He replied ;

"During four winters, I have traveled for a business purpose two months each winter in Mississippi. I have generally spent the night at houses with whose inmates I had some previous acquaintance. Where I had business transactions, especially where debts were due me, which could not be paid, I sometimes neglected to offer payment for my night's lodging, but in no other case, and never in a single instance, so far as I can now recollect, where I had offered payment, has there been any hesitation in taking it. A planter might refrain from asking payment of a traveler, but it is universally expected. In New England, as far as my limited experience goes, it is not so. I have known New England farmers' wives take a small gratuity after lodging travelers, but always with apparent hesitation. I have known New England farmers refuse to do so. I have had some experience in Iowa ; money is there usually (not always) taken for lodging travelers. The principal difference between the custom at private houses there and in Alabama and Mississippi being, that in Iowa the farmer seems to carefully reckon the exact value of the produce you have consumed, and to charge for it at what has often seemed to me an absurdly low rate ; while in Mississippi, I have usually paid from four to six times as much as in Iowa, for similar accommodations. I consider the usual charges of planters to travelers extortionate, and the custom the reverse of hospitable. I knew of a Kentucky gentleman traveling from Eutaw to Greensboro [twenty miles] in his own conveyance. He was taken sick at the crossing of the Warrior River. It was nine o'clock at night. He averred to me that he called at every plantation on the road, and stated that he was a Kentuckian, and sick, but was refused lodging at each of them."

This the richest county of Alabama, and the road is lined with valuable plantations.

The following is an extract from a letter dated Columbus, Mississippi, November 24, 1856, published in the London *Daily News*. It is written by an Englishman traveling for commercial purposes, and tells what he has learned by experience of the custom of the country :

"It is customary in traveling through this country, where towns are few and taverns scarce and vile, to stop at the planters' houses along the road, and pay for your bed and board in the morning just as if you had staid at an inn. The custom is rather repugnant to our Old World notions of hospitality, but it appears to me an excellent one for both the host and his guest. The one feels less bored by demands upon his kindness, as soon as it ceases to be merely a kindness to comply with them, and the other has no fear about intruding or being troublesome when he knows he will have to pay for his entertainment. It is rarely, however, that the *entrée* can be obtained into the houses of wealthy planters in this way. They will not be bothered by your visits, and if you apply to them, have no hesitation in politely passing you on to such of their neighbors as have less money or more generosity."

The same writer afterwards relates the following experience :

"About nineteen miles from Canton, I sought lodging at nightfall at a snug house on the roadside, inhabited by an old gentleman and his two daughters, who possessed no slaves and grew no cotton, and whose two sons had been killed in the Mexican war, and who, with the loudest professions of hospitality, cautiously refrained from giving himself any personal trouble in support of them. He informed me that there was corn in the husk in an almost inaccessible loft, there was fodder in an un-get-at-able sort of a cage in the yard, water in a certain pond about half a mile off, and a currycomb in a certain hole in the wall. Having furnished me with this intelligence, he left me to draw my own conclusions as to what my conduct ought to be under the circumstances."

A naturalist, the author of a well known standard work, who has made several tours of observation in the slave States, lately confided to me that he believed that the popular report of southern hospitality must be a popular romance, for never, during all his travels in the South, had he chanced to be entertained for a single night, except by gentlemen to whom he was formally presented by letter, or who had previously been under obligations to him, without paying for it in money, and to an amount quite equal to the value received.' By the wealthier, a night's entertainment had been frequently refused him, under circumstances which, as must have been evident to them, rendered his further progress seriously inconvenient. Once, while in company with a foreign naturalist—a titled man—he had been dining at the inn of a small county-town, when a certain locally distinguished judge had seen fit to be eloquent at the dinner-table upon the advantages of slavery in maintaining a class of "high-toned gentlemen," referring especially to the proverbial hospitality of southern plantations, which he described as quite a bewilderment to strangers, and nothing like which was to be found in any country unblessed with slavery, or institutions equivalent to it. It so happened that the following night the travelers, on approaching a plantation mansion in quest of lodging, were surprised to find that they had fallen upon the residence of this same judge, who recognized them, and welcomed them and bade them be at home. Embarrassed by a recollection of his discourse of hospitality, it was with some difficulty that one of them, when they were taking leave next morning, brought himself to inquire what he might pay for the entertainment they had received.   He was at once relieved by the judge's prompt response, "Dollar and a quarter apiece, I reckon."

It is very true that the general custom of the South which leads a traveler to ask for a lodging at any private house he may chance to reach near nightfall, and to receive a favorable answer not merely as a favor but as a matter of business, is a convenient one, is one indeed almost necessary in a country so destitute of villages, and where, off certain thoroughfares of our merchants, there are so few travelers. It is a perfectly respectable and entirely sensible custom, but it is not, as it is commonly represented to be, a custom of hospitality, and it is not at all calculated to induce customs of hospitality with the mass of citizens. It is calculated to make inhospitality of habit and inhospitality of character the general rule ; hospitality of habit and of character the exception. Yet the common misapplication of the word to this custom is, so far as I can ascertain, the only foundation of the arrogant assumption of superiority of character in this respect of the southerners over ourselves—the only ground of the claim that slavery breeds a race of more generous and hospitable citizens than freedom.

OF SOUTHERN BREEDING.

The difficulty of giving any thing like an intelligent and exact estimate of the breeding of any people or of any class of people is almost insurmountable, owing to the vagueness of the terms which must be used, or rather to the quite different ideas which different readers will attach to these terms. The very word which I have employed to designate my present subject has itself such a varied signification that it needs to be defined at the outset. I mean to employ it in that sense wherein, according to Webster, it covers the ground of " nurture, instruction, and the formation of manners." It is something more than " manners and customs," then, and includes or may include qualities which, if not congenital, are equally an essential part of character with those qualities which are literally in-bred of a man. Such qualities are mainly the result of a class of circumstances, of the influence of which upon his character and manners a man, or a child growing to a man, is usually unconscious, and of which he can not be independent if he would.

The general difficulty is increased in dealing with the people of the slave States, because among themselves all terms defining social rank and social characteristics are applied in a manner which can be understood only after considerable experience; and also because the general terms of classification, always incomplete in their significance, fail entirely with a large class of southerners, whose manners have some characteristics which would elsewhere be thought "high bred," if they had not other which are elsewhere universally esteemed low and ruffianly.

I do not feel myself competent, therefore, to thoroughly analyze southern breeding; but I propose, while giving my impressions for what they may be considered worth, and claiming but little value for them, to demonstrate clearly the error of certain views on this subject, which have been popularly held at the South, and are still advanced with great confidence by many writers and orators.

There are undoubted advantages resulting from the effects of slavery upon the manners of some persons. The same results to manners, the same sort of breeding, I have thought that I perceived to have arisen in the free States, where a family has been educated with every advantage which wealth would be likely to secure, when judiciously used, in a frontier community. There is boldness, directness, largeness, confidence, with the effect of the habitual sense of superiority to most of the community; not superiority of wealth, and power from wealth merely, but of a mind well-stocked and refined by such advantages of education as only very unusual wealth can procure in a scattered and frontier community. When to this is added the effect of visits to the society of the wealthy of denser communities; when refined and polished manners are grafted on a

natural, easy abandon; when there is high culture without effem-
inacy either of body or mind, as not unfrequently happens, we
find a peculiarly respectable and agreeable sort of men and women.
They are the result of frontier training under the most favorable
circumstances. In the class furthest removed from this on the
frontier—people who have grown up without civilized social
restraints or encouragements, and always under what in a well-
conditioned community would be esteemed great privations—
happens, on the other hand, the most disagreeable specimen of
mankind that the world breeds; men of a sort almost peculiar to
America and Australia; border ruffians, of whom the "rowdies"
of our eastern towns are tame reflections. Cooper has well
described the first class in many instances. I know of no picture
of the latter which represents them as detestable as I have
found them.

The whole South is maintained in a frontier condition by the
system which is apologized for on the ground that it favors
good breeding. This system, at the same time, tends to concentrate wealth in a few hands. If there is wisdom and great care
in the education of a family thus favored, the result which we
see at the North, under the circumstances I have described, is
frequently reproduced. This is the whole story of the advantages
of slavery on manners. There are many more such fruits of
frontier life at the South than the North, because there is more
frontier life. There is also vastly more of the other sort, and
there is everything between, which degrees of wealth and degrees
of good fortune in education would be expected to occasion. The
bad breed of the frontier, at the South, however, is probably far
worse than that of the North, because any effort toward something
better which it may be inclined to make, is so effectually snubbed

in most cases by the tendencies described in a former chapter and
because the frontier condition of the South is everywhere permanent. The child born to-day on the northern frontier, in
most cases, before it is ten years old, will be living in a well
organized and tolerably well provided community; schools,
churches, libraries, lecture and concert halls, daily mails and
printing presses, shops and machines in variety, having arrived
within at least a day's journey of it; being always within an in-
fluencing distance of it. There are improvements, and communities loosely and gradually cohering in various parts of the
South, but so slowly, so feebly, so irregularly, that men's minds
and habits are knit firm quite independently of this class of
social influences.

There is one other grand ruling characteristic of the southerner, which I here state as a fact, without pretending to state it
clearly, and without undertaking to account for it, merely observing that it is far more decided than the difference of climate
merely would warrant. It is intensity of impulse—willfulness.
Every wish of the southerner is, for the moment at least, more
imperative than of the northerner, every belief more undoubted,
every hate more vengeful, every love more fiery. Hence, for
instance, the scandalous fiend-like street fights of the South.
If a young man feels offended with another, he does not incline
to a ring and a fair stand-up set-to, like a young Englishman;
he will not attempt to overcome his opponent by logic; he will
not be content to vituperate, or to cast ridicule upon him; he is
impelled straightway to kill him with the readiest deadly
weapon at hand, and with as little ceremony and pretense of
fair combat as the loose organization of the people against violence will allow. He seems crazy for blood. Intensity of per-

sonal pride—pride in anything a man has, or which connects itself with him, is more commonly evident; hence intense partisanship; hence rashness and overconfidence; hence visionary ambition; hence assurance and violence in debate; hence assurance in society : no matter how ignorant, how out of place, self-assurance seldom fails—partisan assurance, never. As self-appreciation is equally with deference a part of what we call good breeding, and as the expression of deference is much more easily reduced to a matter of manners and forms, in the commonplace intercourse of society, than self-appreciation, this characteristic quality of the southerner needs to be borne in mind in considering the port and manners he commonly has, and judging from them of the effects of slavery. What a man shows that he thinks of himself is certainly of considerable consequence in estimating his value to others. But it is not every thing, or most essential. What he wishes to be, labors to be, is, perhaps, of more consequence, and this is not to be as quickly and as certainly understood from his own presentation of himself.

This much I have written in explanation of what is usually assumed by southerners to be the common opinion of the superior breeding of the South. I will now consider what is the general fact.

In the North, at the Revolution, we scarcely had a distinct class corresponding to the lowest white class of Virginia, as described by Jefferson, our laborers being less ignorant and coarse in their habits, and associating much more familiarly with their betters. We have now a class more nearly corresponding to it, furnished by the European peasant immigration. It is, however, a transient class, somewhat seldom including two generations, and, on an average, I trust, not one. It is, therefore, practically not an additional class, but, overlooking the aged and diseased, a supplement to our lowest normal class.   Out of twenty Irish proletaires, of whose history for five years after their arrival and removal to the country I have been intimately cognizant, only two, both of whom were over fifty years of age, have lived out that period without beginning to acquire wealth and becoming superior in their ambition and habits to the lowest order, which I believe to include a majority of the whites in the plantation districts of the South.*   Our lowest class, therefore, has a higher standard than the lowest class of the slave States.   This, I understand, is made very evident where the two come together at the West, as in southern Illinois.   The very poorest and lowest New England women who go there, are frequently offended by the inconsiderate rudeness and coarseness of the women immigrating from the South, and shocked by their "shiftless," comfortless, vagrant habits, so much so that families have often removed, after having been once established, to escape being bored and annoyed by their southern-born neighbors.

Referring to the lowest class, North and South, as the fourth, I class as third, the lowest rank in society, North or South, in which regard is had by its members to the quality of their associates from other than moral motives, or the prejudices of locality, race, sectarianism, and politics.   In other words, that in which there is a distinct social selectiveness and pride.   I think that everywhere in the free States men of this class would almost universally feel their position damaged—be a little ashamed—if

* I fear that it must be confesed that this general rule has now a multitude of exceptions in our large towns, where, in New York, especially, we seem taking some pains to form a permanent lower class.   With the present great and apparently permanent falling off in the European emigration, it can hardly last, however.

obliged to confess that they did not take a newspaper, or were unable to read it with a clear understanding of the intelligence it was intended to communicate. Allusions to the main facts of American history, to any clause of the Bible, to the provisions of the Constitution, and the more important laws, State and national, would be understood in most cases by those whom I refer to as the third class in northern society. In few families of this class would you fail to find some volumes of the English poets, or some works of great novelists or renowned travelers. Nothing like this would you find in the third class at the South.

The ratio of the number of the citizens who can not read at all to the whole, appears, by the census returns, to be only three times larger at the South than at the North. I believe it to be much greater at the South than these returns indicate.* The comparative cultivation of the third class "North" and of the third class "South," however, can not be at all judged from these statistics, supposing them correct. Those who can read and who do not read, or whose reading is confined within extremely narrow limits, are a much larger number at the South than at the North, owing to the much poorer supply of books and newspapers which commerce can afford to put within the reach of the former. The census returns two million newspapers, for instance, printed annually in Virginia, one hundred and fifteen million in

---

* The ratio of white illiterate to white population, per cent., as returned,

is, { free States, 3.36
     { slave   "   8.27 of the native population, over twenty years old, it

is, { free States, 4.12
     { slave   "   17.23 (Census Compendium, pp. 152, 153.) The ability to

merely read and write may itself be of little value, but the fact of a child's having had the pains-taking necessary to so far instruct him is in some degree a means of measuring his other inherited wealth, and thus his breeding.

New York. There is a post office to every fourteen square miles in New York, one to forty-seven square miles in Virginia; over five hundred publishers and booksellers in New York, but forty in Virgina. Thirty thousand volumes in public libraries in Virginia, eight hundred thousand in New York. The area occupied by the population of Virginia being much the largest, it may be inferred that with the disposition and the ability to read any thing in particular, the Virginian of the third class will have to travel more than thirty times as far as the New Yorker to procure it. The same proposition will hold good in regard to most other means of cultivation, and the third class of the South generally has seemed to me to be as much more narrow-minded, rude, coarse, "dangerous," and miserable, than the third class of the free States, as the most sanguine friend of popular education could anticipate from these facts.

The great difference in character between the third class of the South and that of the North, as indicated by their respective manners, is found in the much less curiosity and ready intelligent interest in matters which have not an immediate personal bearing in that of the South. Apathetic carelessness rather than simple indifference, or reckless incivility as to your comfort, is what makes the low southerner a disagreeable companion. It is his impertinent shrewdness which makes you wish to keep the Yankee at a distance. The first seems without object, spiritless; the latter keen to better himself, if with nothing else, with information which he can draw from you, and by gaining your good opinion.

The next or second class would include, both North and South, those with whose habits and character I am most familiar, and of whom I can speak with the best right to confidence. It would

include in New England and New York the better educated farmers—these owning, I should say, half the agricultural land—the
permanently established manufacturers and merchants of moderate
capital; most of the shop-keepers and the better-educated master
mechanics and artisan foremen; most of the preachers, physicians, and lawyers (some ranking higher). It would correspond
most nearly to what in England would be called the lower-middle
class, but any higher grade being very ill-defined, existing distinctly but in few localities, and rarely recognized as existing at
all, it is in a great measure free from the peculiar vulgarity of its
English parallel.

The number of those at the South who correspond in education and refinement of manners and habits to the average of this
class of the North, it will be evident, from a similar mode of
reasoning to that before employed, must be very much smaller relatively, either to the territory or the whole white population of
their respective regions.

In the comparison commonly made by southern writers between the condition of the people of a sparsely-settled country and
another, it is usually assumed that the advantages of the latter
are confined exclusively to towns, and to large and crowded
towns. By contrasting the evils which concentrate in such
towns with the favorable circumstances of life, where at least
wood, water, and air are abundant, and corn is usually comparatively cheap, an argument of some force to ignorant people is
easily presented. The advantages possessed by a people living
in communities, or in moderately well occupied rural districts,
who are even more free from the evils of great towns than their
own people, are entirely overlooked by most southern writers.
Such is the condition, however, of more white people in the free

States than the whole white population of the slave States. A majority of our farmers' daughters can walk from their dwellings to schools of a quality such as at the South can be maintained not twice in five hundred square miles. These schools are practically a part of their homes. Probably, in more than half the families of the South, the children of which are instructed to the least degree which would be considered "respectable," among this second class of the North, private governesses are obliged to be employed, or the children must be for many years at boarding-schools. We all know that the young women who go to the South, to meet the demand thus occasioned for home education, are not generally, though they may be in cases, our own most esteemed and successful instructresses; and we also know from their report that their skill and labor has necessarily to be long chiefly employed in laying those simple foundation habits of *instructability*, which our northern children acquire imperceptibly from association with those of the neighborhood slightly in advance of them. Churches and the various suborganizations centering in them, in which class distinctions are much lost sight of, to the great advantage of the manners of the lower classes, and little chance of injury to the higher; libraries, literary societies, lecture arrangements, dramatic and musical, art and scientific entertainments, and also highly educated professional men, with whom, for various purposes, many persons are brought often in contact, are correspondingly more frequent at the North, correspondingly more accessible; in other words, the advantages to be derived from them are cheaper, and so more influential on the manners of the people at large.

The common opinion has been that the southerners or planters of the class now under consideration, are more social, more generous, more heartily kind and genial than northerners.   According to my experience, the reverse of all this is true, as a general rule.   Families live so isolatedly at the South, that any social contact, out of the family, is of course much more eventful and stimulating than it is ordinarily at the North, and this accounts for the common opinion.   I could not but think, however, that most persons at the South looked to the voluntary good offices and conversation of others, both within and without their families, for their enjoyment of the world, much less than most at the North.   It may be that when in towns they attach a greater value to, and are more careful to make use of the opportunities for social gathering afforded by towns, than are northerners.   In towns they attach more consequence to forms, are more scrupulous in matters of etiquette, more lavish in expenditure for dress, and for certain other things which are the signs of luxury rather than luxury itself, such as plate and fancy brands of wines.   They make less show of fine art, and less pretense of artistic judgment.

As to manner or deportment simply, with the same impulse and intention, that of the southerner will be best, more true, more quiet, more modestly self-assured, more dignified.   I have said that the second class at the North is without the pervading vulgarity of the class to which it most nearly corresponds in England, the reason being that those which constitute it seldom wish or attempt to appear to belong to a superior class, not clearly recognizing a superior class.   Individuals, however, very generally have a strong desire to be thought better informed, more ingenious, more witty, as well as more successful in their enterprises than they are, and this stamps them with a peculiar quality of manners vulgarly called " smartness," the absence of which makes southern men and women generally much more agreeable companions than northerners of the same degree of education and accomplishments in other respects. Not but that snobs abound; of these it will be more convenient to speak under the next division, however.

We have next to consider the somewhat famous First Families.

The traditional "family," stately but condescending, haughty but jovial, which has long kept open house for all comers on the old plantations of Virginia or South Carolina, is not wholly a myth.

There really was something which, with some sort of propriety, could be termed a gentry in Carolina and Virgina in their colony days; yet of the names which are now thought to have belonged to it, as descended of brave, loyal, and adventurous cavaliers, some I once saw in London upon an old freight-list of a ship outward bound for Virginia, with the addition of tinker and tailor, poacher and pickpocket, all to be sold for life, or a term of years, to the highest bidder when they should arrive.

What was properly to be termed the gentry in Virginia and South Carolina previous to the Revolution, was much smaller in number than is, I believe, commonly supposed. A large proportion of the families who composed it and who remained after the Revolution in the country (for many were tories), have since passed in all their branches through a poverty-stricken period, very dissipating in its influence upon hereditary breeding, novelists and dramatic old servants to the contrary notwithstanding. Many of those who have retained wealth and family pride in succession to the present time, have undeniably, from various causes, degenerated wofully in breeding. Coarse tastes and brutal dispositions can not be disguised under a cavalier address, and the most assured readiness in the established forms of polite society. Of the real " old families" which remain at all "high bred" in their qualities, habits, and manners, I think it will be difficult for most readers who have not studied the matter at all to form a sufficiently small estimate. Some may be supposed, however. Associating with these are many new or recuperated families, in which there is also the best breeding, and in certain few parts or districts of the South, to be defined and numbered without difficulty, there is unquestionably a wealthy and remarkably generous, hospitable, refined and accomplished first class, clinging with some pertinacity, although with too evident an effort, to the traditional manners and customs of an established gentry. I speak of them as a class with some question of the propriety of the term, for I do not much doubt that, as I was told at the South, old ladies may easily be found who will give you a complete census of the whole really " first class people," between the courses of a well-served dinner.

There was a gentry in the North as well as in Virginia and Carolina in the colony period, though a less important and numerous one. As the North has been much more prosperous, as the value of its property has much more rapidly increased than that of the South, the advantages of wealth have, I believe, been more generally retained in families, and probably the number of those who could trace their breeding in an uninterrupted parental influence from the colonial gentry, is now larger at the North than the South.

Including new families, in whose habits and manners and conversation the best bred people of Europe would find nothing more offensive and inharmonious with themselves than might be ascribed to local fashion or a desire to avoid the responsibility of social leadership, there is unquestionably at this time a very much larger number of thoroughly well bred and even high bred people in the free than in the slave States. It is equally certain that the proportion of such people to the whole population of whites is larger at the North than the South.

The great majority of wealthy planters who at the present day assume for themselves a special social respectability and superiority to the class I have defined as the second, are, as a general rule, not only distinguished for all those qualities which our satirists and dramatists are accustomed to assume to be the especial property of the newly rich of the Fifth Avenue, but, as far as I have had opportunity to observe both classes, are far more generally and ridiculously so than the would-be fashionable people of New York, or of any other part of the United States. It is a part of the *rôle* they undertake to act, to be hospitable and generous, as it was lately that of our fops to be sleepy and critical. They are not hospitable and generous, however; they know not the meaning of these terms. They are absurdly ostentatious in entertainment, and extravagant in the purchase of notoriety; possibly they have more tact in this than our Potiphars, but such has not been my personal observation.

It is only at a few centers of commerce in the South that there is a permanent class of merchants and functionaries such as chiefly lead in northern society, and at these the characteristics of society are foreign. With the lawyers, merchants, and functionaries of the interior of the South, I have had little to do. I judge them to be superior very much to the planting class, on an average, yet in several instances where I have been introduced to them, I have found them to be of such habits and manners as would have prevented them from occupying satisfactorily, similar stations at the North. Speaking of merchants, I am reminded of an amusing experience in my journey, which I relate not so much with the intention of instructing the reader as to the mercantile customs of the South, as for his entertainment. It illustrates, however, the wonderful liberality and hospitality to strangers which is supposed to be only born of slavery.

Changing my plans of travel in Mississippi, I pursued a route to Virginia for which I had not previously provided myself with letters. The day after I reached Tuscaloosa I asked advice of the landlord of my inn as to how I could best obtain money by drafts on New York. He seemed surprised at the inquiry; there was but one man who was known to do any thing like an exchange business in the town. On this man, who had some title, judge or governor, I think, I accordingly called. He told me that he was in the habit of selling drafts on New York; they had a certain value when any one wished to pay a bill there. I stated my circumstances, and with much difficulty got him to examine various letters which I carried with me; some of them were from distinguished men, both of the North and South, with whom he professed to have an acquaintance. He did not for a moment doubt that I was the man I assumed to be, or that I was "good" for a much larger amount than I desired him to favor me with. He politely informed me that he did not make a business of furnishing money to travelers; and when I asked if he could not recommend me to some one in the town who would so far accommodate me, he said that he did not think I would find any one to do so. I reminded him that this would leave me in a very unpleasant predicament. He was sorry for it, he replied, but he did not see that he could help it, and as he had

other business he would wish me good morning. I called with
no better success upon two merchants, and then making a close
calculation, I concluded that with good luck I could pay my way,
by traveling in the most carefully frugal manner on the course I
intended pursuing, to Chatannooga in Tennessee, and that by the
time I reached that point I might expect to be supplied with
funds in answer to a letter.

I succeeded in reaching Chatannooga, but with quite an empty
purse. My letters informed me that I was accredited to the post-
master. This gentleman received me cordially, and at once
offered to introduce me to the bank. At the bank, after a little
general conversation with a polite cashier, I asked him to cash a
draft on New York for two hundred dollars. He withdrew, and
presently desired to see the postmaster in a private apartment.
Soon after this, I was called in and presented to the president, who,
after some polite inquiries about my health, wished to know what
friend I had in town who could identify me. None, but here
was the postmaster with a letter— Ah! but what assurance had
they—(that this letter had not been sent the postmaster by an
accomplice, he meant); how, in fact, it was mildly asked, was it
to be known that I was not a swindler? I presented a circular
letter of credit of Duncan, Sherman & Co. on their Mexican
correspondents, and a general letter of credence by the Gov-
·ernor of New York. But who knew their signatures to be genuine, who could identify me as the Frederick Law Olmsted spoken
of in them? I offered to show various letters of introduction,
and twenty letters received by me at post offices on the route
which I alleged that I had followed from Mexico; I proposed to
show the marks on my linen, my engraved cards, my Mexican
passport. But how were they to be made secure that I came

honestly by these things ? It was my intention to remain a day
or two, would I be so good as to leave my letters and papers, and
allow them time for consideration ?

When I called again at the banking establishment, which was
a very commodious and handsome one, the cashier received me
with consideration. They had had a meeting of their directors,
he said, at which my request had been the subject of debate, and
it had been determined, inasmuch as it seemed that I would not
otherwise be able to pursue my journey, to cash a draft on New
York for me, but the directors thinking that two hundred dollars
was a larger amount than I should find absolutely necessary, he
was only authorized to furnish me with one hundred, which he
accordingly did in new notes of the bank.

I was subsequently kept in funds by southern bank-notes,
bought in New York and sent by mail to a designated point on
my route.

Of course, there was nothing wrong in all this—or if there
was, it was with myself and my friends—but if a southerner had
had anything like such an experience in New England, would he
have said nothing about wooden nutmegs, and so forth ? Com-
parisons of this kind are anything but agreeable to draw. They
will be necessary, however, and it will be necessary that the removal of much popular delusion be seriously and systematically
undertaken, if the future discussion of the slavery question is
to have the character which, of late, southern writers have attempted to give it. I find no more foundation for the assumption
of a greater habitual liberality or a more thorough-going honesty,
than of a more general hospitality having been produced by slavery, even upon the planters, than exists among ourselves. To say
nothing more of my personal experience, I will drop this disagree-

able subject after giving two short paragraphs from southern newspapers, and a third, merely by way of explanation, from a foreign periodical.

RELIGIOUS CONTRIBUTIONS.

" In looking over the annual statement of the Board of Foreign Missions, there is a fact that strikes us painfully. By summing up the entire contributions of the Synod of Virginia, we find them to be $3,475 65. Those of the Synod of North Carolina amount to $5,000 90. By referring to the report of contributions from New York, we find that the First Church (Dr. Philips') has given $6,386 60, and the Fifth avenue and Nineteenth street (Dr. Alexander's), $7,648 74—each of them more than all the churches in both of these Synods ! Brethren, why is this ? Is one church in New York richer than both these large and prosperous Synods ? Why, then, this fact ?"—*Richmond Central Herald.*

THE HONEST PLANTER AT HOME.

" The editor of *The Savannah Republican* is in receipt of a letter from one of the cotton manufacturing companies in Georgia, mentioning the purchase of a crop of cotton at Macon, which, from actual weight, contained fifty-five per cent. of sand, leaving but forty-five per cent. of cotton."

THE HONEST PLANTER ABROAD.
Ten Million Dollars Per Annum.

" When the spinner comes to open and inspect his purchases at the mill, he frequently finds concealed therein substances which are certainly not cotton. Formerly flint stones were the principal articles selected as substitutes; and the manufacturer used often to discover that instead of the "fair bowed" which he had bought and paid for, he was favored with a considerable weight of geological specimens. But it seems at length to have struck certain individuals on the other side of the Atlantic, that this was at best but a coarse and vulgar fraud, unworthy of an enlightened age and people, and that it was possible to carry out the principle of sophistication on a far more extended scale, and in a much more refined manner.

Accordingly the system of "sanding" sprung up, and instead of bales consisting of American cotton they are frequently found to consist of America itself, to the extent of ten, twenty, or in many instances of more than thirty per cent.

The extent to which this practice has reached may be imagined, when it is known that, taking the adulteration at ten per cent. on the import of the last crop, which is stated to be a very low estimate, a quantity of sand equal in weight to more than two hundred thousand bales, or forty thousand tons, is found to have been bought and paid for as cotton by Great Britain, *at an expense of upwards of* £2,000,000 sterling; and that there are now lying at Liverpool at least one hundred thousand bales of this sanded cotton which spinners will not buy at any price.

But it may be asked, " can not they purchase it at an allowance in price proportionate to the amount of adulteration?" To this it must be answered that cotton is now bought by sample and not by inspection of the bulk of the article, which indeed would be almost impracticable from the nature of the packages and other causes. When the cotton is warehoused, on its arrival from abroad, a sample is taken from each of the bales, but these are pressed so hard that it is impossible to penetrate more than a few inches into them. If, therefore, as is generally the case, the surface layer be clean cotton, it is evident that the sample can be of no value as an index of quality; but supposing the sample when first drawn to be fair, in the very act of drawing, and at every subsequent examination it is liable to lose some of the sand which it contains, and very shortly to become nothing better than " a delusion, a mockery and a snare."

This sandy adulteration, too, is more difficult to deal with than the simpler one before mentioned: when stones are found in cotton bales, it is at once evident that they have no business there; they were not represented in the sample, and were, therefore, not expected; consequently an affidavit is made of their presence, and a claim for compensation is preferred. It is true that a spinner has occasionally suffered the inconvenience of having his mill burned down, in consequence of contact between a flint and the iron machinery; but as this is not of *very* frequent occurrence, it may, perhaps, be taken out of the account.

But as regards sand, which is nominally, if not actually or fairly, represented in the sample, it is plain that if the spinner make a claim on this score, he is liable to be told that the price he paid was calculated upon the fact of the presence of this sand, and that it would be a point of no small difficulty to settle such a claim equitably if allowed at all. No wonder, therefore, that there are so many bales of cotton at Liverpool which manufacturers decline to touch.

The money actually paid to America for this stuff does not represent the extent of the evil; freight, warehouse rent, and other charges are all incurred on this mass of useless earth, just as though it were what it ought to be; to say nothing of the damage caused to machinery, and the detriment to the health of the work-people in factories where the adulterated cotton is used.

This fraud has assumed such proportions that active steps are taking for its abatement. It is clear that the check must ultimately come from the consumer, for as long as a market exists for such cotton, so long will people be found to supply it. Whatever may be the result of the means adopted with a view to the suppression of this gigantic

swindle, it can not be denied that its perpetration is a strong argument
against our remaining, longer than can be avoided, dependent upon
one country for the largest supply of so important an article as cotton.

It is stated by those whose assertions are worthy of respect, that
cotton could be grown in Africa, and laid down in England at considerably lower prices—quality for quality—than that brought from
New Orleans. No doubt time and capital are requisite to render Africa to any extent available as a source of supply; but most certainly
£2,000,000 sterling might have been far better spent in this direction
during the past year, than in paying for an enormous quantity of useless and mischievous rubbish, and in thus helping to encourage and
support a shameful and systematic fraud."—*C. P. William.*

CHAPTER X.

THE DANGER OF THE SOUTH.

"BEFORE the advent of modern science, any idea of systematic laws of human improvement would have been deemed alike impossible and absurd; but the constant observation of facts, the exact statistics recorded, the progress of science in all departments, has made it possible to conceive of, and probable that there actually exist *uniform laws of social movements*, based upon any given condition of society. If the *elementary social* condition be different in regard to religion, government, arts, science, industry, the resulting movements of society will be different. Hence, when we have ascertained by accurate observation upon and record of the social phenomena, that the social movement is uniformly in a certain direction, and that certain results uniformly follow, we shall know in what *elements* the conditions of society must be changed, in order to change the results. Hence, when this law of social movements is ascertained, the philanthropist, legislator, and jurist will know precisely what must be done, and how in order to remove the evils, or reform the wrongs, or produce the results they desire. They will know that *certain elementary conditions of society* must be changed, and they well know that by removing temptations, or laying restraints, or enlightening the mind, or changing the course of industry, or producing new arts, they will change the social tendency, and thus change the results. * * * Society, or that part of it which thinks and acts, can change the results by changing the elementary conditions which produce them. When you know exactly what the change ought to be, it is not very difficult to produce it; nor does it follow that because a thousand crimes must be committed in Ohio, that a thousand particular individuals *must* commit them. It is true that the individual frequently acts from motives, but is it not just as true that the individual frequently seeks these motives, and presents them to himself."—*From the Report of the Ohio State Commissioner of Statistics*, 1859.

"If there is a first principle in intellectual education it is this—that the discipline which does good to the mind is that in which the mind is active, not that in which it is passive. The secret for developing the faculties is to give them much to do, and much inducement to do it.—*Mill's Political Economy.*

The field-hand negro is, on an average, a very poor and very bad creature, much worse than I had supposed before I had seen him and grown familiar with his stupidity, indolence, duplicity, and sensuality. He seems to be but an imperfect man, incapable of taking care of himself in a civilized manner, and his presence in large numbers must be considered a dangerous circumstance to a civilized people.

A civilized people, within which a large number of such creatures has been placed by any means not within its own control, has claims upon the charity, the aid, if necessary, of all other civilized peoples in its endeavors to relieve itself from the danger which must be apprehended from their brutal propensities, from the incompleteness of their human sympathies—their inhumanity—from their natural love of ease, and the barbaric want of forethought and providence, which would often induce desperate want among them. Evidently the people thus burthened would have need to provide systematically for the physical wants of these poor creatures, else the latter would be liable to prey with great waste upon their substance. Perhaps the very best thing to do would be to collect them into small herds, and attach each herd to a civilized family, the head of which should be responsible for its safe keeping. Such a superintendent should of course contrive, if possible, to make his herd contribute in some way to the procuring of its necessary sustenance ; and if, besides this, he even turned their feeble abilities to such good account by his superior judgment, that they actually procured a considerable surplus of food and clothing for the benefit of others, should not christendom applaud and encourage his exertions, even if a certain amount of severity and physical constraint had been found necessary to accomplish this success?

Let us endeavor to assume a similar difficulty for ourselves. Let us suppose that a large part—the proportion varying with the locality—of our own community should next year suffer from some new malady, the result of which should in no case be fatal, but which should, like the *goitre* of Savoy, leave all who were affected by it permanently injured in their intellects, with diminished bodily activity, and fiercer animal propensities. (I take this method of stating the case, because some of us who only see the negro as he exists at the North might find it difficult to imagine him as he is known to the planters.)

Suppose, further, that this malady should be confined to certain families, as if its seed had been received hundreds of years ago by numerous individuals, and only their descendants (but all cf these to the most distant trace of the blood), now suffered from it. Also, that some of our doctors should be of the opinion that the effects of the malady upon the intellect would descend to the children, and to all descendants of those who suffered. Suppose that these unfortunates should be subject to certain hallucinations, that they should be liable to think themselves sane and quite able to take care of themselves, and that when possessed with these ideas that they should be quite cunning and dangerous in attempting to exercise the usual prerogatives of sane men.

What should we do with them?

Finding them ordinarily tractable and sensible enough, after all, to yield readily, if not cheerfully, to superior force, we might herd them together on a sort of farm-hospitals, and let them earn their living, giving especially capable men charge of many, and rewarding them with good salaries, and ordinary small farmers, smaller numbers, with smaller compensations for overseeing them?

Of course, we should place every possible legislative guard and check upon these superintendents and overseers to secure fair and honest dealing, to prevent them from making perquisites for themselves at the expense of a reasonable comfort in their institutions. Careful instructions to secure economical sustenance, and how to turn such labor as could be got from the unfortunates to the best account, in defraying the cost of their keeping, would also be framed by talented men and furnished each keeper.

And having regard to national wealth, to the temporal good of the commonwealth, this is about all that common sense would lead us to do, at least through the agency of government.

Is this all, reader?

You have too much overlooked our small matters of State, if you think so. We have a few crazy people, a few fools, not enough to be a matter of much consideration to our statesmen or legislators, yet we have a State system in our dealing with them, such as it is, and such as it is, it puts our dealing with them on a little different footing than would the system I have above imagined. What I have imagined is not quite all we have for some time been in the habit of doing when we did anything with this class. And judging from what we have done, it does not seem as if it would be all that we should do in such an emergency as I have supposed, engaging as it would all the talent of the country to diminish as much as possible the necessary results of the calamity.

We should, it appears, call upon our learned doctors eagerly to study ; we should each of us eagerly observe for ourselves whether the fearful infirmity by which so many were incapacitated for their former usefulness, were not only absolutely incurable, but also absolutely not possible to be alleviated. And if our observation should satisfy us, if our doctors could not deny that, with judicious treatment, a considerable alleviation could be effected, so much so indeed, that with a very large part a close approximation to the normal condition of sane and capable mankind could be obtained, there are doubtless those amongst us who would think this a dangerous and an infidel presumption. Just as every year some miserable wretch is found in our dark places to have a crazy father or brother whom he keeps in a cage in his garret, and whose estate he takes care of, and who is of the opinion that it will be of no use, but, on the contrary, a manifest defiance of Divine Providence, and most dangerous to life and property to let this unfortunate out of his cage, to surround him with comforts, and contrive for him cheerful occupation, as our State requires shall be done. But would the average common sense and humanity of the people of the free States allow them to refuse all reduction from their usual annual incomes ; refuse to suffer all necessary addition to their usual taxes ; refuse to burden their minds with the difficulties of the all-absorbing problem, in order to initiate a remedial system ?   Our worst and most cowardly legislature would never dare adjourn leaving this duty incompletely performed. There are thousands on thousands of our citizens who would not only spare from their incomes, but would divide their estates for such a purpose. There is not a county that would not submit to the highest war taxes for it.

Suppose that the doctors and that the universal observation of the community should determine that the defective class were not only capable of being improved, but that so far as their limited intellects permitted, the laws of improvement were the same for them as for healthy men; that they were found to be influenced by a liking for food and drink, for the society of each other and of sane men, for the admiration and respect of each other and of sane men, for their ease, for dancing, for music and other amusements; and that their imperfect natures could be acted upon, drawn out and enlarged by means of these likings. Suppose that it were found that nearly all of them had still some knowledge of religion, that although they were inclined sometimes to consider sane men as their enemies, they were still, in most cases, by judicious play upon their inclinations and disinclinations, capable of being trained quite beyond the most sagacious of our domestic animals, even to read intelligently. Should we, because there were so many of them, go back two hundred years in our civilization, denying ourselves the addition which this capacity would give to their powers of usefulness, and consequently of economy of maintenance; denying them the advantages for improvement which we now in every State give to our hopelessly insane, to our blind and mute, to our fools, to our worst and most dangerous criminals?

Why do we not pass laws forbidding criminals and maniacs to read? Our fathers did not allow them to read when negroes were introduced in Virginia. But every man among us whom we call well informed, now knows that it is a profitable business for the State, which has so little profitable business, even to provide teachers and books for a portion of her criminals, to allow books and encourage reading with all. To provide books, to provide physicians, to provide teachers, to provide halls and gardens of recreation, as stimulants to healthful thought for our madmen and our fools; to this the State is impelled equally by considerations of safety and of economy. Even Kentucky has its State institution for the development of manhood in fools born of white women.

Does not every such man know, too, that given an improvable mind with a sound body, possessed of the natural instincts, the usual desires, appetites, aversions, no matter if, at starting, the being is even what we call an idiot, a driveling imbecile, disgusting all who see him, a sheer burden upon society, the process of making him clean in his habits, capable of laboring with a good and intelligent purpose, and of associating inoffensively with others, is just as certain in its principles and in its progress—infinite progress—as the navigation of a ship or the building of a house?

This is even so with a cretin, whose body is deformed beyond remedy, whose brain is contracted, whose face is contorted, whose limbs are half paralyzed, whose every organ is defective, and who has inherited these conditions from goitrous parents and grandparents.

Dr. Seguin says: "The idiot wishes for nothing; he wishes only to remain in his vacuity."

Even so thinks Dr. Cartwright of the negro, and surely nothing worse can be thought of him.*

But Dr. Seguin adds: "To treat successfully this ill-will [indisposition to take care of himself], the physician wills that the idiot should act *and think himself, of himself, and, finally, by*

---

* "The negro, docile in subjection, attached like the household dog to his master, only in proportion to his intellect, in a far higher grade of being, is satisfied and happy in the half-civilized condition which, with us, his *imitativeness* enables him to attain."—*De Bow's Resources*, vol. ii., p. 203.

himself. The incessant volition of the moral physician urges incessantly the idiot into the sphere of activity, of thinking, of labor, of duty, and affectionate feelings."

Is there no such law of progression of capacity for the black imbeciles? All the laws of the South have the contrary aims; to withdraw them as much as possible from the sphere of self-willed activity, thought, labor—to prevent the negro from thinking by himself, of himself, for himself; and the principle on which these laws are based is thus defined by Mr. De Bow:

" The Almighty has thought well to place certain of His creatures in certain *fixed positions* in this world of ours, for what cause He has not seen fit to make quite clear to our limited capacities; and why an ass is not a man, and a man is not an ass, will probably forever remain a mystery." " God made the world; God gave thee thy place, my hirsute brother, and, according to all earthly possibilities and prob-abilities, it is thy destiny there to remain, bray as thou wilt. From the same great power have our sable friends, Messrs. Sambo, Cuffee & Co., received their position also. . . . . Alas, my poor black brother, thou, like thy hirsute friend, must do thy braying in vain."*

Are there laws on our statute books to prevent asses from being taught to read?

The Richmond *Examiner* says:

" These immigrants do not, like our ancestors, fly from religious and political persecution; they come merely as animals in search of a richer and fresher pasture. They come to gratify physical want—for moral, intellectual, or religious wants they have not acquired. They will settle in large masses, and, for ages to come, will practice and inculcate a pure (or rather impure) materialism. Mormonism is a fit exponent, proof, and illustration of our theory. The mass of them are sensual, groveling, low-minded agrarians, and nine tenths of them would join the Mormons, or some such brutal, leveling sect, if an opportunity offered to do so.

" European writers describe a large class of population throughout England and the Continent as being distinguished by restless, wander-ing, nomadic habits, and by a peculiar conformation of the skull and face. Animal and sensual nature largely predominates, with them, over the moral and intellectual. It is they who commit crimes, fill

* " Resources," vol. ii., pp. 197, 198.

prisons, and adorn the gallows. They will not submit to the restraints of law or religion, nor can they be educated. From their restless and lawless habits, we should infer they composed a large part of the northern immigration."

If all this were true, and were felt by us to be true, should we think it necessary to put the minds of these beings in fetters? Should we hold it to be dangerous if one should undertake to strengthen their intellects, to give them larger ideas?

If all the slaves in the United States were "real Congo niggers," which not one in one thousand is, and if all real Congo niggers were as incapable, and as beastly, and as savage in their propensities as the very worst of them are asserted to be, would the method of dealing with them which the legislation of the slave States, and which a large part of the labor of the Congress and Executive of our confederation is directed to the purpose of perpetuating, be felt to be strictly in accordance with sound and well established economico-political principles? The purpose of that legislation is avowed to be merely to secure safety with economy. Would a project for establishing an institution planned upon the principles of the ancient Bedlam and the ancient Bridewell be felt to-day to be completely justified among us, by the statement that highwaymen and maniacs will endanger life and the security of our property if they are not somehow taken care of?

If there had been no Mettray with its Demetz, no Norfolk Island with its Machonochie, no Hanwell with its Connolly, no Abendberg with its Guggenbuhl; if the courage, devotion, and labor of Pinel, Sicard, and Seguin had been in vain; if there had been no progress in the science of civilized society since the days of Howard, we might listen with merely silent sadness to such an excuse for debilitating the weak, for holding down the fallen; for permitting brutal keepers to exasperate the mad and mercenary nurses to stupefy the idiotic; we might, if we saw it to be necessary to preserve a civilized community from destruction, even give its object our aid, but with the knowledge which in our time is everywhere else acted upon, it is impossible for us not to feel that such an argument is a specious and a fallacious one, and that no State can long act upon it with safety, much less with economy.

And surely the system by which intellectual demands and ambition are repressed in the negro is as little calculated to produce the security which is its object, as it is to turn his physical abilities to the most profitable use for his owner. How far it fails in this respect, the extra legal measures of safety and the semi-instinctive habits of unconscious precaution which pervade southern society evince. I say unconscious precaution, because southerners themselves seem to have generally a very inadequate idea of the influence of slavery upon their habits in this way, and this is very natural.

"Every habit breeds unconsciousness of its existence in the mind of the man whom it controls, and this is more true of habits which involve our safety than of any others. The weary sailor aloft, on the lookout, may fall asleep; but, in the lurch of the ship, his hands will clench the swaying cordage only the more firmly, that they act in the method of instinct. A hard-hunted fugitive may nod in his saddle, but his knees will not unloose their hold upon his horse. Men who live in powder-mills are said to lose all conscious feeling of habitual insecurity; but visitors perceive that they have acquired a constant softness of manner and of voice.

If a laborer on a plantation should insolently contradict his master, it may often appear to be no more than a reasonable precaution for his master to kill him on the spot; for, when a slave has acquired such boldness, it may be evident that not merely is his value as property seriously diminished, but that the attempt to make further use of him at all, as property, involves in danger the whole white community. " If I let this man live, and permit him the necessary degree of freedom to be further useful to me, he will infect with his audacity all my negro property, which will be correspondingly more difficult to control, and correspondingly reduced in value. If he treats me with so little respect now, what have I to anticipate when he has found other equally independent spirits among the slaves? They will not alone make themselves free, but will avenge upon me, and my wife, and my daughters, and upon all our community, the injustice which they will think has been done them, and their women, and children." Thus would he reason, and shudder to think what might follow if he yielded to an impulse of mercy.

To suppose, however, that the master will pause while he thus weighs the danger exactly, and then deliberately act as, upon reflection, he considers the necessities of the case demand, is absurd. The mere circumstance of his doing so would nourish a hopeful spirit in the slave, and stimulate him to consider how he could best avoid all punishment. Hence the instinct-like habit of precaution with individuals, and hence the frenzy which often seizes whole communities.

But, " planters sleep unguarded, and with their bedroom doors open." So, as it was boasted, did the Emperor at Biarritz, last summer, and with greater bravery, because the assassin of Napoleon would be more sure, in dispatching him, that there would be no one left with a vital interest to secure punishment for such a deed : and because, if he failed, Napoleon dare never employ such exemplary punishment for his enemies as would the planters for theirs.   The emperors of the South are the whole free society of the South, and it is a society of mutual assurance.   Against a slave who has the disposition to become an assassin, his emperor has a body-guard, which, for general effectiveness, is to the Cent Garde as your right hand is to your right hand's glove.

It is but a few months since, in Georgia or Alabama, a man treated another precisely as Mr. Brooks treated Mr. Sumner— coming up behind him, with the fury of a madman, and felling him with a bludgeon; killing him by the first blow, however, and then discharging vengeance by repeated strokes upon his senseless body.*   The man thus pitifully abused had been the master of the other, a remarkably confiding and merciful master, it was said—too much so; "It never does to be too slack with niggers."   By such indiscretion he brought his death upon him.

---

* The late Mr. Brooks' character should be honestly considered, now that personal enmity toward him is impossible.   That he was courteous, accomplished, warm-hearted, and hot-blooded, dear as a friend and fearful as an enemy, may be believed by all; but, in the South, his name is yet never mentioned without the term gallant or courageous, spirited or noble, is also attached to it, and we are obliged to ask, why insist on this?   The truth is, we include a habit of mind in these terms which slavery has rendered, in a great degree, obsolete in the South.   The man who has been accustomed from childhood to see men beaten when they have no chance to defend themselves; to hear men accused, reproved, and vituperated, who dare not open their lips in self-defense or reply ; the man who is accustomed to see other men whip women without interference, remonstrance, or any expression of indignation, must have a certain quality, which is an essential part of personal honor with us, greatly blunted, if not entirely destroyed.   The same quality which we detest in the assassination of an enemy, is essentially constant in all slavery.   It is found in effecting one's will with another, when he can not, if he would, defend himself.   Accustomed to this in every hour of their lives, Southerners do not feel magnanimity and the "fair-play" impulse to be a necessary part of the quality of "spirit," courage, and nobleness.   By spirit they apparently mean only passionate vindictivenss of character, and by gallantry mere intrepidity.

But did his assassin escape? He was roasted, at a slow fire, on the spot of the murder, in the presence of many thousand slaves, driven to the ground from all the adjoining counties, and when, at length, his life went out, the fire was intensified until his body was in ashes, which were scattered to the winds and trampled under foot. Then "magistrates and clergymen" addressed appropriate warnings to the assembled subjects. It was not thought indiscreet to leave doors open again that night.

Will any traveler say that he has seen no signs of discontent, or insecurity, or apprehension, or precaution; that the South has appeared quieter and less excited, even on the subject of slavery, than the North; that the negroes seem happy and contented, and the citizens more tranquilly engaged in the pursuit of their business and pleasure? Has that traveler been in Naples? Precisely the same remarks apply to the appearance of things there at this moment. The massacre of Hayti opened in a ball-room. Mr. Cobden judged there was not the smallest reason in the French king's surrounding himself with soldiers the day before the hidden force of insubordination broke forth and cast him forth from his kingdom. It is true, however, that the tranquility of the South is the tranquility of Hungary and of Poland, rather than of France or the Two Sicilies; the tranquility of hopelessness on the part of the subject race. But, in the most favored regions, this broken spirit of despair is as carefully preserved by the citizens, and with as confident and unhesitating an application of force, when necessary to teach humility, as it is by the army of the Czar, or the omnipresent police of the Kaiser. In Richmond, and Charleston, and New Orleans, the citizens are as careless and gay as in Boston or London, and their servants a thousand times as childlike and cordial, to all appearance, in their relations with them as our servants are with us. But go to the bottom of this security and dependence, and you come to police machinery such as you never find in towns under free government: citadels, sentries, passports, grape-shotted cannon, and daily public whippings of the subjects for accidental infractions of police ceremonies. I happened myself to see more direct expression of tyranny in a single day and night at Charleston, than at Naples in a week; and I found that more than half the inhabitants of this town were subject to arrest, imprisonment, and barbarous punishment, if found in the streets without a passport after the evening "gun-fire." Similar precautions and similar customs may be discovered in every large town in the South.

Nor is it so much better, as is generally imagined, in the rural districts. Ordinarily there is no show of government any more than at the North: the slaves go about with as much apparent freedom as convicts in a dock-yard. There is, however, nearly everywhere, always prepared to act, if not always in service, an armed force, with a military organization, which is invested with more arbitrary and cruel power than any police in Europe. Yet the security of the whites is in a much less degree contingent on the action of the patrols than upon the constant, habitual, and instinctive surveillance and authority of all white people over all black. I have seen a gentleman, with no commission or special authority, oblige negroes to show their passports, simply because he did not recognize them as belonging to any of his neighbors. I have seen a girl, twelve years old, in a district where, in ten miles, the slave population was fifty to one of the free, stop an old man on the public road, demand to know where he was going, and by what authority, order him to face about and return to his plantation, and enforce her command with turbulent anger, when he hesitated, by threatening that she would have him well whipped if he did not instantly obey. The man quailed like a spaniel, and she instantly resumed the manner of a lovely child with me, no more apprehending that she had acted unbecomingly, than that her character had been influenced by the slave's submission to her caprice of supremacy; no more conscious that she had increased the security of her life by strengthening the habit of the slave to the master race, than is the sleeping seaman that he tightens his clutch of the rigging as the ship meets each new billow.

There is no part of the South in which the people are more free from the direct action of slavery upon the character, or where they have less to apprehend from rebellion, than Eastern Tennessee. Yet, after the burning of a negro near Knoxville, a few years ago, the deed was justified as necessary for the maintenance of order among the slaves, by the editor of a newspaper (the *Register*) which, owing to its peculiarly conservative character, I have heard stigmatized as "an abolition print." "It was," he observed, "a means of absolute, necessary self-defense, which could not be secured by an ordinary resort to the laws. Two executions on the gallows have occurred in this county within a year or two past, and the example has been unavailing. Four executions by hanging have taken place, heretofore, in Jefferson, of slaves guilty of similar offenses, and it has produced no radical terror or example for the others designing the same crimes, and hence any example less horrible and terrifying would have availed nothing here."

The other local paper (the *Whig*), upon the same occasion, used the following language :

"We have to say, in defense of the act, that it was not per-

petrated by an excited multitude, but by one thousand citizens—
good citizens at that—who were cool, calm, and deliberate."

And the editor, who is a Methodist preacher, presently adds,
after explaining the enormity of the offense with which the vic-
tim was charged—" We unhesitatingly affirm that the punishment was unequal to the crime. Had we been there we should
have taken a part, and even suggested the pinching of pieces
out of him with red-hot pincers—the cutting off of a limb at a
time, and then burning them all in a heap. The possibility of
his escaping from jail forbids the idea of awaiting the tardy
movements of the law." [Although one thousand trusty citizens
volunteered to guard him at the stake.]

How much more horrible than the deed are these apologies
for it. They make it manifest that it was not accidental in its
character, but a phenomenon of general and fundamental significance. They explain the paralytic effect upon the popular conscience of the great calamity of the South. They indicate a
necessary tendency of people living under such circumstances to
return in their habits of thought to the dark ages of mankind.
For who, from the outside, can fail to see that the real reason
why men, in the middle of the nineteenth century, and in the
center of the United States, are publicly burned at the stake, is
one much less heathenish, less disgraceful to the citizens than that
given by the more zealous and extemporaneous of their journal-
istic exponents—the desire to torture the sinner proportionately
to the measure of his sin. Doubtless, this reverend gentleman
expresses the uppermost feeling of the ruling mind of his community. But would a similar provocation have developed a
similar avenging spirit in any other nominally Christian or
civilized people? Certainly not. All over Europe, and in every

free State—California, for significant reasons, temporarily excepted—in similar cases, justice deliberately takes its course; the accused is systematically assisted in defending or excusing himself. If the law demands his life, the infliction of unnecessary suffering, and the education of the people in violence and feelings of revenge, is studiously avoided. Go back to the foundation of the custom which thus neutralizes Christianity among the people of the South, which carries them backward blindly against the tide of civilization, and what do we find it to be? The editor who still retains moral health enough to be suspected— as men more enlightened than their neighbors usually are—of hetrodoxy, answers. To follow the usual customs of civilization elsewhere would not be felt safe. To indulge in feelings of humanity would not be felt safe. To be faithful to the precepts of Christ would not be felt safe. To act in a spirit of cruel, inconsiderate, illegal, violent, and pitiless vengeance, must be permitted, must be countenanced, must be defended by the most conservative, as a "means of absolute, necessary self-defense." To educate the people practically otherwise would be felt to be suicidal. Hence no free press, no free pulpit, no free politics can be permitted in the South. Hence every white stripling in the South may carry a dirk-knife in his pocket, and play with a revolver before he has learned to swim."*

I happened to pass through Eastern Tennessee shortly after this tragedy, and conversed with a man who was engaged in it— a mild, common-sense native of the country. He told me that there was no evidence against the negro but his own confession. I suggested that he might have been crazy. "What if he was?" he asked, with a sudden asperity. What if he was, to be sure?

* From the Introduction to THE ENGLISHMAN IN KANSAS.

The slaves who were brought together to witness his torture were not insane. They were at least capable of instruction. That day they were given a lesson; were taught to know their masters better; were taught that when ordinary and legal discipline failed, resort would be had to more potent means of governing them. A better informed man, having regard to the ignorance of a stranger, might have answered me: "It was of no consequence, practically, whether he were sane or mad. We do not wish our slaves to study the right and the wrong of every exciting occurrence. To say that being mad the negro was not responsible, therefore not guilty of a crime, therefore not to be punished, would be proclaiming to them that only that which is wrong is to be dreaded. Whatever offends us, whatever is against our will and pleasure, is what a slave must be made to dread."

Constantly, and everywhere throughout the South, are there occurrences of this significance. I do not say as horrible, though no year in the last ten has passed without something as bad— but, constantly and everywhere, of the same nature, of the same impulse, the same reasoning, the same purposes, the same disregard of principles of society, which no people can ever set aside and not have reason to feel their situation insecure. It is false, it is the most dangerous mistake possible to assume that this feeling of insecurity, this annihilation of the only possible basis of security in human society, is, in the slightest degree, the result of modern agitation. It is the fundamental law of slavery, as distinctly appears in the decision of Justice Ruffin, of North Carolina, in the case of the State vs. Mann.* The American system of slavery from its earliest years (as shown p. 496, " Seaboard

* 2 Devereaux's North Carolina Reports, 263.

Slave States"), and without cessation to the present time, has had this accompaniment. Less in the last twenty years, if anything, than before. Would it not be more just to say that this element of the present system was the cause of agitation? Must not the determined policy of the South to deal with slavery on the assumption that it is, in its present form, necessary, just, good, and to be extended, strengthened, and perpetuated indefinitely, involve constant agitation as a necessary incident of the means used to carry it out? I do not say with you or with me, reader, but with a goodly number of any civilized community? Do you not, who wish to think otherwise, consider that it will always require what you must deem a superior mind not to be overcome by incidents necessary to the carrying out of this determination? And will not such agitation give renewed sense of danger, and occasion renewed demands for assurance from us?

I have remarked before that in no single instance did I find an inquiry of the owner or the overseer of a large plantation about the poor whites of its vicinity fail to elicit an expression indicating habitual irritation with them. This equally with the polished and tranquil gentleman of South Carolina and the rude pioneer settler of Texas, himself born a dirt-eating sand-hiller. It was evident in most cases, and in one it was distinctly explained to me by a Louisianian planter (as narrated, p. 674, " Seaboard Slave States"), that the reason of this was not merely the bad effect upon the discipline of the plantation, which was had by the intercourse between these people and the slaves, but that it was felt that the contrast between the habits of the former—most of the time idle, and when working, working only for their own benefit and without a master—constantly offered suggestions and temptations to the slaves to neglect their duty, to run away and live a vagabond life, as these poor whites were seen to. Hence, one of the acknowledged advantages of very large and isolated plantations, and hence, in part, the desire of every planter to get possession of the land of any poor non-slaveholding neighbor.

As few southern writers seem to have noticed this, I suppose that few southerners are aware how universal with planters is this feeling. My attention being early directed to the causes of the condition of the poor whites, I never failed to make inquiries of planters, and of intelligent men especially, about those in their neighborhood, and being soon struck by the constant recurrence of similar expressions with regard to them, I was the more careful to introduce the subject at every proper opportunity, and, I repeat, always with the same result. I am afraid that the feeling of the South to the North is (more or less defined in individual minds) of the same nature, and that the contiguity of a people whose laborers take care of themselves, and labor industriously without being owned—that intimate relations and intercourse with such a people can never be felt to be safe by slaveholders. That it must always be looked upon with apprehension, with a sense of danger, more or less vague, more or less well defined, but always sufficient to lead to efforts intended to counteract its natural influence—its influence not so much with slaves, certainly not alone with the slaves, but also with that important element of population which reaps no profit from the good behavior of the slaves.

In *De Bow's Review* for January, 1850, will be found the following passage in an article discussing the practicability of employing the non-slaveholding whites in factories, the argument being that there will be less danger of their becoming "abolitionists" under such circumstances than at present exists :

" The great mass of our poor white population begin to understand that they have rights, and that they, too, are entitled to some of the sympathy which falls upon the suffering. They are fast learning that there is an almost infinite world of industry opening before them by which they can elevate themselves and their families from wretchedness and ignorance to competence and intelligence. It is this great upheaving of our masses that we have to fear, so far as our institutions are concerned."

It is, in the nature of things, while slaveholders refuse the slightest concession to the spirit of the age—while, in their legislation, they refuse to recognize, in the slightest degree, the principles of social science under which we live and must live, and which every civilized people has fully adopted, that they should endeavor to make it appear the fault of others that they do not feel assured of safety and at ease with themselves; that they should try to make their own ignorant people believe that it is from without all danger is to be apprehended—all assurance of safety to be clamored for—that they should endeavor to make themselves believe it.*

Those who seriously propose to stop all agitation on the subject of slavery, by causing the abolitionists to refrain from proceedings which cause apprehension at the South, by silencing all who entertain sentiments the utterance of which is deemed a source of " danger to southern institutions," by refraining themselves from all proceed-

* The real object of the systematic mail robbery which is maintained throughout the South, and of the censorship of the press which is otherwise attempted, was once betrayed by a somewhat distinguished southern editor, Duff Green, in the United States Telegraph, in the following words :

"The real danger of this [slave insurrection] is remote. We believe we have most to fear from the organized action upon the consciences and fears of the slaveholders themselves; from the insinuation of their dangerous heresies into our schools, our pulpits, and our domestic circles. It is only by alarming the consciences of the weak and feeble, and diffusing among our people a morbid sensibility on the question of slavery, that the abolitionists can accomplish their object."

ings which will be looked upon with alarm by their fellow-citizens of the slave States, can know very little of what would be required before the South were satisfied. The destruction of some million dollars' cost in school and text-books would be one of the first and yet a small item in the undertaking. Books which directly comment upon slavery are considered comparatively safe by those who think that they comprehend the situation of the South, because their purpose being defined, they can be guarded against. As is well understood, it is the insidious attacks of a free press that are most feared. But is it well understood what are felt to be " insidious attacks ?" Some idea may be formed from the following passages which I take, not from the heated columns of a daily newspaper, but from the cool pages of the deliberate *De Bow's Review*. The apprehension they express is not of to-day; in the first article from which I quote (which was published in the middle of Mr. Pierce's presidential term) reference is made to warnings of the same character which have been sounded from time to time before; and this very number of the *Review* contains a testimonial from fifty-five southern senators and representatives in Congress to the "ability and accuracy" of its "exposition of the working of the system of polity of the southern States."

" Our text books are abolition books. They are so to the extent of their capacity." . . . . " We have been too careless and indifferent to the import of these things."

" And so long as we use such works as ' Wayland's Moral Science,' and the abolition geographies, readers, and histories, overrunning, as they do, with all sorts of slanders, caricatures, and blood-thirsty sentiments, let us never complain of their [northern Church people's] use of that transitory romance [Uncle Tom's Cabin]. They seek to array our children, by false ideas, against the established ordinance of God; and it sometimes takes effect. A professor in one of our southern seminaries, not long since, placed in the hands of a pupil ' Wayland's Moral Science,' and informed her that the chapter on slavery was heretical and unscriptural, and that she would not be examined on that chapter, and need not study it. *Perhaps* she didn't. But on the day

of examination she wished her teacher to tell her 'if that chapter was
heretical how she was to know but they were all so?' We might enumerate many other books of similar character and tendencies. But we
will refer to only one more—it is 'Gilbert's Atlas'—though the real
author's name does not appear on the title page. On the title page it
is called 'Appleton's Complete Guide of the World;' published by D.
Appleton & Co., New York. This is an elegant and comprehensive
volume, endorsed by the Appletons and sent South, containing hidden
lessons of the most fiendish and murderous character that enraged fanaticism could conceive or indite. It is a sort of literary and scientific
infernal machine. And whatever the design may have been, the tendency is as shocking as the imagination can picture.* . . . . This
is the artillery and these the implements England and our own recreant
sister States are employing to overturn the order of socity and the
established forms of labor that date back beyond the penning of the
decalogue. . . . . This book, and many other northern school
books scattered over the country, come within the range of the stat-
utes of this State, which provide for the imprisonment for life or the
infliction of the penalty of death upon any person who shall 'publish
or distribute' such works; and were I a citizen of New Orleans, this
work should not escape the attention of the grand jury. But need I
add more to convince the skeptical of the necessity there is for the
production of our own text-books, and, may I not add, our own literature? Why should the land of domestic servitude be less productive
in the great works of the mind now than when Homer evoked the
arts, poetry, and eloquence into existence? Moses wrote the Genesis
of Creation, the Exodus of Israel, and the laws of mankind? and when
Cicero, Virgil, Horace, St. John, and St. Paul became the instructors
of the world?† . . . . They will want no cut-throat literature, no
fire-brand moral science . . . . nor Appleton's 'Complete Atlas,'
to encourage crimes that would blanch the cheek of a pirate, nor any
of the ulcerous and polluting agencies issuing from the hot-beds of
abolition fanaticism."

From an article on educational reform at the South, in the
same *Review*, 1856, I take the following indications of what,
among other northern doings, are considered to imperil the
South :

---

* Elsewhere the Messrs. Appleton are spoken of as "THE GREAT ABOLI-
TION PUBLISHERS OF NEW YORK."

† Note the argument, I pray you, reader. Why, indeed? Why is there
not a Feejee Iliad? Are not the Feejees heathen, as Homer was? Why
should not the Book of Mormon be as good a thing as the Psalms of David?
Was not Joseph Smith also a polygamist?

" 'Lovell's United States Speaker,' the 'National Reader,' the 'Young Ladies' Reader,' 'Columbian Orator,' 'Scott's Lessons,' the 'Village Reader,' and numerous others, have been used for years, and are all, in some respects, valuable compilations. We apprehend, however, there are few parents or teachers who are familiar with the whole of their contents, or they would demand expurgated editions for the use of their children. The sickly sentimentality of the poet Cowper, whose ear became so 'pained,' and his soul 'sick with every day's report of wrong and outrage,' that it made him cry out in agony for 'a lodge in some vast wilderness,' where he might commune with howling wolves and panthers on the blesssings of *liberty* (?), stamps its infectious poison upon many of the pages of these works." . . . .

"From the American First Class Book, page 185, we quote another more modern sentiment, which bears no less higher authority than the name of the great Massachusetts statesman, Mr. Webster :"

Having burnt or expurgated Webster and Cowper, is it to be imagined that the leaders of opinion in the South would yet be willing to permit familiar intercourse between themselves and a people who allowed a book containing such lines as these to circulate freely :

> " What is a man
> If his chief good and market of his time
> Be but to sleep and feed ? A beast, no more.
> Sure, He that made us with such large discourse,
> Looking before and after, gave us not
> That capability and Godlike reason,
> To rust unused."

What a dangerous sentiment to come by any chance to a slave ! Is it not ? Are you, then, prepared to burn your Shakspeare ? I will not ask if you will have another book " expurgated" of all passages the tendency of which is to set the bondmen free.

If the security of life and property at the South must for ever be dependent on the thoroughness with which the negro population is prevented from acquiring knowledge, from thinking of themselves and for themselves, it will never be felt to be greater than it is to-day. Efforts made to increase this security will of

themselves occasion agitation, and agitation must counteract
those efforts. Knowledge, knowledge of what is going on elsewhere, of the condition of men elsewhere, of what is thought
elsewhere, must have increased currency with every class of mankind in all parts of this continent, as it increases in population,
and the movements of its population increase in activity and importance. No human laws, embargoes, or armies and navies can
prevent it. Do our utmost, we can not go back of the steam-
engine, the telegraph, the cotton-gin, and the cylinder-press.
The South has admitted steamboats and railroads. It was not
practicable to stop with these, and bar out all the rest that is
peculiar to the nineteenth century. Is it practicable to admit
the machinery of modern civilized life, and not stir up its free
people? Is it practicable to stir up its intermediate class, and
keep its lowest torpid? Assuredly the security which depends
upon preventing either of these steps can never be permanently
increased; spite of all possible further extension of slave territory,
and dispersion and disconnection of plantations, it must gradually lessen. As it lessens, the demand upon the nation to supply
new grounds of security must increase—increase continually,
until at length, this year, next year, or another, they conclusively
and hopelessly fail. It may cost us much or it may cost us little
to reach that point, but it is inevitably to be reached. It may
be after long and costly civil war, or longer and more costly
foreign wars, or it may be peaceably, sensibly, and soon, but it
must come. The annexation of Cuba, international fugitive
slave laws,* the African slave trade, judgments of the Supreme

---

* From the *Columbia* (S. C.) *Times*, quoted without dissent in the conservative South Carolina paper, the *Charleston Mercury* :
"The loss that the South annually sustains by the running of slaves into

Court, and whatever else may be first asked and given, will not
prevent it —nothing the North will do, nothing the North can
do will prevent it.   The proximity of a people who can not hold
labor in contempt; who can not keep laborers in ignorance and
permanent dependence each upon another man; who can not
have an effective censorship of the press, or a trustworthy army
of *mouchards*, prevents, and must always prevent, the South from
standing with the slightest confidence of safety on that policy
which it proclaims to be its only ground of safety.   Nothing but
a reversal of the current of our northern history for half a century, nothing in fact but the enslavement of labor at the North,
could in the nature of things, give that security, even temporarily, to the capitalists of labor at the South which they need.*

Canada, is of sufficient importance to justify her public men in insisting upon
some action of the Government of the United States in the premises.   And
we confess our surprise that southern statesmen have submitted with so
much patience to the annual robbery of thousands of dollars worth of property to which she has as good a right as the land they cultivate.   The
time is propitious for the acquisition of all disputed rights from European powers.   They can not afford to break just now with the United
States.   Let our public men move in the matter, and we question not but
that the President and the American Minister at St. James will give the
movement a cordial support.   Besides, this is a golden moment which may
never return.   Before we get another sound man in the presidential chair,
peace may be made in Europe, and the European powers be less inclined to
look with favor upon the demands of America."

*   " While it is far more obvious that negroes should be slaves than
whites, for they are only fit to labor, not to direct; yet the principle of
slavery is itself right, and does not depend upon difference of complexion.
Difference of race, lineage, of language, of habits, and customs, all tend to
render the institution more natural and durable; and although slaves have
been generally whites, still the masters and slaves have generally been of
different national descent.   Moses and Aristotle, the earliest historians, are
both authorities in favor of this difference of race, but not of color."—*Richmond Enquirer.*

Some demand of the South upon the nation, acquiescence in which it holds essential to its safety, must then at length be distinctly refused. And when, ten or twenty years hence, if so be, this shall come to pass, what then is to happen us?

Dissolution?

This is what many southern politicians avow, whenever they contemplate such a contingency.

Why?

Because it is known that the people of the North are unwilling that the Union should be dissolved whereas they have no indisposition to the only course which it will then be possible for the South to adopt, for the sake of increasing the security of its citizens, against insurrectionary movements of its slaves. This plainly would be to arrange a systematic opportunity and method for the slaves to labor, whenever they chose, and as much as they might choose, in an orderly, peaceable, and wise way, for their own release and improvement, each man for himself and those most dear to him; each man by himself, independently, openly, with no occasion for combination, secrecy, plots, or conspiracy. To prepare, for those disposed to avail themselves of it, a field, either here or elsewhere, in which their capability and Godlike reason, such as it may be, little or great, need not be forced by law to rust unused, or brighten *only* to the material advantage of a master. This I must think to be consciously, even now, the only final course of safety before every reflective southern mind. This, or——dissolution, and the chances of war.

Which will be chosen?

Which is chosen?

The gambling propensity is always strong with those who, like the wealthy southerners, leave the details of their business wholly to others, and who, seldom taking the trouble to reckon beyond next year's crop, are frequently in want of occupation of mind. Gambling is a prevalent vice at the South.   It assumes all forms, and it is not to be wondered at that some intelligent men, feeling this to be true which I have said, are willing, with their eyes open, to stake their fortunes on the chances of war.   Whatever comes of it, the leaders would probably be able to make terms for themselves.   These intelligent men, if they can be leaders, are ready with their stakes—other men, who do not think so far, dissatisfied with the hand they have, are willing to try a new shuffle.   In the quadrennial howl for dissolution, hosts of other intelligent men may unite, because it helps, or is supposed to help, to force the North to yield whatever may be the specific demand of the South at the time, whether it be for a measure or a man antecedent to a measure.   There remains, then, the larger part of the population, poor, ignorant people, whose condition could not be made worse by a war.   They have nothing to sell ; they buy nothing ; they have nothing which an enemy would want ; nothing to fear from devastation.   At best they are indifferent.   Add to these a number of wrongheaded rich men, for want of occupation also leads to impracticable and imaginative thinking, and this invariably, with cultivated men, to dogmatism and wrongheadedness, and we have the elements of strength for disunion at the the South—elements, it must be admitted, of a strong party, because, for the present, nobody can experience direct harm from it.

The substantial, intelligently occupied men, the busy, industrious, improving poor men, form the dormant union party.   It will cohere and quicken never sooner than is necessary to reëstablish

what alone now gives any degree of confidence to industrial un-
dertakings dependent on the labor of slaves, or the demand which
arises therefrom.   What its strength is likely to be when the
question of union or separation comes to be a practical and immediate question, will depend mainly on what the people of the
South then perceive to be their highest interest.   How they will
then look at it, can, I think, be predicted with some confidence.
Let us consider some of the probable consequences of separation
or dissolution.

   I couple the chances of war with disunion, not because I
think no State or number of States have the abstract right to
peaceably secede from the confederation, but because no possible
motive can be imagined for such a secession which does not involve a state of war.   It is not a negative the South wants.   The
threat of disunion is used only to compel the North to yield or
undertake something to which the North must be disinclined.
Withdraw Southern representatives from our Congress, release us
from our constitutional obligations, and how are the demands of
the South to be enforced except by arms?   What would the
South have of honor, or safety, or profit, out of the Union that
she has not in it, except it were obtained by arms?   I never
heard the question of disunion referred to at the South, that it was
not assumed to involve something of war, assumed to be in itself
a demonstration of war—war to compel the North to give better
protection, better profit to property in slaves.   An argument for
disunion is always an argument *ad hominem ;* an appeal to the
warlike impulse and the warlike pride and confidence of the
South.   When I was in the South, there was in all classes an impression, sometimes uttered to me with distinctness and elabora-
tion, more frequently implied, that the working agricultural class,

who mainly own the land, and all the working-people, of the North, were demoralized, like slaves, by their occupation, and disinclined as much as they were unfitted to engage in war, and that as the property of the rich was mainly of a destructable form, and much of it (as factories and buildings) not of a movable character, these would all come to their knees at the slightest appearance of invasion, and by throwing the poor out of employment, soon compel the whole people, not otherwise so inclined, to sue for peace on whatever terms the South should determine that its interests required. I know that many rather well-informed men have this idea, and I presume it is universal with the active disunionists. It plainly underlies all their arguments, and pervades all their demonstrations which are not obvious gasconade.

THE MILITARY CONDITION OF THE SOUTH.

It is undoubtedly true that the southerners, compared with ourselves, are more ready to violence, more familiar with deadly weapons, and more accustomed to resort to physical means of self-defense. It is also true that they are generally less accustomed to luxury, and are more ready for camp life than we are. Probably, also, they are more generally ambitious of martial glory, and more inclined to engage in war—especially so the wealthy young men. The latter class have likewise been more " accustomed to command" than the corresponding class with us, and if these conditions constitute a warlike people, or a military people, then the southerners have a fair claim to be so designated, and to look upon us as, comparitively speaking, a patient, peaceible, and materialistic people. This being so, it may still remain a question whether a " warlike" and " military" people is safer from the evils and dangers of war than a people ordinarily devoted in excess to the arts and industrious occupations of peace. I believe that it is an error to suppose that the latter, however reluctant they may be to engage in war, however even pusillanimous they may ordinarily appear to be, are a poor stock for soldiers when compelled, or induced by sufficient motive, to engage in war. How was it with the greedy, phlegmatic, hardworking, and unambitious Hollanders (who could afford, rather than fight, to supply a foreign tyrant and usurper—the head of a rich empire—with two-fifths of his annual revenue) when at last roused to resist the demands of Philip II.? The pale weavers withdrew reluctantly from their looms, the farmers from their dikes, the laborers from the puddle-banks, the boatmen from the canals, the clerks from the counting-rooms, the haberdashers, smiths, cutlers, and cobblers, all from their shops, took up the tools and machines of war, enrolled themselves, disciplined themselves, drilled early and late, and, when the shock came, stood firm and cool as veterans, so that the inflexible Alva was compelled to exclaim, "These men," crooked, grim, pale, peaceable plodders as they were, and were willing to be, "these men are equal to the best of soldiers," and again to acknowledge " never was a city defended with such skill and bravery" as the manufacturing town of Harlem, chiefly by its own operatives.*

How was it at our own Revolution? The characteristics of the North and South then differed only from the present in degree, as clearly appears on reading Jefferson's notes on the Virginians

There was probably more plodding industry and less chivalrous

* Motley's Dutch Republic, pages 440, 444.

adventure and martial ambition in Connecticut than in any other colony. Yet when, at length, success was earned, Washington, looking back with pain upon what it had cost, said : " If all had done their duty as well as the little State of Connecticut, the war would have ended long ago."* The people of South Carolina were probably the most warlike of all, as, for the present, we use that term. But Governor Rutledge could not even get the militia to muster in defense of their own houses. Marion did bravely with a small body of skirmishers, but confessed and bewailed the fact, that the people in general had not the spirit to defend themselves, and that the State was lost through their own stupidity and factiousness, which he attributed directly to the general enslavement of the working classes, and the ignorance, idleness, and selfishness of the free.† It was much the same throughout the slaveholding and chivalric districts ; better in the free hill country. General Greene wrote, when in command of the southern army, and stationed in the Carolinas, " The back-country people are brave and daring, but the people on the sea-coast are sickly, and but indifferent militia."

The independence of this country is due chiefly to the good fighting qualities of what had been its most quiet, peaceable, hard-working, and plodding citizens before the war. Since the Revolution, the real military strength of the North has never been for a moment engaged. It is its yeomanry—men who have been accustomed to labor with their own hands, who have no impatient personal ambition, and who will not leave their farms, and their shops, and their families until the demand is urgent— that a hard-pressed nation always finally depends upon. And

* Irving's Washington, vol. iii., p. 130.
† See extract, Sea-board Slave States, p. 503.

there is nowhere else in the world so numerous, or so generally intelligent, or so every way.capable a yeomanry as that of our Northern States. It was by seamen out of this class that our navy was chiefly manned during the second English war, their ordinary occupations having been interrupted by it (as those of the yeomanry proper were not), and it was precisely in the qualities of cool, deliberate, and determined application of means to ends, and of steadiness under fire, that they were found to excel even the British sailor, whose ardor and neglect to make the most of his advantages repeatedly occasioned his defeat when engaged with them.

I will not refer to the facts of the Mexican war, because there are yet no authorities whose statements upon the details would be generally accepted. I have never conversed with an officer of the line who held the popular view of the value of the services of either the southern or the northern volunteers; and I have been told by one of the comrades of the "young gentlemen of good family," who came in the ranks to Vera Cruz from Mississippi and South Carolina, and of whom we have heard so much, that the larger part were constantly in hospital while they remained, and scarcely any "stood it through." As at the Revolution, they were "sickly and but indifferent militia."

"THE HABIT OF COMMAND."

Professor Tucker, in a "Treatise on Political Economy," says :

"The habit of command to which the master of slaves has been familiarized from his infancy, peculiarly fits him for many of the higher duties of civilized life. He is thus likely to be better qualified for exercising authority, both in the army and navy, and even in the civil department. It is, perhaps, thus that the Southern States have furnished more than their proportion of those who have held the higher offices of the government."*

This is at the bottom identical with the aristocratic theory of government. Is it to be trusted?

The sum of the intellectual wealth possessed by the South, if it could be measured, would undoubtedly be found small, compared with that of the North, and the intellectual wealth employed in all other avocations at the South, except that of the politician, is, I should think, not equal to that of some one of the States of the North. It would be true to say that the South employs an immensely larger proportion of its whole wealth of intellectual talent in politics than the North. Englishmen, as well as southerners, commonly consider this to be evidence, so far as it goes, of a better state of society. In my judgment, it is quite otherwise. The talent of the North is not engrossed with politics, because it is much less required in politics than in other departments of service to the public. Our method of government has this advantage, it is less dangerous than any other. It is not a religion; it does not form society. It is the agent of society for certain limited, and, compared with the aggregate of other business which society has in hand, extremely unimportant duties. Consider the wealth which has been developed, the talent which has been called into active use for the benefit of mankind, the convenience for comfortable and intelligent living, which have been established for the use of millions of people, through the agency of some score of the leading merchants and capitalists of the city of New York, and ask whether it would not have been a most unfortunate waste of their talent, had these men been all their time in Con-

* Political Economy for the People. By George Tucker, formerly Representative in Congress from Virginia, and Professor of Moral Philosophy in the University of Virginia.

gress or at European courts—at the bar or on the bench? Fulton and Whitney alone have done ten thousand times more for the wealth, and power, and respectability of the South than John C. Calhoun. Two northern railroad builders have done more, by their individual energy and good judgment, for the State of Georgia, during the last fifteen years, than all its politicians in a century; and Mr. Erricson will probably have accomplished infinitely more in the next ten years for the power of the South, through the bravery, pride, perseverance and inflexible will with which he has made his invention of the caloric engine successful, than will have resulted from the labors of all the piratico-political bullies, like Walker and Lamar, of our generation. Is not the President of the Illinois Central Railroad Company rightly a man of more consequence in that State than its so entitled Governor? One is paid, I suppose, two thousand dollars a year, the other, perhaps twenty thousand, for his services, and the intellectual wealth required to satisfactorily discharge the functions of the two offices is thus very fairly represented. Could the talent which has been applied to the commercial enterprise of the *London Times*, during the last fifty years, have been devoted with half the effect upon the condition of England which it has had, if it had been employed in Parliament? And yet the English, being a centralized government, touching the details of its duty only by the most tedious processes, and encumbered with old machinery of forms and etiquette, which would be like gloves to a type-setter, for ordinary men of business, needs a much greater withdrawal of talent from other offices of society than ours.

We hear from Europe much reflection upon the tendency of democratic institutions to produce corruption in office, injustice, and violence. The examples of this country which lead to these reflections, truly show the necessities of springing nations with an echoing frontier of savage and lawless life on one side, and a continent draining life from under hard pressure, on the other. The evidence of governmental corruption, injustice, and violence which we display (and we take no care to conceal it), is trivial compared with that which escapes from the more distinctly aristocratically governed countries of Europe in an average of twenty years. I have traveled a good deal in both continents, and I can not doubt that, spite of the general intensity and recklessness which belongs to our position in the world, there is no country in Europe where men and women may follow personal inclinations which should be harmless, with as much freedom and safety, as, on an average, in the free States of our Republic. I make this comparison with England with the most confidence, because I have lived there for more than a year, attentively regarding the common life of the common people.

Unquestionably there are great evils arising from the lack of talent applied to our government, from the lack of real dignity of character and respectability of attainments in many government offices, but is there not quite as much of evil to the commonwealth arising from the lack of talent and of sound judgment and severe fidelity to duty in the officers of our railroad and banking systems? What losses, what untold misery has been occasioned by the ignorance, the credulity, the want of judgment of those who have formed our railroad system. Has ignorance, and folly, and carelessness occasioned half the suffering to our citizens or to the people of Europe in dealings with the bank, the tariff, the sub-treasury, or any other measure of civil government or laws? If some of our policemen are loafers, and some of our senators blackguards, how is it with our switchmen and our editors, and in which class does any one of us, who reads a newspaper as he speeds upon his business, prefer to have thorough discipline and good manners? What we have to do on this continent is everywhere found a heavy task; we can't afford to employ a heavy proportion of talent or honesty about the little share of our business which is done at the capital, much less can we spare it for the State house or city hall.

Do I write as if it were to be conceded that the South really did get more talent applied to government than we do? This I by no means believe. The South sends more "orators" to Washington than the North, and the nuisance of Washington is "bunkum" oratory. The South speaks more Greek at Washington than the North. The valuable men at Washington are not speakers of Greek or aught else, but the diggers and builders of the committees, and the clerks of the departments, and the best of these are men trained in habits of business by the necessities of what is called private business, and who have been drawn directly from this private business.

It is a pleasant habit, in which most southerners freely indulge, both in literature and in conversation, to repeat phrases of the significance of that of Professor Tucker, "the habit of command to which the master of slaves has been familiarized from infancy," and it seems to be generally imagined that the unmethodical, irresponsible power of compelling negro slaves to perform menial duties, must have the effect of producing a character similar to that which obtains the instinctive respect of powerful disciplined bodies of freemen. The condition of a wealthy slaveholder has some advantages, undeniably, as a preparation for civil duties, for it insures leisure for calm study and deliberate reflection to those so inclined. If it do not also lead to idle and perverse habits of mind, to Quixotic theorizing and exciting speculations, it may produce some valuable fruit in civil public life. I can see no way in which a man's character could be much affected by it favorably for military duties. It is true that a certain kind of "commanding manners" may be acquired on the plantation; that something which may be called "self-confidence in command" may be acquired, by being personally served by slaves; but if these be valuable, as a preparation for the duties of military officers, other qualities and attainments are not less so. The country is at no little pains to select men who possess these, or will most assuredly acquire them. Our wisest and most successful officers and statesmen have formed the system in use for this purpose, and it is probably the best in the world. It begins by annually assembling a body of young men, who are inspired with the ambition, and believe themselves well prepared and adapted to be trained for the duties of officers, who are, moreover, approved each by a member of Congress, from among all similarly disposed in his district, as the most worthy (except a certain number, nominated by the President, and supposed to be taken in equal numbers from each part of the country, and who, for the present purpose, may be left out of account). A preliminary examination is had, and if any of those selected have not been able, before the time of life at which they are allowed to present themselves, to acquire the elements of a common school education, or if any appear physically incompetent to undertake soldierly duties, they are at once set aside. No record is kept, as I am informed by the commanding officer at West Point, of these preliminary examinations.

For four years afterwards, sometimes five, those who are found so far capable as to be worth the trouble, are kept in training

and on trial for competency as soldiers and officers.   Once a year
the result is published, the names of a certain number, who are
entitled the "most distinguished," being officially announced in
the *Army Register*.   So far as it has been possible to construct a
rule for the measurement of the qualifications needed for military command, these young men are the best which our government, acting under the advice of our most experienced military men, has been able to obtain in the country.   I have
examined the Registers as far back as 1848, and find that in the
eight years following,* the first distinction has been gained by
twenty-four entered from the free States, and by two entered
from the slave States.   Of all those obtaining official honors in
the same time, one hundred and eight entered from the free
States, and thirty-four from the slave States.   Of those who,
during the same period, were either discharged, sent back, or
barely whipped through (being the lowest ten of each class, including those thrown out), a minority of all were from the free
States.

Certainly there are qualities of the highest value for conducting military operations, which the West Point sifting can not
catch; and it is not impossible that the men who have been
most punctual, most exact, most thorough, indefatigable, and
tenacious in all the opportunities there offered them to develop
the most necessary qualities and obtain the most necessary ac-
quirements of modern warriors, may be most deficient in the
native talent which overcomes that class of difficulties for which
there can be no sufficient preparation until they arise on the
field.   What are these other qualities, and how can they be

---

* Subsequent registers I had not been able to obtain when this chapter
was prepared.   They would not alter the general indications of these.

manifested? They are mainly included under a single phrase— fertility of resource; in other words—inventive genius. How stands the evidence as to the respective strength of the free and slave States in this quality? The record at Washington shows, in a single year, two thousand original inventions from the free States, established before the patent office examiners, to less than three hundred from the slave States.

A very well informed writer has observed that military quali- ties, both as regards bravery and fitness for the work, are, upon the whole, pretty evenly distributed among civilized nations; that it is not so much the degree as the special nature of the qualifi- cation which distinguishes the soldier of different nationalities— each having some advantages and disadvantages over all others.* It is hardly necessary to say anything of courage. It is rarely, except from want of *esprit de corps,* and, with new soldiers, faith- less in their organization, that cowardice becomes an important element in determining the result of a warlike struggle. If the southerner has more ardor and readiness for deeds of arms, if he has more personal military ambition, more dash and reckless daring, the northerner has more stanchness, and, once roused, more un- tiring, sober, and trustworthy enthusiasm. If the South has the most squirrel shooters, street skirmishers, and duelists, the North has the most men who have proved themselves heroes in con- tests with the elements, and who appreciate and are accustomed to the benefits resulting from the subordination of the individual will to the corporate. The North has also much the largest force of enrolled militia :

North, number............ 1,381,843
South, "   792,876

* Putnam's Monthly, August, 1855.

A mere enrollment is of little value without organization and equipment. There is no doubt that a far larger proportion of the northern enrolled militia is in some degree organized, equipped, drilled, and accustomed to act under its officers, than of the southern.

The comparative material resources of the two parts of our country, really the most important circumstance by which to determine their comparative ability to endure war—having been much discussed and set forth with other purposes—it is unnecessary to more than remind the reader of the entirely overwhelming power the North controls in this respect. The census returns indicate the

REAL AND PERSONAL PROPERTY :

In the Free States................ $4,102,172,108
"   Slave States (including slaves).. 2,936,081,731

But, for war purposes, it is certainly absurd to hold slaves at a higher valuation than free men. Considering negroes, then, as no more to be reckoned a part of the wealth of the country than other men, the comparison will stand :

REAL AND PERSONAL PROPERTY :

Free States..................... $4,102,172,108
Slave States (slaves not included).... 1,336,090,737*

The present actual revenue of the free States is to that of the slave States as eighteen to eight.

The purely military resources are certainly not less preponderating in the free States than might be presumed from these figures; the stock of saltpetre, lead, hospital stores, etc., being always far

* Slaves valued at a trifle over five hundred dollars a head; a low estimate.

larger, and the principal manufactories of arms, vehicles, etc.—not considering those of the government—being in the free States.

In means of rapidly concentrating land forces, the advantage of the North is sufficiently indicated by a comparison of the extent of

COMPLETED RAILROADS:

Free States, miles (1857)............. 17,855
Slave States, "   "   6,859

The latter being much more poorly equipped, and rarely double-tracked. The cost of the northern roads has been more than five times those of the South.

Still more, by a comparison of the cost of transporting the mails, which is more than four times as much at the South, relatively to the amount carried, as at the North:

MAIL TRANSPORTATION—COST FOR EVERY DOLLAR RECEIVED

IN POSTAGE:

Free States............. 56 cts.
Slave States............. $1.51

As to marine resources for the purpose, more than nine tenths of all the shipping and boats of the United States (tonnage capacity) have been built, and are now owned north of the Potomac and the Ohio.

Whether the fact that a large constituent of the working force of the South is the offspring of a subjected foreign people, itself held to labor without stipulated wages, not connected by marriage with the citizens, owning nothing of the property, having no voice in the State, in the lowest degree ignorant, and yet half barbarous in disposition and habits—whether this fact is an element of strength or weakness in a civilized war—can it be a question?

Certainly not, in the minds of the gentlemen in our confederate employment, who are also engaged in the work of " preparing the South for its destiny," as the following extracts from De Bow's " Resources of the South" will indicate:

" If any thing is certain in human affairs, it is certain, and from the most obvious considerations, that we are more secure in this respect than any civilized and fully peopled society on the face of the earth. In every such society there is a much larger proportion than with us of persons who have more to gain than to lose by the overthrow of government and the embroiling of social order." . . . . "It is almost physic- ally impossible that there should be any very extensive combination among the slaves." . . . . " The efficiency of an army is determined by the qualities of its officers. And may we not hope to have a greater proportion of men better qualified for officers, and possessing the true spirit of military command." . . . . " The Helots were a regular con- stituent of the Spartan armies. Thoroughly acquainted with their characters and accustomed to command them, we might use any strictness of discipline which would be necessary to render them effec- tive, and from their habits of subordination already formed this would be a task of less difficulty." . . . . " With white officers, *and accom- panied by strong white cavalry*, there are no troops in the world from which there would be so little reason to apprehend insubordination or mutiny."

The opinion here indicated, that the slaves are a thoroughly subjected race, that they recognize and quail instinctively before their masters, is a correct one, generally speaking, as I have often noticed; but that this " instinct"—that is to say, instinct-like habit of mind—can be depended upon at all times is far from being true, as also I have seen abundant evidence. Let the negro have a strong scent of freedom, and how the real instinct of manhood, which has been dormant perhaps for generations, may chance to take possession of him the editor of the *Feliciana Whig* (Louisiana newspaper), with the simple eloquence of a pure savage, shall testify:

" On Saturday last, a runaway negro was killed in the parish of East Baton Rouge, just below the line of this parish, under the following circumstances : .Two citizens of Port Hudson, learning that a negro was at work on a flat boat, loading with sand, just below that place, who was suspected of being a runaway, went down in a skiff for the purpose of arresting him.

" Having seized him and put him into the skiff they started back, but had not proceeded far when the negro, who had been at the oars, seized a hatchet and assaulted one of them, wounding him very seriously. A scuffle ensued, in which both parties fell overboard. They were both rescued by the citizen pulling to them with the skiff. Finding him so unmanageable, the negro was put ashore, and the parties returned to Port Hudson for arms and a pack of negro dogs, and started again with the intention to capture him. They soon got on his trail, and when found again he was standing at bay upon the outer edge of a large raft of drift wood, armed with a club and pistol.

" In this position he bade defiance to men and dogs—knocking the latter into the water with his club, and resolutely threatening death to any man who approached him. Finding him obstinately determined not to surrender, one of his pursuers shot him. He fell at the third fire, and so determined was he not to be captured, that when an effort was made to rescue him from drowning he made battle with his club, and sunk waving his weapon in angry defiance at his pursuers. He refused to give the name of his owner."*

So far as I could ascertain, there are but few districts in which, ordinarily, insurrection is much or constantly, at present, apprehended. Yet there is no part of the South where the slave population is felt to be quite safe from a contagion of insurrectionary excitement. Any great event having the slightest bearing upon

---

* That the reader may appreciate more perfectly the condition of the soul which could describe in these terms such a glory of mankind as this nigger, who—by the grace of God, a true nobleman—made and kept himself a free man, I quote from *Norman's New Orleans and its Environs*, an account of the leading class of Feliciana :

" This latter received its beautiful and expressive name from its beautifully variegated surface of hills and valleys, and its rare combination of all the qualities that are most desired in a planting country. It is a region of almost fairy beauty and wealth. Here are some of the wealthiest and most intelligent planters and the finest plantations in the State, the region of princely taste and more than patriarchal hospitality," etc.

It is the region and the people, in short, I described in the first chapter of this volume.

the question of emancipation is known to produce an "unwholesome excitement," even in parts of the country where the slave population is, and has least reason not to be, peculiarly contented with its condition. The last presidential election was followed by the discovery of conspiracies and insurrectionary symptoms in all but, I believe, three of the slave States. It was estimated at the time that, altogether, not less than sixty slaves were put to death; some by hanging, but many by torture, in the efforts to check the supposed contagion of revolt. The danger seemed at this time to be about equal in the farming and in the planting districts. In but one or two of those districts in which the danger is ordinarily considered greatest, did evidence of unusual excitement among the slaves become public, undoubtedly because, in those districts, the precautions had been strenuous and sufficient—that is to say, because the white population was vigilant, and the slaves felt themselves under a strong hand.

An armed citizens' police, having a military organization, is, as I have before said, sustained in all parts of the South where there are many slaves. It is more or less efficient according to the necessities of the case, but any long continued entire neglect usually results in general insubordination and much inconvenience, as is indicated in the following remarks upon a robbery in his neighborhood by a Texas editor :

"While all the men were gone from the place, a negro described as being bare headed, thick set, and having on a blue blanket coat and a pair of blue cottonade pants, came to the house, and seeing a double-barrel gun in the corner took it. He then ordered Mrs. Krouse to get him some ammunition, threatening to kill her if she refused. Having got this, he warned her to make no alarm or he would come back and shoot her down. He then made the best of his way off.

" We can but say in connection with this affair that the patrols of the various parts of the county are getting to be lamentably lax in their duty. There are at this time at least a dozen runaway negroes that we know of in the county. We hear of thieveries committed by them every day or two. The above is the boldest act we have yet heard of, and yet that may be followed by yet bolder ones, if this state of things is not checked. When it comes to this, that our property is not secure in our houses, in broad day light, from the incursions of these vagabonds, and that even the lives of defenseless women are threatened by them, it is time something was done. Let the captains of the patrol look to their duty."

It must be borne in mind that throughout the South slaves are accustomed to " run away." On every large or moderate plantation which I visited, I had evidence that in peace, with, south of Virginia and east of Texas, no prospect of finding shelter within hundreds of miles, or of long avoiding recapture and severe punishment, many slaves had a habit of frequently making efforts to escape temporarily from their ordinary condition of subjection. I have shown that this is so common that southern writers gravely describe it as a disease—a monomania, to which the negro race is peculiarly subject, making the common mistake of attributing to blood that which is much more rationally to be traced to condition.

This is the difference between slave and other property. Ships, goods, buildings, machinery, stores may be destroyed, and to some extent, with labor and hazard, carried off. Hence those interested to maintain these things are most anxious to prevent invasion— to annoy and check the progress of invaders by any available means. Slaves may carry themselves off, and with themselves may carry off much other property, which, under ordinary circumstances of war, is not accessible by an enemy. When a slave now runs for the frontier, he seldom neglects the attempt to despoil his master, in some way or other, of movable property, justifying himself with himself on the ground that he has earned wages which have been withheld from him. In a large proportion of all cases, Texas runaways are advertised as having taken a horse, a gun, money, and clothes.

To suppose that in case of a war, either foreign or civil, the slaves would be an element of strength to the South, or that an enemy could not easily turn them to account, seems to me to be, on the face of it, a foundation upon which only the maddest theorist or the most impracticable of abstractionists could found a policy. Whether, finally, in case of the civil war with a threat of which we have so often been threatened, and the periodical suggestion of which will, in the ordinary course of events, soon be presented to us again, northern men are likely to be more influenced by the cost of extra-hazardous insurance policies on their manufactures and stores, than southern gentlemen by the dread of losing the services of their slaves, we can best judge by reference to the past.

During the Revolution, the British ships on the coast, at times offered protection to runaway slaves; and it was estimated that they carried away from Virginia alone not less than thirty thousand of them.* Washington demanded the restoration of one hundred and fifty taken at one time to Nova Scotia, which was refused by Sir Guy Carlton.† John Jay, writing to John Adams, says: "Great numbers of slaves were carried away by the British forces from other ports beside New York."‡ In the second English war, the enemy had too few ships to spare, and little opportunity to adopt the same means of annoyance; but a proclamation of Admiral Cochrane in the spring of 1814, caused great alarm at the South, it being addressed to the slaves, under the denomination " of all persons desirous to emigrate from the United States." These were informed that they would receive protection on board any of his majesty's ships, and be given free pas-

---

* Hildreth, vol. iii., p. 355.   † Spark's Dip. Cor., vol. iv., p. 173.
‡ Spark's Dip. Cor., vol. iv., p. 358.

sage to free soil, if they desired it.* A large sum was afterwards claimed as indemnity for slaves so carried away, and the claim referred to Russia as arbiter.†

The testimony of Mr. Madison, given in a debate in Congress, 1797, on a proposition to impose a duty upon the importation of slaves,‡ is as follows :

"It is to be hoped that by expressing a natural disapprobation of this trade we may destroy it, and save ourselves from reproaches, and our posterity the imbecility ever attendant on a country filled with slaves. I do not wish to say anything harsh to the hearing of gentlemen who entertain different sentiments from me, or different sentiments from those I represent, but if there is any one point in which it is clearly the policy of this nation, so far as we constitutionally can, to vary the practice obtaining under some of the State governments, it is this. But it is certain a majority of the States are opposed to this practice, therefore, upon principle, we ought to discountenance it as far as it is in our power.

"If I were not afraid of being told that the representatives of the several States are the best able to judge of what is proper and conducive to their particular prosperity, I should venture to say that it is as much the interest of Georgia and South Carolina as of any in the Union. *Every addition they receive to their number of slaves tends to weaken and render them less capable of self-defense. In case of hostilities with foreign nations, they will be the means of inviting attack instead of repelling invasion.* It is the necessary duty of the general government to protect every part of the empire against danger, as well internal as external. Every thing, therefore, which tends to increase this danger, though it may be a local affair, yet if it involves national expense or safety, becomes of concern to every part of the Union, and is a proper subject for the consideration of those charged with the general administration of the government."

The most conclusive evidence, however, is that given by that sound and clear-headed patriot, Marion, whose words in reply to De Kalb's inquiry, why the South Carolinians were all "running to take British protections," I again quote :

"We told him the reason was very plain to us who were inhabitants of that country, and knew very well the state of things there. . . .

* Hildreth, vol. vi., p. 483.   † Hildreth, vol. vi., p. 660.
‡ Barton's Debates, p. 75.

The people of Carolina form two classes, the rich and the poor. The poor are generally very poor, because not being necessary to the rich, who have slaves to do all the work, they get no employment of them. Being thus unsupported by the rich, they continue poor and low spirited. They seldom get money, and, indeed, what little they do get is laid out in brandy to raise their spirits, and not on books and newspapers to get information. Hence, they know nothing of the comparative blessings of our country or of the dangers which threaten it, and, therefore, care nothing about it. As to the other class, the rich, they are very rich, and, consequently, *afraid to stir, unless a fair chance offer, lest the British should burn their houses and furniture, and carry off their negroes and stock.*"

And South Carolina is far weaker on these grounds to-day than she was at the Revolution. So is all the cotton region. The border States on the North are possibly stronger, but if English ships drew slaves from their masters to be transported to Nova Scotia, what would England itself brought along side of Virginia have done?

Chancellor Harper, of South Carolina, after claiming that there would be less danger from insubordination of the slaves, if the South were engaged in war, than usual, because there would then be a larger force of armed men a-foot within the country than usual, by which they would be overawed, urges that it is practicable and may be found best to put arms in the hands of the slaves themselves and lead them against the enemy, but concludes that if this were attempted it might be dangerous, after a peace had again been obtained, to attempt to reduce them " to their former condition of laborers." " It might be necessary," he says, "when once embodied, to keep them so, and subject to military discipline—a permanent standing army. This, in time of peace, would be expensive, if not dangerous."

Few northern readers can read this conclusion, reflecting that the contingency it supposes is coolly discussed as one of the probable necessities of a severe campaign of war by one of the oftestquoted authorities of the extreme southern party, and hold the common sense of the South in so little respect as to apprehend that an actual fighting war has ever been contemplated in earnest as a means of strengthening slavery. They will be more likely to believe, that while a warlike demonstration is intended, nothing like a war in earnest is presumed by those whose voice renders the threat of secession worthy of our notice. This is my own judgment. With few exceptions—madder enthusiasts than any we can set against them—these men pledge, and swear, and solemnly vow themselves to the alternative of secession, in the belief that should the presumed condition arise, and should they be forced to attempt to fulfill their vows, commercial interests, under the instant check to trade which would occur at the first demonstration of arms, would prevail, the North recede, and a new confederate constitution be obtained, giving new national securities for slavery.

This error is to be attributed to the prevalent opinion of the South, by which the most intelligent must be affected, that labor begets pusillanimity, and commercial habits unfitness for war, and hence that a real danger of war would bring the South the immediate moral support of a host of people who now resist the demands of the South.

The fact is, that the native rural population of the North is a peculiarly law-loving, and, in this way, a peace-loving people; the strength of the party which the South has agreed to deal with as an enemy is mainly with this class of people. That party can, in the nature of things, never undertake to accomplish its purposes by illegal or unconstitutional acts without losing the support of a large proportion of the rural voters of the North.

Whatever their personal views may be, the leaders of the free soil army of the North know this, and will be governed as politicians and as statesmen by it. On the other hand, no party could exist in an effective form for political action at the North, which supported men who were avowedly acting disloyally to the constitution at the South. A secession movement at the South, based on anything but an unquestionable act of unconstitutional aggression against the South, would then, as soon as it began to be regarded with respect at the North, find few apologists, no practical supporters. Long before it brought about a serious passage of arms, the North would be practically united in one party against it, and in support of the government to which it was opposed. Evidence of this would alone be necessary to convince any intelligent man at the South of the folly of the attempt to coerce the North, and of the necessity for the adoption at home of a new policy—a policy by which the South should no longer depend upon the coöperation of the North in providing against the dangers of slavery. Of necessity, the reactionary party would represent and embody the strength of the nation, that is to say, of the entire North added to itself, in carrying out its policy. Thus, I see no cause for alarm, but only for hope of a peaceful end to our great national squabble, in the most violent and solemn determination for dissolution and war which can be exhibited at the South.

As the present policy so madly pursued has departed from the principles of Democracy and the old Democratic party, so that the words of Jefferson would now hang a man anywhere at the South, I do not much doubt that when reaction comes, the principles on which Jefferson desired to deal with slavery will be found eminently safe and profitable. There would still be extremists; there would be fanatics and fools; there would be

great difference of opinion as to the ultimate destiny of the negro
race, and as to the final disappearance of slavery, and difference
of judgment among moderate men as to measures; but the common sense of the South would be seconded by the common sense
of the North, and would receive the respect of the world, when
it had established a policy the tendency of which would be to
encourage slaves to form industrious habits and exercise intelligence, by securing them palpable benefits therefrom; which would
discourage idleness and improvidence, as well as other vices, by
punishments which they would dread, making grades, perhaps,
from the utterly low slave upward, to what rank here, those governing would determine, but to freedom and the most complete
fair play somewhere else if not here; and every step upward,
an object to be desired by those below; every lapse through the
vices of slavery, or the weaknesses alleged of the negro nature,
distinctly and surely to be apprehended disagreeably.   And
together with this, the encouragement of denser and more
completely furnished communities of citizens.   (Jefferson proposed to the constitutional convention of Virginia to give free
passage, and offer special inducements to whites to come to
Virginia.)

It will be said, of course, that however practicable in Jefferson's time, nothing of this kind is so now, since the demand for
cotton has quadrupled the value of slaves.   It is for this reason
now practicable, if not before.   There is no slave so valuable
that he could not make himself more valuable, if he knew how,
and chose to be more valuable.   Increase his industry and intelligence, and he becomes more valuable.   Punish him as now,
but more systematically and effectually for laziness, stupidity,
and carelessness, but hold before him a sure reward for industry,

study of his allotted duty, and perseverance in it, and he will
share all the larger interests of his master, and be equally anxious with him for the suppression of disorder in lower and more
vicious classes than his own. There is many a negro who is now
considered a dangerous, or at least a "rascally" fellow, whose
labor brings not four bales of cotton a year, who, if he saw hard
fare and a well organized and thorough penal system on one
side, and freedom, or a sure progress toward it for himself and his
family on the other, with luxuries meanwhile, could and would
make his labor worth as much as seven bales of cotton a year.
In half a dozen years, the difference would be equal to his present value. At the same time, his personal interest at stake in
the maintenance of the existing system of government, and of
peace and order, would be yearly and daily increasing.

The task method of working slaves which prevails in much of
South Carolina and Georgia, proves, in my judgment, that what
would seem the most serious difficulty in such a system amounts
to nothing, when self-interest is once felt to be engaged in its
success, for the common overseers, men who can not read and
write themselves, allot the tasks to the slaves, and seldom fail to
have them executed.* On the other hand, where the system has
once become established, it is found very difficult and not very
profitable, to force the slaves to work more for their master than
the custom. Give custom the sanction and penalties of law, and
let the community feel its peace to be endangered by a disregard
of the law, and there would be certainly less knavery and cruelty
to the negro than now; more wealth with less care to the master.

* See pages 434 to 446, Sea-board Slave States.

INDEX.

A.